AN INTRODUCTION
TO
CONSTITUTIONAL LAW

100 Supreme Court Cases
Everyone Should Know

Praise for Barnett & Blackman's

An Introduction to Constitutional Law:
100 Supreme Court Cases Everyone Should Know

"The descriptions by Professors Barnett and Blackman emphasize what students need to know in order to master this material for their exams and for their careers. Professors Barnett and Blackman present the material with great clarity. The videos provide the students another way of learning the material and wonderfully complement the textual descriptions. Although many of the cases are controversial, Professors Barnett and Blackman present them in an unbiased and ideologically neutral manner."

Erwin Chemerinsky
University of California, Berkeley School of Law

"Randy Barnett and Josh Blackman have created a remarkable guide to what they label the 100 most important Supreme Court cases in our history. Students (and their teachers) should especially profit from the multimedia blend of information and analysis. Inevitably there will be quibbles about some few cases included and, therefore, others left out, but if I am typical, most legal academics will agree with at least 90% of their choices, which is impressive indeed. This may prove to be a true event in legal education—and not only for law students."

Sanford V. Levinson
University of Texas at Austin School of Law

"Barnett and Blackman have made learning the basics of American constitutional law as painless and as fun as possible. The case discussions are concise; the videos are full of fascinating pictures and historical details. If you think you might be interested in Constitutional Law, this is a great way to get started."

Jack M. Balkin
Yale Law School

"The pithy, lively, and occasionally opinionated, but always fair-minded chapters and videos provide all of the essentials of the key cases of the constitutional canon, clarifying and summarizing without ever dumbing down."

Michael Dorf
Cornell Law School

"A very accessible guide by two outstanding constitutional scholars to many cases that are taught in almost every class in constitutional law and a few cases that should be taught in almost every class in constitutional law."

Mark Graber
University of Maryland School of Law

"A useful, impressive, and innovative introduction to the history of American constitutional law. Accessible to the beginning student and still helpful to the advanced student. A new approach for a new generation of students. Raises the bar on how to make these complex cases understandable."

Keith E. Whittington
Princeton University

"Randy Barnett and Josh Blackman have done it again! Two of our nation's most brilliant scholars and teachers of the Constitution have teamed up to create a magnificent set of new teaching materials. *100 Supreme Court Cases Everybody Should Know* is an endlessly rich and deeply rewarding resource for understanding the U.S. Constitution. Novices and experts alike will benefit from the Barnett-Blackman treasure trove."

Michael Stokes Paulsen
University of St. Thomas School of Law

"A strong supplement that provides the legal and political context for the most significant Supreme Court cases. It provides important background for all constitutional law students."

William Baude
University of Chicago Law School

AN INTRODUCTION
TO
CONSTITUTIONAL LAW
100 Supreme Court Cases
Everyone Should Know

RANDY E. BARNETT

Carmack Waterhouse Professor of Legal Theory
Georgetown University Law Center

JOSH BLACKMAN

Associate Professor of Law
South Texas College of Law Houston

Published by Wolters Kluwer in New York.

Wolters Kluwer Legal & Regulatory U.S. serves customers worldwide with CCH, Aspen Publishers, and Kluwer Law International products. (www.WKLegaledu.com)

Back cover image: Matt Wood

To contact Customer Service, e-mail customer.service@wolterskluwer.com, call 1-800-234-1660, fax 1-800-901-9075, or mail correspondence to:

Wolters Kluwer
Attn: Order Department
PO Box 990
Frederick, MD 21705

Printed in the United States of America.

5 6 7 8 9 0

ISBN 978-1-5438-1390-6

Library of Congress Cataloging-in-Publication Data

Names: Barnett, Randy E., author. | Blackman, Josh., author.
Title: An introduction to constitutional law: 100 Supreme Court cases
  everyone should know / Randy E. Barnett, Carmack Waterhouse Professor of
  Legal Theory, Georgetown University Law Center; Josh Blackman, Associate
  Professor of Law, South Texas College of Law, Houston.
Description: New York: Wolters Kluwer, [2019]
Identifiers: LCCN 2019021381 | ISBN 9781543813906
Subjects: LCSH: Constitutional law — United States — Digests. | United States.
  Supreme Court. | LCGFT: Law digests.
Classification: LCC KF4547.4.B37 2019 | DDC 342.73 — dc23
LC record available at https://lccn.loc.gov/2019021381

SUSTAINABLE FORESTRY INITIATIVE Certified Sourcing www.sfiprogram.org SFI-00756

About Wolters Kluwer Legal & Regulatory U.S.

Wolters Kluwer Legal & Regulatory U.S. delivers expert content and solutions in the areas of law, corporate compliance, health compliance, reimbursement, and legal education. Its practical solutions help customers successfully navigate the demands of a changing environment to drive their daily activities, enhance decision quality and inspire confident outcomes.

Serving customers worldwide, its legal and regulatory portfolio includes products under the Aspen Publishers, CCH Incorporated, Kluwer Law International, ftwilliam.com and MediRegs names. They are regarded as exceptional and trusted resources for general legal and practice-specific knowledge, compliance and risk management, dynamic workflow solutions, and expert commentary.

Summary of Contents

Contents

PART VII

EXPANDING THE SCOPE OF THE DUE PROCESS CLAUSE

PART VIII

EQUAL PROTECTION OF THE LAW: DISCRIMINATION ON THE BASIS OF RACE

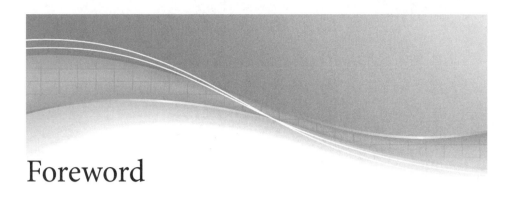

Foreword

Professors Randy Barnett and Josh Blackman have created an innovative study aid for students to help them understand constitutional law. They take the 100 most important Supreme Court cases and provide students a wealth of useful information about them, including questions to focus their understanding, clear narrative explanations of the decisions, and videos about the rulings.

Their choice of cases is impeccable. In each area of constitutional law, they have selected the cases that students and practitioners must know. Although not every constitutional law class will cover each of these cases, Professors Barnett and Blackman have included the most important cases that are covered in any constitutional law course. Indeed, my hope would be that every law graduate — and for that matter every person in the country — be familiar with most of these crucial rulings. These are the cases that define the structure of American government and that affect all of us, often in the most intimate and important aspects of our lives.

Their materials on each case are sure to enhance the student's understanding of the decision and its significance. Like all student aids, this book is no substitute for students reading the primary sources: the cases themselves. But Supreme Court decisions are often hard to comprehend. The descriptions by Professors Barnett and Blackman emphasize what students need to know in order to master this material for their exams and for their careers. Professors Barnett and Blackman present the material with great clarity. The videos provide the students another way of learning the material and wonderfully complement the textual descriptions. Although many of the cases are controversial, Professors Barnett and Blackman present them in an unbiased and ideologically neutral manner.

There, of course, are many study aids to help students learn the material covered in their courses. But I never have seen one like this and believe that it will be tremendously helpful to students in the entire range of constitutional law courses that are part of the undergraduate and law school curriculum. In fact, anyone seeking to learn more about American constitutional law would benefit from these materials.

Erwin Chemerinsky
Dean and Jesse H. Choper Distinguished Professor of Law
University of California, Berkeley School of Law

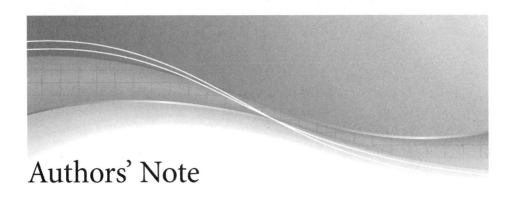

Authors' Note

We developed this multimedia platform to innovate how constitutional law is studied. First, *An Introduction to Constitutional Law* will teach you the narrative of constitutional law as it has developed over the past two centuries. All students — even those unfamiliar with American history — will learn the essential background information to grasp how this body of law has come to be what it is today. Second, the online video library will bring to life the *100 Supreme Court Cases Everyone Should Know*. To make the content more engaging, we've embedded photographs, maps, and even audio from the Supreme Court.

We've made the book and videos accessible for all levels of study: law school, college, high school, home school, and independent study. Students can read and watch these materials before class to prepare for lectures. Or students can utilize the platform after class to fill in any gaps in their notes. And most likely, come exam time, students can *binge-watch* the entire canon of constitutional law in less than 12 hours.

We hope you enjoy using *An Introduction to Constitutional Law: 100 Supreme Court Cases Everyone Should Know* as much as we enjoyed preparing it.

Randy E. Barnett
Washington, D.C.
Josh Blackman
Houston, TX
July 2019

AN INTRODUCTION
TO
CONSTITUTIONAL LAW
100 Supreme Court Cases
Everyone Should Know

FOUNDATIONAL CASES ON CONSTITUTIONAL STRUCTURE

Part I will focus on five cases from the early days of our Republic: *Chisholm v. Georgia* (1793), *Marbury v. Madison* (1803), *McCulloch v. Maryland* (1819), *Gibbons v. Ogden* (1824), and *Barron v. City of Baltimore* (1833). These cases provide the foundation for modern constitutional law.

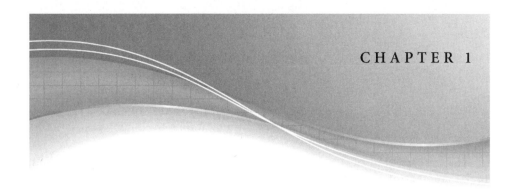

CHAPTER 1

Chisholm v. Georgia (1793)

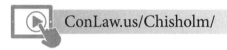 ConLaw.us/Chisholm/

In 1793, the Supreme Court decided its first major constitutional controversy. *Chisholm v. Georgia* considered whether a state could be sued in federal court by a citizen of another state. The facts of this case arose before the Constitution was even ratified.

During the Revolutionary War, the Executive Council of Georgia authorized the purchase of clothing from Robert Farquhar, a South Carolina merchant. After receiving the supplies, Georgia did not deliver the payments as promised. Soon, Farquhar died. In 1793, the executor of his estate, Alexander Chisholm, filed suit against Georgia in the Supreme Court's original jurisdiction. At the time, the Supreme Court convened in Old City Hall in Philadelphia.

This suit raised an important question of first principles: Could an individual like Chisholm sue a state like Georgia? Article III, Section 2 listed several *heads* of the federal courts' jurisdiction. One portion of this clause provided that "[t]he *judicial power* shall extend . . . to controversies . . . between a *state and citizens of another state*. . . ." Chisholm, a citizen of South Carolina, sought to sue Georgia, another state.

STUDY GUIDE

Article III, Section 2 lists "a state" first and "citizens of another state" second. Does it matter whether the state is the plaintiff or the defendant?

Georgia objected to being a defendant in such a lawsuit. The state argued that it could not be sued in federal court without its consent because Georgia was a "sovereign." Indeed, Georgia refused to make an appearance because it took the position that the Supreme Court lacked jurisdiction over the state.

The five Justices on the Court wrote five separate opinions. At this time, the Supreme Court did not issue a single opinion of the Court. Instead, each Justice wrote his own opinion to explain his vote. The opinions were published *seriatim*, that is, in the order they were delivered in court.

The first opinion by a Justice in the majority was delivered by Justice John Blair. The text of the Constitution, he contended, did not recognize the doctrine of sovereign immunity that existed in England. "The Constitution of the United States," he wrote, "is the only fountain from which I shall draw; the only authority to which I shall appeal." Whatever sovereignty the states gained following the Revolution, he explained, was surrendered when they adopted the Constitution.

Justice James Wilson, who was a lead drafter of the Constitution, wrote the second majority opinion. He relied primarily on "the principles of general jurisprudence." "To the Constitution of the United States," he wrote, "the term SOVEREIGN, is totally unknown." Rather, Wilson characterized the individual free man as an original sovereign. The states were mere aggregations of individuals: a collection of original sovereigns. "[L]aws derived from the pure source of equality and justice," he wrote, "must be founded on the CONSENT of those whose obedience they require. The sovereign, when traced to his source, must be found in the man." The Preamble to the Constitution begins, "We the People." With these three words, he explained, "our national scene opens with the most magnificent object which the nation could present. 'The PEOPLE of the United states' are the first personages introduced." Finally, Wilson turned to the text of Article III, Section 2. The people of Georgia, who ratified this provision, had consented to the Supreme Court's jurisdiction over Chisholm's suit. "As to the purposes of the Union," Wilson concluded, "Georgia is NOT a sovereign state."

STUDY GUIDE

How does Justice Wilson's conception of "popular sovereignty" differ from how that term is often used today?

Justice William Cushing authored the third majority opinion. He focused on the wording of Article III, Section 2. That provision made no reference to whether a state was the plaintiff or defendant. From that text, he concluded that states could sue, or be sued, in federal court.

The fourth majority opinion came from John Jay, our first Chief Justice. Jay was the third co-author of *The Federalist Papers* along with Alexander Hamilton and James Madison. Chief Justice Jay explained that, before 1776, Americans were subjects of the King and owed allegiance to him. From this history, Jay concluded "that fellow citizens and joint sovereigns cannot be degraded by appearing with each other in their own courts to have their controversies determined."

STUDY GUIDE

Did Chief Justice Jay articulate an individual or collective conception of "We the People"?

Justice James Iredell was the lone dissenter. Yet his seriatim opinion appeared first because he likely delivered it before the others. In England, the King had absolute sovereign immunity and could not be sued. After the Revolution, Iredell observed, sovereignty was transferred from the King to the states. Subsequently, neither the Constitution nor Congress expressly abandoned the concept of sovereign immunity. Therefore, Iredell concluded, following the principles of old law, the suit against Georgia should not be permitted.

Chisholm was decided in February 1793. The decision quickly became unpopular among the state legislatures. In March 1794, Congress introduced an amendment to the Constitution that would have made it impossible for Chisholm to sue Georgia. In February 1795, two years after the decision in *Chisholm*, the proposed amendment was ratified as the Eleventh Amendment. It provided, "The Judicial power of the United States shall not be construed to extend to any suit in law or equity, commenced or prosecuted against one of the United States by Citizens of another State, or by Citizens or Subjects of any Foreign State." The Eleventh Amendment modified Article III, Section 2 of the Constitution. Originally, the judicial power expressly extended to controversies between *a state and a citizen of another state*. Now, while a state can be a *plaintiff* in a suit against another state or a citizen thereof, a state cannot be a *defendant* in a suit by a citizen "of another state."

After the ratification of the Eleventh Amendment, it would be impossible for a citizen of one state to sue another state. However, the text of the Amendment did not expressly address the opinions of the *Chisholm* majority, which concluded that states lacked sovereign immunity. Indeed, the Eleventh Amendment, like the original Constitution, does not invoke the concept of sovereign immunity at all! The Eleventh Amendment simply bars states from being sued by citizens of another state.

STUDY GUIDE

Does the Eleventh Amendment bar a citizen from suing his or her own state?

This question would not be addressed by the Supreme Court until *Hans v. Louisiana* (1890). We will study that case in Chapter 19.

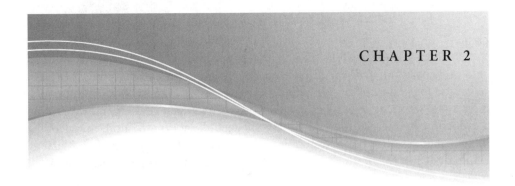

CHAPTER 2

Marbury v. Madison (1803)

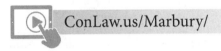 ConLaw.us/Marbury/

Our study of *Marbury v. Madison* begins with the presidential election of 1800. In that race, candidates Thomas Jefferson and Aaron Burr received the same number of electoral votes. This tie threw the election into the House of Representatives, which was still controlled by the outgoing Federalist party. Ultimately, Jefferson was elected President on the thirty-sixth ballot, a mere two weeks before Inauguration Day.

Before the inauguration, the *lame duck* Federalist Congress enacted several last-minute laws to preserve its power. For example, the Judiciary Act of 1801 created forty-two new federal judgeships. President John Adams nominated Federalist supporters to fill these positions. The Federalist-controlled Senate promptly confirmed the so-called "midnight judges." On the eve of Jefferson's inauguration, President Adams signed the judges' commissions.

At the time, John Marshall served as both the Chief Justice and the Secretary of State. In his latter role, Marshall was responsible for delivering the signed commissions to the new judges. However, Marshall failed to deliver several signed commissions. In particular, William Marbury, who was nominated as a Justice of the Peace in the District of Columbia, never received his commission.

After the inauguration, President Jefferson instructed James Madison, his new Secretary of State, not to deliver Marbury's commission. Congress, now controlled by Jefferson's new Republican party, repealed the Judiciary Act of 1801. Congress also eliminated the Supreme Court's 1802 term so it could not review the new legislation. This move sent a clear warning to the Supreme Court.

William Marbury sued Secretary of State James Madison. He asked for a *writ of mandamus*. This order would have directed, or *mandated*, Madison to deliver the commission. However, Marbury did not begin his case in a lower court. Rather, he filed suit directly in the Supreme Court.

Chief Justice Marshall wrote the majority opinion. He divided his opinion into three parts. First, does Marbury have the right to his commission? The Court answered the first question yes. After President Adams signed Marbury's commission, then-Secretary of State Marshall put the Great Seal of the United States on the document. This act, the Court held, finalized the appointment. Delivery of the actual commission, a mere formality, was not necessary. (In his opinion, Marshall omitted the fact that it was his fault that the commission was never delivered.)

STUDY GUIDE

Should Chief Justice Marshall have even been sitting on a case in which he was so intimately involved?

Second, is Marbury entitled to a legal remedy in the courts? Marshall answered yes. The Court distinguished between two types of actions by executive branch officials. In the first category, the heads of departments are acting "merely to execute the will of the President," as his "political or confidential agents," or are acting "in cases in which the executive possesses a constitutional or legal discretion." Such so-called *political questions* are "only politically examinable," and courts may not provide any legal relief. However, in the second category, "where a specific duty is assigned by law, and individual rights depend upon the performance of that duty, it seems equally clear, that the individual who considers himself injured, has a right to resort to the laws of his country for a remedy." The Court found that the delivery of the commission was a ministerial task, not a political question. Therefore, Marbury's claim could be reviewed. But that analysis did not end the case.

Third, Marshall turned to the question of whether the Supreme Court could issue a writ of mandamus to order Madison to deliver Marbury's commission? Here the answer was no. Section 13 of the Judiciary Act of 1789, which was enacted by the first Congress, provided that the Supreme Court "shall have power to issue . . . writs of mandamus." However, the Court concluded that this provision was unconstitutional.

Marshall's analysis turned on the distinction between the Supreme Court's "original" and "appellate" jurisdiction. The court where a lawsuit originates — typically a trial court — has what is called *original jurisdiction*. In contrast, a court that reviews the rulings of a lower court is said to have *appellate jurisdiction*. Marshall held that a writ of mandamus can only properly be issued by a court of original jurisdiction.

Yet Article III, Section 2 of the Constitution limited the Supreme Court's "original jurisdiction" to "Cases affecting Ambassadors, other public Ministers and Consuls, and those in which a State shall be Party." None of these heads of jurisdiction covered Marbury's case. Article III, Section 2 continues, "In all the other Cases before mentioned, the Supreme Court shall have *appellate Jurisdiction*."

Marshall reasoned that Congress could not give the Supreme Court the power to issue writs of mandamus in its original jurisdiction — that is, in cases *not* involving ambassadors, public ministers, or disputes against states. The Judiciary Act purported to give the Supreme Court an authority that was prohibited by the Constitution. Marshall concluded that only an amendment to the Constitution, and not a mere statute, can modify the Supreme Court's original jurisdiction.

Ultimately, Marshall held that the Supreme Court could not issue the writ Marbury sought, even though a duly enacted statute gave it that power. In a crucial passage, he wrote:

> The powers of the legislature are defined and limited; and that those limits may not be mistaken, or forgotten, the constitution is written. To what purpose are powers limited, and to what purpose is that limitation committed to writing, if these limits may, at any time, be passed by those intended to be restrained? The distinction between a government with limited and unlimited powers is abolished, if those limits do not confine the persons on whom they are imposed, and if acts prohibited and acts allowed, are of equal obligation. It is a proposition too plain to be contested, that the constitution controls any legislative act repugnant to it; or, that the legislature may alter the constitution by an ordinary act.

An "act" of a legislature is not a valid *law* if it conflicts with the limits imposed by a written constitution. Marshall then asked, "If an act of the legislature, repugnant to the constitution, is void, does it, notwithstanding its invalidity, bind the courts, and oblige them to give it effect? Or, in other words, though it *be not law*, does it constitute a rule as operative as if it was a law?" His answer? No.

In one of the most famous passages in all of constitutional law, Marshall affirmed, "It is emphatically the province *and duty* of the judicial department to say what the law is." What happens when a judge is faced with the choice of following the text of the Constitution or following the text of an act of Congress? Marshall answered, "If two laws conflict with each other, the courts must decide on the operation of each. So if a law be in opposition to the constitution; if both the law and the constitution apply to a particular case, so that the court must either decide that case conformably to the law, disregarding the constitution; or conformably to the constitution, disregarding the law; the court must determine which of these conflicting rules governs the case." This role, he said, was "the very essence of judicial *duty*."

He then concluded that "if courts are to regard the constitution, and the constitution is superior to any ordinary act of the legislature, the constitution, and not such ordinary act, must govern the case to which they both apply." For this reason, Marshall held that it was the province and duty of the Supreme Court to say that the Judiciary Act's grant of a power to issue a writ of mandamus to the Supreme Court was not a valid law. Rather, the statute was null and "void." Therefore, Marbury must be denied the remedy Congress otherwise authorized.

In *Marbury v. Madison*, the Court asserted what is today called the power of judicial review to declare the law unconstitutional. However, contrary to common misconception, Marshall did not invent the concept of judicial review. Both the idea and the practice had existed for some time in the Anglo-American tradition. Alexander Hamilton articulated this philosophy as Publius in *Federalist No. 78*. Indeed, Marshall's reasoning in many regards echoed Hamilton's.

This concept was not, however, called the "*power* of judicial review." It was referred to as the "judicial *duty*" to follow the higher law of the Constitution. An office-holder has the discretion to exercise a "power." In contrast, an office-holder must perform a "duty." It is nondiscretionary, and simply must be done. (As we shall see, in *McCulloch v. Maryland* (1809), Marshall refers to this role as "the *painful duty* of this tribunal . . . to say that such an act was not the law of the land.")

In one of the most famous "jiu jitsu" maneuvers in legal history, Marshall asserted the power of the Court to declare legislation unconstitutional. At the same time, he avoided the possibility that President Jefferson would ignore an adverse ruling by the Court. In the end, Marbury's suit was dismissed for lack of jurisdiction.

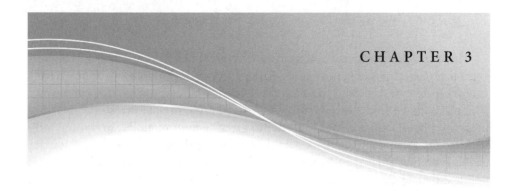

CHAPTER 3

McCulloch v. Maryland (1819)

 ConLaw.us/McCulloch

Following the ratification of the Constitution, our young Republic faced serious financial problems. Alexander Hamilton, the Secretary of the Treasury, proposed a solution to address these problems: The federal government should Charter a national bank. This institution would have branches throughout the United States that could establish credit, accept deposits, and lend money to the new national government.

STUDY GUIDE

Did the Constitution give Congress the enumerated power to incorporate the national bank?

Article I, Section 1 of the Constitution explains that "All legislative Powers *herein granted* shall be vested in a Congress of the United States." In other words, if a legislative power is not enumerated *somewhere* in the Constitution, then Congress does not have that power.

Most of Congress's enumerated powers can be found in Article I, Section 8, which lists eighteen separate clauses. The power to incorporate a bank cannot be found in the first seventeen clauses of Article I, Section 8. Hamilton's proposal does not require the collection of direct taxes. So that power is out. Nor does the bill borrow money or regulate commerce. All of the other express powers are likewise out. Only Clause 18, the Necessary and Proper Clause, could possibly empower Congress to incorporate the bank.

Members of Congress and officers in the executive branch debated about an important constitutional question: Is it "necessary and proper" for Congress to charter a bank in order to execute its powers to collect taxes, borrow money, and regulate commerce?

Unlike the Federal Reserve bank that exists today, private investors held stock in the first national bank. Was it proper to grant such monopolies to favored individuals? Opponents of the bank feared creating a privileged, monied aristocracy of the type that existed in Europe. These populist concerns created a white-hot political debate. Soon, the controversy about the bank's constitutionality focused on Congress's power to grant such a monopoly.

Representative James Madison delivered an important speech to Congress. He argued that the power to incorporate a bank was not incident to any of the enumerated powers. Therefore, the power to charter the bank was a "great and important power" that needed to be enumerated in the text of Article I. In addition, Madison contended that it was not *necessary* to incorporate a bank in order to collect taxes, borrow money, or regulate commerce. He concluded that Congress lacked the power to incorporate the bank.

Despite Madison's opposition, Congress enacted the bank bill. Subsequently, President Washington asked members of his cabinet for their opinions on its constitutionality. Thomas Jefferson, the Secretary of State, took an even more stringent view of the Necessary and Proper Clause than did Madison. Jefferson contended that "the constitution restrained [Congress] to the necessary means" of executing its powers. This power was limited to "those means without which the grant of the power would be nugatory." Because Congress's goals could be accomplished in other ways, Jefferson contended, a bank charter was not "necessary."

Alexander Hamilton, who first proposed the idea of the national bank, strongly rejected Jefferson's strict reading of *necessary*. Instead he offered a broader definition of *necessary*: "needful, requisite, incidental, useful, or conducive." In other words, if it is "useful" for Congress to charter a bank in order to collect taxes or borrow money, then Congress has the power to charter the bank.

Hamilton rejected any test of constitutionality that rested on the "degree in which a measure is necessary," or "the more or less of necessity or utility" of a measure. Yet he did not say that Congress had the discretion to adopt *any* means that, in its sole judgment, would be convenient to carry into execution its other powers. Instead he offered the following test: "The relation between the measure and the end; between the nature of the mean employed toward the execution of a power, and the object of that power must be the criterion of constitutionality." Today, we would call this approach *means-ends scrutiny*.

In 1791, President Washington signed the bill that chartered the first bank of the United States. He either agreed with Hamilton's constitutional opinion or he agreed with Jefferson that, because the decision was a close one, he should defer to Congress. The federal bank would remain in business for two decades.

In 1816, Congress chartered a second bank of the United States. President James Madison, who had opposed the bank two decades earlier, signed the bill into law. Did his opinion about the Necessary and Proper Clause change from the view he had articulated as a congressman? In private correspondence, Madison defended the consistency of his approaches: It was proper to defer to the judgment of several Congresses on the question of whether a bank was truly necessary to execute its powers. Madison said this deference was especially appropriate given the bank's "almost necessity."

Soon, the Bank of the United States became very unpopular. In 1818, the Maryland General Assembly imposed a tax on the branch in Baltimore. The bank's cashier, James William McCulloch, refused to pay the tax. Maryland sued McCulloch to recover the money. The Maryland Court of Appeals ruled for the state. McCulloch then appealed the case to the Supreme Court. He argued that the state could not tax the federal institution. However, the Court first had to decide if Congress had the power to charter the federal bank before resolving whether the state tax was constitutional.

In *McCulloch v. Maryland*, the Supreme Court resolved the debate from two decades earlier between Jefferson and Madison on one side and Hamilton on the other. Chief Justice Marshall wrote the majority opinion. He rejected Maryland's very narrow reading of *necessary*. Though Marshall did not cite Hamilton, the Chief Justice copied several portions of the Treasury Secretary's opinion on the bank almost verbatim.

Recall that Hamilton defined *necessary* as "needful," "requisite," "useful," and "conducive." Marshall used the same four adjectives, but added another definition that Hamilton did not: "convenient." That is, *McCulloch* can be read as saying that Congress could do whatever is "convenient" in order to execute its other enumerated powers. Indeed, Marshall described the creation of a bank as "a convenient, a useful, and essential instrument in the prosecution of [Congress's] fiscal operations" and "an appropriate mode of executing the powers of government." He rejected the notion that the bank must be an "absolute physical necessity."

What about the objection that the Constitution did not specify a power to create a bank? Marshall responded that such specificity "would partake of the prolixity of a legal code." Instead, in a much-repeated phrase, he declared, "we must never forget that it is a constitution we are expounding." Our Constitution, he explained, is "intended to endure for ages to come, and consequently, to be adapted to the various crises of human affairs." In other words, the Constitution speaks in more general terms to avoid growing outdated quickly.

Next, Marshall provided a test that the Supreme Court still uses to determine the scope of Congress's implied powers: "Let the end be legitimate, let it be within the scope of the constitution, and all means which are appropriate, which are plainly adapted to that end, which are not prohibited, but consist with the letter and spirit of the constitution, are constitutional." Does the criteria of "means which are . . . plainly adapted to the end" include the sort of *means-ends scrutiny* that Hamilton advocated for? Probably, but it is not entirely clear.

STUDY GUIDE

Does Marshall's interpretation of the Necessary and Proper Clause give Congress a blank check? If not, what are the limits of Congress's implied powers?

Ultimately, *McCulloch* held that the Necessary and Proper Clause gave Congress a sufficient power to incorporate the bank. As a result, Maryland could not tax the federal bank. Why? Marshall explained that "the power to tax involves the power to destroy."

McCulloch soon became very controversial. Chief Justice Marshall defended his opinion in a series of pseudonymous columns published in two Virginia newspapers. Specifically, he sought to rebut the charge that the Court had read the Necessary and Proper Clause to authorize an "unlimited power of congress to adopt any means whatever." Marshall highlighted a portion of his opinion that does not always receive attention today. He explained that the Court would still have to set aside a law "should congress under the pretext of executing its powers, pass laws for the accomplishment of objects, not entrusted to the government, [because] it would become the painful duty of this tribunal . . . to say that such *an act* was not *the law* of the land." (Notice Marshall distinguished between a mere legislative "act" and "the law of the land." This distinction helps to explain the original meaning of the "due process *of law*.")

Even though he equated "necessary" and "convenient," Marshall still maintained that the Supreme Court had a role to scrutinize federal statutes before they can be considered part of the law of the land. Is Congress carrying into execution an enumerated power *in good faith*? Or is Congress's justification instead a mere *pretext* for exercising a power that has not been entrusted to the national government?

STUDY GUIDE

How would the Supreme Court identify when Congress was acting pretextually and not asserting an enumerated power in good faith?

Thirteen years later, in 1832, President Andrew Jackson vetoed the renewal of the national bank. Unlike Marshall, Jackson concluded that the bank was not "necessary" for Congress to execute its other enumerated powers. Therefore, the federal charter was unconstitutional.

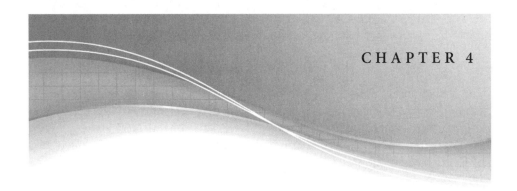

CHAPTER 4

Gibbons v. Ogden (1824)

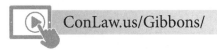

ConLaw.us/Gibbons/

New York law gave Aaron Ogden a monopoly. Only his firm could operate steamboats within New York waters. Another businessman, Thomas Gibbons, disregarded that law. He operated steamboats that travelled from New Jersey to New York.

Ogden sued to halt Gibbons's steamboat business. He contended that New York law gave him a monopoly. Gibbons countered that the New York law interfered with a federal law that licensed him to operate his ships. If Congress had the power to license ships that travelled between one state and another, then the New York law would be preempted, and thus unconstitutional. The New York courts rejected Gibbons's constitutional argument and enjoined his operations. In turn, Gibbons appealed the case to the United States Supreme Court. He argued that the federal law was supported by Congress's power under the *Commerce* Clause. Article I, Section 8, Clause 3 gives Congress the power "[t]o regulate Commerce with foreign Nations, and *among the several States*, and with the Indian Tribes." Gibbons contended that a state cannot regulate interstate commerce.

In *Gibbons v. Ogden*, the Supreme Court agreed. Chief Justice Marshall's majority opinion provided the Court's first major interpretation of the words "commerce" and "among" in the Commerce Clause.

Ogden argued that the New York monopoly law was constitutional because Congress lacked the power to regulate boats travelling between New York and New Jersey. *Commerce*, he contended, was limited to "traffic, to buying and selling, or the interchange of commodities, and . . . it [did not] comprehend[] navigation." Therefore, the New York law should control.

As in *McCulloch v. Maryland*, Chief Justice Marshall rejected the narrowest interpretation of Congressional power in favor of a somewhat broader one. He explained that Ogden's construction would "restrict a general term," that is *commerce*, which is "applicable to many objects, to one of its significations" — meaning trade or traffic. Instead, Marshall adopted a broader interpretation of the meaning of the word *commerce*. He concluded that, "[c]ommerce, undoubtedly, is traffic, but it is something more: it is intercourse. It describes the commercial intercourse between nations, and parts of nations, in all its branches, and is regulated by prescribing rules for carrying on that intercourse." This conclusion is also supported by compelling evidence that the original meaning of "commerce" included laws governing navigation.

STUDY GUIDE

Is *intercourse* broader than *commerce*?

Next, Marshall explained that the word *among* in the Commerce Clause is defined as "intermingled with." Marshall wrote that "[c]omprehensive as the word 'among' is, it may very properly be restricted to that commerce which concerns more States than one." The word "concerns" is another broadening term.

When the words of the Commerce Clause in the Constitution are replaced by the synonyms used by Marshall ("commerce" with *intercourse* and "among" with *intermingled with*), the power seems to be broader — or so later courts would rule.

STUDY GUIDE

Is there anything Congress cannot regulate?

However, like in *McCulloch v. Maryland*, Marshall placed an important *limiting principle* on the scope of Congress's powers. The Commerce Clause enumerated three specific powers: to regulate commerce with foreign nations, among the several states, and with Indian tribes. Therefore, that "enumeration presupposes something *not* enumerated." In other words, Congress can't regulate any other type of commerce than the three that are listed. Specifically, Marshall found that the Constitution does not give Congress the power to regulate the "exclusively internal commerce of a state." Such "exclusively internal commerce," he added, "may be considered as reserved for the State itself."

The text of the Tenth Amendment supports Marshall's conclusion. It provides that: "The powers not delegated to the United States by the Constitution, nor prohibited by it to the States, are reserved to the States respectively, or to the people." If an enumerated power is not delegated to Congress, then it is reserved to the states.

STUDY GUIDE

Could Congress *ever* regulate commerce that takes place entirely within a state? Could Congress sometimes regulate that intrastate commerce pursuant to its authority under the Necessary and Proper Clause?

With this broad reading of "commerce" and "among," the Court found that Congress had the power to enact the federal law that licensed Gibbons's boats. As a result, the state law that limited boats from entering New York waters was preempted, and was unconstitutional.

Like in *McCulloch v. Maryland*, Marshall can be accused of casually employing expansive and comparatively imprecise rhetoric concerning the scope of Congress's enumerated powers. Yet, once again, Marshall in fact reaffirmed limits on these powers. Future decisions would rely on Marshall's broad definition of "commerce" and "among," yet ignore his limitations on federal power.

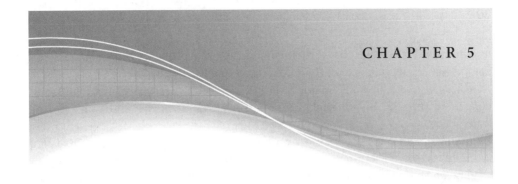

CHAPTER 5

Barron v. Baltimore (1833)

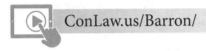 ConLaw.us/Barron/

The proposed federal Constitution was submitted to the states in 1787. Many states ratified the Constitution on the condition that certain amendments would be added later. In 1789, the first Congress introduced twelve proposed amendments, ten of which were ratified. Today, these ten amendments are known collectively as the "Bill of Rights."

STUDY GUIDE

The first eight amendments to the Constitution put limits on the powers of the federal government. Did they also limit the powers of the state governments?

The First Amendment begins, "*Congress* shall make no law respecting an establishment of religion." There is no question that this provision limits Congress's powers. But what about the Fifth Amendment's Takings Clause? It provides "nor shall private property be taken for public use, without paying just compensation." The Clause does not specify whether the state governments are also prohibited from taking private property without just compensation. *Barron v. City of Baltimore* (1833) would resolve this question.

John Barron owned a profitable wharf in Baltimore's harbor. The City of Baltimore diverted the flow of streams near the harbor. This construction created mounds of sand and earth near Barron's wharf. As a result, the water became too shallow for most vessels to dock. Barron sued the mayor of Baltimore for damages. He claimed that the City took his private property without paying just compensation, in violation of the Fifth Amendment.

Chief Justice Marshall's majority opinion rejected Barron's claim. The Court concluded that the Bill of Rights limited only federal power and did not limit state power.

Marshall's analysis was based on inferences from the Constitution's text. For example, Article I, Section 9 provides that "no Bill of Attainder or ex post facto Law shall be passed" by Congress. This provision appears in a section that limits federal powers. In contrast, Article I, Section 10 provides that "no state shall . . . . pass any Bill of Attainder [or] ex post facto Law." This provision appears in a section that limits state powers.

When the Framers sought to restrict state power, Marshall reasoned, they did so expressly. He added that if states wanted to provide "additional safeguards to liberty," then the "remedy was in their own hands." That is, they could have amended their own state constitutions. This process was far easier than amending the federal Constitution.

Finally, Marshall made a historical claim: The Bill of Rights was aimed at assuaging Anti-Federalist concerns about the extent of the new national government's powers. However, "[t]hese amendments contain no expression indicating an intention to apply them to the State governments."

Chief Justice Marshall's reasoning in *Barron* came to be the settled view of how and why the first eight amendments did not apply to the states. This view would change, however, with the ratification of the Fourteenth Amendment. Indeed, the Thirty-ninth Congress drafted the Fourteenth Amendment, in part, to reverse *Barron*.

Today, almost all of the provisions of the Bill of Rights have now been extended to the states by *incorporating* them into the Due Process Clause of the Fourteenth Amendment.

A Brief History of Implied Powers

	Broader Reading of Implied Powers →
Founding	First Bank of the United States (1791)
Marshall Court	*McCulloch v. Maryland* (1819) →
	Gibbons v. Ogden (1824)
Taney Court	*Prigg v. Pennsylvania* (1842) → → → → → → → →
Chase Court	*U.S. v. Dewitt* (1869) ←
	Hepburn v. Griswold (1870)
	Knox v. Lee (1871) → → → → → → → →
Progressive Era	*U.S. v. E.C. Knight* (1895) ←
	Champion v. Ames (1903) → →
	Hammer v. Dagenhart (1918)
	Schechter Poultry Corp. v. U.S. (1935)
New Deal	*NLRB v. Jones & Laughlin Steel. Corp.* (1937) → →
	U.S. v. Darby (1941) → →
	Wickard v. Filburn (1942) → →
Warren Court	*Heart of Atlanta Motel v. U.S.* (1964)
	Katzenbach v. McClung (1964) → →
Rehnquist Court	*U.S. v. Lopez* (1995)
	U.S. v. Morrison (2000)
	Gonzales v. Raich (2005) → →
Roberts Court	*NFIB v. Sebelius* (2012)

ENUMERATED POWERS

Part II provides an introduction to the doctrine of enumerated powers, which governs the scope of Congress's regulatory power. We begin with the Fugitive Slave Act and the Taney Court's decision in *Prigg v. Pennsylvania* (1842). Next, we discuss how the Chase Court interpreted the scope of Congress's enumerated powers in three cases: *United States v. Dewitt* (1869), *Hepburn v. Griswold* (1870), and *Knox v. Lee* (1871).

We then consider three cases in which the Supreme Court's enumerated powers doctrine fluctuated during the Progressive Era: *United States v. E.C. Knight* (1895), *Champion v. Ames* (1903), and *Hammer v. Dagenhart* (1918). *Schechter Poultry Corp. v. United States* (1935) was a high-water mark for the judiciary's enforcement of the enumerated powers doctrine.

Subsequently, in three cases, the Court developed the "substantial effects" test: *NLRB v. Jones & Laughlin Steel Corp.* (1937), *United States v. Darby* (1941), and *Wickard v. Filburn* (1942).

We then jump ahead to analyze how the Warren Court approached the doctrine of enumerated powers. Two cases considered the constitutionality of the Civil Rights Act of 1964: *Heart of Atlanta Motel v. United States* (1964) and *Katzenbach v. McClung* (1964).

Finally, we conclude Part II with a study of five cases that identified limits on the growth of federal power: *South Dakota v. Dole* (1987), *United States v. Lopez* (1995), *United States v. Morrison* (2000), *Gonzales v. Raich* (2005), and *NFIB v. Sebelius* (2012).

CHAPTER 6

Prigg v. Pennsylvania (1842)

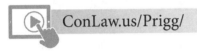 ConLaw.us/Prigg/

Most students study *Dred Scott v. Sandford* (1857), but few students are familiar with *Prigg v. Pennsylvania* (1842). This case considered the constitutionality of the Fugitive Slave Act, which Congress enacted in 1793. It authorized slave catchers to travel across state lines and arrest runaway slaves. This federal law was very unpopular in northern states that opposed slavery. Pennsylvania and other abolitionist states enacted so-called *personal liberty laws.* These laws prevented a person from being removed from the state without a full judicial proceeding — including a jury trial — to determine whether or not that person was in fact a fugitive slave. These state laws conflicted with the federal act, which afforded only minimal procedural protections to alleged runaway slaves. In *Prigg v. Pennsylvania*, the Supreme Court found that the federal law was constitutional and superseded, or preempted, any state laws to the contrary.

At this time, Maryland was a slave state, and Pennsylvania was a free state. In 1832, Margaret Morgan, a slave, left Maryland to marry a free black man in Pennsylvania. (She apparently did so with the acquiescence of her owner, John Ashmore.) Five years later, after John Ashmore's death, his widow sent Edward Prigg — a slave catcher — from Maryland to Pennsylvania. Prigg soon captured Morgan and brought her back to Maryland. After a public outcry, the governor of Maryland agreed to allow Prigg to be extradited to Pennsylvania where he was tried and convicted for kidnapping. But the governor refused to return Morgan, the person Prigg had kidnapped.

Prigg appealed his conviction to the Supreme Court. He argued that the federal Fugitive Slave Act preempted the state personal liberty law. Prigg cited the Supremacy Clause in Article VI, which provides "This Constitution, *and the Laws of the United States* which shall be made in Pursuance thereof . . . shall be the *supreme Law of the Land*; and the Judges in every State shall be bound thereby, any Thing in the Constitution or Laws of any State to the Contrary notwithstanding."

To resolve this dispute, the Supreme Court had to decide whether the federal Fugitive Slave Act was constitutional — that is, whether it was "made in Pursuance" of the Constitution. *McCulloch v. Maryland* (1819) and *Gibbons v. Ogden* (1824) held that Congress can only enact laws pursuant to its delegated powers.

STUDY GUIDE

What provision of the Constitution gave Congress the power to enact the Fugitive Slave Act?

One possible candidate is the Fugitive Slave Clause in Article IV, Section 2. It provides, "No Person held to Service or Labour in one State . . . escaping into another, shall . . . be discharged from such Service . . . but shall be delivered up on Claim of the Party to whom such Service or Labour may be due." (Do not confuse the Fugitive Slave *Clause* with the Fugitive Slave *Act*.)

STUDY GUIDE

Does the Fugitive Slave Clause actually grant Congress the power to enact the Fugitive Slave Act?

Salmon Chase, who would later become the Chief Justice, argued as an attorney that the Fugitive Slave Clause did not expressly grant Congress any new powers. Because the text in Article IV did not expressly give Congress an enforcement power, he argued, then Congress lacked the power to enact the Fugitive Slave Act.

Compare two provisions of the Constitution that appear next to each other. Article IV, Section 3 expressly states that "Congress shall have power" to make rules governing the territories. However, the Fugitive Slave Clause in Article IV, Section 2 merely describes the relationship between states. It does not grant an express enforcement power to Congress. Therefore, Chase concluded, the Fugitive Slave Act was unconstitutional.

In *Prigg v. Pennsylvania*, the Supreme Court rejected the argument that Congress lacked the enumerated power to enact the Fugitive Slave Act. Justice Story wrote the majority opinion. He held that the Fugitive Slave Act was constitutional because the Fugitive Slave Clause "was *intended*" to prevent free states from "intermeddling with, or obstructing, or abolishing the rights of the owners of slaves." He doubted that the Union could have even been formed if the Fugitive Slave Clause had not been added to the Constitution.

But what about Chase's argument that Article IV, Section 2 did not grant Congress an enforcement power? Justice Story responded that the Necessary and Proper Clause provides Congress with the authority. He wrote, "The end being required, it has been deemed a just and necessary implication, that the means to accomplish it are given also; or, in other words, that the power flows as a necessary means to accomplish the end."

Story's broad interpretation of the Necessary and Proper Clause gave Congress far more authority than did Chief Justice Marshall's analysis in *McCulloch v. Maryland*. *Prigg* remains one of the most expansive readings of the Necessary and Proper Clause ever adopted by the Supreme Court.

On the other hand, Justice Story also maintained that the states cannot be "compelled to enforce" the Fugitive Slave Act. Rather, the national government is responsible for carrying into effect its own policies. This limitation on congressional power would provide the foundation for the so-called "anti-commandeering doctrine." This modern doctrine holds that Congress lacks the power to "commandeer," or *force*, states to implement federal programs. (See Chapters 17 and 18.)

In sum, Story found that the Fugitive Slave Act was made "in pursuance of" the Fugitive Slave Clause, and in conjunction with the Necessary and Proper Clause. Therefore, the Act was "supreme" and preempted the Pennsylvania personal liberty law. Prigg's conviction was reversed.

After the Supreme Court upheld the Fugitive Slave Act of 1793, Congress would pass an even more draconian Fugitive Slave Act in 1850.

STUDY GUIDE

We have come to associate the Southern side of the Civil War with that of "states' rights." Does Congress's assertion of the power to enact the Fugitive Slave Act, and the outcome of *Prigg*, cloud that picture?

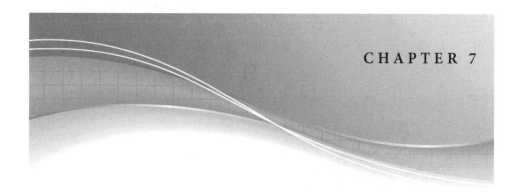

CHAPTER 7

Enumerated Powers on the Chase Court (1869-1871)

In different eras, the Supreme Court has interpreted the scope of Congress's enumerated powers in different ways. In *McCulloch v. Maryland* (1819), the Marshall Court's interpretation of the Necessary and Proper Clause gave Congress broad discretion to implement its other enumerated powers. And in *Gibbons v. Ogden* (1824), the Marshall Court defined "commerce" as "intercourse" and interpreted "among the several states" as "concerning more states than one."

The Taney Court continued the trend set by the Marshall Court. In *Prigg v. Pennsylvania* (1842), Justice Story upheld the constitutionality of the Fugitive Slave Act. He interpreted Congress's implied powers under the Necessary and Proper Clause even more broadly than Marshall had in *McCulloch*.

After Chief Justice Roger Taney died in October 1864, President Lincoln appointed his Secretary of the Treasury, Salmon P. Chase, as the Chief Justice. This nomination was fitting. Chase had earned the nickname "the attorney general for runaway slaves" because of his work as an antislavery lawyer. He argued that the Fugitive Slave Act was unconstitutional based on a narrow reading of congressional power.

In the span of three years, the Chase Court would decide three cases that interpreted the scope of Congress's enumerated powers: *United States v. Dewitt* (1869), *Hepburn v. Griswold* (1870), and *Knox v. Lee* (1871).

United States v. Dewitt (1869)

 ConLaw.us/Dewitt

In 1867, Congress criminalized the sale of oil that was made from petroleum—including transactions that were completed entirely within a single state. Mr. Dewitt was indicted for selling oil in Detroit, Michigan. His case was appealed to the Supreme Court.

STUDY GUIDE

Which enumerated power gave Congress the power to criminalize the sale of oil?

Chief Justice Chase wrote the majority opinion in *Dewitt*. He held that Congress's authority under the Commerce Clause, by itself, was not enough to enact the statute. Chase wrote that the Commerce Clause is a "virtual denial [to Congress] of any power to interfere with the internal trade and business of the separate states." This passage echoes Chief Justice Marshall's opinion in *Gibbons*.

However, there is an important exception to the rule. Congress can interfere with internal trade when it is a "necessary and proper means for carrying into execution some other power expressly granted or vested." Chase's opinion teaches the vital lesson: when considering the scope of Congress's enumerated powers, the courts cannot stop with their analysis of the Commerce Clause. Courts must also consider the Necessary and Proper Clause.

Chase then rejected the claim that it was "necessary and proper" for Congress to criminalize the sale of petroleum-based oils to more effectively enforce its "Power To lay and collect Taxes" on the local sale of oils. Chase applied Marshall's construction from *McCulloch*, and concluded that this "consequence is too remote and too uncertain to warrant us in saying that the prohibition is an appropriate and plainly adapted means for carrying into execution the power of laying and collecting taxes." Today, many scholars contend that the Supreme Court did not adopt a narrow interpretation of the Commerce Clause until the Progressive Era during the early twentieth century. *Dewitt*, however, proves otherwise.

Hepburn v. Griswold (1870)

 ConLaw.us/Hepburn

Without question, Congress has the power to issue paper notes as currency. However, during the Civil War, Congress debated whether it could make this paper currency a *legal tender*. That is, could Congress require everyone to accept the government's paper currency as payment for a debt, even if a contract called for payment with gold or silver. At the time of the framing, the term "dollar" in the Constitution referred to a unit of silver — in particular to the Spanish Dollar coin, which was in wide circulation. It was a big deal to force people to accept dollar bills in place of silver or gold. Does the Constitution give Congress this power?

In 1862, Congress determined that it had such a power, and enacted the Legal Tender Act. Secretary of the Treasury Salmon Chase supported the constitutionality of the law. The federal government even put his face on the $1 bill, known as a greenback.

However, eight years later, Chase changed course as Chief Justice. He wrote the majority opinion in *Hepburn v. Griswold* (1870). That decision held that Congress lacked the power to require people to accept paper currency as legal tender. The Court observed that there is "no express grant of legislative power" to create paper legal tender. The federal government has the power to "regulate commerce," "to coin Money," or "to borrow money." But the Constitution does not give Congress an express power to make people accept paper currency. Nor does the Necessary and Proper Clause give Congress an implied power to make paper currency a legal tender.

Chief Justice Chase reasoned that the power to require people to accept paper money is not incidental to the power to "regulate commerce," or "to coin Money," or to "to borrow money." (James Madison, who opposed the national bank, relied on the concept of "incidental" powers to interpret the scope of the Necessary and Proper Clause.) Chase concluded that "an act making mere promises to pay dollars a legal tender in payment of debts previously contracted, is not a means appropriate, plainly adapted, really calculated to carry into effect any express power vested in Congress."

Now comes the fun part. When *Hepburn* was argued in November 1869, there were only eight Justices on the bench. After arguments the vote was 5-3. The majority concluded that the Legal Tender Act was unconstitutional. However, in January 1870, Justice Grier resigned due to his poor health before the decision was formally announced. This vacancy made the final vote 4-3.

After *Hepburn* was decided, President Grant appointed Justices Strong and Bradley. They were known to support paper money as legal tender, which Grant also favored. Following their confirmations there were now five Justices who thought that the Legal Tender Act was constitutional. Sure enough, the Court reversed itself a year later.

Knox v. Lee (1871)

 ConLaw.us/Knox

Knox v. Lee held that the Legal Tender Act was constitutional. *Hepburn* was now overturned by a 5-4 vote. In *Knox*, the majority found that the Legal Tender Act was made "necessary" by the shortage of gold and silver during the Civil War.

STUDY GUIDE

After the Civil War concluded, and the currency emergency subsided, did Congress lose the power to enact the Legal Tender Act?

Knox did far more than uphold the Legal Tender Act. The decision also adopted a construction of the Necessary and Proper Clause that was even broader than Justice Story's analysis in *Prigg v. Pennsylvania*. The "non-enumerated powers" granted by this Clause, Justice Strong wrote, "reach beyond the mere execution of all powers definitely intrusted [sic] to Congress and mentioned in detail." Indeed, Justice Strong stated it was "not indispensable" that an implied power "be found specified in the words of the Constitution, or clearly and directly traceable to some one of the specified powers." The existence of such a power "may be deduced fairly from more than one of the substantive powers expressly defined, *or from them all combined*. It is allowable to group together any number of them and infer from them all that the power claimed has been conferred." In *Knox*, the Court found that Congress's implied powers included "the power of self-preservation."

This reading of the Necessary and Proper Clause may be the most capacious reading the Supreme Court has ever articulated. Now in dissent, Chief Justice Chase lamented that, under the majority's approach, the "powers [of] the government become[] practically absolute and unlimited." Indeed, *Juilliard v. Greenman* (1884) held that Congress could make government notes "a legal tender for the payment of private debts" in the absence of any emergency "as incident to the power of borrowing money, and issuing bills or notes of the government for money borrowed."

Chase died in 1873. The narrower construction of enumerated powers he articulated in *Dewitt* would be echoed during the Progressive Era in the early twentieth century. However, *Prigg* and *Knox* foreshadowed how the Supreme Court would eventually treat the scope of Congress's enumerated and implied powers following the New Deal.

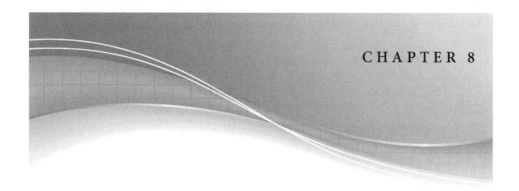

CHAPTER 8

Enumerated Powers in the Progressive Era (1895-1918)

As the nineteenth century drew to a close, the Progressive Movement successfully lobbied the states, and later Congress, to enact new political, economic, and social reforms. In Part VII, we will study how *state* progressive laws were challenged as deprivations of liberty without the "due process of law." In this chapter, we will study three cases in which *federal* progressive laws were challenged for exceeding the scope of Congress's enumerated powers: *United States v. E.C. Knight* (1895), *Champion v. Ames* (1903), and *Hammer v. Dagenhart* (1918).

United States v. E.C. Knight (1895)

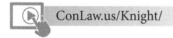 ConLaw.us/Knight/

The first case began after the American Sugar Refining Company purchased its competitors, including E.C. Knight. The federal government charged that the new firm would monopolize the sugar market nationwide, in violation of the Sherman Antitrust Act. The Supreme Court considered whether Congress had the power to criminalize this conduct based on its power to "regulate Commerce . . . among the several states," together with its power "to make all Laws which shall be necessary and proper for carrying into Execution the foregoing Powers."

The Supreme Court does not always explicitly consider both provisions. However, you should. Even in cases where the Court only discusses the Commerce Clause, the Necessary and Proper Clause is also working in the background.

33

Chief Justice Fuller wrote the majority opinion in *E.C. Knight*. He held that Congress could not regulate the local manufacture of sugar, even if the sugar produced would be exported to other states. "Commerce," he wrote, "succeeds to manufacture, and is not a part of it." In other words, commerce involves the sale or movement of an item *after* it is manufactured.

STUDY GUIDE

Compare the interpretation of "commerce" in *E.C. Knight* and in *Gibbons v. Ogden*.

Although the majority opinion did not discuss the Necessary and Proper Clause, Justice John Marshall Harlan's dissent did. He found that this provision empowered Congress to regulate the local manufacture of sugar. He contended that the Constitution "did not define the means that may be employed to protect the freedom of commercial intercourse." Rather, it gave Congress the "authority to enact all laws necessary and proper for carrying into execution the power to regulate commerce." Justice Harlan then applied the means-ends scrutiny test from *McCulloch v. Maryland*.

What are the ends, or goals, the government is trying to achieve? The "protection of trade and commerce among the States against unlawful restraints." Harlan concluded that the ends are legitimate. What means did the government choose? "Suppression of monopolies." Are those means appropriate? Harlan said they were. Because the means fit the ends, Congress could regulate the local manufacture of sugar.

Champion v. Ames (1903)

ConLaw.us/Champion/

In *E.C. Knight*, Chief Justice Fuller was in the majority and Justice Harlan was in dissent. In *Champion v. Ames*, the roles reversed. Justice Harlan wrote the majority opinion for a 5-4 Court. Chief Justice Fuller dissented. *Champion v. Ames*, also known as the *Lottery Cases*, considered whether Congress could prohibit the interstate shipment of lottery tickets. *Champion* turned on the meaning of the words "commerce" and "regulate" in the Commerce Clause. Is the movement of lottery tickets from one state to another "commerce"? Justice Harlan answered yes: "Lottery tickets are subjects of traffic and therefore are subjects of commerce, and the regulation of the carriage," or transportation, "of such tickets from State to State, at least by independent carriers, is a regulation of commerce among the several States."

STUDY GUIDE

Does the power to "regulate" commerce give Congress the power to *prohibit* commerce?

Justice Harlan concluded that it does. By way of analogy, he observed that states have the police power to prohibit the intrastate sale of lottery tickets. If the states have that power, he asked, "why may not Congress, invested with the power to regulate commerce among the several States, provide that such commerce shall not be polluted by the carrying of lottery tickets from one State to another?" In short, just as a state has a police power over intrastate commerce — which includes the power to prohibit such commerce — Congress also has a police power over interstate commerce. To this day, *Champion v. Ames* is cited for the principle that the power to "regulate" commerce includes the power to prohibit some forms of commerce.

The Court did, however, adopt a *limiting principle* based on the Tenth Amendment. Harlan acknowledged that Congress cannot "interfere with traffic or commerce in lottery tickets carried on exclusively within the limits of any State." Three decades later during the New Deal, the Supreme Court would abandon Harlan's limiting principle. We will discuss these cases in Chapter 10.

STUDY GUIDE

Compare the interpretation of "commerce" in *Champion v. Ames*, in *E.C. Knight*, and in *Gibbons v. Ogden*.

Chief Justice Fuller dissented in *Champion*. The power to prohibit lotteries, he wrote, "belongs to the states." A congressional "general police power" over interstate commerce, he contended, would "defeat the operation of the Tenth Amendment."

STUDY GUIDE

What is the police power? Does the federal government have a police power? If the states are barred from policing interstate commerce, does that power fall to Congress?

Hammer v. Dagenhart (1918)

 ConLaw.us/Hammer/

Champion established the rule that Congress's power to regulate commerce includes the power to prohibit commerce. In *Hammer v. Dagenhart*, the Court considered whether Congress could prohibit the shipment of products manufactured by children.

Hammer divided the Court 5-4. Justice Day wrote the majority opinion. He considered why Congress enacted the child labor law. The federal law, he said, "does not regulate transportation among the States, but *aims to* standardize the ages at which children may be employed." Day added that Congress can "regulate commerce." However, the federal government cannot "control the States in their exercise of the police power over local trade."

Critics of the Progressive Era Court often assert that the conservative Justices found that *state* child labor laws violated the Due Process Clause of the Fourteenth Amendment. This claim is false. *Hammer* only found that Congress lacked the power to prohibit the interstate shipment of goods made by child labor, when the true "aim" was to intrude into the state's police power.

Justice Oliver Wendell Holmes dissented in *Hammer*. He argued that *Champion v. Ames* allowed the federal government to prohibit the interstate shipment of goods manufactured by child labor. Congress's aims or motives, he contended, were irrelevant.

E.C. Knight and *Hammer* would be overturned following the New Deal. The Supreme Court would hold that Congress's commerce power was not limited by the state's police power. *Champion v. Ames*, which allowed Congress to prohibit interstate commerce, remains good law.

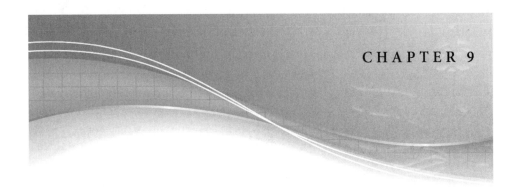

CHAPTER 9

Schechter Poultry Corp. v. United States (1935)

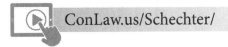 ConLaw.us/Schechter/

In 1932, Franklin D. Roosevelt was elected President. Roosevelt's legislative agenda pushed the boundaries of how much local conduct Congress could regulate. One of the most significant of these laws was the National Industrial Recovery Act (NRA). Under the NRA, private businesses and unions could adopt "Codes of Fair Competition" that would become legally enforceable once approved by the President.

STUDY GUIDE

The challenge to the NRA also raised a separation of powers question: Can Congress can delegate to the President the power to make laws? This principle is known as the *nondelegation doctrine*.

President Roosevelt adopted the Live Poultry Code for New York City. The code regulated labor conditions in slaughterhouses and specified how chickens could be slaughtered. The Schechter Brothers operated a Kosher slaughterhouse in Brooklyn. They did not ship their chickens out of state. The federal government prosecuted them for violating the code.

The Court unanimously concluded that Congress lacked the power to enact the NRA. Even Justice Louis Brandeis, a progressive, agreed that the NRA gave the federal government too much power to regulate local activities. Chief Justice Hughes wrote the majority opinion in *Schechter Poultry*. He found that "neither the slaughtering nor the sales by defendants [of chickens] were transactions in interstate commerce." This finding was true, he said, even if live chickens were imported from other states.

The NRA, however, did more than allow the federal government to regulate commerce between one state and another. The law also empowered the executive branch to regulate "any transaction in or *affecting* interstate or foreign commerce."

STUDY GUIDE

What is the significance of the word "affecting"?

The word "affecting" suggests that Congress's *enumerated* powers under the Commerce Clause are being supplemented by Congress's *implied* powers under the Necessary and Proper Clause. *United States v. Darby* (1941) would clarify that the word "affecting" implicates the Necessary and Proper Clause. We will discuss this case in Chapter 10.

Although the NRA was halted, the Justices still gave the Roosevelt administration a small but important victory: The Court agreed that Congress can regulate local transactions that merely "affect" commerce. Rather, the Court found that the local sale of chickens did not *directly* "affect" interstate commerce. The effect was only *indirect*. Therefore, Congress could not regulate those local transactions because they were too remote from interstate commerce. Chief Justice Hughes recognized that if Congress could regulate activities that *indirectly* affected interstate commerce, then "there would be virtually no limit to the federal power, and, for all practical purposes, we should have a completely centralized government."

However, Congress could regulate other types of local activities that have a *more direct* effect on interstate commerce. *Schechter Poultry* offered a limiting principle to preserve federalism, similar to those advanced in *E.C. Knight* and *Hammer*: "[T]he authority of the federal government may not be pushed to such an extreme as to destroy the distinction, which the commerce clause itself establishes, between commerce 'among the several States' and the internal concerns of a State." Chief Justice Marshall invoked a similar distinction in *Gibbons v. Ogden* (1824).

Schechter Poultry, decided in 1935, was one of the last major defeats President Roosevelt suffered at the Supreme Court. Subsequent New Deal legislation, however, never went as far as the NRA had gone. Starting in 1937, the Supreme Court began to consistently uphold federal and state Progressive laws. By and large, these decisions did not expand the scope of Congress's enumerated powers under the Commerce Clause. Rather, these cases expanded the scope of Congress's implied powers under the Necessary and Proper Clause.

CHAPTER 10

The Substantial Effects Doctrine (1937-1942)

The Commerce Clause gives Congress the power to regulate *inter*state commerce. However, the Supreme Court has found that the Commerce Clause, working in conjunction with the Necessary and Proper Clause, allow Congress to regulate certain types of *intra*state activity. For example, Congress can regulate local activity that is not "among" one state and another.

Throughout the twentieth century, the Supreme Court adopted different tests to determine what kinds of intrastate activity Congress could regulate. During the Progressive Era the Court used the so-called *direct effects* test. In *E.C. Knight* (1895), *Hammer v. Dagenhart* (1918), and *Schechter Poultry* (1935), the Court held that Congress could only regulate local activity that had a *direct* effect on interstate commerce.

However, after 1937, the New Deal Court replaced the *direct effects* test with the new *substantial effects* test. In three decisions the Court held that Congress can regulate local activity that had a *substantial* effect on interstate commerce: *NLRB v. Jones & Laughlin Steel Corp.* (1937), *United States v. Darby* (1941), and *Wickard v. Filburn* (1942). These cases are still good law.

NLRB v. Jones & Laughlin Steel Corp. (1937)

 ConLaw.us/NLRB/

In 1935, President Roosevelt signed into law the National Labor Relations Act (NLRA). This statute gave the National Labor Relations Board (NLRB) the power to punish "unfair labor practices *affecting* commerce."

The Jones & Laughlin Steel Corporation argued that the NLRA was "an attempt to regulate all industry, thus invading the reserved powers of the States over their local concerns." On this question, the Court split 5-4. Chief Justice Hughes wrote the majority opinion. He acknowledged that the federal government could not regulate "all labor relations, but only what may be deemed to burden or obstruct that commerce." This test allowed Congress to protect interstate commerce from "burdens and obstructions." Hughes found that Congress may regulate local activity that has "such a close and substantial relation to interstate commerce that their control is essential or appropriate to protect that commerce from burdens and obstructions."

However, he qualified this holding with a limiting principle: The scope of the power to regulate intrastate activity "must be considered in the light of our dual system of government, and may not be extended so as to embrace effects upon interstate commerce so indirect and remote that to embrace them, in view of our complex society, would effectually obliterate the distinction between what is national and what is local and create a completely centralized government. The question is necessarily one of degree." The majority did not reject the distinction between "direct" and "indirect" effects. Rather, the Court found that Congress could prohibit local activities that "burden[] or obstruct[]" — that is, have a "direct" effect on — interstate commerce.

United States v. Darby (1941)

 ConLaw.us/Darby/

The second case, *United States v. Darby* (1941), unanimously upheld Congress's power to regulate the wages of local lumber workers. *Darby* rejected the *direct effects* test and introduced the *substantial effects* test. This framework recognized that Congress could do more than simply protect interstate commerce from being burdened or obstructed. Congress also had the power to regulate "intrastate activities where they have a substantial effect on interstate commerce." The Court's analysis, by Justice Stone, relied on *McCulloch v. Maryland* (1819).

STUDY GUIDE

What clause of the Constitution did *McCulloch*, and in turn *Darby*, rely on?

By citing *McCulloch*, the Court indicated that the substantial effects test was based on the Necessary and Proper Clause. *Darby* did not expand the meaning of the word "commerce" in the Commerce Clause. Rather, under the substantial effects test, Congress could now regulate local activities — even if those activities were not commerce — if the law was a "necessary and proper" means to regulate interstate commerce.

Though *Darby* cited *McCulloch*, the New Deal Cout did not follow Chief Justice Marshall's reasoning. Justice Stone stated that it did not matter whether Congress was in fact motivated by a desire to regulate local activities. "*Whatever their motive and purpose*," he wrote, "regulations of commerce which do not infringe some constitutional prohibition are within the plenary power conferred on Congress by the Commerce Clause." Compare that passage with the limiting principle in *McCulloch v. Maryland*. Chief Justice Marshall maintained that the Court had a duty to declare unconstitutional a law "should congress under the pretext of executing its powers, pass laws for the accomplishment of objects, not entrusted to the government."

STUDY GUIDE

Can *Darby* be reconciled with *McCulloch's* limiting principle?

Finally, the Court held that the Tenth Amendment "states but a truism that all is retained which has not been surrendered." As a result, the Court would no longer consider whether Congress's implied powers under the Necessary and Proper Clause would intrude on a state's police power. *Darby* accordingly overruled *Hammer v. Dagenhart* (1918).

Wickard v. Filburn (1942)

 ConLaw.us/Wickard/

The third case was *Wickard v. Filburn*. The Agricultural Adjustment Act restricted the amount of wheat that farmer Roscoe Filburn could grow to a specified quota. Secretary of Agriculture Claude Wickard administered this regulatory scheme. The law restricted the supply of wheat as a means to increase prices, thereby benefiting farmers. According to the record, Filburn used the bulk of the wheat he grew in excess of this quota on his farm to feed his livestock. This way, Filburn could use his own home-grown wheat to feed his livestock at a lower cost, and still benefit by selling his "quota" wheat on the market for a higher price.

The Justices considered this case to be so controversial that they asked the parties to reargue it. While deliberating over the decision, Justice Jackson initially favored an opinion that would have abandoned all scrutiny concerning the scope of Congress's commerce power. In other words, the Court would uphold any economic regulation that Congress deemed reasonable. But even the New Deal Court was not prepared to take such a momentous step. Instead, Jackson's majority opinion expanded the substantial effects test. The Court acknowledged that Filburn's small amount of locally consumed wheat did not *by itself* have a "substantial effect" on interstate commerce. Yet, when all of the locally consumed wheat nationwide is considered together, *in the aggregate*, those intrastate activities have a substantial effect on interstate commerce. Thus Congress can regulate the locally consumed wheat. This doctrine became known as the *aggregation principle*.

The Court considered evidence that home-grown wheat used to feed livestock affected national wheat prices. Even though Filburn's "own contribution to the demand for wheat may be trivial by itself," the Court found that this fact was "not enough to remove him from the scope of federal regulation where, as here, his contribution, taken together with that of many others similarly situated, is far from trivial." *Darby* introduced the substantial effects test, and *Wickard* added the aggregation principle.

It is a myth that the Court in *Wickard* was concerned with the home-grown wheat that Filburn and his family consumed at the dinner table. "The total amount of wheat consumed as food varies but relatively little," the Court said. In contrast, the wheat that farmers like Filburn grew to feed their livestock, which they would then send to market, "constitutes the most variable factor in the disappearance of the wheat crop." The Court found that this latter activity — in the aggregate — had a substantial effect on the interstate price of wheat. The locally consumed wheat thereby undercut the Agricultural Adjustment Act's plan to maintain higher interstate wheat prices.

STUDY GUIDE

Did *Wickard* retain any role for the Court to scrutinize laws that Congress enacts pursuant to its powers under the Necessary and Proper Clause?

Nearly six decades would pass before the Rehnquist Court provided a limiting principle for the substantial effects doctrine that expanded Congress's powers under the substantial effects test.

CHAPTER 11

Enumerated Powers on the Warren Court (1964)

The Civil Rights Movement of the 1950s and 1960s is sometimes referred to as the Second Reconstruction. This era ushered in monumental improvements for the rights and equality of African Americans in the United States. The elected branches, and not the courts, were the primary drivers in this revolution. In particular, the Civil Rights Act of 1964, and its ensuing enforcement by the executive branch, played an important role to reduce segregation. Title II of the law guaranteed "full and equal enjoyment . . . of any place of public accommodation . . . without discrimination or segregation on the ground of race, color, religion, or national origin." Title II applied to a business "if its operations affect commerce." Congress made many findings about the "burdens that discrimination by race or color places upon interstate commerce." For example, segregationist policies impeded interstate travel. The *Green Book* listed hotels and restaurants African Americans could use while traveling.

Soon, opponents of the Civil Rights Act filed two test cases: *Heart of Atlanta Motel v. United States* (1964) and *Katzenbach v. McClung* (1964).

Heart of Atlanta Motel v. United States (1964)

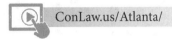

ConLaw.us/Atlanta/

The Heart of Atlanta Motel refused to rent rooms to African-American patrons. Its owner challenged the constitutionality of Title II. He argued that Congress lacked the power to prohibit segregation in a local motel.

The Warren Court unanimously rejected this claim. Justice Clark's majority opinion was based on the substantial effects test: "[T]he power of Congress to promote interstate commerce also includes the power to regulate the local incidents thereof, including local activities in both the States of origin and destination, which might have a *substantial and harmful effect* upon that commerce." Clark found that the motel was available to travelers and solicited customers from the national media. Indeed, 75 percent of its guests were from out of state. Therefore, the motel's segregationist policies, though local, had a substantial effect on interstate commerce.

STUDY GUIDE

Is *Heart of Atlanta*'s application of the substantial effects test broader than that of the New Deal Court? Or does the Civil Rights Act regulate the channels and instrumentalities of commerce?

The Court did not rest its entire decision on Congress's powers under the Commerce Clause. The Necessary and Proper Clause provided Congress with additional authority to prohibit local segregation: "How obstructions in commerce may be removed — what *means* are to be employed — is within the sound and exclusive discretion of the Congress. It is subject only to one caveat — that the means chosen by it must be *reasonably adapted* to the end permitted by the Constitution. We cannot say that its choice here was not so adapted." The Court's approach required a fit between the means and the ends. This analysis follows from Chief Justice Marshall's opinion in *McCulloch v. Maryland*. *Heart of Atlanta* is also a Necessary and Proper Clause case.

When Congress enacted the Civil Rights Act of 1964, it did not rely solely on the Commerce and Necessary and Proper Clauses. Congress also invoked Section 5 of the Fourteenth Amendment, which gave it an important new enumerated power: "The Congress shall have power to enforce, by appropriate legislation, the provisions of this article."

What are "the provisions of this article"? That phrase refers back to Sections 1 through 4 of the Fourteenth Amendment. Section 1 contains the Equal Protection

Clause: "nor shall any state . . . deny to any person within its jurisdiction the equal protection of the laws." If a "state" denies a person the "equal protection of the laws," Congress would have the power to enact "appropriate legislation" to enforce that person's civil rights. The key word is "state."

In the *Civil Rights Cases* (1883), the Supreme Court held that Congress's enforcement powers under Section 5 of the Fourteenth Amendment were limited. (See Chapter 29.) The federal government could only protect people from "state action" — meaning actions by state governments. As a result, Congress could not use its Section 5 enforcement powers to prohibit segregation by private businesses.

In *Heart of Atlanta Motel*, only Justice William O. Douglas found that Congress could enact the Civil Rights Act based on its Section 5 powers. Such a justification, he thought, would make it unnecessary to litigate "whether a particular restaurant or inn is within the commerce definitions of the Act or whether a particular customer is an interstate traveler." Because this authority "would apply to *all* customers in *all* the enumerated places of public accommodation," he contended, it "would put an end to all obstructionist strategies, and finally close one door on a bitter chapter in American history."

The other eight Justices relied solely on Congress's powers under the Commerce and Necessary and Proper Clauses, and not its Section 5 enforcement powers.

STUDY GUIDE

Would there be any advantages if the Court upheld the Civil Rights Act based on Congress's enforcement powers, rather than its power to regulate interstate commerce? Any disadvantages? Is it more fitting — and also more limited — to base a Civil Rights law on the Fourteenth Amendment than on the Commerce Clause?

Katzenbach v. McClung (1964)

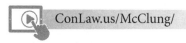 ConLaw.us/McClung/

The second test case, *Katzenbach v. McClung*, involved Ollie's Barbecue. This restaurant in Birmingham, Alabama, would not serve African-American customers. Unlike the Heart of Atlanta Motel, however, Ollie's Barbecue did not serve out-of-state customers. Nonetheless, the Court found "that a substantial portion of the food served in the restaurant had moved in interstate commerce."

Here, the Court recognized what is sometimes called a *jurisdictional hook*: Congress had jurisdiction to regulate local activity that utilized items that had previously travelled in interstate commerce. Professor David Engdahl has dubbed this approach the "herpes theory" of jurisdiction: Items that travel in inter-state commerce forever retain that trait.

In this regard, *McClung* represented an expansion of congressional power beyond the limits identified by the New Deal Court in *NLRB*, *Darby*, and *Wickard*. Today, Congress often relies on these expanded powers when regulating local conduct.

South Dakota v. Dole (1987)

ConLaw.us/Dole/

The Constitution gives Congress the power "to lay and collect taxes, duties, imposts and excises, to pay the debts and provide for the common defense and general welfare of the United States." This authority is known as the *Taxing Power*. However, this provision is also known as the *Spending Clause*, even though the text affords Congress no explicit authority to spend money.

The absence of an expressly enumerated spending power gave rise to a constitutional debate in the early days of our Republic: Are there any limits on what Congress can spend money on?

Alexander Hamilton argued that Congress could spend money in a broad fashion in order to "provide for the common defense and general welfare of the United States." In other words, this portion of the Spending Clause identified the appropriate *purpose* of federal spending.

James Madison, however, took a narrower view. He argued that the "common defense and general welfare" portion of the Clause limited Congress's power. Taxes, duties, imposts, and excises could only be used to benefit the whole country, rather than to benefit a faction. Madison contended that Congress's spending power stemmed from, and was limited by, the Necessary and Proper Clause. This provision empowered Congress to spend money as a necessary and proper means to execute its *other* enumerated powers in Article I, Section 8, such as the power to establish courts or post offices. Madison thought that Hamilton's alternative reading of the Spending Clause would undermine the enumerated powers scheme on which our federalism is based.

In *United States v. Butler* (1936), the Supreme Court essentially adopted the Hamiltonian approach. This case upheld a very broad exercise of the spending power. The Supreme Court, however, has also acknowledged Madison's federalism concerns. The Justices have imposed certain limits on Congress's power to attach *strings* on money given to the states. *South Dakota v. Dole* (1987) summarized these limitations.

In 1984, Congress enacted a law to encourage states to raise their drinking age. That statute allowed Elizabeth Dole, the Secretary of Transportation, to withhold a percentage of federal highway funds from states with a drinking age lower than twenty-one. South Dakota, which allowed nineteen-year-olds to purchase light beer, sued the Secretary. In Chapters 17 and 18 we will study *New York v. United States* (1992) and *Printz v. United States* (1997). These cases held that Congress lacks the power to direct, or *commandeer*, states to take certain actions. Because Congress could not force the state legislature to raise its drinking age, South Dakota argued that Congress could not accomplish that same objective by taking away federal funds.

The Supreme Court rejected this argument. Chief Justice Rehnquist wrote the majority opinion. He explained that "[t]he spending power is of course not unlimited, but is instead subject to [four] general restrictions." First, "the exercise of the spending power must be in pursuit of 'the general welfare.'" The Court found that the federal law satisfied this first factor. Teenagers could decide to drink and drive in South Dakota because of the lower drinking age. "The means [Congress] chose to address this dangerous situation were reasonably calculated to advance the general welfare."

Second, Congress must place conditions on the funds "unambiguously." States need to know what they are getting into when they accept federal money. In this case, the condition on highway funds was clear and unambiguous.

Third, the conditions must relate to "the federal interest" for which the spending program was established. Chief Justice Rehnquist found that "[t]he condition imposed by Congress is directly related to one of the main purposes for which highway funds are expended—safe interstate travel." The majority opinion did not define how closely "related" the condition must be to Congress's "purpose." Justice O'Connor's dissent provided a more narrow test for "relatedness," or "germaneness."

Fourth, "[o]ther constitutional provisions may provide an independent bar to conditional grant of federal funds." The Court held that the Twenty-First Amendment, which allows states to regulate alcohol, was not such a bar. And neither was the Tenth Amendment.

In addition to these four limitations, Chief Justice Rehnquist identified a fifth factor: A condition becomes unconstitutional when "the financial inducement offered by Congress might be so coercive as to pass the point at which 'pressure turns into compulsion.'" Such coercion would, in effect, commandeer the state legislature to comply with the condition. In this case, however, South Dakota would only lose 5 percent of "certain federal highway funds." This incentive was "relatively mild encouragement." Therefore, the condition was constitutional.

STUDY GUIDE

According to *South Dakota v. Dole*, are there any limits on Congress's power to place conditions on spending?

Justice Sandra Day O'Connor authored a solo dissent. She agreed with the majority that the Constitution imposes four limits on Congress's spending power. The third condition, she found, was violated. Why? "[T]he establishment of a minimum drinking age of twenty-one is *not sufficiently related* to interstate highway construction to justify so conditioning funds appropriated for that purpose." She added that Congress cannot impose conditions "because of an attenuated or tangential relationship to highway use or safety."

Justice O'Connor wrote that raising the drinking age was not "fairly" related, or "germane," to the expenditure of highway funds. She explained that "if the rule were otherwise, the Congress could effectively regulate almost any area of a State's social, political, or economic life on the theory that use of the interstate transportation system is somehow enhanced."

Justice O'Connor's approach to "germaneness" turns on the difference between a spending requirement and a regulation. She explained that the former is permissible. The federal government can mandate "*how* the money should be spent, so that Congress' intent in making the grant will be effectuated." For example, Congress can restrict, or "condition," federal funding for specific projects, and not other goals. That is, Congress can give the states money to improve highways, on the condition that the highways are improved in a certain way.

However, Justice O'Connor contended, "Congress has no power under the Spending Clause to impose requirements on a grant that go beyond specifying *how* the money should be spent." In other words, Congress cannot give the states money to improve highways on the condition that the state raises its drinking age. Here, no federal money was being spent on establishing a twenty-one-year-old drinking age. Instead, the threat to withhold highway funds was made solely to induce the South Dakota legislature to *regulate* its people in the way Congress desired. Because Congress lacked the power to enact a stand-alone bill to raise the state's drinking age, Justice O'Connor reasoned, it could not accomplish that same goal by placing conditions on a state's federal funding.

The majority, however, did not adopt Justice O'Connor's approach. In cases decided after *Dole*, the Supreme Court would primarily focus on the fifth factor — whether a spending condition was coercive. And twenty-three years later, in *NFIB v. Sebelius* (2012), the Supreme Court finally identified such a coercive condition.

CHAPTER 13

United States v. Lopez (1995)

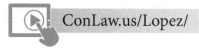

ConLaw.us/Lopez/

The Supreme Court's interpretation of the phrase "commerce among the several states" in the Commerce Clause has not changed much since the Founding. To this day, Congress's authority to regulate interstate commerce is still largely confined to trade and transportation of people and things from one state to another. (There is one outlier decision, *United States v. South-Eastern Underwriters Association* (1944), which held that "commerce" includes insurance.) However, the Court's construction of Congress's implied powers based on the Necessary and Proper Clause has fluctuated greatly. Under the Court's modern doctrine, the federal government can regulate local activity that is not interstate commerce.

Consider this brief history of implied congressional powers. (See Timeline — A Brief History of Implied Powers on page 22.)

- First, in 1791, President Washington determined that Congress had the implied power to create the First Bank of the United States. At the time, James Madison and Thomas Jefferson objected to this broad reading of the Necessary and Proper Clause.
- Second, during his tenure as Chief Justice, John Marshall adopted the broader Hamiltonian reading of implied federal powers in cases like *McCulloch v. Maryland* (1819) and *Gibbons v. Ogden* (1824) (Chapters 3 and 4).
- Third, we studied *Prigg v. Pennsylvania* (1842). This case, decided by the Taney Court, embraced an even broader construction of the Necessary and Proper Clause. *Prigg* held that Congress had the implied power to enact the Fugitive Slave Act (Chapter 6).
- Fourth, we studied *United States v. Dewitt* (1869) and *Hepburn v. Griswold* (1870). In these cases, Chief Justice Chase narrowed the Court's approach to Congress's implied powers. After President Grant appointed new Justices, however, in *Knox v. Lee* (1871) the Court adopted perhaps its broadest interpretation of the scope of Congress's implied powers (Chapter 7).

- Fifth, during the Progressive Era, the Court flip-flopped. In *United States v. E.C. Knight* (1895) and *Hammer v. Dagenhart* (1918), the Court adopted a more narrow approach to Congress's implied power to regulate local business transactions. But in *Champion v. Ames* (1903), the Court permitted Congress to prohibit the sale of foreign lottery tickets (Chapter 8). Then, in *Schechter Poultry Corp. v. United States* (1935), the Court reasserted a limit on Congress's implied powers: The National Industrial Recovery Act violated the *direct effects* test (Chapter 9).
- Sixth, the New Deal Court ushered in a radical redefinition of implied federal powers. *United States v. Darby* (1941) adopted the *substantial effects* test. The Court further expanded this doctrine in *Wickard v. Filburn* (1942), by adopting the *aggregation principle* (Chapter 10).
- Seventh, the Warren Court continued the New Deal Court's approach to implied federal powers. *Heart of Atlanta Motel v. United States* (1964) relied on these precedents to uphold the Civil Rights Act of 1964. And in *Katzenbach v. McClung* (1964), the Court held that Congress could regulate intrastate activity that used items that had travelled in interstate commerce, so long as the statute included a "jurisdictional hook" (Chapter 11).

Nearly six decades would pass before the Supreme Court reviewed a law that exceeded Congress's powers under the Commerce and Necessary and Proper Clauses. The federal government's winning streak came to an end with *United States v. Lopez*.

In 1990, Congress enacted the Gun-Free School Zones Act. This law made it a federal crime "for any individual knowingly to possess a firearm" within 1,000 feet of a school zone. The law did not purport to regulate any commercial activity. Additionally, the government did not need to show that the firearm had traveled in interstate commerce — the so-called *jurisdictional hook*.

In March 1992, Alfonso Lopez carried a concealed handgun into Edison High School in San Antonio. Initially, the high school senior was charged with violating a Texas law that banned the possession of firearms in schools. The next day, the state charges were dismissed after federal agents charged Lopez with violating the Gun-Free School Zones Act. He was tried and found guilty. On appeal, the Fifth Circuit declared the statute unconstitutional.

The United States appealed the case to the Supreme Court. During oral arguments the Solicitor General was unable to articulate what limits existed on the scope of Congress's powers. Justice Ginsburg asked the Solicitor General, "What are the limits, then?" and "What would be a case that would fall outside" the scope of federal powers? After an uncomfortable pause, he replied, " — I don't have — ." Justice Scalia then interjected, "Don't give away anything here." There was audible laughter in the Court. The Solicitor General was unable to identify a limiting principle for the scope of congressional powers. His inability to answer the question proved fatal to the government's case.

By a 5-4 vote, the Supreme Court held that the Gun-Free School Zones Act exceeded Congress's power under the Commerce Clause. Chief Justice William Rehnquist wrote the majority opinion. "We start with first principles," he explained. "The Constitution creates a Federal Government of enumerated powers." Next, the Court quoted from James Madison in *Federalist No. 45*: "The powers delegated by the proposed Constitution to the federal government are few and defined. Those which are to remain in the State governments are numerous and indefinite." Chief Justice Rehnquist added, "This constitutionally mandated division of authority was adopted by the Framers to ensure protection of our fundamental liberties."

The Court acknowledged that *Jones & Laughlin Steel*, *Darby*, and *Wickard* had "ushered in an era of Commerce Clause jurisprudence that greatly expanded the previously defined authority of Congress under that Clause." Yet, Chief Justice Rehnquist observed, "even these modern-era precedents which have expanded congressional power under the Commerce Clause confirm that this power is subject to outer limits."

The Court then identified "three broad categories of activity that Congress may regulate under its commerce power." You can remember them with the helpful acronym *CIA*.

- First, "Congress may regulate the use of the *channels* of interstate commerce." In *Darby* and *Heart of Atlanta*, for example, the Court upheld Congress's authority to keep "the channels of interstate commerce free from immoral and injurious uses." In such cases, Congress can regulate local activities that block the flow of interstate commerce.
- Second, "Congress is empowered to regulate and protect the *instrumentalities* of interstate commerce, or persons or things in interstate commerce, even though the threat may come only from intrastate activities." For example, Congress could protect ports and railroads from foreign terrorist attack, even though these hubs are entirely intrastate.
- Third, Congress had the "authority to regulate those . . . [intrastate] *activities* that substantially affect interstate commerce." *Darby* and *Wickard* established the substantial effects test. Those decisions found that Congress could regulate such *intrastate* activity as a necessary and proper means of regulating *interstate* commerce.

Lopez attempted to synthesize nearly a century of precedent with these three categories. Chief Justice Rehnquist explained that the government could only defend the Gun-Free School Zones Act under the third category. He then added something new to the doctrine: an outer limit of the substantial effects test. Congress could only regulate intrastate activity that substantially affects interstate commerce if the intrastate activity is *economic* in nature. "Even *Wickard*," he observed, "which is perhaps the most far reaching example of Commerce Clause authority over intrastate activity, involved *economic* activity in a way that the possession of a gun in a school zone does not."

The Gun-Free School Zones Act, he concluded, "has nothing to do with 'commerce' or any sort of economic enterprise, however broadly one might define those terms." Nor is the federal law "an essential part of a larger regulation of economic activity, in which the regulatory scheme could be undercut unless the intrastate activity were regulated." For this reason, the Act "cannot . . . be sustained under [the] cases upholding regulations of [intrastate economic] activities . . . which viewed in the aggregate, substantially affects interstate commerce."

In Chapter 10, we explained that the substantial effects test was based on the Necessary and Proper Clause. *Lopez* held that the substantial effects test could only be used to uphold regulations of intrastate *economic* activity. This case limited the scope of Congress's powers under the Necessary and Proper Clause. Specifically, *Lopez* restricted the circumstances when it would be "necessary" for Congress to regulate *intrastate* economic activity as a means to regulate *interstate* commerce. However, Chief Justice Rehnquist did not make this point explicitly. He didn't even cite the Necessary and Proper Clause.

Why did *Lopez* limit the substantial effects test to intrastate economic activity? Perhaps because such local economic activity — like manufacturing and agriculture — will likely be closely related to the regulation of interstate commerce. Conversely, local non-economic activity is likely to be quite *remote* from interstate commerce. This distinction between economic and non-economic activity allows the Court to separate "what is national and what is local." This limiting principle prevents Congress from "creat[ing] a completely centralized government." *NLRB v. Jones & Laughlin Steel* (1937).

Justice Kennedy wrote a concurring opinion, which Justice O'Connor joined. If Congress took "over the regulation of entire areas of traditional state concern," he worried, "the boundaries between the spheres of federal and state authority would blur and political responsibility would become illusory."

Justice Thomas wrote a separate concurring opinion. "In a future case," he hoped, the Court "ought to temper [its] Commerce Clause jurisprudence in a manner that both makes sense of our more recent case law and is more faithful to the original understanding of that Clause." Justice Thomas would abolish the substantial effects test altogether.

There were three separate dissents. First, Justice Stevens wrote, "Whether or not the national interest in eliminating that market [for guns in schools] would have justified federal legislation in 1789, it surely does today." Justice Souter's dissent extolled "[t]he practice of deferring to rationally based legislative judgments [as] a paradigm of judicial restraint." Justice Breyer's dissent found that the Gun-Free School Zones Act "falls well within the scope of the commerce power as this Court has understood that power over the last half century."

In September 1994, six months before *Lopez* was decided, Congress enacted a new version of the Gun-Free School Zones Act that included a jurisdictional hook. Now, to be convicted of violating this law, the government had to prove that the firearm in question "has moved in or otherwise affects interstate commerce." As amended, the law remains in force.

Nevertheless, *Lopez* sent a shock wave through the legal academy. Many law professors questioned whether the Court intended to draw this bright line between economic and non-economic activity. Critics asserted that Congress had become complacent. The statute lacked factual findings to connect the possession of a gun to interstate commerce. Had Congress included such a jurisdictional hook, perhaps the Court would have upheld the law. Did *Lopez* represent a step towards repudiating a century of Commerce Clause precedent? Or did the Court merely put a halt on the further expansion of federal power?

The Court would answer these questions in the next two cases: *United States v. Morrison* (2000) and *Gonzales v. Raich* (2005).

CHAPTER 14

United States v. Morrison (2000)

ConLaw.us/Morrison/

In *United States v. Lopez* (1995), the Supreme Court declared unconstitutional the Gun-Free School Zones Act. One year earlier, Congress enacted the Violence Against Women Act (VAWA). This legislation created a cause of action that allowed victims of "gender-motivated violence" to sue in federal court. Recall that the Gun-Free School Zones Act did not include any factual findings: The congressional record did not demonstrate that possessing a gun in a school zone had a substantial effect on interstate commerce. In contrast, Congress conducted extensive hearings when it enacted VAWA. The record showed that violence against women has extensive economic effects nationwide. Nevertheless, *United States v. Morrison* (2000) found that this evidence was not sufficient to support the constitutionality of VAWA's federal cause of action.

In 1994, Christy Brzonkala was a student at Virginia Tech. She alleged that two members of the varsity football team, Antonio Morrison and James Crawford, raped her. The local prosecutor in Virginia never brought criminal charges against the players. Brzonkala alleged that she was a victim of "gender-motivated violence." As a result, she relied on VAWA's federal cause of action to sue the state university, as well as Morrison and Crawford, in federal court.

The Supreme Court held that Congress lacked the power to create VAWA's federal cause of action. *Morrison*, like *Lopez* five years earlier, yielded a 5-4 split. Chief Justice Rehnquist wrote the majority opinion. He applied the economic/non-economic distinction: "Gender-motivated crimes of violence are not, in any sense of the phrase, economic activity." For this reason, Congress had stepped beyond the line that the

Court had drawn in *Lopez*. Remember, VAWA was enacted one year before *Lopez* was decided.

Morrison was significant for three reasons:

- First, the decision reaffirmed *Lopez*'s distinction between economic activity and non-economic activity. Once again, the Court seemed serious about maintaining that line.
- Second, *Morrison* found that Congress's factual findings about the economic effects of violence against women nationwide were not relevant. This opinion clarified that Congress may not regulate wholly intrastate *non*-economic activity *regardless* of its effects on interstate commerce.
- Third, the Court explained that it was not repudiating any of the New Deal precedents. Rather, the Court would not go beyond those cases. Chief Justice Rehnquist explained, "thus far in our Nation's history our cases have upheld Commerce Clause regulation of intrastate activity *only* where that activity is economic in nature." In other words, *this far, and no farther* without a judicially administrable limiting principle.

The Rehnquist Court's jurisprudence came to be known as the *New Federalism*. This approach did not seek to restrict the exercises of federal implied powers that were upheld by the New Deal and Warren Courts. Instead, *Morrison* adhered to the reasoning in *NLRB v. Jones & Laughlin Steel* (1937): The Court would *limit* the *further* expansion of Congress's implied powers in "light of our dual system of government." A precedent that failed to limit this expansion of federal power would "effectually obliterate the distinction between what is national and what is local and create a completely centralized government."

Morrison was based on the fundamental premise that Congress lacks a general police power. Because of this *first principle*, the Court would reject any proposed expansion of congressional power that lacked a judicially administrable *limiting principle*. In other words, the Court sought to identify a categorical distinction that judges are capable of applying to particular facts. The *Morrison* majority thought that it was able to distinguish between the category of economic activity and the category of non-economic activity. This distinction would ensure that Congress could not regulate local activities that were too remote from interstate commerce.

Morrison would not be the last word on the scope of Congress's implied power. *Gonzales v. Raich* (2005), considered whether Congress could regulate locally grown medical marijuana — wholly intrastate activity — under its Commerce and Necessary and Proper Clause powers.

CHAPTER 15

Gonzales v. Raich (2005)

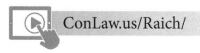

ConLaw.us/Raich/

In 1996, California voters passed the Compassionate Use Act, which legalized and regulated marijuana for medical use. The activities authorized by California's law, however, still violated the Controlled Substances Act (CSA). This federal law banned the cultivation, possession, and distribution of marijuana. In 1998, the federal government sued to enjoin the operation of the Oakland Cannabis Buyers Cooperative (OCBC). Randy Barnett was part of the legal team that represented the OCBC. OCBC argued that the CSA exceeded Congress's powers under the Commerce Clause. However, there was an obstacle to this claim: Since money and marijuana was clearly changing hands in the Cooperative, there was clearly *economic* activity. Indeed, these payments were in fact intrastate commerce.

Robert Raich, a member of the OCBC team, proposed an alternate strategy to Barnett: bring a lawsuit on behalf of Californians who cultivated and possessed marijuana, as authorized by California law, but who did not buy or sell the drug. Barnett agreed, and became lead counsel in the new case.

As it happened, Robert's wife, Angel Raich, was suffering from several intractable illnesses — including a brain tumor — which had caused a wasting syndrome. Her weight loss threatened her life. A nurse suggested that she try marijuana. The controlled substance allowed Raich to regain weight and strength. Diane Monson, another Californian, used medical marijuana to relieve her back pains and spasms, which had not responded to conventional therapy. Because the federal government seized Monson's plants, she had a concrete injury, and "standing," to bring the challenge.

Barnett and his legal team filed a civil suit to halt the enforcement of the CSA against Angel and Diane. Critically, neither Plaintiff purchased marijuana. Angel's caregivers grew the cannabis and gave it to her at no charge. Diane grew her own plants, and thus did not have to buy it. The plaintiffs contended that, under the limiting principle established by *Lopez* and *Morrison*, Congress could not regulate this entirely *intra*state *non*-economic activity. Furthermore, because no items used to cultivate the marijuana had ever traveled in interstate commerce, there was no *jurisdictional hook*.

Angel and Diane lost in the Northern District of California but prevailed in the Ninth Circuit Court of Appeals. On appeal, Barnett argued on behalf of Angel and Diane before the Supreme Court. The Bush administration was represented by Solicitor General Paul Clement. The government contended that *Wickard v. Filburn* (1942) supported the constitutionality of the CSA. Clement argued that the local cultivation of marijuana was an "economic activity" because home-grown marijuana substituted for marijuana that could have been purchased on the interstate marketplace. For example, because Roscoe Filburn grew wheat on his own farm to feed his livestock, he did not need to purchase that wheat on the interstate marketplace. Likewise, because Diane Monson grew her own cannabis, she did not have to buy marijuana on the interstate marketplace. This framework was known as the market substitute theory: An activity is "economic" when it substitutes for a market activity

Barnett responded that *Wickard* was distinguishable. Unlike Angel and Diane, Filburn was engaged in *commercial* farming. Specifically, the feeding and marketing of his livestock were economic activities. Furthermore, *United States v. Lopez* (1995) and *United States v. Morrison* (2000) had already rejected any theory of enumerated powers that lacked a judicially administrable limiting principle (Chapters 13 and 14). If anything that serves as a substitute for goods or services obtained in the market can be considered "economic," Barnett contended, there would be no limit on Congress's power. Nearly any activity we do for ourselves can also be provided by a commercial service.

During oral argument, some of the justices seemed open to the market substitute theory. Justice Souter suggested that an activity could be "economic" if it had an economic effect on the national economy. He then equated the economic effect that Angel and Diane's home-grown marijuana had on the interstate marketplace with that of Filburn's home-grown wheat. Barnett replied that the mere fact that activities may have an economic effect on the market does not make them economic activities. To identify "whether an activity is economic," he explained, "you have to look to the activity, itself." What is an economic activity? An activity that is "associated with sale, exchange, barter" or an activity associated with "the production of things for sale, exchange, barter."

Barnett offered a hypothetical. He observed that "prostitution is an economic activity." However, "marital relations is not an economic activity," even though "we could be talking about virtually the same act." The fact that "there is a market for prostitution," Barnett explained, does not make any substitute for what can be obtained in that market — marital sex for example — an "economic activity." After this exchange, the Justices dropped the market substitute theory of economic activity.

Ultimately, the Court ruled for the government by a 6-3 vote. The four progressive justices were joined by two of the conservative justices from the *Lopez* and *Morrison* majority: Justices Scalia and Kennedy.

Justice Stevens wrote the majority opinion. He did not adopt the government's market substitute theory of economic activity. Instead, he found that *Lopez* and

Morrison authorized Congress to regulate the local cultivation of marijuana. To support this broad conception of economic activity, Justice Stevenes relied on *Webster's Third New International Dictionary*. It defined "economic" as "the production, distribution, and consumption of commodities." Because Angel's caregivers and Diane were engaged in the activity of producing marijuana, according to *Webster's*, they were engaged in "economic" activity. Therefore, under *Morrison* and *Lopez*, Congress could regulate their intrastate activity. As a result, the CSA was constitutional as applied to the locally cultivated marijuana.

Justice Stevens also adopted an alternative holding. In *Lopez*, Chief Justice Rehnquist mentioned in passing that the Gun-Free School Zones Act was not "an essential part of a larger regulation of economic activity, in which the regulatory scheme could be undercut unless the intrastate activity were regulated." In *Raich*, Justice Stevens announced a new rule based on this observation: "Congress has the power to regulate purely local activities" when doing so is necessary to implement a comprehensive national regulatory program. Unlike the Gun-Free School Zones Act, the Controlled Substances Act was such a comprehensive program.

Justice Scalia did not join the majority opinion, which relied on *Webster's* definition of "economic." He only concurred with the Court's judgment that the CSA could be applied to both Angel and Diane. Nor did Justice Scalia adopt the government's market substitute theory of economic activity. Rather, according to Justice Scalia, Congress could regulate some local *non-economic* activity if those laws are "essential" to a broader regulatory scheme. Under this theory, Congress can regulate local non-economic activity as part of a larger regulation of interstate commerce, whether or not that local activity has a substantial effect on interstate commerce.

Crucially, Justice Scalia thought that the courts must defer to Congress's judgment. The legislature, and not the judiciary, should decide whether the regulation of local non-economic conduct — in this case, the local cultivation of marijuana that was neither bought nor sold — was essential to the CSA's regulatory scheme. "Congress could reasonably conclude," Justice Scalia wrote, "that its objective of prohibiting [local] marijuana from the interstate market 'could be undercut' if those activities were excepted from its general scheme of regulation." Justice Scalia stressed that this doctrine derived from the limits of Congress's powers under the Necessary and Proper Clause, not the Commerce Clause. That is, the Court should ask if a local activity was essential, or *necessary*, to a broader regulatory scheme.

Justice O'Connor dissented in *Raich*. She rejected the Court's broad definition of "economic," which "threaten[ed] to sweep all of productive human activity into federal regulatory reach." She also objected to the Court's use of "a dictionary definition of economics to skirt the real problem of drawing a meaningful line between 'what is national and what is local.'" Here, Justice O'Connor cited *NLRB v. Jones & Laughlin Steel* (1937). She also questioned whether the Court should defer to Congress's claim that reaching local activity was essential to the CSA's regulatory scheme: "If the Court always defers to Congress as it does today, little may be left to the notion of enumerated powers."

Chief Justice Rehnquist joined Justice O'Connor's dissent. At the time he was too ill from cancer to attend oral argument. He likely participated in the Court's private conference by telephone. Chief Justice Rehnquist died in September 2005, three months after *Raich* was decided.

Justice Thomas also dissented. In his separate opinion, he repeated his view from both *Lopez* and *Morrison*: The Court should abandon the substantial effects test altogether. That approach was not consistent with the original meaning of Congress's enumerated powers. He wrote, "Respondents Diane Monson and Angel Raich use marijuana that has never been bought or sold, that has never crossed state lines, and that has had no demonstrable effect on the national market for marijuana." Thomas continued, "If Congress can regulate this under the Commerce Clause, then it can regulate virtually anything — and the Federal Government is no longer one of limited and enumerated powers."

Lopez and *Morrison* represented an effort to put the brakes on any further expansion of New Deal and Warren Court doctrines governing implied federal powers. Congress could only regulate intrastate activity that had a substantial effect on interstate commerce if the activity was economic in nature. However, *Raich* modified that doctrine. Now, Congress can regulate even non-economic activity as part of a broader regulatory scheme.

In *Raich*, the Court seemed to authorize an expansion of congressional power beyond that which the New Deal Court had recognized in *Wickard*. Barnett predicted as much during oral argument in *Raich*. He told the Justices that if they accepted the government's rationales to uphold the regulation of home-grown marijuana, then *Gonzales v. Raich* "will replace *Wickard v. Filburn* as the most far-reaching example of Commerce Clause authority over intrastate activity." And so it did.

After *Raich*, one might have agreed with Justice Thomas that there was no activity Congress could not regulate so long as it was an essential part of a "larger . . . regulatory scheme." Then, in 2010, Congress passed a comprehensive regulatory scheme called the Patient Protection and Affordable Care Act. *NFIB v. Sebelius* (2012) would consider the constitutionality of that law.

NFIB v. Sebelius (2012)

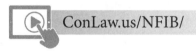

ConLaw.us/NFIB/

In 2010, Congress passed the Patient Protection and Affordable Care Act (ACA). The ACA, also known as Obamacare, regulated the private health insurance marketplace. Through the so-called individual mandate, the ACA *required* most Americans to maintain health insurance. Additionally, the law required states to make more low-income people eligible for Medicaid, a state-run insurance program. States that refused to expand their Medicaid programs would lose all the funding they were receiving for their existing Medicaid program, which was billions of dollars.

The attorneys general of twenty-six states and the National Federation of Independent Business (NFIB) challenged the ACA's constitutionality. Randy Barnett eventually became a member of NFIB's legal team.

In 2012, a sharply divided Supreme Court upheld most of the ACA. Chief Justice Roberts provided the fifth swing vote. It is commonly claimed that the Chief Justice found the individual insurance mandate to be constitutional as a tax on going uninsured. Your authors disagree.

Chief Justice Roberts noted that the Court's previous Commerce Clause decisions — from *Wickard v. Filburn* (1942) to *United States v. Lopez* (1995) — all concerned the regulation of "activity." In contrast, he observed, the individual mandate "compels individuals to become active in commerce by purchasing a product, on the ground that their failure to do so affects interstate commerce." This requirement was *unprecedented*: Congress had never before mandated that people engage in economic activity, and then regulate that mandated activity. Although the Commerce Clause gives Congress the power "to regulate," or prohibit activity,

Chief Justice Roberts held that this provision did not authorize Congress to compel people to engage in activity.

The Chief Justice also found that Congress could not enact the mandate pursuant to its powers under the Necessary and Proper Clause. He explained that the Court must consider separately whether a law is both a "necessary" *and* a "proper" means for Congress to carry into execution its other enumerated powers. (Justice Scalia had previously employed this same distinction in *Printz v. United States* (1997), which we will study in Chapter 18.) "Even if the individual mandate is 'necessary' to" prevent insurers from discriminating against people with pre-existing conditions, Roberts reasoned, "such an expansion of federal power is not a 'proper' means for making those reforms effective." The law was improper because it was not the sort of "incidental" power authorized by the Necessary and Proper Clause. Rather, a power to compel people to do business with a private company was a "great substantive and independent power" that was "beyond those specifically enumerated." (Chief Justice Marshall offered this test two centuries earlier in *McCulloch v. Maryland*.) Chief Justice Roberts explained that "the Government's theory" of enumerated powers "would give Congress the same license to regulate what we do not do, fundamentally changing the relation between the citizen and the Federal Government."

STUDY GUIDE

What exactly did Chief Justice Roberts think was not "proper" about the individual mandate?

Next, the Chief Justice found that a legally enforceable *requirement* to purchase insurance was not authorized by the taxing power. Instead, he adopted a saving construction. He observed that the monetary "penalty" for failing to maintain insurance was low and not coercive. Therefore, it was "reasonably possible" to construe the ACA as affording people an *option* either to buy insurance or to pay a modest and noncoercive *tax*. As a result, the law need not be read as imposing a *mandate enforced by a penalty*, which he conceded was the most "natural" construction of the statute. Yet he felt duty-bound to defer to Congress if the mandate could be read in a way to uphold the ACA.

The Chief Justice upheld the law under the saving construction, in which the ACA gave people an option to buy insurance or pay a modest tax. He rejected the government's argument that Congress could impose a purchase mandate under its Commerce Clause powers. This decision was significant. Consider a hypothetical: The Supreme Court holds that Congress cannot criminalize the possession of drugs, but instead can only tax those who possess controlled substances. In that alternate world, Congress could not imprison people for merely possessing or using a controlled substance. It would be perfectly legal for them to do so, provided they pay a noncoercive tax. The federal government could only punish those who fail to pay the tax. This alternate approach to federal powers would result in a revolutionary change in how federal drug laws are enforced. If the Supreme Court suddenly extended *NFIB*'s reasoning to the Controlled Substances Act (CSA), for example, countless federal prisoners would have to be released.

STUDY GUIDE

Did Chief Justice Roberts rule that Congress could have enacted the individual *mandate* under its taxing power?

Next, Chief Justice Roberts upheld the ACA's Medicaid expansion, in part. First, he declared that the expansion was unconstitutional to the extent that the ACA withdrew from the states their existing level of Medicaid funding. Some states could lose more than "10 percent of [their] overall budget." He found that "penaliz[ing] States that choose not to participate in the Medicaid expansion," was "economic dragooning that leaves the States with no real option but to acquiesce in the Medicaid expansion." This extreme penalty violated the fifth limit on the spending power that was identified in *South Dakota v. Dole* (1987): "the financial inducement offered by Congress [was] so coercive [that it] pass[ed] the point at which 'pressure turns into compulsion.'" The ACA, therefore imposed an impermissible condition on federal funding.

Seven Justices agreed that the expansion coerced the states, in violation of *Dole*'s limits. But not all seven agreed on the remedy. Chief Justice Roberts, joined by Justices Breyer and Kagan, applied yet another saving construction. To uphold the expansion, they found that the ACA must be read to give the states a choice: The states could (a) accept the new Medicaid funding, or (b) decline the new Medicaid funding, without having to give up existing federal funding. The trio recognized that the ACA, as written, did not afford the states this option. As a result, they removed the condition from the statute altogether. Justices Scalia, Kennedy, Alito, and Thomas would have declared the Medicaid expansion unconstitutional in its entirety.

NFIB's holding is complicated:

- A majority of the Court held that Congress lacked the power to impose the individual mandate under the Commerce and Necessary and Proper Clauses, as well as the taxing power.
- Four of the more progressive Justices would have upheld the individual mandate under any or all of these enumerated powers.
- Four of the more conservative Justices would have declared the individual mandate, as well as the Medicaid expansion, unconstitutional in their entirety.
- Chief Justice Roberts was somewhere in the middle. He upheld the individual mandate by changing it into an option. Furthermore, the Chief Justice deleted Congress's threat to withhold Medicaid funding. Ultimately, the Chief Justice was able to keep the rest of the ACA in place by changing these two key provisions.

Let's conclude Part II by revisiting the Court's precedents concerning the Commerce and Necessary and Proper Clauses. In *Lopez v. United States* (1995) and *United States v. Morrison* (2000), the Rehnquist Court attempted to put the brakes on any further expansion of Congress's implied federal powers, as they were interpreted by the New Deal and Warren Courts. In light of these cases, Congress could only regulate intrastate *economic* activity that had a substantial effect on interstate commerce. Congress could not regulate non-economic intrastate activity on the ground that it substantially affects interstate commerce.

Gonzales v. Raich (2005) added an exception to the Court's implied powers doctrine that had been hinted at in *Lopez*. In *Raich*, the Court allowed Congress to regulate intrastate *non-economic* activity, if that regulation was part of a broader regulatory scheme. *Raich*'s exception expanded Congress's powers beyond the high-water mark established by the New Deal Court. *Wickard v. Filburn* (1942) only concerned Congress's powers to regulate local economic activity.

In *NFIB*, however, the Court drew a line. The federal government could regulate intrastate economic and non-economic activity, but it could not take the unprecedented step of regulating *inactivity*. *NFIB* did not repudiate the New Deal Court's jurisprudence. Rather, Chief Justice Roberts followed the Rehnquist Court's approach: this far, and no farther without a judicially administrable limiting principle. In other words, the Court would not go beyond the line drawn in *Wickard* and extended in *Raich*.

Chief Justice Roberts explained in his announcement of *NFIB* that the Court's decision was not "based on our judgment about whether the Affordable Care Act is good policy. That judgment is for the people acting through their representatives." Five years later, in December 2017, Congress made a different judgment about the ACA. Through the Tax Cuts and Jobs Act, Congress set the penalty to $0. As a result, there were no financial consequences for going uninsured.

When he signed the tax reform bill, President Trump contended that even though the Supreme Court did not declare unconstitutional the ACA's individual mandate, Congress had now done just that. "Many people thought it should have been overturned in the Supreme Court. It didn't quite make it. Almost — but didn't quite make it. But now we're overturning the individual mandate, the most unpopular thing in Obamacare. Very, very unfair."

Congress only zeroed out the penalty enforcing the individual mandate. The ACA's individual mandate, the Medicaid expansion, and many other health insurance regulations, remain on the books.

FEDERALISM LIMITS ON CONGRESSIONAL POWER

Part III will focus on seven important federalism cases decided by the Rehnquist Court. *New York v. United States* (1992) and *Printz v. United States* (1997) developed the anti-commandeering doctrine. *Seminole Tribe of Florida v. Florida* (1996) analyzed the Eleventh Amendment and state sovereign immunity. Finally, the Court considered Congress's powers under Section 5 of the Fourteenth Amendment in four cases: *City of Boerne v. Flores* (1997), *United States v. Morrison* (2000), *University of Alabama v. Garrett* (2001), and *Nevada Department of Human Resources v. Hibbs* (2003).

CHAPTER 17

New York v. United States (1992)

 ConLaw.us/NY/

In 1985, only three states had facilities that disposed of low-level radioactive waste. In response to this critical shortage, Congress created incentives for states to provide for waste generated within their borders. The most severe incentive was the so-called "Take Title" provision. If a state could not provide a disposal facility, the state must take title, or ownership, of waste generated by private parties in the state. Furthermore, the state would be liable for all damages that resulted from the waste.

New York challenged the constitutionality of this law. The state acknowledged that the federal government could regulate the interstate waste market. However, New York maintained that Congress could not force the state to take ownership of private radioactive waste.

The Supreme Court agreed. Justice O'Connor wrote the majority opinion. She explained that "Congress may not simply 'commandeer,'" or mandate, "the legislative processes of the States by directly compelling them to enact and enforce a federal regulatory program." In other words, Congress could not force the state legislature to enact new laws that authorized the government to assume liability for the radioactive waste.

Congress could use other means to encourage the states to take title of radioactive waste. For example, the federal government could provide money to the states with strings attached, as in *South Dakota v. Dole* (1987). Or Congress could preempt state waste disposal laws and impose a uniform federal standard nationwide. But Congress could not force the state legislatures to enact such legislation itself.

Justice O'Connor recognized the importance of federalism in our system of government. "The Constitution divides authority between federal and state governments," she said, "for the protection of individuals."

The anti-commandeering line of cases, including *New York*, are often described as Tenth Amendment cases. The Tenth Amendment provides, "The powers not delegated to the United States by the Constitution, nor prohibited by it to the States, are reserved to the States respectively, or to the people."

STUDY GUIDE

Is the Tenth Amendment relevant to the Court's analysis?

Justice O'Connor observed that the Tenth Amendment is not relevant, directly at least. "The Tenth Amendment likewise restrains the power of Congress," she wrote, "but this limit is *not* derived from the text of the Tenth Amendment itself, which, as we have discussed, is essentially a tautology."

In what way is the Tenth Amendment a "tautology"? The Tenth Amendment has three premises:

- First, we ask if a power is delegated to Congress. For example, can Congress use its authority under the Commerce and Necessary and Proper Clauses to require New York to take title of the waste? If the answer is yes, then Congress can exercise that power. However, in *New York*, the Court answered that question no.
- Second, we ask if the Constitution prohibits the state from taking that action. The Constitution lists several prohibitions in Article I, Section 10. For example, states cannot enact bills of attainder or ex post facto laws. However, the Constitution says nothing about how New York can or cannot deal with waste.
- Third, therefore, the decision of how to deal with the waste is reserved to the state. Congress lacks the power to tell the state how to make that decision.

The Tenth Amendment does not add anything to the Court's analysis. Generally, if Congress has the power to enact a statute, then states' rights do not affect the scope of that power. But Congress lacks the power to force New York to pass the statute; New York retains the power to deal, or not deal, with the waste. Again, the Tenth Amendment plays no role in this analysis.

Justice Stevens dissented in *New York*: "The notion that Congress does not have the power to issue 'a simple command to state governments to implement legislation enacted by Congress' is incorrect and unsound." He added that "there is no such limitation in the Constitution."

STUDY GUIDE

Is there any textual support for the anti-commandeering doctrine?

Textual support for the anti-commandeering doctrine can be found in the Necessary and Proper Clause. *New York* implicitly stands for two important propositions. First, the "Take Title" provision may be a "necessary" means to regulate the interstate waste market. Second, however, such an intrusion into state sovereignty is not a "proper" exercise of federal power because the law requires a state legislature to legislate. That the anti-commandeering doctrine rests on the meaning of "proper" in the Necessary and Proper Clause would not become explicit until *Printz v. United States* (1997), which we will study in Chapter 18. That case considered whether Congress could commandeer state executive branch officials to implement a federal program. *NFIB v. Sebelius* (2012), which we studied in Chapter 16, further clarified the distinction between "necessary" and "proper."

Printz v. United States (1997)

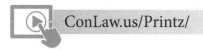 ConLaw.us/Printz/

New York v. United States (1992) held that Congress could not commandeer, or force, state legislatures to take certain actions, such as enacting new legislation. *Printz v. United States* (1997) extended the anti-commandeering doctrine. This decision held that Congress could not commandeer state executive-branch officials, such as sheriffs, to implement a federal program.

Printz began in 1993, when Congress enacted the Brady Handgun Violence Prevention Act. The law proposed a national database that would allow federal firearm dealers to instantly check the background of prospective handgun purchasers. That system, however, would take some time to develop. During this time gap, the federal law commanded the "chief law enforcement officer" (CLEO) of each local jurisdiction to conduct background checks.

The law was challenged by several sheriffs, including Jay Printz of Ravalli County, Montana, and Richard Mack of Graham County, Arizona. They argued that the federal government could not force them to perform background checks, which could delay or even prevent people in their communities from purchasing firearms.

On this question, the Supreme Court divided 5-4. Justice Scalia wrote the majority opinion. Justice Stevens wrote the principal dissent. They disagreed on everything.

First, Justice Stevens wrote that in the early days of the Republic, Congress enacted statutes that required state officials to implement federal law. Justice Scalia, however, countered that these federal obligations were imposed only on state judges, who could be forced to apply federal law. Justice Scalia cited the Supremacy Clause in Article VI, Clause 2. It provides that "the Laws of the United States . . . shall be the supreme Law of the Land; and the *Judges in every State shall be bound thereby.*" In contrast, Article VI, Clause 3 states that "*executive and judicial Officers* . . . of the several States, shall be *bound* by Oath or Affirmation, to support this Constitution." Based on this textualist argument, Scalia concluded that the Constitution imposes an obligation to follow Congressional commands on state judges, but not on state executive-branch officials.

Second, the dissent contended that, even if *New York v. United States* was correct that state legislatures cannot be commandeered, state executive-branch officials can be commandeered. "The fact that the Framers intended to preserve the sovereignty of the several States," Justice Stevens wrote, "simply does not speak to the question whether individual state employees may be required to perform federal obligations." Legislatures make laws. In contrast, the central role of all executive-branch officials — whether federal or state — is to execute those laws.

Justice Scalia rejected this distinction. "While the Brady Act is directed to 'individuals,'" he wrote, the law "is directed to them in their official capacities as state officers; it controls their actions, not as private citizens, but as the agents of the State."

STUDY GUIDE

Is there any principled distinction between Congress's power to commandeer state legislatures and its power to commandeer state executive-branch officials?

Third, Justice Stevens cited recent examples where Congress may have ordered state executive-branch officials to take certain actions. Justice Scalia dismissed the relevance of these recent practices. "Their persuasive force," he said, "is far outweighed by almost two centuries of apparent congressional avoidance of the practice."

Finally, the dissent argued that the Brady Act was valid "because the Tenth Amendment imposes no limitations on the exercise of delegated powers." Furthermore, Justice Stevens found that the Necessary and Proper Clause was an "affirmative delegation of power in Article I" that "provides ample authority for the congressional enactment."

Justice Scalia colorfully responded that the Necessary and Proper Clause was "the last, best hope of those who defend ultra vires congressional action." He stated explicity what Justice O'Connor had implied in *New York v. United States*: Courts must separately ask whether a law is both "necessary" *and* "proper." Justice Scalia stated the rule succinctly: "When a 'Law . . . for carrying into Execution' the Commerce Clause violates the principle of state sovereignty . . . it is not a 'Law . . . proper for carrying into Execution the Commerce Clause,' and is thus, in the words of The Federalist, 'merely [an] ac[t] of usurpation' which 'deserve[s] to be treated as such.'"

The Brady Act provision may have been a "necessary" means to regulate the interstate firearms marketplace. But forcing the Sheriffs to perform background checks was not a "proper" exercise of federal power. This "usurpation" *violates the principle of state sovereignty* reflected in the Tenth Amendment and other structural provisions of our Constitution.

The Supreme Court would reaffirm this distinction between "necessary" and "proper" fifteen years later in the Affordable Care Act decision, *NFIB v. Sebelius* (2012).

CHAPTER 19

The Eleventh Amendment

In Chapter 1, we studied *Chisholm v. Georgia* (1793). This case held that a South Carolina citizen could sue the state of Georgia in federal court. Four Justices held that the states were not sovereign and could be sued in federal court without their consent: Blair, Wilson, Cushing, and Chief Justice Jay. Justice Iredell was the lone dissenter. He found that the states, as sovereigns, retained their immunity following the ratification of the Constitution. Therefore, they could not be sued without their consent. *Chisholm* was met with widespread opposition by state governments.

Two years later, the Eleventh Amendment was ratified. It provides, "The Judicial power of the United States shall not be construed to extend to any suit in law or equity, commenced or prosecuted against one of the United States by Citizens of another State, or by Citizens or Subjects of any Foreign State."

This provision modified Article III, Section 2 of the Constitution. Originally, the judicial power expressly extended to controversies "between a State and Citizens of another State." The Eleventh Amendment changed that rule. A state could still sue a citizen of another state in federal court. That is, the state could be the plaintiff. However, a state could not be made a defendant in federal court by a citizen "of another state" unless the state consented.

The text of the Eleventh Amendment answered some questions but left many other questions unresolved. First, could a citizen of one state sue another state? That is, could a resident of South Carolina sue Georgia in federal court? The answer is clearly no. Second, could a citizen sue his own state? That is, could a citizen of Louisiana sue Louisiana in federal court? The text does not address that question. Third, did the Eleventh Amendment reverse the *Chisholm* majority's holding that states lacked sovereign immunity? Again, the text does not address that question—at least not expressly.

These final two questions would be resolved a century later by *Hans v. Louisiana* (1890).

Hans v. Louisiana (1890)

 ConLaw.us/Hans/

After Reconstruction concluded, the state of Louisiana failed to pay interest on certain bonds. Hans, a citizen of Louisiana, sued Louisiana in federal court. He claimed that the state had violated the Contracts Clause. Article I, Section 10 of the Constitution provides that "No State shall . . . make any . . . Law impairing the Obligation of Contracts." Hans argued that Louisiana's violation of this Clause gave rise to *federal question* jurisdiction under Article III, Section 2. It provides, "The judicial Power shall extend to all Cases, in Law and Equity, arising under this Constitution, the Laws of the United States, and Treaties made . . . under their Authority." Federal courts have *federal question* jurisdiction when a plaintiff alleges that the government violated the Constitution, such as the Contracts Clause, or a federal statute or treaty. In such cases, the federal courts have the "judicial Power" to resolve the dispute. Article III, Section 2 also establishes *diversity* jurisdiction. Federal courts can hear a case "between Citizens of different States," or a case brought by a state against a citizen of another state. The federal courts can exercise diversity jurisdiction regardless of the subject matter of the legal claims being made.

STUDY GUIDE

Does it make a difference whether a citizen sues a state based on federal question or diversity jurisdiction?

The Supreme Court found that it lacked jurisdiction, and unanimously rejected Hans's claim. Justice Bradley wrote the majority opinion. He acknowledged that the text of the Eleventh Amendment does not prohibit a citizen from suing his own state. It only applied to suing "another state." "It is true," he wrote, "the amendment does so read." But this reading would lead to an "anomalous result" in cases involving federal question jurisdiction. Specifically, "a State may be sued in the federal courts by its own citizens, though it cannot be sued for a like cause of action by the citizens of other States, or of a foreign State."

Justice Bradley concluded that the text of the Eleventh Amendment was not to be read literally: "The letter is appealed to now, as it was [in *Chisholm*], as a ground for sustaining a suit brought by an individual against a State. The reason against it is as strong in this case as it was in that." What was that reason? "It is inherent in the nature of sovereignty," Justice Bradley observed, for a state "not to be amenable to the suit of an individual without its consent."

The *Hans* Court answered the two questions left open by *Chisholm* and the Eleventh Amendment. Can a citizen sue his own state in federal court for violating the Constitution, a federal statute, or a treaty? The *Hans* Court answered no. Did the

Eleventh Amendment reverse the *Chisholm* majority's holding that states lacked sovereign immunity? The *Hans* Court answered yes. In sum, after *Hans* a citizen could not sue his own sovereign state without its consent.

STUDY GUIDE

Does the text of the Eleventh Amendment say anything about sovereign immunity? Did the Eleventh Amendment correct a mistake in the original Constitution, or did it correct the Supreme Court's mistaken interpretation in *Chisholm*?

Justice John Marshall Harlan concurred. He agreed that "a suit directly against a State by one of its own citizens is not one to which the judicial power of the United States extends, unless the State itself consents to be sued." However, he stated that *Chisholm* "was based upon a sound interpretation of the Constitution" prior to the ratification of the Eleventh Amendment. In other words, he thought it was the Constitution, not the Court, that needed to be corrected by the Eleventh Amendment.

Seminole Tribe of Florida v. Florida (1996)

 ConLaw.us/SeminoleTribe/

Even after *Hans*, there are still two ways a state can be sued in federal court. First, a state can waive its own sovereign immunity by consenting to citizen-suits in federal court. State governments, like the federal government, have enacted *Claims Acts* that waive their sovereign immunity and enable some types of citizen-suits. Second, even if the state does not consent to citizen-suits in federal court, Congress has the power to override, or abrogate, a state's sovereign immunity. Through the Indian Gaming Regulatory Act, Congress attempted to do just that.

In our second case, the Seminole Tribe of Florida sued the state of Florida in federal court for violating the Indian Gaming Regulatory Act. Here, the state did not wave its sovereign immunity. The Supreme Court held that Congress could not use its Commerce Clause powers to abrogate Florida's sovereign immunity.

Chief Justice Rehnquist wrote the majority opinion for a 5-4 Court. He quoted *Hans v. Louisiana*'s rejection of a literal interpretation of the Eleventh Amendment: "Although the text of the Amendment would appear to restrict only the Article III diversity jurisdiction of the federal courts, 'we have understood the Eleventh Amendment to stand *not so much for what it says*, but for the presupposition . . . which it confirms.'" That presupposition, or assumption, "has two parts."

First, that "each State is a sovereign entity in our federal system." Second, that "'[i]t is inherent in the nature of sovereignty not to be amenable to the suit of an individual without its consent." From these two premises, Chief Justice Rehnquist concluded that the Indian Gaming Regulatory Act's waiver of sovereign immunity was unconstitutional: "Even when the Constitution vests in Congress complete lawmaking authority over a particular area," he wrote, such as the regulation of interstate or Indian commerce, "the Eleventh Amendment prevents congressional authorization of suits by private parties against unconsenting States." When Chief Justice Rehnquist cited "the Eleventh Amendment," he was not referring to its text but to the "presuposition" for which it stands. According to the majority, "federal jurisdiction over suits against unconsenting States 'was not contemplated by the Constitution when establishing the judicial power of the United States.'"

Justice Souter wrote a lengthy dissent that recounted the history of the Eleventh Amendment. On its face, he explained, the text appears to limit only the Article III diversity jurisdiction of the federal courts. Article III specifically refers to a citizen of one state suing another state, which is what makes the parties diverse. The text of the Eleventh Amendment does not reference the Court's jurisdiction to hear cases involving federal questions; for example, whether Congress has enacted a law that exceeds its powers under the Commerce Power. According to Justice Souter, "we have two Eleventh Amendments, the one ratified in 1795, the other (so-called) invented by the Court nearly a century later in *Hans v. Louisiana*."

STUDY GUIDE

Who is the originalist in *Seminole Tribe*? Is it Justice Souter, who relies on the original meaning of the text of Article III and the Eleventh Amendment? Or is it Chief Justice Rehnquist who relies on what was "contemplated by the Constitution"?

Regardless of what the Eleventh Amendment says, however, the Court later held that Section 5 of the Fourteenth Amendment expressly gave Congress an enumerated power to override a state's sovereign immunity. But there are limits on when Congress can exercise that authority. The Court considered this issue in *City of Boerne v. Flores* (1997), which we will discuss in Chapter 20.

Section 5 of the Fourteenth Amendment

Hans v. Louisiana (1890) held that the Eleventh Amendment presupposed that the states had sovereign immunity. In later cases, however, the Court held that Section 5 of the Fourteenth Amendment gave Congress the authority to override, or abrogate, a state's sovereign immunity. In other words, Congress can make the state vulnerable to citizen lawsuits in federal court.

Section 5 gives Congress the "power to enforce, by appropriate legislation, the provisions of this article." What are "the provisions of this article"? That phrase refers back to Sections 1 through 4 of the Fourteenth Amendment. Section 1 of the Fourteenth Amendment contains the Due Process Clause: "nor shall any State deprive any person of life, liberty, or property, without due process of law." If a "state" "deprive[s]" a person of "liberty" "without due process of law" — a violation of Section 1 — then Congress has the power under Section 5 to enact "appropriate legislation" to enforce that person's civil rights.

STUDY GUIDE

Is there a parallel between the phrase "appropriate legislation" in Section 5 of the Fourteenth Amendment and the Necessary and Proper Clause in Article I, Section 8?

The Free Exercise Clause of the First Amendment provides, "Congress shall make no law . . . prohibiting the free exercise" of religion. In 1940, the Supreme Court held that the phrase "liberty" in the Due Process Clause of the Fourteenth Amendment "embraces the liberties guaranteed by the First Amendment." Under the modern *incorporation doctrine*, the Due Process Clause of the Fourteenth Amendment prevents states from violating rights enumerated in the first eight amendments.

STUDY GUIDE

Can you see how expanding or contracting the scope of Section 1 of the Fourteenth Amendment affects the scope of Section 5?

What does it mean for Congress to "enforce" the First Amendment with "appropriate legislation"? *Katzenbach v. Morgan* (1966) held that Section 5 gives Congress the power to "remedy or prevent unconstitutional actions." In *City of Boerne v. Flores* (1997), however, the Court held that Section 5 does not give Congress the power to "make a substantive change" to the Supreme Court's interpretation of the scope of Section 1.

City of Boerne v. Flores (1997)

 ConLaw.us/Boerne/

To understand *Boerne* we have to review how the Supreme Court has interpreted the Free Exercise Clause. (We will consider this doctrine in Chapter 57.) *Sherbert v. Verner* (1963) held that the government *cannot* substantially burden the free exercise of religion unless the government shows that it has a compelling interest to impose that burden. Nearly three decades later, the Supreme Court changed course in *Employment Division v. Smith* (1990). The Court held that a state *can* substantially burden the free exercise of religion, even if the government lacks a compelling interest to impose that burden, so long as the law was "neutral" towards religion. A law is "neutral" if it imposes the same burden on all religions.

Smith proved to be very unpopular among both Democrats and Republicans. In 1993, Congress enacted the Religious Freedom Restoration Act (RFRA). The House passed RFRA unanimously. In the Senate, the vote was 97-3. President Clinton signed RFRA into law. (We will study RFRA in Chapter 58.)

As its name suggests, RFRA sought to restore *Sherbert's* more protective test. Specifically, under RFRA, once again, a law could not "substantially burden" the free exercise of religion unless the state can show it had a compelling interest for doing so. States that violated RFRA could be sued in federal court. Congress used its Section 5 powers to abrogate state sovereign immunity.

After RFRA was enacted, the city of Boerne, Texas denied a building permit to St. Peter's Catholic Church. Generally, the city — a subdivision of the state — could not be sued in federal court. However, Archbishop Flores was able to sue the city because of RFRA. He claimed that the denial of the building permit substantially burdened his free exercise of religion and that the city failed to show that it had a compelling interest to deny the permit.

STUDY GUIDE

Could Congress require Texas to provide greater protections for the Free Exercise of Religion than what *Employment Division v. Smith* required?

The Supreme Court held that Congress lacked this power. Justice Kennedy wrote the majority opinion. He found that Congress's enforcement powers under Section 5 could only "remedy" constitutional violations of Section 1, as Section 1 had been interpreted by the Supreme Court. Section 5 does not give Congress "the power to decree the substance of the Fourteenth Amendment's restrictions on the States." Congress may only remedy violations of Section 1 as it has been defined by the Court.

STUDY GUIDE

How does the Court draw the line between "remedial" legislation and "substantive" legislation? How does the Court assess whether Congress has gone beyond its remedial power?

The Court draws this line by measuring the fit between the "injury to be prevented" and the "means adopted to that end." After *Smith* defined the meaning of "free exercise" of religion, Congress could not use its Section 5 enforcement power to expand the scope of that right. Justice Kennedy explained, "There must be a congruence and proportionality between the injury to be prevented or remedied and the means adopted to that end. Lacking such a connection, legislation may become substantive in operation and effect."

Let's apply this framework to RFRA. What is the injury Congress attempted to prevent? A state law that substantially burdens the free exercise of religion—a right that is protected by Section 1 of the Fourteenth Amendment. What are the means Congress adopted to prevent such a violation of Section 1? When sued by a citizen, the state must show a compelling interest that justifies the burden. Is the fit between the means and the ends "congruent and proportional"? The Court answered no. *Smith* already held that the State need not show a compelling interest to justify a burden on free exercise, if that burden was imposed by a "neutral" law.

Therefore, RFRA was not *remedial* legislation. It changed the *substance* of Section 1 of the Fourteenth Amendment, as defined by the Court. As a result, the Court held that Section 5 did not give Congress the power to waive a state's sovereign immunity pursuant to RFRA. Justice Kennedy explained, "when the court has interpreted the Constitution, it has acted within the province of the Judicial Branch which embraces the duty to say what the law is. . . . [A]s the provisions of the federal statute here invoked are beyond congressional authority, it is this Court's precedent and not RFRA which must control."

RFRA could not be used to restrict a state's police power. However, the Court found that RFRA was constitutional as applied to the federal government. Why? Congress could limit its own powers as a means to provide greater protection for the free exercise of religion.

Over the next decade, the Rehnquist Court would consider three other federal laws in which Congress purported to use its Section 5 power to override, or abrogate, state sovereign immunity.

United States v. Morrison (2000)

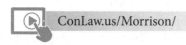 ConLaw.us/Morrison/

First, *United States v. Morrison* (2000) considered the constitutionality of the Violence Against Women Act (VAWA). In Chapter 14, we discussed how Congress lacked the powers under the Commerce and Necessary and Proper Clauses to create a federal cause of action for gender-motivated violence. *Morrison* also held that Section 5 did not give Congress the power to create the federal cause of action. Therefore, the state university that violated VAWA could not be sued in federal court.

Board of Trustees of University of Alabama v. Garrett (2001)

 ConLaw.us/Garrett/

Second, *Board of Trustees of University of Alabama v. Garrett* (2001) held that a state university that violated the Americans with Disabilities Act (ADA) could not be sued for money damages in federal court.

Nevada Department of Human Resources v. Hibbs (2003)

 ConLaw.us/Hibbs/

In the third case, however, the Rehnquist Court changed course. Over the prior decade, Chief Justice Rehnquist had consistently declared unconstitutional federal waivers of state sovereign immunity. But in *Nevada Department of Human Resources v. Hibbs* (2003) he found that Congress *could* abrogate a state's sovereign immunity to remedy violations of the Family Medical Leave Act (FMLA). This law allowed "eligible employees to take up to 12 work weeks of unpaid leave annually." Employers that denied that benefit — including state government agencies — could be sued in federal court for damages. In this case, William Hibbs sued the Nevada Department of Human Resources for violating FMLA.

By a 6-3 vote, the Supreme Court found that FMLA's waiver of sovereign immunity was constitutional. Chief Justice Rehnquist wrote the majority opinion. He concluded that *FMLA* was different from *RFRA* and the ADA.

Further, unlike with the history of the ADA, when FMLA was enacted, "Congress had before it significant evidence of a long and extensive history of sex discrimination with respect to the administration of leave benefits by the States, which is weighty enough to justify the enactment of prophylactic § 5 legislation." Therefore, FMLA's waiver of sovereign immunity was "congruent and proportional" to Congress's goal of reducing sex-based discrimination with respect to leave benefits.

Justice Kennedy dissented in *Hibbs*. He found that with FMLA, "Congress was not responding with a congruent and proportional remedy to a perceived course of unconstitutional conduct. Instead, it enacted a substantive entitlement program of its own."

STUDY GUIDE

Can *Hibbs* be reconciled with *Boerne*? Justice Ginsburg hinted that Chief Justice Rehnquist joined the majority in *Hibbs* due to "life experience." His daughter was a recently divorced single mother with a demanding career.

THE EXECUTIVE POWER

Article II of the Constitution vests "the executive power" in "a President of the United States of America." Part IV studies three cases that explore the scope of presidential power. *Ex Parte Merryman* (1861) analyzes the President's power to suspend the writ of *habeas corpus* during the Civil War. *Youngstown Sheet & Tube Company v. Sawyer* (1952) rebuffed the President's effort to seize private property during the Korean War. *Korematsu v. United States* (1944) affirmed the President's power to exclude Japanese-Americans from their homes during World War II.

CHAPTER 21

Ex Parte Merryman (1861)

ConLaw.us/Merryman/

In the contentious election of 1860, Republican Abraham Lincoln was elected President without receiving a single electoral vote from a Southern state. After his election, but before he took office, seven Southern states seceded from the Union: South Carolina, Mississippi, Florida, Alabama, Georgia, Louisiana, and Texas.

On March 4, 1861, Chief Justice Roger Brooke Taney issued the oath of office to Lincoln. During his inaugural address, Lincoln assured the remaining slave states, which had not yet seceded, that he would not disturb their institutionalized slavery. His promises, however, would not be effective. On April 12, 1861, Confederate forces fired on Fort Sumter in South Carolina. Unable to receive federal reinforcements, the fort was surrendered three days later. Soon, the slave states of Virginia, North Carolina, Tennessee, and Arkansas joined the Confederacy.

Though the conflict is called the Civil War, Congress never formally voted on a declaration of war. Rather, President Lincoln prosecuted the military campaign through broad and largely unprecedented assertions of executive powers. *Ex Parte Merryman* (1861), decided by Taney, considered whether the President could deny a prisoner the right to ask a judge to determine the legality of his confinement.

In the Anglo-American tradition, a prisoner can petition a judge for what is known as a writ of *habeas corpus*. This term is part of a Latin phrase that means "produce the body." This writ refers to a judicial order to a jailer to produce the prisoner's body to the court. The Suspension Clause in our Constitution recognizes this tradition. Article I, Section 9 provides, "The privilege of the writ of habeas corpus shall not be suspended, unless when in cases of rebellion or invasion the public safety may require it." This Clause presupposes both the availability of such a writ and that it may sometimes be suspended. But the Constitution does not specify who may suspend it: Is it the President, Congress, or both acting in concert? The Framers did include this provision in Article I, which concerns the legislature's authority. It does not appear in Article II, which concerns the President's powers. The Clause's placement in Article I suggests that Congress has the power to suspend the writ.

Often, courts rely on a textualist argument, where the express text of the Constitution supports a certain result. *Merryman*, however, relied on a structural argument to address an issue on which the text of the Constitution was silent: Which branch can suspend the writ? Because the power appears in Article I rather than in Article II, Chief Justice Taney found that the structure or organization of the Constitution implies that this power belongs to Congress, and not to the President.

President Lincoln disagreed. After hostilities began, he unilaterally suspended the writ of habeas corpus and imposed martial law in areas that had not seceded from the Union, including the slave state of Maryland. At the time, Congress was not in session.

STUDY GUIDE

Did President Lincoln have the unilateral power to suspend the writ? Does it matter that Congress was not in session at the time and was therefore unable to act?

In *Merryman*, Chief Justice Taney sharply criticized Lincoln's suspension of the writ as unconstitutional. The facts of this case are quite curious. On May 25, 1861, John Merryman, a citizen of Maryland, was arrested by a military force and detained at Fort McHenry in Baltimore. On May 26, Chief Justice Taney issued a writ of habeas corpus directing General George Cadwalader to produce Merryman's body. By issuing a writ, Taney did not order that Merryman must be released. The Chief Justice only ordered that the prisoner should be brought to court for a hearing. General Cadwalader declined to produce Merryman. Instead, he sent the Chief Justice a letter that explained his rationale. When informed that the general had not delivered Merryman's body, the Chief Justice ordered the marshal of the court to arrest the General, so Cadwalader could be held in contempt. That effort was unsuccessful. Taney then issued a written opinion.

STUDY GUIDE

Notice that this opinion is rendered by Taney while he was serving at the Circuit Court, District of Maryland, and not at the Supreme Court. In what capacity did Taney render his decision?

Taney relied on the stuctural argument, and concluded that the President could not suspend the writ of habeas corpus. Only Congress had that power. He wrote:

> I can see no ground whatever for supposing that the president, in any emergency, or in any state of things, can authorize the suspension of the privileges of the writ of habeas corpus, or the arrest of a citizen, except in aid of the judicial power. He certainly does not faithfully execute the laws, if he takes upon himself legislative power, by suspending the writ of habeas corpus, and the judicial power also, by arresting and imprisoning a person without due process of law.

Taney then took an unusual step. He ordered that his written opinion should "be laid before the president, in order that he might perform his constitutional duty, to enforce the laws, by securing obedience to the process of the United States." It is commonly argued that President Lincoln invoked his executive power to defy Taney's order. Some scholars use this "fact" to criticize Lincoln; others use this position to justify broad presidential power today.

Recently, however, this claim has been challenged as among several myths surrounding the facts of *Merryman*. According to Professor Seth Barrett Tillman, Taney merely transmitted his opinion to the President. "Taney issued no order to release Merryman," Tillman wrote. "It follows, therefore, that Lincoln could not have ignored or defied it, nor could anyone else for that matter."*

Following Taney's decision, Merryman was detained at Fort McHenry until he was transferred to the federal civilian authorities. He was indicted for treason, and shortly thereafter was released on bail. Six years later, in 1867, all charges against Merryman were dropped.

The President never formally acknowledged Taney's opinion. Lincoln did, however, defend his decision to suspend the writ of habeas corpus. On July 4th, 1861, he delivered a message to a special session of Congress. Lincoln sought approval for actions he had taken in Congress's absence, including the suspension of habeas corpus. Congress agreed and formally enacted a statute "approving, legalizing, and making valid all the acts, proclamations, and orders of the President, &c., as if they had been issued and done under the previous express authority and direction of the Congress of the United States."

STUDY GUIDE

Is this act of Congress relevant to an assessment of Lincoln's previous actions?

Taney died in office three years later in 1864. Lincoln fittingly replaced the author of *Dred Scott v. Sandford* (1857) with antislavery lawyer Salmon P. Chase.

---

* *See* Seth Barrett Tillman, *Ex Parte Merryman*: Myth, History, and Scholarship, 224 Mil. L. Rev. 481 (2016).

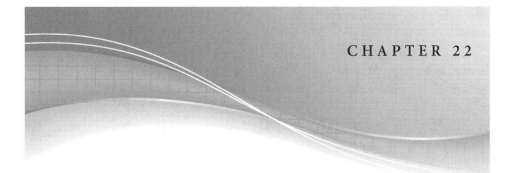

CHAPTER 22

Youngstown Sheet & Tube Company v. Sawyer (1952)

ConLaw.us/Youngstown/

Youngstown Sheet & Tube Company v. Sawyer (1952) is one of the Supreme Court's most important decisions concerning the separation of powers between the President, the Congress, and the judiciary. The Supreme Court resolved the *Steel Seizure Case*, as the case is also known, in less than two months between April and June 1952. To understand this case, we first have to recount the history of the Korean War — one of our most forgotten wars.

From 1950-1953, the United States was engaged in a military conflict on the Korean Peninsula. Congress did not declare war on Korea. Instead, the United Nations Security Council authorized the conflict. The United States became a member of the United Nations after the Senate approved a treaty in 1945. President Harry S. Truman's administration argued that this treaty gave him the power to prosecute the *conflict* in Korea even in the absence of a formal declaration of war.

Soon, a labor crisis arose on the homefront that threatened to disrupt the war effort. Due to a wage dispute, the United Steelworkers union announced that it would halt work — or *strike* — at steel mills across the country. President Truman determined that the strike would frustrate the war effort in Korea because there would not be enough steel to manufacture tanks, planes, and other munitions. On April 8, 1952, one day before the planned strike, President Truman signed Executive Order 10340.

STUDY GUIDE

What is an executive order? How does it differ from a bill approved by the House and Senate that the President signs into law?

The executive order authorized Charles Sawyer, the Secretary of Commerce, to take control of steel mills nationwide that would be affected by the strike. The plant managers were ordered to "continue their functions."

STUDY GUIDE

What would have happened if managers refused to comply with the executive order?

President Truman sent two messages to Congress about the seizure. But the President never asked for permission or authorization. Instead, he said that "the Congress can, if it wishes, reject the course of action I have followed in this matter." During this time Congress took no action to approve, or disapprove, the executive order.

One of the seized mills was the Youngstown Sheet and Tube Company in Youngstown, Ohio. Thirty minutes after the seizure, the mill's owner challenged the constitutionality of the executive order. On April 29, three weeks after the executive order was issued, the district court halted the seizure. The following day, the Court of Appeals put the lower court ruling on hold, so long as the government immediately appealed the case to the Supreme Court. On May 2, attorneys for the federal government and the steel industry filed petitions for writs of certiorari with the Supreme Court.

The following day, the Supreme Court granted those petitions. On May 12 and 13, the Supreme Court heard oral arguments. And on June 2, 1952, the Supreme Court decided the case—less than a month after oral arguments and less than two months after the steel seizure. But there was a cost to resolving the case so quickly: The final opinion was extremely fragmented. Six Justices found that the seizure was unconstitutional. Justice Black wrote the majority opinion. Five other Justices joined him, and each wrote a separate concurring opinion: Justices Frankfurter, Douglas, Jackson, Burton, and Clark. Three Justices voted to uphold the seizure. Chief Justice Vinson wrote the dissenting opinion, which was joined by Justices Reed and Minton.

Text. Justice Hugo Black wrote a textualist majority opinion. He explained that "the President had no power to act except in those cases expressly or implicitly authorized by the Constitution or an act of Congress." In other words, because the President had no inherent or *unenumerated* power to seize a private company, he could only seize the mills if the Constitution or Congress authorized that action.

President Truman argued that three provisions of the Constitution gave him the power to issue the executive order: (1) the Vesting Clause in Article II, Section 1, (2) the Commander in Chief Clause in Article II, Section 2, and (3) the Take Care Clause in Article II, Section 3. Justice Black found that none of those clauses gave the President the power to seize private property on the homefront.

Did any act of Congress give President Truman the authority to seize the steel mills? Justice Black answered no. In fact, he explained, "Congress rejected an amendment which would have authorized such governmental seizures in cases of emergency." In short, the President lacked both the constitutional and statutory authority to issue the executive order. Therefore, the seizure violated the separation of powers.

Past practice. Justice Frankfurter wrote the first concurring opinion. He explained that the scope of presidential power cannot be defined solely by the text of the Constitution, such as the Vesting Clause. Rather, the meaning of "the executive power" should be understood based on past presidential practice.

STUDY GUIDE

What is the relationship between "the executive power" and how executives have exercised their power?

For example, imagine if there were a 150-year-long tradition of Presidents seizing private property. What if President Washington had seized private property, and Congress did not object? And President Adams did the same, as did Presidents Jefferson and Madison, and *every other* President leading up to President Truman's steel seizure in 1952. Justice Frankfurter explained that such a "systematic, unbroken, executive practice, long pursued to the knowledge of the Congress and never before questioned . . . may be treated as a *gloss* on 'executive power' vested in the President by § 1 of Art. II." In other words, Presidents Washington, Adams, Jefferson, and Madison, through their actions, added a new *gloss*, or a supplement, to the Constitution. Because Congress approved of these long-standing practices, courts should hesitate before disturbing that settlement. Unfortunately for President Truman, however, Justice Frankfurter found that there was no "systematic, unbroken, executive practice" of past Presidents seizing private property. Therefore, he concluded, President Truman did not have the "executive power" to seize the steel mills.

Structure. Justice Douglas wrote the second concurring opinion. It was based on the structure of the Constitution. The Fifth Amendment requires that the government must pay "just compensation" when it takes "private property." Because the seizure of the steel mills was a "tak[ing]," the government had to pay the steel companies "just compensation." However, "[t]he President has no power to raise revenues," Justice Douglas explained. "That power is in the Congress by Article I, Section 8 of the Constitution." Therefore, he concluded, "[t]he branch of government that has the power to pay compensation for a seizure is the only one able to authorize a seizure or make lawful one that the President has effected." In other words, the seizure was a taking, and the Constitution entrusted this quintessentially legislative act to the Congress. Moreover, Congress had not authorized the President to seize the mills. Therefore, Justice Douglas found that the taking was unconstitutional.

The Twilight Zone. Justice Jackson wrote the third, and most influential concurring opinion. Justice Jackson had previously served as President Roosevelt's Attorney General. He admitted that there was a "poverty of really useful and unambiguous authority applicable to concrete problems of executive power." As a result, he reasoned, "isolated clauses" of the Constitution cannot resolve most problems. Instead, Justice Jackson explained there are three *zones* of presidential authority.

In the first zone, the President can always rely on all constitutional authority "that he possesses in his own right" pursuant to Article II. And in this first zone he can also rely on the power he has been given by the "express or implied authorization of Congress" pursuant to its Article I lawmaking power. Because the President possesses power from both sources, in this first zone he has "maximum" authority. Therefore, in the first zone the Court should review the executive action with the "strongest presumption[]" of constitutionality. We call this tier the *daylight zone*, where the sun of congressional power shines on presidential power.

STUDY GUIDE

What is a *presumption of constitutionality*? Randy Barnett has written that the opposite of the *presumption of constitutionality* is the *presumption of liberty*. Although *Youngstown* is not a traditional *rights* case based on the Due Process Clause, does the constitutional separation of powers protect individual liberty? If so, whose liberty?

We'll come back to the second category in a moment.

In the third zone, the President can rely only on his own constitutional authority. But that's it. Congress has not delegated any additional legislative authority. Therefore, the President's "power is at its lowest ebb." In this third zone, the judiciary must "scrutinize[]" all executive actions "with caution." We call this tier the *nighttime zone,* where the President acts alone based on his own authority, without any light cast by Congress.

But what about a case where the scope of the congressional delegation of authority is unknown? In the second category, Justice Jackson said, the President's authority is in "a zone of twilight" — that is, when it is not quite night, but not quite day. How should courts review executive actions taken in the *twilight zone*? Justice Jackson explained, "any actual test of power is likely to depend on the imperatives of events and contemporary imponderables rather than on abstract theories of law." In sum, the Court must rely on practical considerations.

Justice Jackson found that, in this case, President Truman's executive order fell within the third zone. Congress did not authorize the President to seize the steel mills, and the President could only act based on his own Article II authority. In this lowest tier, Justice Jackson applied a form of *strict* scrutiny. That is, he scrutinized the executive order with great caution to identify any flaws or defects. After this rigorous review, Justice Jackson found that the executive order was unconstitutional. In *Dames & Moore v. Regan* (1981), the Supreme Court would adopt Justice Jackson's three-zone framework as the definitive approach to analyze separation of powers issues.

Past Practice. Chief Justice Vinson wrote the dissent. He was joined by Justices Reed and Minton. They looked at history very differently than did Justice Frankfurter. Chief Justice Vinson explained that Presidents Washington, Jefferson, Lincoln, Roosevelt, and others "dealt with national emergencies by acting promptly and resolutely to enforce legislative programs," even when they lacked "explicit statutory authorization."

STUDY GUIDE

Do the President's authorities expand during an emergency? Do those powers contract after the emergency concludes?

Chief Justice Vinson concluded that President Truman could "faithfully execute the laws by acting in an emergency to maintain the status quo, thereby preventing collapse of the legislative programs until Congress could act."

Minutes after the Supreme Court decided *Youngstown*, President Truman ordered Secretary Sawyer to return the steel mills to the owners.

STUDY GUIDE

What would have happened if President Truman ignored the Supreme Court's order?

The labor strike would last fifty days as the Korean War continued. Contrary to the government's concerns, there was no apparent disruption to the military's steel supply lines.

CHAPTER 23

Korematsu v. United States (1944)

ConLaw.us/Korematsu/

On December 7, 1941, Japan launched a surprise attack on the Pacific Fleet of the U.S. Navy, which was docked in Pearl Harbor, Hawaii. The following day, Congress declared war against Japan. Over the next three years, the Supreme Court would consider the legality of three executive actions taken by the Roosevelt administration during the war against Japan. First, in *Hirabayashi v. United States* (1943), the Justices unanimously upheld a curfew imposed against American citizens of Japanese ancestry on the West Coast. Second, in *Ex parte Endo* (1944), the Court unanimously halted the military's detention of Japanese-Americans in detention camps. In the third case, *Korematsu v. United States* (1944), the Justices upheld the military's exclusion of Japanese-Americans from certain "zones" on the West Coast. This 6-3 decision upheld Fred Korematsu's conviction for violating the exclusion order.

Justice Black wrote the majority opinion in *Korematsu*. He explained that the Supreme Court would be suspicious of all racial classifications:

> It should be noted, to begin with, that all legal restrictions which curtail the civil rights of a single racial group are immediately suspect. That is not to say that all such restrictions are unconstitutional. It is to say that courts must subject them to the most rigid scrutiny. Pressing public necessity may sometimes justify the existence of such restrictions; racial antagonism never can.

Justice Black's approach came to be known as *strict scrutiny*. This promising beginning, however, quickly gave way to judicial restraint. Justice Black ultimately deferred to the Roosevelt administration's defense of the policy: "We cannot say that the war-making branches of the Government did not have ground for believing that in a critical hour such persons could not readily be isolated and separately dealt with." The "exclusion from a threatened area," Black observed, "has a definite and close relationship to the prevention of espionage and sabotage." In other words, the means chosen were sufficiently tailored to accomplish the compelling state interest of protecting national security. At bottom, the majority was not willing to second-guess the military: "We cannot — by availing ourselves of the calm perspective of hindsight — now say that at that time these actions were unjustified."

There were three separate dissenting opinions. Justice Roberts wrote the first dissent. He contended that "the indisputable facts exhibit a clear violation of Constitutional rights." Excluded people could only challenge the order by breaking the law and refusing to leave their homes. This dilemma, Justice Roberts concluded, violated the liberty protected by the Fifth Amendment's Due Process Clause.

Justice Murphy wrote the second dissent. He observed that "this exclusion of 'all persons of Japanese ancestry' . . . goes over 'the very brink of constitutional power,' and falls into the ugly abyss of racism." Because "no reliable evidence is cited to show that such individuals were generally disloyal," he reasoned, the government did not satisfy the burden to justify this "obvious racial discrimination."

STUDY GUIDE

Does Justice Murphy rely on hindsight in his dissent?

Justice Murphy concluded that the exclusion of Japanese-Americans "deprives all those within its scope of the equal protection of the laws as guaranteed by the Fifth Amendment."

STUDY GUIDE

Does the Fifth Amendment have an Equal Protection Clause?

Justice Jackson wrote the third dissent. He explained that the exclusion order determined a person's guilt solely because he was "born of different racial stock." Unlike the majority, Justice Jackson was willing to second-guess the military commanders, especially when there was no evidence in the record to justify the policy. Yet he was still hesitant to abandon the presumption of constitutionality. Ultimately, Justice Jackson found that the government's use of racial classifications violated the Fifth Amendment's Due Process Clause.

Korematsu, as well as *Ex parte Endo*, were both decided on December 18, 1944. The day before, however, the Western Defense Command lifted the exclusion order on the West Coast. Japanese-Americans would be allowed to return to their homes. That notice, however, was not published until three weeks later. There is some evidence that Chief Justice Stone, who was in touch with the executive branch, delayed the release of *Korematsu* and *Endo*, possibly to induce the administration to lift its order.

STUDY GUIDE

Were *Korematsu* and *Endo* moot before the cases were even decided?

In 1983, a federal court vacated Fred Korematsu's conviction. In 2011, the Solicitor General's office confessed that it had committed error. Specifically, six decades earlier, the federal government failed to disclose to the Court a report showing that "only a small percentage of Japanese Americans posed a potential security threat." In *Trump v. Hawaii* (2018), Chief Justice Roberts wrote that "*Korematsu* was gravely wrong the day it was decided, has been overruled in the court of history, and — to be clear — has no place in law under the Constitution."

STUDY GUIDE

What does Chief Justice Roberts mean by "overruled in the court of history"?

Korematsu is one of the most reviled Supreme Court opinions of all time, standing alongside *Dred Scott v. Sandford* (1857) and *Plessy v. Ferguson* (1896) in the *anti-canon*.

THE SEPARATION OF POWERS

Part V focuses on two important structural cases concerning the scope of presidential power. *Morrison v. Olson* (1988) discusses the scope of the President's removal power. *NLRB v. Noel Canning* (2014) analyzes the scope of the President's recess appointment power.

CHAPTER 24

Morrison v. Olson (1988)

ConLaw.us/Olson/

Morrison v. Olson involved a constitutional challenge to the Ethics in Government Act (EIGA) of 1978. To understand why this federal law was enacted, we need to recount the history of the Watergate scandal.

President Nixon ran for re-election in 1972, with support from the Committee for the Re-election of President Nixon. CREEP, as critics dubbed it, hired several men to surreptitiously enter the Democratic National Headquarters, which were located at the Watergate Hotel complex in Washington, D.C. What they were searching for remains a matter of controversy. Following the break-in, the men were arrested and charged with burglary. Nixon had no role in, or even knowledge of, the break-in. However, based on recordings of White House conversations, we know that Nixon later became aware of the break-in. Specifically, the President and his closest advisors discussed raising money to pay the burglars in return for their silence about CREEP's involvement. This unsuccessful effort became known as "the cover-up."

The press reported on the burglary before the election. However, President Nixon's involvement in the cover-up was not uncovered until after he won re-election in a landslide victory. As evidence of Nixon's misbehavior mounted, the House Judiciary Committee began public impeachment hearings on May 9, 1974.

The Constitution provides a two-step process for Congress to impeach and remove the President. First, "[t]he House of Representatives . . . shall have the sole Power of Impeachment." Art. I, Sec. 2, Cl. 5. The House approves, by majority vote, "Articles of Impeachment" that charge the President with engaging in "Treason, Bribery, or other high Crimes and Misdemeanors." Art. II, Sec. 4. An "impeachment" resembles an indictment in a criminal case.

Second, "The Senate shall have the sole Power to try all Impeachments." Art I, Sec. 3, Cl. 6. After the House impeaches the President, the Senate functions as a court, where the President is tried. "When the President of the United States is *tried*, the Chief Justice shall preside." Removing the President requires "the Concurrence of two thirds of the [Senators] present." Art. I, Sec. 3, Cl. 6.

Ultimately, the House would never vote on articles of impeachment. On August 9, 1974, three months after the impeachment hearings began, President Nixon resigned from office. He stepped down in the aftermath of the so-called "Saturday Night Massacre," which had occurred the prior fall. In May 1973, President Nixon nominated Elliott Richardson as Attorney General. During his confirmation hearing, the Senate pressured Richardson to appoint a special prosecutor to investigate the Watergate incident. Once confirmed, Richardson appointed Archibald Cox to perform the investigation. Cox issued a subpoena to President Nixon for secret recordings made in the Oval Office.

Under the regulations in effect at the time, Nixon could not fire the special prosecutor; only the Attorney General could. On the evening of Saturday, October 20, 1973, Nixon ordered Richardson to dismiss Cox. Richardson refused to fire Cox, and instead resigned. At the time, William Ruckelshaus was the number-two person at the Justice Department. After Richardson's resignation, Ruckelshaus was elevated to the post of Acting Attorney General. Nixon then ordered Ruckelshaus to fire Cox. Ruckelshaus had also promised the Senate that he would support the independent investigation. As a result, he refused to fire Cox, and instead resigned.

The process would repeat itself one more time. After Ruckelshaus's resignation, Solicitor General Robert Bork was third in line at the Justice Department. Now, Nixon ordered Bork to fire Cox. Unlike Richardson and Ruckelshaus, Bork never pledged to the Senate that he would support Cox's investigation. Bork, as Acting Attorney General, followed Nixon's order, and removed the special prosecutor. This rapid sequence of events, which all transpired on Saturday, October 20, 1973, came to be known as the "Saturday Night Massacre."

This saga was far from over. Subsequently, Nixon authorized Bork to appoint Leon Jaworski as the new special prosecutor. In turn, Jaworski subpoenaed the White House for the secret Oval Office recordings. President Nixon refused to produce the tapes. He argued that the separation of powers, and the principle of "executive privilege," prevented the courts from enforcing the subpoena.

The Supreme Court disagreed—unanimously. *United States v. Nixon*, decided on July 24, 1974, held that the subpoena could be enforced. Less than three weeks later, Nixon became the first President to resign from office. In the wake of the Watergate scandal, Congress enacted the Ethics in Government Act of 1978 (EIGA). This history brings us to the facts that gave rise to *Morrison v. Olson*.

During the Reagan administration, Assistant Attorney General Theodore Olson was alleged to have testified untruthfully to a Congressional committee. After a lengthy investigation, the House of Representatives submitted a report to the Attorney General. It alleged that Olson violated the law. This report triggered a process, pursuant to the EIGA, that resulted in the appointment of an "independent counsel."

First, based on the committee report, the Attorney General determined that there were "reasonable grounds to believe that further investigation or prosecution is warranted." Second, when such a finding is made, the EIGA called for a special three-judge panel of the Court of Appeals for the D.C. Circuit to "appoint an appropriate independent counsel" and "define that independent counsel's 'prosecutorial jurisdiction.'" In 1986, a three-judge panel appointed Alexia Morrison as the independent counsel.

Olson argued that Morrison's appointment was unconstitutional for two reasons. First, she was appointed by judges, not the President. Second, the Senate did not vote to confirm her. Olson claimed that the Appointments Clause required that vote. This conflict gave rise to *Morrison v. Olson*. By a vote of 7-1, the Supreme Court rejected Olson's challenge. Chief Justice Rehnquist wrote the majority opinion. Justice Scalia was the lone dissenter.

Morrison presented three important separation-of-powers questions.

First, did the three-judge panel's appointment of the independent counsel violate the Appointments Clause? The Appointments Clause provides two paths to appoint federal officers, depending on whether they are "principal" or "inferior" officers. *Principal officers*, including "Ambassadors, other public Ministers and Consuls, Judges of the supreme Court, and all other Officers of the United States," must be nominated by the President and confirmed by the Senate. Alternatively, "Congress may by Law vest the Appointment of such *inferior Officers*, as they think proper, in the President alone, in the Courts of Law, or in the Heads of Departments." The majority opinion determined that the independent counsel was an "inferior officer." Therefore, Congress could vest the power to make that appointment in the "Courts of Law" — that is, the three-judge panel of the special division.

Chief Justice Rehnquist wrote that the independent counsel is "an inferior officer because she is inferior in rank to the Attorney General." Moreover, Morrison has "limited jurisdiction" and "the office of independent counsel is of limited duration in tenure." Therefore, the special division could appoint the independent counsel, an inferior officer. Justice Scalia vigorously disagreed. "The independent counsel," he insisted, "is not an inferior officer because she is not subordinate to any officer in the Executive Branch (indeed, not even to the President)."

Morrison presented a second important separation of powers question: Did the fact that the independent counsel could only be removed for "good cause" impermissibly interfere with the President's duty to take care that the laws be faithfully executed? Chief Justice Rehnquist, who announced the majority opinion from the bench, found that it did not: "We do not think that in this case the good cause removal restriction contained in the Act unduly interferes with the President's exercise of executive power and his constitutional duty to ensure that the laws are faithfully executed." Justice Scalia once again disagreed. He responded that "limiting [the] removal power to 'good cause' is an impediment to, not an effective grant of, Presidential control."

Finally, *Morrison* presented a third important separation of powers question: Was the Act unconstitutional because it reduced the President's ability to control the prosecutorial powers wielded by the independent counsel? Again, Chief Justice Rehnquist answered that it was not. He conceded that "the counsel is to some degree 'independent' and free from executive supervision to a greater extent than other federal prosecutors." Nevertheless, the Court maintained that "these features of the Act give the Executive Branch sufficient control over the independent counsel to ensure that the President is able to perform his constitutionally assigned duties."

Justice Scalia once again disagreed. He quoted Article II, Section 1, Clause 1, which provides, "The executive Power shall be vested in a President of the United States." Justice Scalia stressed that *the executive power* "does not mean *some* of the executive power, but *all* of the executive power." The "[g]overnmental investigation and prosecution of crimes," he wrote, "is a quintessentially executive function." As for the question of whether the EIGA "deprives the President of exclusive control over that quintessentially executive activity: the Court does not, and could not possibly, assert that it does not. That is indeed the whole object of the statute."

Justice Scalia closed with a warning about the dangers of the independent counsel statute:

> Frequently an issue of this sort will come before the Court clad, so to speak, in sheep's clothing: the potential of the asserted principle to effect important change in the equilibrium of power is not immediately evident, and must be discerned by a careful and perceptive analysis. But this wolf comes as a wolf.

More than two decades after Justice Scalia's solo dissent in *Morrison v. Olson*, politicians on both sides of the aisle came to see the wisdom and foresight of his analysis. In 1994, a three-judge panel appointed Ken Starr as independent counsel. Over the next four years, Starr investigated President Clinton and his associates. Ultimately, Starr's report led to Clinton's impeachment by the House of Representatives in 1998. After the Senate acquitted Clinton, politicians on both sides of the aisle soured on the independent counsel statute. The Ethics in Government Act that authorized Starr's appointment had a "sunset" provision: Congress had to re-approve it every five years. In 1999, Congress allowed the law to lapse.

CHAPTER 25

NLRB v. Noel Canning (2014)

ConLaw.us/NoelCanning/

The National Labor Relations Board (NLRB) is an independent agency that enforces federal labor law. The Board has five members who serve staggered five-year terms. The President can appoint, with the advice and consent of the Senate, three members from his own political party and two members from the opposite political party. The Board requires a quorum of three members to operate. If three members depart — due to resignation or the expiration of their terms — the short-handed Board is unable to enforce federal labor law.

Towards the end of the George W. Bush administration, Senate Democrats blocked the President's appointments to the NLRB. The goal was simple: deny the now-conservative NLRB a quorum. Unsurprisingly, the roles reversed after the 2008 presidential election. Now, Senate Republicans filibustered President Obama's appointments to the NLRB.

In response, President Obama made two appointments to the NLRB while the Senate was in recess. Subsequently, the Republican-controlled House relied on another provision of the Constitution to prevent the Democratic-controlled Senate from taking a long recess. Art. I, Sec. 5, Cl. 4 provides that "[n]either House, during the Session of Congress, shall, without the Consent of the other, adjourn for more than three days. . . ." The goal was simple: prevent President Obama from making any more recess appointments. Or at least that was the plan.

Because of this strategy, in January 2012, the Democratic-controlled Senate would convene every three days. During these brief *pro forma* sessions, business was transacted very rarely. The Senate held a pro forma session on January 3rd, and then adjourned until the next pro forma session on January 6th.

On January 3rd, after the pro forma session began, NLRB member Craig Becker's term expired. At that point, the two-member Board lacked a quorum to conduct business. The following day, President Obama purported to make three "recess appointments" to the NLRB. Subsequently, the Board acted as if it had a quorum, based on the assumption that the three new appointments were valid.

Later that year, the NLRB found that Noel Canning, a bottling company in Washington State, violated federal labor laws. Noel Canning argued that the judgment was invalid because the NLRB lacked a quorum. Specifically, the firm contended that President Obama's three appointments to the NLRB were not made during "the recess of the Senate," as required by Article II, Section 2, Clause 3.

The Supreme Court agreed. *NLRB v. Noel Canning* ruled unanimously that President Obama's appointments were unconstitutional because they were not made during "the recess of the Senate." However, the Court divided 5-4 on exactly why the appointments were invalid. Justice Breyer wrote the majority opinion. Justice Scalia wrote an opinion concurring in judgment, which was joined by Chief Justice Roberts, and Justices Alito and Thomas. They agreed that the recess appointments in this case were unconstitutional, but they disagreed on three important questions about the Recess Appointments Clause.

First, what type of recess did the phrase "the recess of the Senate" refer to? Did it only empower the President to make appointments during the *inter*-session recess? (There is only a single break between sessions of Congress.) Or did the Clause also apply to *intra*-session recesses? (That is, the various breaks during a particular session, such as summer or Christmas vacation.) Justice Scalia found that the President could only make appointments during the single inter-session recess.

In contrast, Justice Breyer concluded that the President could make appointments during *both* the intra-session recess as well as inter-session recesses. Justice Breyer found that the original meaning of the phrase "the recess of the Senate" was ambiguous and could refer to either inter- or intra-session recesses:

> In our view, the phrase "the recess" . . . taken literally can refer to both types of recess. Founding-era dictionaries define the word "recess," much as we do today, simply as "a period of cessation from usual work." The Founders themselves used the word to refer to intra-session, as well as to inter-session, breaks . . . .
> The constitutional text is thus ambiguous.

Justice Breyer then resolved this ambiguity by relying on the function, or purpose, of the Clause: He explained that the power to make recess appointments was given to the President so he could "ensure the continued functioning of the Federal Government when the Senate is away." During that time, Congress would be unable to vote on the President's nomination and fill the vacancy.

Justice Breyer supported his functionalist analysis with an appeal to historical practice. As intra-session breaks began to grow longer and inter-session breaks began to grow shorter, Presidents began to make intra-session recess appointments. Since the end of World War II, the Court observed, there have been thousands of such appointments.

Justice Scalia contended that the original public meaning of "the recess of the Senate" was not ambiguous. It referred to the period of time between two of the Senate's official sessions. That phrase did not mean "any break in the Senate's proceedings." Because the original public meaning was unambiguous, the Court should not have based its ruling on the purpose of the Clause, or historical practice. Therefore, he rejected the need to resort either to the purpose of the Clause or to historical practice. Justice Scalia maintained that the unambiguous original meaning of the phrase, "the recess of the Senate," referred to the period of time between two of the Senate's official sessions. That phrase did not mean "any break in the Senate's proceedings."

Next, Justice Scalia explained that, at the founding, as today, the word "recess" had both a formal meaning and a colloquial meaning. First, formally, it meant the period of time between two of the Senate's official sessions. Justice Scalia explained that was how the phrase "the recess," was generally used in governmental practice, and in the Recess Appointments Clause. Second, colloquially, a recess could mean "any break" in the Senate's proceedings.

Under the majority's reading, he explained, "a half-hour lunch break," for example, could be called a recess. Adopting the colloquial meaning would be "absurd." In contrast, the original meaning of the text was clear and unambiguous. Therefore, Justice Scalia hewed to the text's original meaning.

Justices Breyer and Scalia also disagreed about a second question: Did the Recess Appointments Clause only empower the President to fill vacancies that came into existence *during* the recess, or did this provision also empower the President to fill vacancies that arose *prior* to the recess? They both agreed that the Clause applied to vacancies that arose during a recess. However, Justice Breyer also found that the Clause applied to vacancies that already existed before the recess.

Justice Breyer acknowledged that, "to a modern ear," the words "vacancies that may happen during the recess" sound as if they refer to vacancies that initially occur during the recess. But here, too, Justice Breyer claimed that the Framers thought the phrase was "ambiguous." And once again, Justice Breyer resolved the ambiguity by relying on executive-branch practice. At least since 1821, he explained, Presidents have thought and acted as if they have the power to fill vacancies that initially arose prior to the recess.

Once again, Justice Scalia argued that the text was not ambiguous. The majority's reading, he contended, effectively reads the word "happen" right out of the Recess Appointments Clause. The Constitution does not say that "the President may fill vacancies 'during the recess.'" Furthermore, Justice Scalia found that Justice Breyer relied on historical executive- and legislative-branch practice that points in the opposite direction: This issue has been the subject "of a long simmering inter-branch conflict" that the Court ought to resolve according to its best lights, rather than by deferring to an overreaching executive branch.

Finally, the Justices disagreed about a third question: Could the President make the appointments during a three-day Senate break sandwiched between two pro forma sessions of the Senate? Justice Breyer once again employed a functionalist approach: "in light of historical practice, . . . a recess of more than 3 days but less than 10 days is presumptively too short to fall within the Clause." Therefore, he held, "for purposes of the Recess Appointments Clause, the Senate is in session when it says it is, provided that, under its own rules, it retains the capacity to transact Senate business. The Senate met that standard here."

In his oral hand-down of his concurring opinion, Justice Scalia ridiculed this Goldilocks standard — not too hot, not too cold — as "just made up." He stated:

> A three day break is too short, a four- to nine-day break is probably too short unless the President can persuade a court that the situation was really urgent, and 10 days is probably long enough, most of the time, although the majority isn't really clear about that. These new rules have no basis whatever in the Constitution.

To the contrary, Justice Scalia explained, the Framers did not specify how long the recess had to be. Why? "Because they were obviously referring to the formal recess" between sessions.

In the end, the Court unanimously held that President Obama's three appointments to the NLRB were unconstitutional. However, the Justices divided over whether the original meaning of the Recess Appointments Clause was determinate enough to resolve the case. Justice Scalia, Chief Justice Roberts, Justice Thomas, and Justice Alito thought the original meaning of the text was determinate. Justices Breyer, Kennedy, Ginsburg, Sotomayor, and Kagan, however, thought the original meaning of the text was ambiguous. And because of that ambiguity, the Court had to consider the Clause's underlying function, or purpose, and its historical practice.

PART VI

SLAVERY AND THE RECONSTRUCTION AMENDMENTS

Our study of slavery begins with the anti-canonical case *Dred Scott v. Sandford* (1857). After *Dred Scott*, we recount the history of the Civil War and the ratification of the Thirteenth and Fourteenth Amendments. Next, we study the Supreme Court's early decisions that narrowly interpreted the Privileges or Immunities Clause of the Fourteenth Amendment: the *Slaughter-House Cases* (1873), *Bradwell v. Illinois* (1873), and *United States v. Cruikshank* (1875). Then we review two cases that construed Congress's enforcement powers under the Thirteenth and Fourteenth Amendments: *Strauder v. West Virginia* (1880) and the *Civil Rights Case* (1883). Finally, we study the Supreme Court's early and conflicted approaches to the Equal Protection Clause of the Fourteenth Amendment: *Yick Wo v. Hopkins* (1886) and *Plessy v. Ferguson* (1896).

CHAPTER 26

Dred Scott v. Sandford (1857)

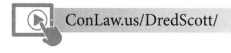 ConLaw.us/DredScott/

The holding of *Dred Scott v. Sandford* (1857) is well known: People of African descent — whether free or enslaved — could *never* be citizens of the United States. However, the facts that gave rise to *Dred Scott* are not well understood. This chapter will consider the specific mechanics of Chief Justice Roger Brooke Taney's opinion.

Following the Constitution's ratification, the slave states and the free states gradually became more bitterly divided. As time went by, each side feared that the other would gain more representation in Congress when new states were admitted to the Union. This fear resulted in the Missouri Compromise of 1820, which prohibited slavery in all new states north of the 36° 30′ line. The compromise was designed to preserve the political equipoise in Congress: For every new slave state that was admitted into the Union, a new free state would also be admitted.

Dred Scott is an infamous decision that belongs in the *anti-canon*. The case began when Dred and his wife Harriet, both slaves, were transported by their owner from Missouri to a U.S. Army fort located in the free Wisconsin territory (present-day Minnesota), and to the free state of Illinois. Eventually, at Harriet's urging, Dred asked a Missouri state court to declare that his family was emancipated by virtue of their presence in the free territory. Initially, Scott won his case. At the time, Missouri case law held that a slave was emancipated by virtue of travelling to a free territory or state. However, the Missouri Supreme Court reversed that precedent and ruled against Scott.

Scott then took his case to federal court and sued his owner, John Sanford. (At some point, his name was misspelled as "Sandford" in the court records.) Federal courts have jurisdiction to hear *diversity* suits that involve "citizens" of different states. (See Chapter 19.) If Scott was in fact a citizen of Missouri, he could sue

Sanford, a citizen of New York in federal court. If Scott was not a citizen, however, the case must be dismissed because the federal court lacked jurisdiction.

The Supreme Court ruled against Scott by a 7-2 vote. Chief Justice Taney wrote the majority opinion, which had two major parts. First, he found that the Court lacked diversity jurisdiction because Scott was not a citizen of Missouri, or of the United States. Taney based his analysis on the history of slavery in America. He contended that descendants of African slaves could never become citizens of the United States — even if they were emancipated under state law and were considered "citizens" by their state.

STUDY GUIDE

Does this decision offer a valid critique of originalist methods of interpretation?

If the Court lacked jurisdiction, the case should have been dismissed. However, Taney decided another important constitutional question: was Scott emancipated when his owner brought him north to a federal free territory. Why did Taney resolve this issue? Because he wanted to provide a definitive resolution to the slavery question. As a result, the second part of *Dred Scott* presumed that the Court had jurisdiction, which Taney already found that it did not.

Through the Missouri Compromise, Congress designated certain territories, including the Wisconsin territory, as "free soil" jurisdictions. The Court found that this arrangement violated the Fifth Amendment. This provision prohibits Congress from depriving any person "of life, liberty, or property, without due process of law."

The majority reasoned that the Missouri Compromise had the effect of emancipating a slave who is taken into a free territory. The Court found that this law would deprive the slave owner of his "property [in his slave] without the due process of law." For this reason, Chief Justice Taney ruled that the Missouri Compromise was unconstitutional.

Dred Scott relied on the Due Process Clause to assess the substantive validity of the Missouri Compromise. The majority did not simply assess what procedures the government followed. During the twentieth century, critics dubbed this approach *substantive due process*.

STUDY GUIDE

Can you see how these critics can use *Dred Scott* to attack substantive due process? It is often argued that Chief Justice Taney invented the doctrine of substantive due process. However, three decades earlier, Congress debated whether a law that deprives slaveholders of their "property" in slaves would violate the Fifth Amendment.

There were two dissents in *Dred Scott*. First, Justice Curtis wrote that the Constitution was not made exclusively for the white race. When that document was ratified, people of African descent could be citizens in at least five states. Justice McLean wrote a separate dissent. He observed, "A slave is not a mere chattel. He bears the impress of his Maker, and is amenable to the laws of God and man."

STUDY GUIDE

Was *Dred Scott* correctly decided at the time?

As a historical matter, *Dred Scott* may well have contributed to the Civil War. During that period, the courts began to protect the rights of Southerners to transport their slaves through free states. Northerners feared that eventually the courts would extend this doctrine and protect the rights of Southerners to settle permanently in free states with their slaves. There was only a short step between these two positions. This fear galvanized popular opinion in the North and led to the electoral success of the new Republican party. Abraham Lincoln's election as President on the Republican party ticket would provoke the South to secede.

Ultimately, *Dred Scott* was reversed not by the Supreme Court but — after a bloody Civil War — by the Thirteenth, Fourteenth, and Fifteenth Amendments.

CHAPTER 27

The History of the Thirteenth and Fourteenth Amendments

ConLaw.us/13thAnd14th/

To understand the history of the Thirteenth and Fourteenth Amendments, we have to trace their origins from the Constitutional Convention in 1787 to *Dred Scott v. Sandford* (1857) to the Reconstruction Period following the Civil War.

The Article IV Privileges and Immunities Clause

Article IV, Section 2 of the Constitution provides, "The Citizens of each State shall be entitled to all Privileges and Immunities of Citizens in the several States." This clause prohibits states from discriminating against citizens from other states. Specifically, a state must guarantee certain fundamental rights, known as "Privileges and Immunities," equally to its own citizens and to citizens from other states. But what are these rights?

Corfield v. Coryell (1823), a circuit court case from Pennsylvania, came to be viewed as the most important judicial interpretation of Article IV. *Corfield* was authored by Justice Bushrod Washington, who was President Washington's nephew. He wrote the opinion while *riding circuit* from the District of Columbia to the District of Pennsylvania. Justice Washington explained that this Clause protects "those privileges and immunities which are fundamental; which belong of right to the citizens of all free governments." He then listed several examples of privileges and immunities, including the "protection by the government" and "the right to acquire and possess property of every kind and to pursue and obtain happiness and safety."

This formulation of fundamental rights was originally developed in May 1776 by George Mason, who wrote the Virginia Declaration of Rights. Mason referred to these liberties as "inherent natural rights." Mason's Declaration inspired the Declaration of Independence, which Thomas Jefferson drafted a few weeks later. Massachusetts, and several other states, incorporated Mason's definition of natural rights into their constitutions. In 1783, the Massachusetts Supreme Judicial Court invoked this language to hold that slavery was unconstitutional in that commonwealth.

Article IV of the Constitution would play an important role in another slavery-related situation. In the nineteenth century, free black sailors from the north were often imprisoned while their ships docked in southern ports. Horace Mann and other antislavery activists argued that the sailors were citizens of their home states. As a result, slave states were required to protect the same "Privileges or Immunities" for their own citizenry, as well as for the black sailors from Northern states. The slave states, however, countered that they could treat the black sailors — citizens from another state — the same way that they treated their own free blacks under the discriminatory Black Codes. The abolitionists replied that Article IV protected all out-of-state citizens from discrimination with respect to a set of *fundamental rights*, of the sort Justice Washington identified in *Corfield*.

Dred Scott v. Sandford (1857)

Dred Scott v. Sandford (1857) held that people of African descent could not be citizens. This argument relied, in part, on the scope of the rights protected by the Privileges and Immunities Clause. Chief Justice Taney contended that if free blacks were citizens, then they would be guaranteed the privileges and immunities in Article IV.

STUDY GUIDE

Does the Privileges and Immunities Clause of Article IV refer to "citizens of the United States"? To whom does it refer?

Chief Justice Taney speculated that Southern states would never have agreed to join the Union had they known that Article IV of the Constitution would compel them to protect the rights of free blacks who traveled from Northern states. Therefore, he reasoned, such persons could not have been considered citizens of the United States. Chief Justice Taney listed examples of privileges and immunities that Southern states never would have wanted to extend to free blacks: "the full liberty of speech in public" and the right "to keep and carry arms wherever they went." These rights are, of course, also protected by the First and Second Amendments, respectively. For Chief Justice Taney's argument to work, at least some of the rights protected by the Bill of Rights must have been thought to be privileges and immunities of U.S. citizens.

In addition, Article IV concerns the rights of "citizens of each state" and "citizens in the several states." It does not establish two classes of citizenship. Yet *Dred Scott* drew a distinction between *state* citizenship, which blacks could possess, and *national* citizenship, which they could never have. (The Fourteenth Amendment eliminated that distinction between state citizenship and national citizenship.)

Dred Scott helped precipitate a bloody Civil War, which began just four years later. And it was this war that led to *Dred Scott*'s repudiation. In April 1865, the Civil War drew to a formal conclusion. Confederate General Robert E. Lee, at long last, surrendered to Union General Ulysses S. Grant.

The Thirteenth Amendment

The Thirteenth Amendment was ratified eight months later in December 1865. Section 1 of the Thirteenth Amendment provides, "Neither slavery nor involuntary servitude, except as a punishment for crime whereof the party shall have been duly convicted, shall exist within the United States." Section 1 did what President Lincoln's war-time Emancipation Proclamation could not: It eliminated slavery nationwide. But the drafters of the Thirteenth Amendment did not trust the states to voluntarily eradicate slavery. They also chose not to rely on Congress's implied powers to enforce the amendment. (In *Prigg v. Pennsylvania*, which we discussed in Chapter 6, the Supreme Court offered an expansive reading of these implied powers to uphold the Fugitive Slave Act.) Instead, Section 2 of the Thirteenth Amendment granted Congress a new *enumerated* "power to enforce this article," that is Section 1, "by appropriate legislation."

The Civil Rights Act of 1866 and the Freedmen's Bureau Act

Three months after the Thirteenth Amendment was ratified, Congress relied on its new power in Section 2 to enact the Civil Rights Act of 1866. The law provided that "all persons born in the United States" were "citizens of the United States." During the Civil War, President Lincoln's Attorney General Edward Bates concluded that free blacks born in the United States were citizens. Therefore, they were therefore eligible to serve in the Union Army. His opinion expressly conflicted with *Dred Scott*.

STUDY GUIDE

Was the Lincoln administration bound to adhere to Chief Justice Taney's opinion about citizenship in *Dred Scott*? Was Congress?

Through the Civil Rights Act of 1866, Republicans in Congress tried to use a statute to overrule *Dred Scott*: Now, people of African descent would be recognized as citizens of the United States.

The Civil Rights Act of 1866 also guaranteed that all "citizens, of every race and color . . . shall have the same right . . . to make and enforce contracts, to sue, be parties, and give evidence, to inherit, purchase, lease, sell, hold, and convey real and personal property, and to full and equal benefit of all laws and proceedings for the security of person and property."

Later that year, Congress enacted the Freedmen's Bureau Act. This law established an administrative agency to advance the interests of the newly freed slaves. The Act also required the President to protect the rights of the freedmen that had been listed in the Civil Rights Act, along with "the constitutional right of bearing arms."

In April 1865, President Abraham Lincoln was assassinated. He was replaced by his Vice President, Andrew Johnson. The Tennessee Democrat came to oppose the Republicans' plan for Reconstruction. Once in office, Johnson vetoed the Civil Rights Act of 1866 and the Freedmen's Bureau Act. He claimed that the laws were unconstitutional. Johnson argued that following the formal abolition of slavery, these measures now exceeded slavery had already been formally abolished, and these measures exceeded Congress's "Section 2" powers to enforce the Thirteenth Amendment.

The House of Representatives and the Senate successfully overrode the vetoes, and both bills became law. But some members of Congress, including Representative John Bingham of Ohio, shared Johnson's constitutional concerns. The Republicans also feared that Southern Democrats would repeal the Civil Rights Act when their representatives returned to Congress. As a result, Bingham and others pushed for the adoption of a constitutional amendment to protect fundamental rights, such as those protected by the Civil Rights Act.

The Fourteenth Amendment

The Fourteenth Amendment was drafted to ensure that Congress had the power to enact the Civil Rights Act. Even if a future Congress repealed the act, the rights it protected would still be enshrined in the Constitution. The Fourteenth Amendment was ratified in 1868.

The Citizenship Clause

Section 1 of the Fourteenth Amendment has four provisions. Section 1 began by repudiating *Dred Scott*. "All persons born or naturalized in the United States and subject to the jurisdiction thereof," it proclaims, "are citizens of the United States and of the State wherein they reside." Section 1 of the Fourteenth Amendment tracks the Civil Rights Act of 1866: Both ensured that those born in the United States, including the freedmen, were now citizens. Moreover, Section 1 eliminated the distinction that Chief Justice Taney drew between state citizenship and national citizenship.

The Privileges or Immunities Clause

The second element of Section 1 of the Fourteenth Amendment is the Privileges or Immunities Clause: "No State shall make or enforce any law which shall abridge the privileges or immunities of citizens of the United States." This provision echoed the Privileges and Immunities Clause of Article IV. However, unlike Article IV and the Civil Rights Act of 1866, the Privileges or Immunities Clause prohibited *any* abridgement of a citizen's "privileges or immunities." The text now barred two types of deprivations of fundamental rights: laws that discriminated against some citizens, as well as laws that discriminated against everyone, equally.

Indeed, the phrase "no state shall" in the Privileges or Immunities Clause is identical to the prohibitions used in Article I, Section 10 of the Constitution. For example, Article I, Section 10, Clause 1 provides "*No State shall* enter into any Treaty, Alliance, or Confederation." Additionally, the phrase "no state shall *make any law*" resembles the First Amendment's command that "*Congress shall make no law* respecting an establishment of religion."

STUDY GUIDE

What rights did "privileges or immunities" refer to?

One source of guidance to undestand the meaning of "privileges or immunities" can be found in the statements of congressional proponents of the Fourteenth Amendment. For example, Michigan Senator Jacob Howard was the Amendment's sponsor. In an important floor speech, he remarked that privileges or immunities fall into two categories. First, he explained, they include whatever rights are protected by Article IV. On the Senate floor, he read Justice Washington's canonical formulation of fundamental "privileges and immunities" in *Corfield v. Coryell*. Moreover, the rights listed in the Civil Rights Act of 1866 generally tracked the fundamental rights identified in *Corfield*. In his notes, Howard even referred to these *Corfield* privileges and immunities as "civil rights."

Next, Senator Howard identified a second category of privileges or immunities: "the personal rights guaranteed and secured by the first eight amendments of the Constitution." He then listed the provisions in the first eight amendments that protect individual rights. In *Dred Scott*, Chief Justice Taney also assumed that the freedom of speech and the right to keep and bear arms were privileges and immunities protected by Article IV. Likewise, the Freedmen's Bureau Act expressly protected the fundamental "constitutional right of bearing arms."

In this way, the Privileges or Immunities Clause overruled *Barron v. Baltimore* (1833). Six decades earlier, Chief Justice Marshall concluded that the Bill of Rights only limited federal power. Now, the state's police powers would also be limited by the fundamental rights in the first eight amendments.

In addition to *Corfield*, the Civil Rights Act of 1866 serves as another source of guidance about the meaning of "privileges or immunities." This federal statute protects certain "fundamental" rights, including the right "to make and enforce contracts" and the right to "convey real and personal property." The Fourteenth Amendment was designed to protect the rights specified in the Civil Rights Act from being repealed by a future Congress. This goal could only be accomplished if the "fundamental" rights listed in the Civil Rights Act were thought to be "privileges or immunities of citizens of the United States." Like the Bill of Rights, the Civil Rights Act provides textual evidence that the rights it contained were so fundamental as to be considered privileges or immunities.

The Due Process Clause

The third element of Section 1 of the Fourteenth Amendment is the Due Process Clause. It provides, "Nor shall any State deprive any person of life, liberty, or property, without due process of law." The Fifth Amendment already prohibited the *federal* government from depriving a person of "life, liberty, or property, without due process of law." Now, under the Fourteenth Amendment, *states* were subject to the same restriction. In Part VII, we will explore what the "due process of law" requires.

The Equal Protection Clause

The fourth element of Section 1 of the Fourteenth Amendment is the Equal Protection Clause. It provides that a state cannot "deny to any person within its jurisdiction the equal protection of the laws." Let's contrast the Equal Protection Clause with the Privileges or Immunities Clause. Which of these provisions prohibits states from enacting discriminatory laws?

According to modern Supreme Court precedent, it's the Equal Protection Clause. The text of the Fourteenth Amendment, however, suggests otherwise: The Privileges or Immunities Clause prohibits two categories of legislation: laws that deprive *everyone equally* of a fundamental right, and laws that deprive *some people* of a fundamental right. Specifically, it prohibited two categories of legislative action: laws that deprive *everyone equally* of a fundamental right, and laws that deprive *some people* of a fundamental right.

The Equal Protection Clause had a very different purpose. Its text does not impose limitations on the enactment of legislation. Rather, "[e]qual *protection* of the law" seems to require the equal *enforcement* of the law. The states now had an affirmative duty to enforce the rights of *all* its people, white and black, male and female. That is, the government had to *protect* them from both governmental and private deprivations of their fundamental rights — including the "privileges or immunities of citizens of the United States." This right of protection mirrored the Civil Rights Act of 1866, which mandated that all citizens were entitled to the "full and equal benefit of all laws and proceedings for the security of person and property."

Section 5

Once again, the drafters did not trust the states to comply with the Fourteenth Amendment. As a result, they added an *enforcement* provision. Recall that Section 2 of the Thirteenth Amendment gave Congress an enumerated power to enforce Section 1 of that provision. Likewise, Section 5 of the Fourteenth Amendment gave Congress an enumerated power to enforce Sections 1 through 4 of that provision. Congress could now enact new "appropriate legislation" to protect a person's rights under the Thirteenth and Fourteenth Amendments.

The Framers of the Fourteenth Amendment did not trust the states to comply with these new restrictions. There were a few exceptions. Article I, Section 10, for example, prohibited states from passing bills of attainder, ex post facto laws, or impairing the obligation of contracts. However, the rest of the Constitution, such as the Establishment Clause, only applied to Congress. That dynamic would change after the Civil War. Soon, Southern resistance to Reconstruction and racial equality grew. The Thirteenth and Fourteenth Amendments greatly expanded Congress's enumerated powers to protect citizens from their own states. These Amendments also empowered the federal Courts to enforce those rights.

The Supreme Court and Reconstruction Amendments

The Reconstruction Amendments were designed to fundamentally change the relationship between the federal government, the states, and the people. Or at least that was the plan. Not everyone agreed that such a great departure from the original constitutional design was a good idea. Over the ensuing three decades, the Supreme Court resisted this alteration to the federal system. In a series of important decisions, the Justices narrowly construed three critical provisions of the Fourteenth Amendment:

- First, the Privileges or Immunities Clause was basically deleted from the text of the Fourteenth Amendment in the *Slaughter-House Cases* (1873), *Bradwell v. Illinois* (1873), and *United States v. Cruikshank* (1875).
- Second, in the *Civil Rights Cases* (1883), the Court limited the Fourteenth Amendment and Congress's Section Five enforcement power to state action.

Under what came to be known as the "state action doctrine," private actors could violate fundamental civil rights so long as the states took no action.

- Finally, in the anti-canonical decision of *Plessy v. Ferguson* (1896), the Court found that the Fourteenth Amendment allowed the government to mandate "separate but equal" accommodations.

Taken together, these decisions enabled the rise of *Jim Crow*. This regime of state-sanctioned racial subordination and discrimination was enacted throughout the Southern states. Critically, this legal regime was reinforced by organized private violence against African Americans, and any white people who stood by them. Notwithstanding the Thirteenth and Fourteenth Amendments, local law enforcement — that is, state actors — refused to protect the civil rights of some of their people.

These decisions also inhibited the fight against public and private racial discrimination throughout the United States. The promise of the Fourteenth Amendment was not fulfilled. Yet, because the Constitution enshrined that promise in its text, that promise could later be kept.

CHAPTER 28

The Privileges or Immunities Clause

Section 1 of the Fourteenth Amendment provides, "No State shall make or enforce any law which shall abridge the privileges or immunities of citizens of the United States." In Chapter 27, we discussed how the framers of the Privileges or Immunities Clause sought to prevent the states from making laws that abridge the fundamental rights of their own citizens. These rights likely included the "privileges and immunities" from Article IV that Justice Washington identified in *Corfield v. Coryell*, the personal guarantees in the Bill of Rights, and the fundamental rights protected by the Civil Rights Act of 1866. Or at least that was the plan.

In three cases decided in a span of three years, the Supreme Court would effectively eliminate the Privileges or Immunities Clause from the Constitution. The *Slaughter-House Cases* and *Bradwell v. Illinois* were both decided in 1873. These decisions held that the privileges or immunities of citizens of the United States were limited to a very narrow subset of *federally created* rights. A state retained the power to violate the great bulk of its citizens' fundamental civil rights. The third case, *United States v. Cruikshank*, was decided in 1875. Here, the Court held that these federally created rights did not include the fundamental rights that were enumerated in the Bill of Rights.

The Slaughter-House Cases (1873)

 ConLaw.us/SlaughterHouse/

Let's start with the facts of the *Slaughter-House Cases*. In 1869, Louisiana's legislature ordered the closure of all private slaughterhouses in New Orleans. The government granted a monopoly to a single, privately owned slaughterhouse. Now, everyone would have to use that facility. A group of butchers sued the state. They argued that the Slaughter-House monopoly that prohibited private butcher shops violated the Privileges or Immunities Clause. Specifically, the law abridged their constitutional "right to exercise their trade" — a right that is not expressly enumerated in the text of the Constitution.

The Court split 5-4, and ruled that the Fourteenth Amendment did not protect this unenumerated right. Justice Miller wrote the majority opinion, joined by Justices Clifford, Strong, Hunt, and Davis. In dissent were Chief Justice Chase, and Justices Field, Bradley, and Swayne.

STUDY GUIDE

What content, or substance, does the *Slaughter-House* majority give the Privileges or Immunities Clause?

The Privileges or Immunities Clause can be read in two different ways. Behind Door #1, the Fourteenth Amendment could be read to protect an *old* group of fundamental rights, "privileges or immunities," that "citizens of the United States" all share in common. Before the Fourteenth Amendment was ratified, Article IV secured privileges and immunities in a limited way. Specifically, a state could not deny the fundamental rights identified in *Corfield* to citizens who traveled from another state. Article IV did not restrict how a state must treat its own citizens. And the rights in the first eight amendments only limited the federal government's powers. After the Fourteenth Amendment was ratified, however, both Congress and the federal courts would be empowered to prevent states from abridging these old fundamental rights of any U.S. citizen. Behind Door #1, the Privileges or Immunities Clause describes *whose* fundamental rights are protected: those of every U.S. citizen.

Alternatively, behind Door #2, the Clause can be read to refer solely to the "privileges or immunities of citizens of the United States." That is, a particular set of distinctly federal or national rights held by virtue of being a "citizen of the United States." This category would not include the rights identified in *Corfield* or in the Civil Rights Act of 1866. Behind Door #2, the Privileges or Immunities Clause describes *what* fundamental rights are protected: a limited set of federal rights.

The four dissenting Justices in the *Slaughter-House Cases* chose Door #1. But the majority opinion chose Door #2. And with that decision, the Supreme Court slammed the door shut on the original meaning of the Privileges or Immunities Clause. The *Slaughter-House* majority found that the Privileges or Immunities Clause protects a very narrow subset of rights, "which owe their existence to the Federal government, its National character, its Constitution, or its laws." For example, a citizen has the right "to come to the seat of government to assert any claim he may have upon that government," "the right of free access to its seaports . . . to the subtreasuries, land offices, and courts of justice in the several States," the right to "care and protection . . . on the high seas," and "[t]he right to use the navigable waters of the United States."

STUDY GUIDE

Did the *Slaughter-House* majority effectively nullify a constitutional amendment?

The Privileges or Immunities Clause, Justice Miller concluded, did not protect the butchers' "right to exercise their trade" or pursue a lawful occupation. These rights, and all other unenumerated natural or civil rights, could only be protected by the states. The majority worried about altering the Constitution's original federalism scheme. Justice Miller observed that the Fourteenth Amendment did not authorize the Supreme Court to become "a perpetual censor upon all legislation of the States, on the civil rights of their own citizens." Such a holding, he concluded, would "radically change[] the whole theory of the relations of the State and Federal governments."

STUDY GUIDE

Was the Fourteenth Amendment designed to fundamentally change the relationship between the federal government, the states, and the people?

Justice Field dissented. He explained that the Privileges or Immunities Clause protected a pre-existing set of fundamental rights. The Fourteenth Amendment, he wrote, "refers to the natural and inalienable rights which belong to all citizens" and "ordains that they shall not be abridged by State legislation." The Privileges or Immunities Clause "does not attempt to confer any new privileges or immunities upon citizens." The majority, he said, rendered the Fourteenth Amendment "a vain and idle enactment, which accomplished nothing." Justice Field concluded, "All pursuits, all professions, all avocations are open without other restrictions than such as are imposed equally upon all others of the same age, sex, and condition."

Justice Bradley wrote a separate dissent. He also rejected the majority's conclusion that protecting fundamental rights would jeopardize federalism. Justice Bradley agreed that "[t]he right of a State to regulate the conduct of its citizens is undoubtedly a very broad and extensive one, and not to be lightly restricted." Nevertheless, "there are certain fundamental rights which this right of regulation cannot infringe." The government "may prescribe the *manner of their exercise*, but it cannot *subvert* the rights themselves." In other words, states may still reasonably regulate the exercise of fundamental rights, so long as the regulation is not in fact a pretext for suppressing the exercise of those rights. Justice Bradley stressed that the rights protected by the Privileges or Immunities Clause were a set of pre-existing rights. That is, "the rights of citizens of any free government. . . . In this free country, the people of which inherited certain traditionary rights and privileges from their ancestors, citizenship means something."

Bradwell v. Illinois (1873)

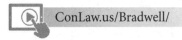 ConLaw.us/Bradwell/

The day after *Slaughter-House* was handed down, the Supreme Court decided *Bradwell v. Illinois*, its second interpretation of the scope of the Privileges or Immunities Clause.

Myra Bradwell was an aspiring attorney and editor of a legal newspaper in Chicago. She argued that the Privileges or Immunities Clause protected the right of "admission to the bar of a State of a person who possesses the requisite learning and character." She noted that the Clause applies to *all* "citizens of the United States," not just to men.

In *Slaughter-House,* the Court divided 5-4 on whether the Fourteenth Amendment protects the right of a *male* butcher "to exercise [his] trade." However, the vote in *Bradwell v. Illinois* was 8-1. The *female* attorney, the Court held, did not have a constitutional right to "exercise [her] trade." Chief Justice Chase was the lone dissenter.

For the *Slaughter-House* majority, *Bradwell* was easy. In both cases, the majority rejected the claim that the "privileges or immunities of citizens of the United States" included an unenumerated right to pursue a lawful occupation, such as a butcher or a lawyer. Justice Miller also wrote the *Bradwell* majority opinion. He explained that the "right to admission to practice in the courts of a State is not a privilege or immunity" because it "in no sense depends on citizenship of the United States."

But Justices Field, Bradley, and Swayne had a tougher job. They contended in *Slaughter-House* that the Privileges or Immunities Clause *did* protect the right to pursue a lawful occupation. As a result, their challenge was greater. The trio had to explain why the right to exercise a trade — which they said existed — was not "abridge[d]" by the exclusion of women from the practice of law.

To address this problem, Justice Bradley wrote a now-notorious concurring opinion, joined by Justices Field and Swayne. He attempted to provide facts that justified different treatment of men and women. "The civil law, as well as nature herself," Justice Bradley wrote, "has always recognized a wide difference in the respective spheres and destinies of man and woman." He added that "[t]he natural and proper timidity and delicacy which belongs to the female sex evidently unfits it for many of the occupations of civil life." Moreover, Justice Bradley noted that under the laws of coverture, a wife has no separate legal identity from her husband. Therefore, "[a] married woman is incapable, without her husband's consent, of making contracts which shall be binding on her or him. This very incapacity was one circumstance which the Supreme Court of Illinois deemed important in rendering a married woman incompetent fully to perform the duties and trusts that belong to the office of an attorney and counselor."

STUDY GUIDE

Which approach is better: a doctrine like Justice Miller's that denies rights to everyone equally, or one like Justice Bradley's that requires a justification as to why some people should be treated differently than others?

Only Chief Justice Salmon Chase dissented in both *Slaughter-House* and *Bradwell*. Indeed, in *Bradwell*, he not only dissented from the opinion of the Court, but he also dissented from Justice Bradley's concurring opinion. The Supreme Court report reads, "THE CHIEF JUSTICE dissented from the judgment of the court, and from *all the opinions*."

Earlier in his career, Chase earned the nickname "the attorney general for runaway slaves." He was also progressive when it came to gender equality. The year before *Bradwell*, Chase wrote, "I have always favored the enlargement of the sphere of women's work and the payment of just compensation for it." However, by 1873, Chase was too weak and ill from a series of strokes to write a dissent in either case. Three weeks after *Slaughter-House* and *Bradwell* were announced, a final stroke took his life.

United States v. Cruikshank (1875)

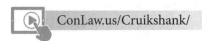 ConLaw.us/Cruikshank/

The first two cases, *Slaughter-House* and *Bradwell*, involved what could be called *unenumerated rights*. That is, privileges or immunities that are not expressly stated in the Constitution. The final case, *United States v. Cruikshank*, held that the Privileges or Immunities Clause also did not bar a state from violating so-called *enumerated rights*: in this case, rights listed in the First and Second Amendments.

The facts of *Cruikshank* are gruesome. In 1872, competing Republican and Democratic factions claimed to have won the office of judge and sheriff in Grant Parish, Louisiana. In March 1873, a Republican faction of African Americans seized the courthouse in Colfax, Louisiana. They were armed with the rifles they carried as Union soldiers. One hundred and fifty white militiamen attacked the courthouse. The militia, unable to overcome the armed resistance of the freedmen within, set the courthouse on fire to smoke the Republicans out. More than one hundred freedmen were shot and killed as they fled the inferno, even after they surrendered to the white militia. The slaughter became known as the Colfax Massacre. William Cruikshank, one of the lynchers, was prosecuted in federal court. The indictment alleged that he interfered with the victims' constitutional rights, including the First Amendment right to peaceably assemble, and the Second Amendment right to keep and bear arms.

Four decades earlier, Chief Justice Marshall concluded in *Barron v. Baltimore* that the Bill of Rights only limited Congress's powers. Under this precedent, the First and Second Amendments did not limit the state's police powers. But was *Barron* still good law following the ratification of the Fourteenth Amendment? During congressional debates, Representative John Bingham of Ohio suggested that it would not be. He stated that there was only one to prevent states from violating the guarantees in the first eight amendments: adopt a constitutional amendment.

The Supreme Court disagreed. Chief Justice Waite wrote the majority opinion in *Cruikshank*. He found that the states were still not bound by the first eight amendments, even after the Fourteenth Amendment's ratification:

> The first amendment to the Constitution prohibits Congress from abridging "the right of the people to assemble and to petition the government for a redress of grievances." This, like the other amendments proposed and adopted at the same time, was not intended to limit the powers of the State governments in respect to their own citizens, but to operate upon the National government alone. *Barron v. The City of Baltimore* (1833). . . . It is now too late to question the correctness of this construction.

Slaughter-House, Bradwell, and *Cruikshank* effectively eliminated the Privileges or Immunities Clause from the Constitution. These three decisions held that the Fourteenth Amendment (1) does not protect the fundamental rights recognized in *Corfield v. Coryell*; (2) does not protect the fundamental rights specified in the Civil Rights Act of 1866; and (3) does not protect the individual rights enumerated in the Bill of Rights. The Clause would only protect an insignificant set of federal rights. To compensate for the deleted Privileges or Immunities Clause, the Supreme Court would gradually expand the scopes of the Due Process and Equal Protection Clauses, far beyond their original meaning. Today, all three cases remain good law.

In 2010, Chicago residents invoked the Privileges or Immunities Clause in an appeal to the Supreme Court. They claimed that Chicago's handgun ban abridged their right to keep and bear arms. To reach that result, they urged the Supreme Court to reverse both *Slaughter-House* and *Cruikshank*. In *McDonald v. Chicago* (2010), however, Chief Justice Roberts, and Justices Kennedy, Scalia, and Alito declined that invitation. Instead, they relied on the Court's modern expanded reading of the Due Process Clause. Only Justice Clarence Thomas based his decision on the original meaning of the Privileges or Immunities Clause. By providing the fifth and decisive vote to enforce a fundamental right against a state, the Privileges or Immunities Clause had finally performed its intended function. We will study *McDonald* in Chapter 61.

CHAPTER 29

The Enforcement Powers of the Thirteenth and Fourteenth Amendments

The Thirteenth, Fourteenth, and Fifteenth Amendments emancipated the slaves and guaranteed the freedmen constitutional rights, including the right to vote. However, states began to enact so-called "Black Codes" that deprived the freedmen of their rights. In addition, the Ku Klux Klan and other terrorist groups resisted reconstruction. They often killed the freedmen in gruesome lynchings, like the Colfax Massacre at issue in *United States v. Cruikshank*.

In response to this resistance, Congress enacted a series of *Enforcement Acts*. These laws empowered the executive branch, as well as the federal judiciary, to protect the civil rights of the freedmen. For example, Congress concluded that, in certain cases, state courts could not be trusted to protect the rights of the freedmen. In 1875, Congress enacted a law that allowed a criminal defendant to transfer, or *remove* his case from state court to federal court if the prosecution deprived him of "the equal civil rights of citizens of the United States."

STUDY GUIDE

What enumerated powers gave Congress the authority to enact this removal law?

Strauder v. West Virginia (1880)

 ConLaw.us/Strauder/

The Supreme Court would consider the constitutionality of this removal law in *Strauder v. West Virginia* (1880). Taylor Strauder was charged with murdering his wife. Both were African Americans. At the time, West Virginia law limited jury service to white males. Strauder argued that this prosecution "denied rights to which he was entitled under the Constitution." Therefore, he contended that his case should be removed to federal court. The trial court denied Strauder's request to remove the case to federal court. Likewise, the West Virginia Supreme Court found no reason "why a jury of white men would not be quite as likely to do justice to the prisoner as a jury of negroes." Moreover, the court found that the Fourteenth Amendment was not "intended to protect the citizens of any State against unjust legislation by their own State."

On appeal, the Supreme Court of the United States reversed by a 7-2 vote. Justice Strong's majority opinion had two parts. First, the Court found that the Fourteenth Amendment's guarantee of equal protection of the laws protects a defendant's "right to a trial . . . by a jury selected and impanelled without discrimination against his race or color."

Second, because Strauder's rights under Section 1 of the Fourteenth Amendment were violated, Congress had the power to remedy the violation pursuant to its powers under Section 5 of the Fourteenth Amendment. That is, Congress had the power to enact "appropriate legislation" to "enforce" the "equal protection of the laws." Therefore, the case should have been removed to federal court. As a result, Strauder's conviction was vacated.

STUDY GUIDE

Did the Supreme Court declare the West Virginia law unconstitutional because it violated the Fourteenth Amendment's Equal Protection Clause? Or did the Supreme Court merely find that the removal law was constitutional, and that Strauder's case should have been removed?

Justice Field dissented. He found that segregating the jury pool would not deprive the defendant of the equal protection of the laws. He wrote, "there is no warrant for the act of Congress under which the indictment in this case was found." Field concluded that the law was unconstitutional because Congress lacked the power to compel the removal of the case from state court.

Strauder was a rare case where the Court upheld an exercise of Congress's enforcement powers under the Fourteenth Amendment. The *Civil Rights Cases* (1883) would take a very different direction.

The Civil Rights Cases (1883)

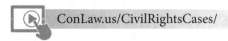

ConLaw.us/CivilRightsCases/

The Civil Rights Act of 1875 was the most significant enforcement act. The law provided:

> That all persons within the jurisdiction of the United States shall be entitled to the full and equal enjoyment of the accommodations, advantages, facilities, and privileges of inns, public conveyances on land or water, theaters, and other places of public amusement; subject only to the conditions and limitations established by law, and applicable alike to citizens of every race and color, regardless of any previous condition of servitude.

What happened if a business subject to the Act excluded a patron on the basis of race? The United States could prosecute the owner for a federal crime. In addition, the excluded patron could sue the business owner for damages in federal court.

STUDY GUIDE

What enumerated powers gave Congress the authority to enact the Civil Rights Act of 1875?

During congressional debates, members of the House and Senate were divided on this very question: Did the federal government have the authority to criminalize segregation in certain private businesses? No one in Congress suggested that its power to regulate interstate commerce could support the Civil Rights Act. (*Heart of Atlanta Motel v. United States* (1964) held that Congress could use its powers under the Commerce Clause to enact a modern version of the Civil Rights Act.) Rather, proponents of the Civil Rights Act of 1875 cited Congress's enforcement powers: Section 2 of the Thirteenth Amendment and Section 5 of the Fourteenth Amendment. The former gave Congress the power to enact "appropriate legislation" to eradicate slavery. The latter gave Congress the power to enact "appropriate legislation" to enforce the guarantees of Section 1 of the Fourteenth Amendment. Ultimately, the Civil Rights Act passed a divided Congress. President Grant signed it into law.

Several years after *Strauder* was decided, federal prosecutors indicted the owners of segregated businesses across the country. Some of the cases involved "denying to persons of color the accommodations and privileges of an inn or hotel." Contrary to common misconceptions, segregation was not limited to the Southern states. For example, Maguire's theater in San Francisco "refus[ed] a colored person a seat in the dress circle." And, the Grand Opera House in New York denied "another person, whose color is not stated, the full enjoyment of the accommodations."

In each prosecution, the business owner raised the same defense: The indictments were unconstitutional because Congress lacked the power to enact the Civil Rights Act of 1875. Each of these appeals was consolidated in a case known, fittingly, as the *Civil Rights Cases*. Eight years after it was enacted, eight Justices voted to declare unconstitutional the Civil Rights Act of 1875. Justice John Marshall Harlan was the lone dissenter.

Justice Bradley wrote the majority opinion. He found that the Fourteenth Amendment's enforcement powers could not be used to regulate private businesses. He explained that "civil rights, such as are guaranteed by the Constitution against State aggression, cannot be impaired by the wrongful acts of individuals, unsupported by State authority in the shape of laws, customs, or judicial or executive proceedings."

Justice Bradley added that the Fourteenth Amendment was only intended to remedy the "abrogation and denial of rights for which the States alone were or could be responsible." This purpose, he wrote, "was the great seminal and fundamental wrong which was intended to be remedied." Justice Bradley also observed that the plain text of the Fourteenth Amendment supported his position: The Privileges or Immunities Clause, the Due Process Clause, and the Equal Protection Clause, he wrote, only restrict "state" action. This principle became known as the *state action* doctrine. Justice Bradley concluded that Congress could not remedy civil rights violations by private parties. Therefore, Congress lacked the authority under Section 5 of the Fourteenth Amendment to enact the Civil Rights Act of 1875.

STUDY GUIDE

Is Justice Bradley's textualist argument persuasive?

The text of the Privileges or Immunities Clause concerns the making and enforcing of "laws," which can only be enacted by the government. This provision, therefore, seems to require state action. Similarly, the Due Process Clause's reference to the "due process of law" is limited to the state mechanisms for how laws are applied. Here, too, there must be state action.

The text of the Equal Protection Clause, however, does not impose limitations on the *enactment* of legislation. Rather, "[e]qual protection of the law" requires equal *enforcement* of the law. This language not only protects rights from state action. It also protects rights against state *inaction*. The states now had an affirmative duty to *enforce* the rights of all people, white and black, male and female. That is, the government had to act to protect everyone from both governmental and private deprivations of their fundamental rights. These rights included the "privileges or immunities of citizens of the United States." This *right of protection* mirrored the Civil Rights Act of 1866, which mandated that all citizens were entitled to the "full and equal benefit of all laws and proceedings for the security of person and property."

STUDY GUIDE

Is state inaction — that is, the failure to provide some people with "protection" —
a violation of the Equal Protection Clause?

Further, Section 5 of the Fourteenth Amendment empowers Congress
to enforce all the rights in Section 1, including the Equal Protection Clause.
Consider a situation where a state fails to protect its people from *private* deprivations of their privileges or immunities. Congress would then have the power
to enact laws to protect the private rights identified by Justice Washington in
Corfield v. Coryell (1823): "the Enjoyment of Life and Liberty, with the Means
of acquiring and possessing Property, and pursueing and obtaining Happiness
and Safety."

But this understanding of the Equal Protection Clause was too radical for
the Supreme Court to adopt. And the Court's narrow reading of the Fourteenth
Amendment from 1883 remains. From that day to the present, the Supreme Court
has maintained that only state action can violate Section 1.

Justice John Marshall Harlan was the lone dissenter. He did not deny the textualist claim that only state action can violate the Fourteenth Amendment. Instead,
Harlan contended that discrimination by the inns, hotels, and theaters, in fact, constituted state action. Under the common law, he wrote, so-called common carriers
and inns were obligated to accept all paying customers from the general public.
Because these businesses each had a monopoly, they had a common-law duty not
to discriminate against potential customers. Justice Harlan admitted that so-called
public amusements, such as theaters, were not traditionally treated like inns or
common carriers. Nevertheless, theaters required a public license to operate, and
the state governments who granted such licenses were servants of all the people.
Justice Harlan concluded that Congress had the power to ensure that all citizens
had access to these public spaces.

STUDY GUIDE

Do you agree with Justice Harlan that discrimination by the inns, hotels, and
theaters constituted state action? Are some of his rationales more persuasive
than others?

Unlike the Fourteenth Amendment, the text of the Thirteenth Amendment
was not limited to state action. Rather, it prohibited slavery, even when enforced
by private individuals. As a result, the Court had to resolve whether the types of
discrimination barred by the Civil Rights Act amounted to the re-institution of
slavery. If it did, then Congress could prohibit such discrimination pursuant to

its powers under Section 2 of the Thirteenth Amendment. The majority and dissent agreed, in the abstract at least, about the appropriate test concerning the Thirteenth Amendment: In addition to barring slavery itself, Congress could also enact laws that were "necessary and proper" to "abolish all badges and incidents of slavery."

STUDY GUIDE

What are the "badges and incidents of slavery"?

The majority inquired whether "the denial to any person of admission to the accommodations and privileges of an inn, a public conveyance, or a theatre [subjects] that person to any form of servitude, or tend[s] to fasten upon him any badge of slavery?" Justice Bradley observed that such segregationist policies did not. The Court noted that discriminatory Black Codes had long existed in some Northern free states where slavery was banned. Justice Bradley worried that enacting federal legislation in response to "every act of discrimination . . . would be running the slavery argument into the ground." He concluded that "mere discriminations on account of race or color were not regarded as badges of slavery."

STUDY GUIDE

Is the prior existence of African slavery in the United States relevant when considering whether disparate treatment of African Americans after their emancipation constitutes a badge or incident of slavery?

Justice Harlan once again disagreed in dissent. He contended that segregation in hotels, inns, and theaters did impose badges of slavery on the freedmen. Therefore, Congress could prohibit those badges. Since slavery "rested wholly upon the inferiority, as a race, of those held in bondage," Justice Harlan observed, "their freedom necessarily involved immunity from, and protection against, all discrimination against them, because of their race, in respect of such civil rights as belong to freemen of other races." Among these "civil rights" was the right of access to common carriers, such as inns and other places of public accommodation.

The majority and the dissent concluded with very different conceptions of how the federal government should treat the freedmen following the abolition of slavery. Justice Bradley contended that Congress had already done enough for African Americans:

> When a man has emerged from slavery, and by the aid of beneficent legislation has shaken off the inseparable concomitants of that state, there must be some stage in the progress of his elevation when he takes the rank of a mere citizen, and ceases to be the special favorite of the laws, and when his rights as a citizen,

or a man, are to be protected in the ordinary modes by which other men's rights are protected.

Justice Harlan vigorously disagreed:

The one underlying purpose of congressional legislation has been to enable the black race to take the rank of mere citizens. The difficulty has been to compel a recognition of the legal right of the black race to take the rank of citizens, and to secure the enjoyment of privileges belonging, under the law, to them as a component part of the people for whose welfare and happiness government is ordained.

Alas, Justice Harlan was the lone dissenter. To this day, the *Civil Rights Cases* remain good law.

Slaughter-House, *Bradwell*, and *Cruikshank* contracted the scope of the Privileges or Immunities Clause. In a similar fashion, the *Civil Rights Cases* contracted the scope of Congress's Section 5 powers. *Plessy v. Ferguson* (1896), which we will study in Chapter 30, would further weaken the Fourteenth Amendment's Due Process and Equal Protection Clauses.

Over time, the Supreme Court would, however, adjust its interpretations of other provisions of the Constitution. First, the Court would compensate for the loss of the Privileges or Immunities Clause by expanding the scope of the Due Process and Equal Protection Clauses. Second, the Court would compensate for the loss of Congress's enforcement powers under Section 5 by relying on an expanded reading of Congress's other enumerated powers in Article I, Section 8. Specifically, the Supreme Court upheld the landmark Civil Rights Act of 1964 as an exercise of Congress's powers under the Commerce and Necessary and Proper Clauses.

CHAPTER 30

The Equal Protection Clause of the Fourteenth Amendment

Under the so-called police power, states can enact laws that regulate health, safety, welfare, and public morals. Though broad, the state police power was limited by the Fourteenth Amendment. Yet, the *Slaughter-House Cases* (1873) rejected a challenge to Louisiana's police power. The Court held that the Privileges or Immunities Clause did not prevent the state from establishing a monopoly slaughterhouse to protect the public's health. In other cases, however, the Court found that the Due Process and Equal Protection Clauses restricted the police power. For example, in *Yick Wo v. Hopkins* (1886), the Court held that the state could not violate the "right to exercise a trade."

Yick Wo v. Hopkins (1886)

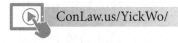
ConLaw.us/YickWo/

In 1880, San Francisco required business owners who operated laundries in wooden buildings to obtain a permit. At the time, about 95 percent of the city's 320 laundries were located in wooden buildings. And approximately two-thirds of those laundries were owned by people of Chinese descent. Yick Wo (whose real name was Lee Yick) had operated a laundry business in a wooden building for more than two decades. In 1884, after an inspection, he received a license. The City determined that his "appliances for heating" were "not dangerous to the surrounding property from fire." Yick sought to renew his license a year later, but the government denied his application.

Why was Yick not allowed to renew his license? The San Francisco ordinance allowed the government to deny the license for any reason, or no reason at all. The Supreme Court observed that even if an applicant was "in every way a competent and qualified person," he could be denied a license "without reason." An ordinance that "acknowledges neither guidance nor restraint," the Court found, is unconstitutional. Why? Because a law with such wide discretion was "purely arbitrary" and, therefore, was beyond the state's police power to enact.

San Francisco's law allowed the government to arbitrarily deprive people of their liberties. When the City can deny rights without establishing a proper justification for doing so, the government can act based on overt racism. Such was the case here. In San Francisco, no permits were granted to Chinese owners. Only one non-Chinese owner was denied a permit. All white operators received licenses.

In a companion case to *Yick Wo*, the federal circuit court observed that the government's licensing scheme was not a means "to regulate the business for the public safety." Rather, its actual purpose was "to drive out of business all the numerous small laundries, especially those owned by Chinese, and [to] give a monopoly of the business to the large institutions established and carried on by means of large associated Caucasian capital." This policy, the court found, likely violated the Fourteenth Amendment. Why? Because it deprived the business owners of their "property" — that is their business and livelihood — "without due process of law." On this point, the Supreme Court agreed, *unanimously*. All nine Justices found that the ordinance violated Yick's rights under the Fourteenth Amendment.

STUDY GUIDE

What constitutional provision does such an arbitrary regime violate?

Justice Stanley Matthews wrote the majority opinion. He cited two provisions of the Fourteenth Amendment that are "not confined to the protection of citizens." First, the Due Process Clause, and second, the Equal Protection Clause. "These provisions," the Court observed, "are universal in their application, to all persons within the territorial jurisdiction, without regard to any differences of race, of color, or of nationality; and the equal protection of the laws is a pledge of the protection of equal laws."

First, let's consider the Due Process Clause. The Court explained that our Constitution protects the "fundamental rights to life, liberty, and the pursuit of happiness, considered as individual possessions." Under the San Francisco ordinance, "no reason whatever, except the will of the supervisors, is assigned why [the laundry owners] should not be permitted to carry on, in the accustomed manner, their harmless and useful occupation, on which they depend for a livelihood." Notice how similar this right is to the right asserted by the butchers in *Slaughter-House* — namely, "the right to exercise their trade." In the United States, the Court observed, no man should be "compelled to hold his life, or the means of living, or any material right essential to the enjoyment of life at the mere will of another." Such an idea "seems to be intolerable in any country where freedom prevails, as being the essence of slavery itself."

Accordingly, Justice Matthews found that the ordinance grants the government "a naked and arbitrary power to give or withhold consent" in violation of these "fundamental" rights. Such an ordinance is not consistent with the Due Process of Law because so arbitrary an exercise of power is not truly a "law." On this account, even if a law is enacted by a majority vote, a purely arbitrary restriction on life, liberty, or property is not a proper exercise of government power. Therefore, the restriction cannot be a *law*. Remember that what we call the Due Process Clause is actually the "Due Process *of Law*" Clause. This provision requires that the government give people not only the process that is due but the process that is due according to a valid law.

STUDY GUIDE

Does the Due Process of Law analysis turn on the race of the business owners? If the government granted licenses to all *large* laundries, but not laundries owned by a *single* person, would that regime also deny the due process of law?

Second, the Court provided this now-famous test to determine whether a law violates the Equal Protection Clause:

Though the law itself be fair on its face, and impartial in appearance, yet, if it is applied and administered by public authority with an evil eye and an unequal hand, so as practically to make unjust and illegal discriminations between persons in similar circumstances, material to their rights, the denial of equal justice is still within the prohibition of the constitution.

The Court's conception of the Equal Protection Clause relates to the *protection* of the laws. In San Francisco, the laws were not being enforced equally. In addition, the content, or *substance*, of the ordinance was itself arbitrary, and thus violated the Due Process Clause.

STUDY GUIDE

How are courts to determine when a law is motivated by "an evil eye and an unequal hand"?

In *Yick Wo*, this test was satisfied: "The facts shown establish an administration directed so exclusively against a particular class of persons as to warrant and require the conclusion that" the government's "mind [was] so unequal and oppressive as to amount to a practical denial by the State of that equal protection of the laws."

The Court concluded that a facially neutral law may be unconstitutional if it is enforced in an unequal fashion. If a law is not enforced equally, some people are being denied the protection of the law that others enjoy. At the same time, licenses were always denied to Chinese applicants. The Court noted, "eighty others, not Chinese subjects, are permitted to carry on the same business under similar conditions." The only justification for this failure to enforce the law equally, the Court concluded, is "hostility to the race and nationality to which the petitioners belong, and which, in the eye of the law, is not justified." Therefore, the discrimination is "illegal, and the public administration which enforces it is a denial of the equal protection of the laws and a violation of the Fourteenth Amendment of the Constitution."

In *Yick Wo*, the Court determined that the law was not enacted to serve the health and safety of the general public. How does the Court reach this conclusion? Justice Matthews looked to both the substance of the ordinance, which was arbitrary, and the discriminatory manner in which the ordinance was enforced. Because the law was not enacted to promote the general welfare, it must have been enacted for *other motives* — in this case racial animus towards Chinese people.

A decade later, the Court decided *Plessy v. Ferguson* (1896). This anti-canonical case adopted a very different and far more deferential approach to scrutinizing exercises of the police power under the Due Process and Equal Protection Clauses.

Plessy v. Ferguson (1896)

 ConLaw.us/Plessy/

In 1890, Louisiana required all trains to "provide equal but separate accommodations for the white, and colored races, by providing two or more passenger coaches for each passenger train." Two years later, Homer Plessy intentionally "took possession of a vacant seat in a coach where passengers of the white race were accommodated." The train conductor ordered Plessy, who was described by the Court as "of mixed descent," to take a seat in the other coach. Plessy refused and was forcibly ejected by a police officer. After his arrest, Plessy posted a $500 bond and was released. There are strong indications that Plessy wanted to get arrested to set up a *test case*. His goal was to challenge the validity of Jim Crow laws. Plessy filed suit against John H. Ferguson, the judge of the criminal court who handed down his sentence.

The Court upheld the Louisiana law by an 8-1 vote. As in the *Civil Rights Cases*, Justice John Marshall Harlan was the lone dissenter.

Justice Henry Brown wrote the majority opinion. It had two parts. First, the Court rejected the argument that Louisiana's segregation law violated the Thirteenth Amendment. "A statute which implies merely a legal distinction between the white and colored races," Justice Brown wrote, "has no tendency to destroy the legal equality of the two races, or reestablish a state of involuntary servitude." The Court explained that "[t]he underlying fallacy of the plaintiff's argument [is] the assumption that the enforced separation of the two races stamps the colored race with a badge of inferiority." Justice Brown observed, "If this be so, it is not by reason of anything found in the act, but solely because the colored race chooses to put that construction upon it."

STUDY GUIDE

If racial separation did not "stamp[] the colored race with a badge of inferiority," why did Louisiana favor it?

Second, the Court turned to the Fourteenth Amendment. Justice Brown explained that "[l]aws permitting, and even requiring, their separation in places" are within "the exercise of [the state's] police power." The Court reasoned that "every exercise of the police power must be reasonable, and extend only to such laws as are enacted in good faith for the promotion of the public good, and not for the annoyance or oppression of a particular class."

STUDY GUIDE

Compare the Court's review of the state's police power in *Yick Wo* and in *Plessy*.

In *Yick Wo*, the San Francisco ordinance violated the Fourteenth Amendment because "it conferred upon the municipal authorities arbitrary power" to deny laundry licenses. This ordinance, was "a covert attempt . . . to make an arbitrary and unjust discrimination against the Chinese race." In *Plessy*, however, the Court found that "the case reduces itself to the question whether the statute of Louisiana is a reasonable regulation, and, with respect to this, there must necessarily be a large discretion on the part of the legislature."

Justice Brown ruled that Louisiana's segregation law was a reasonable exercise of the state's police power in light of "the established usages, customs, and traditions of the people, and with a view to the promotion of their comfort, and the preservation of the public peace and good order." The *Plessy* Court did not cite any evidence to support the claim that "the public peace and good order" had been disrupted by integrated passenger cars. Justice Brown added that the Fourteenth Amendment was never "intended to abolish distinctions based upon color, or to enforce . . . a commingling of the two races upon terms unsatisfactory to either." But the law did not enforce any commingling of the races. Instead, it was the law that prevented people of different races from *choosing* to commingle.

Finally, the Court noted, "the separation of the two races in public conveyances" is no "more obnoxious to the fourteenth amendment than the acts of congress requiring separate schools for colored children in the District of Columbia, the constitutionality of which does not seem to have been questioned." (*Brown v. Board of Education* (1954) will revisit Congress's decision to segregate schools in the federal District of Columbia.) Therefore, the Court found that the Louisiana segregation law did not violate the Thirteenth or the Fourteenth Amendments.

As in the *Civil Rights Cases*, Justice Harlan was the lone dissenter. First, he observed that "[t]he arbitrary separation of citizens on the basis of race while they are on a public highway is a badge of servitude." Therefore, Lousiana's law violated the Thirteenth Amendment. Second, Justice Harlan turned to the Fourteenth Amendment's Equal Protection Clause. He wrote that the Constitution does not "permit any public authority to know the race of those entitled to be *protected* in the enjoyment of such rights." Justice Harlan stated, "Our Constitution is color-blind, and neither knows nor tolerates classes among citizens." This passage would become very famous. In this country, he observed, there is "no superior, dominant, ruling class of citizens." Rather, "in respect of civil rights, all citizens are equal before the law.

STUDY GUIDE

Can you see why modern Supreme Court justices may object to viewing the Constitution as a "color-blind" document? For example, does the Constitution allow the government to adopt race-conscious measures to *help*, rather than to *hurt*, racial minorities?

Justice Harlan did not attempt to determine why Louisiana enacted the law. Instead, he measured the *fit* between the *ends* the government was trying to achieve, and the *means* it employed. He found that segregating train cars is not "at all germane" — that is, related — "to an end to which the legislature was *competent*" — for example, protecting the health and safety of the public. Because this connection was not close enough, the segregation law was not a reasonable exercise of the police power. Justice Harlan believed that the state could only exercise its police power to achieve goals "to which the legislature was competent." This approach is reminiscent of Justice Samuel Chase's description of the "legislative" power in *Calder v. Bull* (1798).

Plessy continued the trend of other decisions that narrowed the scope of the Reconstruction Amendments. Like *Slaughter-House*, *Cruikshank*, and the *Civil Rights Cases* before it, *Plessy* substantially weakened the Fourteenth Amendment. While these three earlier cases remain good law, *Plessy* is not. Justice Harlan predicted that *Plessy* would become "as pernicious" as *Dred Scott v. Sandford*. He was right. Today, *Plessy v. Ferguson* and *Dred Scott* are part of the *anti-canon*.

More than a century later, Phoebe Ferguson and Keith Plessy, descendants of the litigants in the infamous case, founded the *Plessy & Ferguson Foundation*. The organization aims to teach the history of the case and explain why it is still relevant today.

PART VII

EXPANDING THE SCOPE OF THE DUE PROCESS CLAUSE

We start our study of the Due Process Clause with *Lochner v. New York* (1905). Next we turn to three *economic* liberty cases decided during the Progressive Era: *Muller v. Oregon* (1908), *Buchanan v. Warley* (1917), and *Adkins v. Children's Hospital* (1923). We then consider three *personal* liberty cases decided during the Progressive Era: *Meyer v. Nebraska* (1923), *Pierce v. Society of Sisters* (1925), and *Buck v. Bell* (1927). Next, we analyze three *economic* liberty cases decided just before and during the New Deal: *O'Gorman & Young, Inc. v. Hartford Fire Insurance Company* (1931), *Nebbia v. New York* (1934), and *West Coast Hotel v. Parrish* (1937). Finally, we study how the Supreme Court approached *economic* liberty in *United States v. Carolene Products* (1938) and *Williamson v. Lee Optical* (1955).

CHAPTER 31

Lochner v. New York (1905)

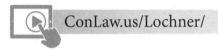

ConLaw.us/Lochner/

In the late nineteenth century, most bakeries in New York City operated in tenement house basements. The rent in these homes were low, and the cellar floors were sturdy enough to support the weight of an oven. These cramped spaces, however, had serious sanitation issues. They were never designed for commercial uses. In 1895, New York enacted the Bakeshop Act to address these problems. The law established a detailed code of sanitation standards for bakeries. One provision was added at the behest of the bakeshop union: Employees could not work more than ten hours per day and sixty hours per week. (The owners of the bakeshops were not subject to this limit.)

At the time, small bakeshops were largely owned and operated by Jewish, German, and other immigrants, who served their own communities. The owners of these businesses fiercely resisted unionization and the maximum hour laws. Their operations required a few employees to operate the ovens over a 24-hour period. The workers could then sleep on the premises while the bread was rising or baking. In contrast, large commercial bakeries could employ shift workers to comply with the maximum-hours law. As a result, the Bakeshop Act had the effect of, and was possibly intended to privilege corporate-owned, unionized bakeries over their small immigrant competitors.

Joseph Lochner, a German immigrant, operated a bakery in Utica, New York. It was located in a nice shop, not in a crowded tenement house in Manhattan. Lochner employed his worker, Arman Schmitter, for more than sixty hours in a week. The lifelong friends likely reached that arrangement so Lochner would be charged with violating the law, thus setting up a test case. Ultimately, Lochner was convicted of violating the Bakeshop Act. He then refused to pay the fifty-dollar fine and was imprisoned. On appeal, he contended that the Bakeshop Act violated the Fourteenth Amendment's Due Process Clause.

All nine Justices agreed that the Bakeshop Act's health and safety regulations were valid exercises of the state's police power. Both the majority and the dissent upheld the regulations concerning ventilation, ceiling heights, the location of washrooms, and the cleanliness of floors in bakeries.

STUDY GUIDE

Does the Court view "freedom of contract" as an absolute right that may never be regulated?

The Justices, however, split 5-4 on whether the state could enact the maximum-hours law pursuant to its police power. Justice Peckham wrote the majority opinion. He was joined by Chief Justice Fuller and Justices Brewer, Brown, and McKenna. Was the maximum- hours law "a fair, reasonable and appropriate exercise of the police power of the State, or [was] it an unreasonable, unnecessary and arbitrary interference with the 'liberty of contract' "? The Court answered that it was the latter.

Justice Peckham rejected the claim that the maximum-hours provision was a genuine health and safety measure. Lochner's lawyer argued that the mortality rate of English bakers was lower than that of the general population, and was about equal to those of cabinetmakers, masons, and clerks. (This mode of argument based on empirical data foreshadowed the so-called "Brandeis briefs," which Louis Brandeis filed to defend progressive legislation.) The majority opinion relied on these statistics. Justice Peckham concluded that "[t]here is no reasonable ground for interfering with the liberty of person or the right of free contract, by determining the hours of labor, in the occupation of a baker." Indeed, Justice Peckham twice suggested that the New York law was enacted for "other motives." In other words, the Bakeshop Act was *class legislation* aimed at helping unions, and harming non-unionized bakeshops and their employees.

Justice Harlan wrote the principal dissent, joined by Justices White and Day. Justice Harlan agreed with the majority that "there is a liberty of contract which cannot be violated." But he contended that "when the validity of a statute is questioned, the burden of proof, so to speak, is upon those who assert it to be unconstitutional." Harlan then cited different statistical sources, which undercut Lochner's claim that the regulation was arbitrary. Harlan thought that Lochner, and not the government, had the burden of proof to argue that the law was unconstitutional.

Justice Holmes wrote a now-famous dissent. He would have upheld the Bakeshop Act if *any* reasonable person could have supported the law. Holmes charged the majority with "decid[ing the case] upon an economic theory which a large part of the country does not entertain," namely, "laissez faire" capitalism. He wrote, "The Fourteenth Amendment does not enact Mr. Herbert Spencer's Social Statics." Some scholars have viewed this passage as a rejection of *Social*

Darwinism — or the survival of the fittest. In fact, Holmes was himself a Social Darwinist. Instead, Holmes was rejecting Herbert Spencer's "law of equal freedom." This work claimed that "each has freedom to do all that he wills provided that he infringes not the equal freedom of any other."

STUDY GUIDE

Do you see any important difference between the approaches favored by the dissents of Justices Harlan and Holmes?

Lochner v. New York was not particularly controversial when it was decided in 1905. Except for critical coverage in union newspapers, the case was generally well received in the press. It only became notorious in 1912 when Theodore Roosevelt attacked *Lochner* during his campaign for President. The former President, who served as a Republican, was now the presidential candidate of the Progressive Party. Roosevelt, who appointed Holmes to the Supreme Court, now praised the dissenter's approach in campaign speeches. Ultimately, Roosevelt's third-party campaign took away votes from the Republican candidate, William Howard Taft. As a result, Woodrow Wilson, the progressive candidate on the Democratic ticket, prevailed.

In 1916, President Wilson nominated Louis Brandeis to the Supreme Court. The progressive jurist shared Holmes's constitutional approach. Before and during the New Deal, Justices appointed by progressive Presidents — Democratic and Republican alike — would repudiate *Lochner*. These progressive Justices followed the approach from Justice Harlan's dissent: The challenger had the burden to show that a restriction on liberty was arbitrary or irrational. After the New Deal, however, in *Williamson v. Lee Optical* (1955), the Supreme Court would adopt something like Justice Holmes's more deferential approach.

CHAPTER 32

"Economic" Liberty in the Progressive Era

At the end of the nineteenth century, the Progressive Movement began to successfully lobby the states, and later Congress, to enact new political, economic, and social reforms. In Part II, we studied how *federal* progressive laws were challenged for exceeding the scope of Congress's enumerated powers. This chapter will discuss how both *state* and *federal* progressive laws were challenged as violations of the Fifth and Fourteenth Amendment's Due Process Clauses. Specifically, the plaintiffs argued that these laws deprived people of their liberty without the due process of law.

In the *Slaughter-House Cases* (1873), the Supreme Court held that the Privileges or Immunities Clause protected only a narrow set of federal rights. As the nineteenth century drew to a close, and the pace of economic regulations increased, the Court began to compensate for the weakened privileges or immunities by expanding the scope of the Due Process Clause. For example, *Lochner v. New York* (1905) held that the Fourteenth Amendment protected the right to contract — not as a "privilege or immunity" of citizenship, but as a "liberty" protected by the Due Process Clause.

Following *Lochner*, the Supreme Court decided three important *economic* liberty cases: *Muller v. State of Oregon* (1908), *Buchanan v. Warley* (1917), and *Adkins v. Children's Hospital* (1923). Our analysis will start with *Muller*.

Muller v. Oregon (1908)

ConLaw.us/Muller/

Oregon made it a crime to employ female workers for more than ten hours a day. The owner of the Lace House Laundry challenged the law as a violation of the

Fourteenth Amendment. Naturally, he relied on the recent precedent of *Lochner*, which found that limiting bakers to ten hours per day violated the Due Process Clause. Yet, only three years later, *Muller* unanimously upheld Oregon's maximum-hour law for women.

STUDY GUIDE

What distinguishes the maximum-hour law upheld in *Muller* from the maximum-hour law declared unconstitutional in *Lochner*? Can these decisions be reconciled?

Justice Brewer wrote the majority opinion in *Muller*. He explained that "the difference between the sexes [can] justify a different rule respecting a restriction of the hours of labor." Here, Justice Brewer relies on the same argument that Justice Bradley invoked in *Bradwell v. Illinois*. That notorious 1873 concurring opinion observed that "[t]he civil law, as well as nature herself, has always recognized a wide difference in the respective spheres and destinies of man and woman."

Justice Brewer drew a distinction between men and women in the workplace based, in large part, on a brief submitted by Louis Brandeis. At the time, Brandeis was one of the most famous progressive litigators. His brief did not make legal arguments. Intead, it presented excerpts from social science writings and other data to support the Oregon statute. For example, Brandeis argued that because of the "physical differences between men and women," there was a "bad effect of long hours on health" on women. Indeed, Brandeis wrote, there were "specific evil effects on childbirth and female functions" from working too long. Based on these alleged facts, he contended that the state had acted reasonably to "protect[] women" and "future generations" by limiting how many hours they could work.

Many of the claims in Brandeis's brief were absurd, even at the time. For example, Brandeis asserted that there is "more water" in women's blood than in men's. Therefore, women were physically "inferior[]" to men. Yet Justice Brewer's majority opinion accepted Brandeis's "sociological" information. The Court even cited Brandeis's brief in a footnote. Such pleadings filed in support of progressive legislation came to be known as "Brandeis Briefs." There was no dissent in *Muller*. In 1916, President Wilson would appoint Brandeis to the Supreme Court.

Buchanan v. Warley (1917)

 ConLaw.us/Buchanan/

In 1917, the Supreme Court decided another economic liberty case unanimously: *Buchanan v. Warley*. However, the outcome of this case was very different from that of *Muller*.

The city of Louisville, Kentucky prohibited black people from buying homes in predominantly white neighborhoods. The law likewise prohibited white people from buying homes in predominantly black neighborhoods. The government defended this "exercise of the police power" on the ground that "maintain[ing] racial purity . . . tends to promote the public peace by preventing racial conflicts." Charles Buchanan, a white man, was prohibited from selling his home to William Warley, a black man.

Buchanan challenged the Louisville ordinance as a violation of the Fourteenth Amendment. The law complied with *Plessy v. Ferguson*'s separate-but-equal rule, because it treated all races equally. Therefore, Buchanan could not state a claim under the Equal Protection Clause. However, he could state a claim under the Due Process Clause. Specifically, Buchanan contended that the ordinance deprived him of "property" without the due process of law. That is, the Louisville law reduced the value of his home by excluding potential buyers of the opposite race.

All nine Justices agreed that the Louisville segregation ordinance violated the Due Process Clause of the Fourteenth Amendment. Justice Day wrote the majority opinion. He explained that "the police power, broad as it is, cannot justify the passage of a law or ordinance which runs counter to the limitations of the Federal Constitution."

First, Justice Day considered the Civil Rights Act of 1866. That precursor to the Fourteenth Amendment protected the right of all citizens, of all races, to "convey real and personal property." Second, he explained that the Fourteenth Amendment, ratified two years later in 1868, was designed to protect the right of "a colored man to acquire property without state legislation discriminating against him solely because of color."

Third, the Court noted that the Fourteenth Amendment did not only protect "persons of color." Remember, Mr. Buchanan, the seller, was white. Rather, "the broad language used was deemed sufficient to protect all persons, white or black, against discriminatory legislation by the States." Therefore, the Louisville ordinance "was not a legitimate exercise of the police power of the State" because it deprived Buchanan of his "property" without the due process of law.

While the final vote in *Buchanan* was unanimous, Justice Holmes had circulated to his colleagues a draft dissent. He was seemingly indifferent to the statute that barred African Americans from living in white neighborhoods. Holmes's draft dissent reflected the same deference towards state police power legislation that he had espoused in *Lochner*. In particular, he questioned whether the Fourteenth Amendment protected the rights of a white person to sell his property. He also seemed troubled that the NAACP engineered this dispute as a test case. Justice Holmes, who apparently could not persuade another justice to join him, withdrew his draft dissent and joined the majority opinion.

STUDY GUIDE

Does *Buchanan* suggest the possibility that the Court's approach to the Due Process Clause in general, and liberty of contract in particular, could be used to protect members of politically disfavored groups?

Adkins v. Children's Hospital (1923)

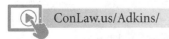 ConLaw.us/Adkins/

Muller and *Buchanan* involved challenges to the state's police power. The next case, *Adkins v. Children's Hospital of the District of Columbia* (1923), involved a challenge to a federal law. So far, we have only considered challenges to state laws for violating the Fourteenth Amendment's Due Process Clause. However, *Adkins* involved the Fifth Amendment's Due Process Clause, which limits Congress's powers.

STUDY GUIDE

Is there any difference between the Court's protection of "liberty" under the Fifth and Fourteenth Amendments?

In Part II, we studied how the federal government lacks a general police power. But Congress does have the power to "exercise exclusive Legislation" over the federal District of Columbia. Art. I., Sec. 8, Cl. 17. The scope of this power is similar to the state's police power to legislate for health, safety, and public morals. Pursuant to its general legislative power, Congress authorized a minimum wage for women and children workers in the District of Columbia. The purpose of the law was "[t]o protect the women and minors of the District from conditions detrimental to their health and morals."

In *Adkins*, the Supreme Court declared the federal minimum wage for women unconstitutional by a 5-3 vote. (The Court did not consider the minimum wage for children.) The Court found that the federal law deprived women of their "liberty" — that is the "right to contract about one's affairs" — without the "due process of law." Justice Sutherland wrote the majority opinion. He explained that the Fifth Amendment gives employers and employees "an equal right to obtain from each other the best terms they can as the result of private bargaining." Justice Sutherland found that the federal law interfered with the right of women to negotiate for a salary that was lower than the minimum wage.

STUDY GUIDE

How does the Court reconcile *Adkins* with *Muller*, which unanimously upheld a maximum-hour law for women?

A political cartoon at the time ridiculed *Adkins* as protecting a "constitutional right to starve." Yet, Justice George Sutherland viewed the situation very differently.

He observed that since *Muller v. Oregon* was decided in 1908, the differences between the sexes "have now come almost, if not quite, to the vanishing point." Justice Sutherland concluded that "women of mature age" cannot "be subjected to restrictions upon their liberty of contract" that "could not lawfully be imposed [on] men under similar circumstances."

During his tenure in the Senate, Sutherland had introduced the Nineteenth Amendment, which extended the vote to women nationwide. He wrote that the Nineteenth Amendment had ushered in "revolutionary changes . . . in the contractual, political, and civil status of women." He added that the "ancient inequality of the sexes" suggested in *Muller* "has continued 'with diminishing intensity.'"

Finally, Justice Sutherland conceded that "[t]here is, of course, no such thing as absolute freedom of contract." However, violations of economic liberty "can be justified only by the existence of exceptional circumstances." And no such circumstances existed here. Rather, the minimum wage law "is so clearly the product of a naked, arbitrary exercise of power that it cannot be allowed to stand under the Constitution of the United States." The *Adkins* Court articulated a presumption in favor of liberty even more clearly than did the *Lochner* Court.

Unlike *Muller*, which was unanimous, *Adkins* had two dissenting opinions. Chief Justice William Howard Taft's dissent echoed Justice Holmes's dissent in *Lochner*. He wrote, "it is not the function of this court to hold congressional acts invalid simply because they are passed to carry out economic views which the court believes to be unwise or unsound."

In his dissent, Justice Holmes once again found that the statute was reasonable and must be upheld. First, he said that the "ends" of the law — that is, the removal of "conditions leading to ill health" — were permissible. Second, he observed that the federal law was a permissible "means" because minimum wages for women were mandated across the country. "When so many intelligent persons, who have studied the matter more than any of us can, have thought that the means are effective and are worth the price it seems to me impossible to deny that the belief reasonably may be held by reasonable men." In conclusion, Justice Holmes could "perceive no difference in the kind or degree of interference with liberty" between the maximum-hour law upheld in *Muller*, and the minimum-wage law declared unconstitutional in *Adkins*.

Less than a decade later during the New Deal, the Supreme Court reversed course on the protection of "economic liberty" and overruled *Adkins*.

CHAPTER 33

"Personal" Liberty in the Progressive Era

The Fourteenth Amendment provides that a state cannot "deprive any person of life, liberty, or property, without due process of law." Since the New Deal, the Supreme Court has tended to provide less protection for *economic* liberty than it does for *personal* liberty. During the Progressive Era, however, the Court did not draw any distinction between economic and personal liberty. But we will still categorize the cases in this chapter as personal liberty cases. Why? While the old cases concerning economic liberty are no longer good law, the old cases concerning personal liberty are still good law today. For this reason, it is helpful to consider the two categories of cases separately.

STUDY GUIDE

Today, the Supreme Court carefully scrutinizes laws that violate personal liberties, but generally defers to laws that violate economic liberties. Is there any principled textual or constitutional reason to justify this distinction?

We have already studied four economic liberty cases decided during the Progressive Era: *Lochner v. New York* (1905), *Muller v. Oregon* (1908), *Buchanan v. Warley* (1917), and *Adkins v. Children's Hospital* (1923). In this chapter, we will study three personal liberty cases from the same period: *Meyer v. Nebraska* (1923), *Pierce v. Society of Sisters* (1925), and *Buck v. Bell* (1927).

Meyer v. Nebraska (1923)

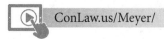 ConLaw.us/Meyer/

Nebraska criminalized teaching to young students "alien speech," such as German, French, Spanish, and Italian. "Ancient languages," such as Latin, Greek, and Hebrew could still be taught. The government was worried that children of "foreign born population[s]" were not being taught to speak English. The state contended that the "public safety [was] imperiled" because these children were "hindered from becoming citizens of the most useful type." The Nebraska law addressed these problems by ensuring that English became "the mother tongue of all children reared in [the] State." Nebraska prosecuted Robert Meyer, who taught at a private Lutheran school. His offense? Teaching German Bible stories to a ten-year-old student.

STUDY GUIDE

Is *Meyer* premised on the First Amendment right to free speech or free exercise of religion? If not, why not?

The Nebraska Supreme Court upheld Meyer's sentence — a twenty-five-dollar fine — because the law "was a valid exercise of the police power." On appeal, the Supreme Court reversed the conviction. Justice McReynolds wrote the opinion for a seven-member majority. Justices Holmes and Sutherland dissented.

The Court found that the Nebraska law deprived Meyer of the liberty protected by the Fourteenth Amendment. Justice McReynolds explained that the concept of "liberty" is not limited to "freedom [from] bodily restraint." Rather, it includes a wide range of freedoms, including: (1) the "right of the individual to contract"; (2) the right "to engage in any of the common occupations of life"; (3) the right "to acquire useful knowledge"; (4) the right "to marry"; (5) the right to "establish a home and bring up children"; (6) the right "to worship God according to the dictates of his own conscience"; (7) and "generally [the right] to enjoy those privileges long recognized at common law as essential to the orderly pursuit of happiness by free men."

STUDY GUIDE

How does Justice McReynolds come up with this list of rights protected by the Due Process Clause? What is the "orderly pursuit of happiness by free men"?

The Supreme Court found that the Nebraska law violated the liberty of the teacher, the student, *and* his parents: The "legislature has attempted materially to interfere (1) with the calling of modern language teachers, (2) with the opportunities of pupils to acquire knowledge, and (3) with the power of parents to control the education of their own."

The Court acknowledged that the statute's goals, or *ends*, were permissible. The state had a legitimate interest to "improve the quality of its citizens, physically, mentally and morally." However, even if the *ends* were legitimate, the *means* were "prohibited." The government could not interfere with liberty "under the guise of protecting the public interest" unless the law had a "reasonable relation to some purpose within the competency of the State to effect." Here, speaking a foreign language is not "so clearly harmful as to justify" this deprivation of rights. Rather, "the statute as applied is *arbitrary* and *without reasonable relation* to any *end within the competency* of the state." Therefore, the Nebraska law "unreasonably infringe[d] the liberty guaranteed" by the Fourteenth Amendment. Meyer's conviction was reversed.

Once again, Justice Holmes dissented, joined by Justice Sutherland. First, he found that the law pursued a "proper" and "desirable" *end*: "that all the citizens of the United States should speak a common tongue." Second, he concluded that the *means* "of reaching the desired result" was a "reasonable or even necessary method" to ensure that "young children . . . shall hear and speak only English at school." Therefore, third, he concluded, the law was not an act of "arbitrary fiat." Here, Holmes echoed his *Lochner* dissent. He wrote that "men reasonably might differ" on the propriety of the law, but the Constitution does not "prevent[] the experiment being tried" by the state.

Pierce v. Society of Sisters (1925)

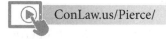 ConLaw.us/Pierce/

During the Progressive Era, state governments did not only regulate *what* students could learn. Progressive laws also regulated *where* students could learn. The Oregon Compulsory Education Act had the effect of requiring all children to attend *public* schools. Specifically, parents who sent their children to *private* schools would be guilty of a misdemeanor. The Society of the Sisters and the Hill Military Academy, two private schools in Oregon, challenged the law as a violation of the Fourteenth Amendment.

STUDY GUIDE

Is a corporation, like a private school, a "person" for purposes of the Fourteenth Amendment? How can a private school assert the constitutional rights of teachers they employ and students they teach?

Justice McReynolds wrote the majority opinion for a unanimous Court. He found that the Oregon statute was unconstitutional. The government can only violate constitutional rights, he found, when the law has a "reasonable relation to some *purpose within the competency* of the state."

STUDY GUIDE

What does the Court mean by a "purpose within the competency of the state"?

Further, the legislature's determination "of what constitutes proper exercise of police power is not final or conclusive but is subject to supervision by the courts." Like the law at issue in *Meyer*, the Oregon law "unreasonably interfere[d] with the liberty of parents and guardians to direct the upbringing and education of children under their control."

STUDY GUIDE

Is *Pierce* premised on the First Amendment right to free exercise of religion? If not, why not?

The Fourteenth Amendment protected more than the rights of parents and their children. Justice McReynolds also found that the Constitution protected the rights of the incorporated private schools: the Society of Sisters and the Hill Military Academy. The Court acknowledged that corporations "cannot claim for themselves the *liberty* which the Fourteenth Amendment guarantees." However, the Fourteenth Amendment protects the *property* owned by the corporations. The Oregon law would result in the "destruction of their business and property" because parents would be required to withdraw their students. Therefore, the Court found, the law deprives the corporations of their property rights, without the due process of law.

STUDY GUIDE

Does *Pierce* involve the *economic* liberty of the school or the *personal* liberty of parents? Or does the case involve both? Why does this distinction matter?

In *Meyer v. Nebraska* and *Pierce v. Society of Sisters*, the Supreme Court closely scrutinized state legislation that restricted liberty. Specifically, the Court assessed whether the restrictions served an *end* that was "within the competency of the state." That is, the health and safety of the public. The Court found that the challenged laws in *Meyer* and *Pierce* could not be justified as health and safety measures. In *Buck v. Bell*, however, the Court found that an even more severe restriction on liberty was a valid exercise of the state's police power.

Buck v. Bell (1927)

ConLaw.us/Buck/

In 1924, Virginia enacted the Sterilization Act and the Racial Integrity Act. The former law allowed the government to forcibly sterilize so-called "imbeciles." The latter law prohibited interracial marriage. (The Supreme Court declared the Racial Integrity Act unconstitutional in *Loving v. Virginia* (1967), which we will discuss in Chapter 38.) Both Acts were designed to promote *scientific eugenics*. Eugenics broadly refers to the idea that mankind can improve the population by reducing the reproduction of undesirable genetic traits. For example, eugenicists wanted to prevent interracial couples from having mixed-race children. They also wanted the state to sterilize those deemed "undesirable," so they could not reproduce. This movement is often associated with Nazi Germany. In fact, decades before the rise of the National Socialist Party in Germany, many Americans accepted eugenics as a scientific truth. This view was especially popular among Progressives, though it enjoyed widespread support throughout the United States.

During the Progressive Era, however, the legality of mandatory sterilization regimes was in doubt. In the early decades of the twentieth century, several state supreme courts declared that such laws violated their state constitutions.*

To resolve this doubt, eugenics advocates in Virginia engineered a test case: They wanted the Supreme Court to uphold their *model* legislation as a legitimate health and safety measure. The Virginia law provided a three-step process by which the government could sterilize a "patient afflicted with hereditary forms of insanity" and "imbecility." First, the government would recommend for sterilization a patient who was institutionalized in the Colony for Epileptics and Feeble Minded. Second, the court would appoint a guardian to advocate on behalf of the patient. Third, if the Colony decided to sterilize the patient, the guardian could appeal that decision to the courts.

The Colony selected Carrie Buck as the first patient to sterilize for a very specific reason. The Colony's doctor determined that the women in Buck's family line were all "feeble-minded." First, Carrie's mother, Emma, was deemed promiscuous because she contracted syphilis and gave birth out of wedlock. Second, Carrie was also deemed promiscuous. She too gave birth out of wedlock. Third, Carrie's six-month-old baby, Vivian, was deemed an "imbecile." Why? She failed a "mental test."

---

* *See* Jeffrey Sutton, 51 Imperfect Solutions: States and the Making of American Constitutional Law (2018).

A coin was held in front of the infant's face, and she did not pay attention to it. The Colony used Carrie to prove that imbecility was hereditary and, in the interest of the public health, sterilization was the only way to stop this line from reproducing.

STUDY GUIDE

What are the possible risks when courts rely on the science of the day to uphold restrictions on individual liberty?

The government's findings about the Buck family were demonstrably false. Carrie attended high school and could read and write. And, according to reports, she became pregnant after she was raped. Carrie was not feeble-minded. But none of these facts was presented to the courts in this test case. Buck's court-appointed attorney served on the Colony's Board of Directors. He deliberately presented a weak defense and did not call any witnesses. His only goal was to ensure that the case could be appealed to the Supreme Court. It is not clear that Carrie even understood what surgery the government sought to perform on her.

On appeal, the Supreme Court upheld Virginia's law. Justice Holmes wrote the majority opinion for eight Justices. He wholeheartedly accepted Virginia's account of the Buck family. In one of the most infamous lines in Supreme Court history, Justice Holmes remarked, "Three generations of imbeciles are enough." Justice Holmes thought that Emma, Carrie, and Vivian were nothing more than imbeciles. Because he was satisfied that Buck was given a proper trial in this case, Justice Holmes focused on whether mandatory sterilization could *ever* be justified. He observed that her challenge was "not upon the procedure" of the law. Buck's lawyer did not dispute the fairness of the trial. Rather, Justice Holmes found that Buck complained about the "substantive law." In other words, she challenged the substance, or content, of the sterilization law.

STUDY GUIDE

Later in the twentieth century, the Supreme Court would distinguish between "substantive due process" and "procedural due process." Virginia's law was properly enacted by the state legislature. If you reject "substantive due process," must *Buck v. Bell* be correct?

Justice Holmes's opinion can be reduced to a simple premise: Because the government has the *greater* power to imprison an "imbecile" in the Colony for life, then the government must have the *lesser* power to sterilize the "imbecile," who can then be "discharged" from the Colony "with safety." Justice Holmes found that the alternative of life imprisonment was far worse. In light of Virginia's law, the state did not have to "wait[] to execute degenerate offspring for crime or to let them starve for their imbecility."

STUDY GUIDE

Which would you choose: Spending the rest of your life in the Colony where you are not allowed to procreate or spending the rest of your life outside the Colony where you are unable to procreate?

Justice Holmes analogized government-compelled sterilization to government-compelled vaccination. The Court upheld the latter practice in *Jacobson v. Massachusetts* (1905). Holmes concluded that "the principle that sustains compulsory vaccination is broad enough to cover cutting the Fallopian tubes." But Holmes didn't stop there. He extended the analogy still further: If the military draft can "call upon the best citizens for their lives," why could the government "not call upon those who already sap the strength of the State for these lesser sacrifices" — that is, mandatory sterilization? In a letter to a friend, Justice Holmes said he was "amused at some of the rhetorical changes" to his opinions suggested by his colleagues "when [he] purposely used short and rather brutal words . . . that made them mad."

STUDY GUIDE

Does the fact that the federal government can draft Americans to fight and die for their country imply that the state can also justly compel Americans to do *anything* short of death for their country?

The vote in *Buck v. Bell* was 8-1. Only Justice Pierce Butler dissented, but he did not write a separate opinion. This practice was somewhat common on the Taft Court. *Buck v. Bell* would cast a long, dark shadow. After the law was upheld by the Supreme Court, state courts began to relax their scrutiny of similar laws. By 1937, thirty-two states enforced their compulsory sterilization laws. This practice would continue until the 1960s. During the Nuremberg trials, attorneys defended Nazis by reading from Justice Holmes's opinion. They sought to demonstrate that Americans, and not Germans, invented eugenics.

We have now concluded our study of seven Due Process cases decided in the Progressive Era. What are their current statuses?

- First, *Lochner* and *Adkins* are no longer good law. Following the New Deal, the Supreme Court held that regulations of *economic* liberty must be upheld if there is any conceivable basis to justify them as reasonable.
- Second, *Meyer* and *Pierce* remain good law. However, these cases are not cited for their broad protection of fundamental liberties under the Due Process Clause. Instead, modern cases have recast both *Meyer* and *Pierce* as decisions that protect First Amendment *personal* rights: speech and the free exercise of religion.

- Third, although *Muller* was premised on blatant sexism, it has been recast as a stepping stone towards enlightened laws that protect the welfare of all employees. Today, *Muller* is considered a *good* case.
- Fourth, *Buchanan* remains good law but has been recast from a Due Process Clause case to an Equal Protection Clause case.
- Finally, *Buck v. Bell* was never overruled. It remains good law. Indeed, Justice Holmes's opinion was favorably cited in *Roe v. Wade* (1973) for the proposition that, under current law, women and men alike do not have an "unlimited right to do with one's body as one pleases."

Despite the fact that the principle upheld in *Buck v. Bell* is considered good law, the case itself is condemned for its reliance on quack science and shoddy fact-finding. Such criticisms render this case part of the Supreme Court's *anti-canon*, along with *Dred Scott*, *Korematsu*, and *Plessy*.

CHAPTER 34

"Economic" Liberty Through The New Deal

Franklin D. Roosevelt was elected President in 1932. His "New Deal" policies aimed to reform the entire American economy. During Roosevelt's first and second terms in office, the Supreme Court radically altered how it reviewed regulations of *economic* liberty. However, even to this day, many lawyers do not know *why* and *when* this change occurred. Our story starts before Roosevelt even took office.

In February 1930, Chief Justice Taft resigned from the Supreme Court due to illness. One month later, Justice Sanford suddenly passed away. President Herbert Hoover nominated Charles Evans Hughes and Owen Roberts to fill the two vacancies. Though a Republican, Hoover was a political progressive. His two appointments began to shift the Court to the left.

O'Gorman & Young, Inc. v. Hartford Fire Insurance Company (1931)

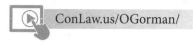

ConLaw.us/OGorman/

Justice Roberts made an immediate impact on the Court in *O'Gorman & Young, Inc. v. Hartford Fire Insurance Company* (1931). Under New Jersey law, commissions on the sale of fire insurance policies were required to be "reasonable." The O'Gorman firm sold Hartford Fire Insurance policies. Their contract provided that the commissions would be priced at "what such services were reasonably worth." O'Gorman asserted that its commission was "reasonably worth" 25 percent of the insurance premiums. Hartford, however, only paid a 20 percent commission. O'Gorman filed suit for breach of contract. The trial court found that under New Jersey law, a 25 percent commission was *unreasonable* and could not be paid.

O'Gorman appealed the case to the Supreme Court. The firm argued that the regulation deprived the company of *property* — that is, the extra commission — without the due process of law. In April 1930, the Court heard oral arguments. At the time, there were only eight members on the bench. Apparently, the Court split 4-4 on whether the regulation was constitutional. Three weeks later, Justice Owen Roberts was confirmed. *O'Gorman* was re-argued the following term. At that time, Justice Roberts cast the fifth and deciding vote to uphold the statute.

The Supreme Court's precedents, including *Lochner*, recognized that the Fourteenth Amendment protected the liberty of contract. That right generally prohibited price regulations. But there was an exception to this general rule: Legislatures could set prices for a business "affected with a public interest." Originally this category was limited to businesses with some kind of monopoly market power. Eventually, the Supreme Court expanded the category to include any business the state wanted to regulate.

Justice Louis Brandeis wrote the majority opinion in *O'Gorman*. He found that "[t]he business of insurance is so far affected with a public interest that the State may regulate the rates." To avoid the "evils" of an "unreasonably high rate level," the state may limit commissions. Therefore, the New Jersey statute is "clearly within the scope of the police power." Second, Justice Brandeis explained that courts must presume the law is constitutional, unless there is a "factual foundation" that the provision was not "an appropriate remedy" for the "evils" in the insurance industry. Here, the Court applied a *presumption of constitutionality*. Nothing on "the face of the" New Jersey statute or the "facts of which the court must take judicial notice," he wrote, could rebut this presumption of constitutionality. Therefore, the regulation was "reasonable."

Justice Van Devanter wrote a dissent. He was joined by Justices Sutherland, Butler, and McReynolds. While the majority presumed the law was constitutional, the dissent required the government to justify why the law was necessary. Justice Van Devanter's dissent offered the following test: The state could deny O'Gorman "the right to make private contracts" only if "some special circumstances" exist that are "sufficient to indicate the necessity" of the statute to eliminate "evils" in the marketplace. The key word is "necessity."

STUDY GUIDE

Compare *O'Gorman* to the three opinions in *Lochner* by Justices Peckham, Harlan, and Holmes, respectively. Which of these three opinions does the *O'Gorman* majority most closely resemble? The *O'Gorman* dissent?

Nebbia v. New York (1934)

 ConLaw.us/Nebbia/

Three years after *O'Gorman* was decided, the Court considered another economic liberty case: *Nebbia v. New York* (1934). The state fixed the price of milk at nine cents per quart. This law, which was designed to help dairy farmers, raised milk prices for everyone — including the poor.

The biggest beneficiaries of the law, however, were large firms that delivered milk directly to homes. Their prices could be undercut by small mom-and-pop stores that did not incur delivery costs. In this way, the minimum price for milk protected the profits of larger milk distributors.

Grocer Leo Nebbia offered his customers a special deal to get around the New York law. If a customer bought two quarts of milk at the regulated price of nine cents each — for a total of eighteen cents — Nebbia would throw in a free loaf of Italian bread, which was worth five cents. With this deal, customers received twenty-three cents of groceries, for only eighteen cents. New York charged Nebbia with violating the price-control law. He was convicted of offering his customers a discount and was sentenced to pay a criminal fine.

Nebbia argued that the law deprived him of liberty and property without the due process of law. The Supreme Court rejected his argument by a 5-4 vote. Once again, Justice Roberts was the swing vote. This time he authored the majority opinion. First, Justice Roberts wrote that states can regulate businesses "affected with a public interest." That category now included even the corner grocery store. As a result, the state had the police power to fix "the prices to be charged for the products or commodities" that the store sells.

Second, the Court reviewed the New York law with the *presumption of constitutionality* that was articulated in *O'Gorman*. Under this approach, the "state [was] free to adopt whatever economic policy may reasonably be deemed to promote public welfare." The "requirements of due process [were] satisfied," Justice Roberts observed, if the law had "a reasonable relation to a proper legislative purpose, and [was] neither arbitrary nor discriminatory." It was not the Court's role to determine if the rule was "unwise."

Third, the Court considered how the law accomplished its purpose — that is, the relationship between the *means* and the *ends*. What "evils" was the government trying to address? "Ruthless competition from destroying the wholesale price structure on which the farmer depends for his livelihood." The Court concluded that the price-control law was not "unreasonable or arbitrary," and it had a "relation to [this] purpose." Therefore, Nebbia's conviction was proper.

As they had in *O'Gorman*, Justices Van Devanter, Sutherland, Butler, and McReynolds dissented together. And, as in *O'Gorman*, the quartet rejected the presumption of constitutionality. In his dissent, Justice McReynolds observed that the stated purpose of the New York law was to "increas[e] milk prices at the farm." Yet, the milk distributors were not required to share their increased revenue with the dairy farmers. For this reason, he questioned whether "the means adopted" — the price controls — bore a "reasonable relation" to the stated purpose of assisting dairy farmers. Justice McReynolds did not assess the legislators' motives directly. Instead, he concluded that the law was arbitrary because the *means* adopted did not *fit* the purported *ends* of the legislation. In other words, the law seemed to be designed to protect large milk distributors from competition rather than to help farmers.

Between 1931 and 1937, Justices Van Devanter, Sutherland, Butler, and McReynolds consistently voted as a bloc to declare unconstitutional progressive federal and state legislation. This conservative quartet was dubbed by their critics as "The Four Horsemen," a reference to the *Four Horsemen of the Apocalypse* from the New Testament's Book of Revelation. During this same period, Justice Roberts was often the "swing" vote. In some cases, he would join the Four Horsemen to give the conservatives a majority. And in other cases, like *O'Gorman* and *Nebbia*, Justice Roberts voted to uphold progressive legislation. In our next case, *West Coast Hotel v. Parrish*, Justice Roberts would once again join the liberal bloc.

West Coast Hotel v. Parrish (1937)

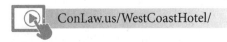

ConLaw.us/WestCoastHotel/

Washington State imposed a minimum wage for women and children, but not for men. Elsie Parrish worked as a chambermaid at the West Coast Hotel in Wenatchee, Washington. Her employer failed to pay her the minimum wage, and she filed suit to recover back pay. The hotel's owner argued that the labor regulation deprived him of the liberty of contract without due process of law.

Over the previous three decades, the Supreme Court had decided several cases concerning economic liberty for women. In *Muller v. Oregon* (1908), the Court upheld a law that limited the hours women could work. The law was deemed reasonable because of the "physical differences between men and women." However, fifteen years later, in *Adkins v. Children's Hospital* (1923), the Court declared unconstitutional a minimum-wage law for women. The federal statute violated the liberty of contract protected by the Fifth Amendment's Due Process Clause. Thirteen years later, in *Morehead v. New York ex rel. Tipaldo* (1936), the Court reaffirmed *Adkins*. The 5-4 decision found that New York's minimum-wage law for women was unconstitutional. In that case, Justice Roberts joined the Four Horsemen. Critically, however, in *Morehead* the Court was not asked to overrule *Adkins*.

But in *West Coast Hotel*, Elsie Parrish asked the Court to expressly overrule *Adkins*. By a 5-4 vote, the Court did exactly that. Justice Roberts once again cast the deciding vote. Chief Justice Hughes — the other Hoover appointee — wrote the majority opinion. He explained that *Adkins*, decided only thirteen years earlier, "was a departure from the true application of the principles governing the regulation by the state of the relation of employer and employed." Furthermore, cases decided since *Adkins* — including *O'Gorman* and *Nebbia* — applied those principles properly through the "presumption of constitutionality." Chief Justice Hughes could not "reconcile" *Adkins* with *O'Gorman* and *Nebbia*. Therefore, the Court overruled *Adkins*.

With *Adkins* out of the way, it was easy for the Court to uphold the Washington minimum-wage law: "[I]f the protection of women is a legitimate end of the exercise of state power," Chief Justice Hughes asked, "how can it be said that the requirement of the payment of a minimum wage fairly fixed in order to meet the very necessities of existence is not an admissible means to that end?" He added, "[e]ven if the wisdom of the policy be regarded as debatable and its effects uncertain, still the Legislature is entitled to its judgment." This deference is especially appropriate, the Court noted, in light of the "unparalleled demands for relief which arose during the recent period of depression." Therefore, the law did not violate the Fourteenth Amendment.

For one of the last times, the Four Horsemen dissented together. Justice Sutherland, who wrote the *Adkins* majority opinion, also wrote the *West Coast* dissent. Here, he questioned the presumption of constitutionality. The dissent explained that a judge has an independent "duty to make up his own mind and adjudge accordingly" whether a law is constitutional. A deferential judge who "automatic[ally] accept[s] the views of others," he lamented, has "surrender[ed] his deliberate judgment."

Justice Sutherland further contended that the Court should not base its ruling on the exigencies of the Great Depression. "The meaning of the Constitution," he stated, "does not change with the ebb and flow of economic events." Rather, he added, "the words of the Constitution [must] mean today what they . . . mean[t] when written." A contrary rule would "rob that instrument of the essential element which continues it in force."

Finally, Justice Sutherland attacked the law because it imposed a minimum wage for women but not for men. As a Senator, Sutherland supported the Ninteteenth Amendment and women's suffrage. In his dissent he boasted, "Women today stand upon a legal and political equality with men." Therefore, "[d]ifference of sex affords no reasonable ground for making a restriction applicable to the wage contracts of all working women from which like contracts of all working men are left free."

STUDY GUIDE

Nearly four decades later, in *Craig v. Boren* (1976), the Supreme Court would hold that the government cannot distinguish between men and women without providing a legitimate basis. (See Chapter 41.)

On March 29, 1937, Justice Roberts joined the majority opinion in *West Coast Hotel,* which overruled *Adkins*. However, only nine months earlier in *Morehead,* Justice Roberts agreed with the Four Horsemen that New York's minimum wage law for women was unconstitutional in light of *Adkins*. How can we explain his change in position? For generations, law students learned that Justice Roberts changed his vote in response to President Franklin Roosevelt's proposal to expand the size of the Supreme Court. On March 9, 1937, three weeks before the decision in *West Coast Hotel* was announced, President Roosevelt released his so-called Court-packing plan. He explained:

> Whenever a judge or Justice of any federal court has reached the age of 70, and does not avail himself of the opportunity to retire on a pension, a new member should be appointed by the President then in office, with the approval as required by the Constitution of the Senate of the United States.

The size of the Supreme Court is not specified in the Constitution. It has always been set by Congress. The number of Justices has varied from as few as six to as many as ten. President Roosevelt was not concerned with the age or the workload of the Court. Rather, he was frustrated that conservative Justices had declared unconstitutional federal and state progressive legislation. President Roosevelt called upon Congress to change the size of the Court for a very specific purpose: appointing new justices who were more amenable to his New Deal policy agenda, and his vision of the Constitution.

On March 29, three weeks after the President's announcement, *West Coast Hotel* was decided. Justice Roberts was in the majority. His apparent reversal from *Morehead* created the appearance that the Court-packing proposal influenced his decision. According to what became the conventional narrative, Justice Roberts voted to uphold the Washington minimum wage law in order to remove the incentives for President Roosevelt to pack the Supreme Court. Since that day, Justice Roberts's vote has been hailed as the so-called "switch in time that saved nine" — a play on the folksy aphorism that "a stitch in time saves nine." In other words, if you mend a small hole now, you won't need to mend a bigger hole later.

However, the conventional narrative — that Justice Roberts changed his vote in response to the Court-packing plan — has been called into question. In 1936, several of the Justices recorded the votes cast at private conferences. Based on the records in the "docket books," we know that Justice Roberts voted to uphold the Washington law in December 1936 — nearly three months *before* President Roosevelt announced his Court-packing plan.

There is a far more mundane explanation for Justice Roberts's switch: In *Morehead*, the Court was not asked to overrule *Adkins*. However, Elsie Parrish asked the Court to expressly overrule *Adkins*. And so it did, relying on prior decisions Roberts had joined: *O'Gorman* and *Nebbia*.

Why does this history matter? According to the conventional narrative, Justice Roberts changed course for political reasons. Therefore, the argument goes, the Supreme Court is an inherently *political* institution. And because the conventional narrative applauds the "switch in time," a political Supreme Court is a *good* thing. The actual history, however, reveals that politics played a different, more subtle role.

President Herbert Hoover, a political progressive, appointed two progressives: Chief Justice Hughes and Justice Roberts. These appointments, unsurprisingly, moved the Court in a progressive direction. Hughes and Roberts simply had different judicial philosophies about the Constitution than those held by more conservative Justices, such as the Four Horsemen, who were appointed by more conservative presidents.

In this way, popular elections — not intimidation by political actors — changed the constitutional balance of the Supreme Court. The political process by which Justices are selected allows for a Justice with one principled vision of the Constitution to be replaced by a Justice holding a different vision. *West Coast Hotel* was a byproduct of President Hoover appointing two progressive Justices in 1931, not President Roosevelt's partisan tactics in 1937.

West Coast Hotel marked the commencement of what is sometimes called the *constitutional revolution of 1937*. Whenever and however it happened, there is no dispute that a constitutional sea change did occur. During the same period, the Supreme Court also approved a vast expansion of Congress's powers under the Commerce and Necessary and Proper Clauses.

Three months after *West Coast Hotel* was decided, the Four Horsemen disbanded. In June 1937, Justice Van Devanter retired. In January 1938, Justice Sutherland retired. Justice Butler stepped down the following year in November 1939. Thirteen months later, in January 1941, Justice McReynolds left the Court.

During his twelve years in office, President Roosevelt made nine Supreme Court nominations. By 1943, during Roosevelt's unprecedented fourth term in office, he had replaced all members of the once-conservative Court from the Progressive Era. Starting with *O'Gorman* in 1931, a constitutional sea change had occurred. Soon, even more radical changes would come.

Throughout the New Deal, the presumption of constitutionality in *O'Gorman*, *Nebbia*, and *West Coast Hotel* was rebuttable. It was still feasible for plaintiffs to challenge the constitutionality of a law that restricted economic liberty. They could present evidence showing that the restriction was arbitrary. Eventually, however, the Warren Court would make the presumption of constitutionality irrebuttable. The constitutional revolution was completed.

CHAPTER 35

"Economic" Liberty After the New Deal

States cannot deprive people of "life, liberty, or property" without the "due process of law." The "due process of law" requires a judicial process to determine whether a law that deprives a person of "life, liberty, or property" has unconstitutionally exceeded the legislature's power. Such an action is not a valid "law." The Supreme Court has adopted four distinct approaches to decide if the police power permits the enforcement of economic regulations.

During the first three decades of the twentieth century, the Supreme Court reviewed economic regulations with a *rebuttable presumption of liberty*. (See Chapter 34.) That is, the Court presumed that an economic regulation was unconstitutional unless the government could provide factual evidence to show that the regulation was reasonable. Under this approach, the *means* must have a reasonable relation to proper *ends*. Furthermore, the legislature must be competent to pursue those ends. In three cases, the government failed to offer enough evidence to rebut the presumption of liberty: *Lochner v. New York* (1905), *Buchanan v. Warley* (1917), and *Adkins v. Children's Hospital* (1923). Therefore, the laws in those three cases violated the Fourteenth Amendment. In *Muller v. Oregon* (1908), however, the Court reached a different result. All nine Justices agreed that the evidence in the "Brandeis Brief" was persuasive enough to justify the maximum-hour law for female employees.

In 1931, the Court began to move away from the presumption of liberty. Instead, the Court established the *presumption of constitutionality*: Economic regulations were now presumed to be constitutional. Yet that presumption could still be rebutted. How? The person whose liberty was being violated had to persuade the Court that the government was acting unreasonably. This approach most closely resembled Justice Harlan's *Lochner* dissent. The Court applied this rebuttable presumption of constitutionality in three cases: *O'Gorman & Young, Inc. v. Hartford Fire Insurance*

Company (1931), *Nebbia v. New York* (1934), and *West Coast Hotel v. Parrish* (1937). And in each case, the Court upheld the economic regulation as a reasonable exercise of the police power.

In this chapter, we will discuss the Court's third and fourth approaches to reviewing economic regulations. In *United States v. Carolene Products* (1938), the Court qualified the presumption of constitutionality. And in *Williamson v. Lee Optical* (1955), the Court made the presumption of constitutionality nearly impossible to rebut.

United States v. Carolene Products (1938)

ConLaw.us/CaroleneProducts/

The Carolene Products company manufactured a product known as "Milnut." This brand of filled milk was made by removing the dairy fat from whole milk and replacing it with coconut oil. Milnut, which did not have any dairy fat, could be stored in cans without refrigeration. Dairy farmers did not welcome this competition. As a result, they exercised their considerable political clout to persuade legislators to prohibit filled milk. In 1923, Congress banned the shipment of filled milk in interstate commerce. The United States indicted Carolene Products for shipping Milnut in interstate commerce. The government alleged that filled milk was "an adulterated article of food, injurious to the public health." Charles Hauser, the president of Carolene Products, argued in court that the Filled Milk Act deprived him of "property without due process of law." By 1938, the Supreme Court had already established the presumption of constitutionality in cases like *West Coast Hotel.*

Hauser had very low odds of persuading the Court that the Filled Milk Act was an unreasonable and arbitrary deprivation of his property. Yet the Justices agreed that Hauser must still be given a chance to make that argument. Justice Stone wrote the majority opinion in *Carolene Products.* He explained that Hauser could rebut the "presumption of constitutionality" with evidence. For example, even if the ban on filled milk was "valid on its face," Hauser could provide "proof of facts" that the "statute would deny due process." This strategy, however, was not successful in *Carolene Products.* The Court found that there was "affirmative evidence [that] sustain[ed] the" law's constitutionality. Specifically, congressional reports concluded that the "use of filled milk as a substitute for pure milk is generally injurious to health and facilitates fraud on the public."

The bulk of *Carolene Products* was fairly mundane: The decision simply restated how the presumption of constitutionality was rebuttable. This case became famous, however, because of its fourth footnote — the most famous footnote in the annals of the Supreme Court. Footnote Four of *Carolene Products* is over 500 words long and spans across two pages. Each of its three paragraphs identifies different circumstances where courts should not apply the presumption of constitutionality.

The first paragraph of Footnote Four stated that courts should not apply the presumption of constitutionality when reviewing legislation that "appears on its face" to violate "a specific prohibition of the Constitution." Specifically, the presumption is not warranted when a law runs afoul of "the first ten Amendments." For example, the Court should not review a law that violates the freedom of speech with the presumption of constitutionality. Instead, the Court should apply a presumption of liberty: The government has the burden to justify why it is violating that enumerated right. This approach would later become known as "strict scrutiny." Justice Stone added this paragraph at the behest of Chief Justice Hughes. He thought that a law that is "directly opposed to [a specific] constitutional guaranty" — like freedom of speech — "has no presumption [of constitutionality] to support it."

STUDY GUIDE

The Ninth Amendment provides, "The enumeration in the Constitution, of certain rights, shall not be construed to deny or disparage others retained by the people." Does Footnote Four "disparage" rights that are "not enumerated in the Constitution" because they are not enumerated?

In the second paragraph of Footnote Four, Justice Stone speculated that "more exacting judicial scrutiny" may be appropriate when courts review "legislation which restricts those political processes which can ordinarily be expected to bring about repeal of undesirable legislation." For example, he listed "restrictions upon the right to vote," "restraints upon the dissemination of information," "interferences with political organizations," and a "prohibition of peaceable assembly." As a general matter, the Court might trust legislators to make laws for the public good. But judges should be more skeptical when legislators seek to change the rules by which they are elected.

In the third paragraph, Justice Stone speculated that "more exacting judicial scrutiny" may also be appropriate when Courts review "statutes directed at particular religious, or national, or racial minorities." Here, the Court cited *Pierce v. Society of Sisters* (1925) and *Meyer v. Nebraska* (1923).

STUDY GUIDE

Did the Court review the challenged laws in *Pierce* and *Meyer* with a presumption of liberty because the government targeted "religious or national minorities"? Recall that one of the parties, the Hill Military Academy, was not religious at all. Was the First Amendment cited in either case?

Justice Stone further speculated in the third paragraph that a "correspondingly more searching judicial inquiry" may be appropriate when Courts review "statutes directed at . . . discrete and insular minorities." Why? Because "prejudice against" such groups "tends seriously to curtail the operation of those political processes ordinarily to be relied upon to protect minorities."

Due to recusals and dissents, Footnote Four was only joined by four Justices on a seven-member Court. Even so, it is probably the most important footnote in Supreme Court history. It introduced an entire theory of constitutional law and would be cited by the Supreme Court time and again throughout the twentieth century.

Most importantly for our purposes, Footnote Four qualified the presumption of constitutionality: Not *all* legislation should be reviewed with deference. Laws that violated certain favored rights — such as those expressly stated in the Bill of Rights — would be strictly scrutinized. Conveniently, economic liberty rights were not enumerated in the Bill of Rights. Under this approach, laws that restrict such unenumerated rights would be reviewed with a presumption of constitutionality.

Justice Stone's description of the presumption of constitutionality in the main text of *Carolene Products* — not in Footnote Four — resembled Justice Harlan's dissent in *Lochner*. The government will get the benefit of the doubt when courts review laws that restrict individual liberties that are not expressly enumerated in the text of the Constitution. Today, such freedoms are called "liberty interests." Yet, this presumption of constitutionality could still be rebutted — in theory at least. *Williamson v. Lee Optical* (1955), however, made the presumption of constitutionality almost *impossible* to rebut.

Williamson v. Lee Optical (1955)

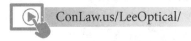 ConLaw.us/LeeOptical/

Before we study *Lee Optical*, let's first settle some vision terminology. *Ophthalmologists* and *optometrists* are licensed doctors. They can perform vision tests, write prescriptions for glasses, and check for eye diseases. In contrast, an *optician* cannot perform vision tests, write prescriptions, or check for diseases. However, an optician can duplicate the prescription from old lenses to new lenses. That service, performed with a device known as a *lensometer*, can be very profitable.

Lee Optical operated a chain of eyeglasses stores throughout the Midwest. Their opticians could independently manufacture new lenses and fit the frames to a customer's face. In response to this new business model, Oklahoma made it illegal for opticians to manufacture new lenses without a prescription from an ophthalmologist or optometrist. Lee Optical argued that the Oklahoma law violated the Fourteenth Amendment's Due Process Clause.

At the time, constitutional challenges to state and federal laws were initially considered by a panel of three federal judges. In *Lee Optical*, the panel reviewed the

Oklahoma law with the rebuttable presumption of constitutionality from *Carolene Products*. The district court recognized that "all legislative enactments are accompanied by a presumption of constitutionality." However, the panel insisted it could still "annul legislative action where it appears certain that the attempted exercise of police power is arbitrary, unreasonable or discriminatory."

Lee Optical was able to present evidence at trial about the *unreasonableness* of the Oklahoma law. In turn, the court could then evaluate the persuasiveness of that evidence. Through this process, Lee Optical could rebut the presumption of constitutionality and prove that the law was unreasonable. Based on Lee Optical's arguments, the panel held that "[t]he means chosen by the legislature" — prohibiting opticians from making lenses — did "not bear 'a real and substantial relation' to the end sought, that is, better vision." Indeed, opticians were *more* qualified than doctors to manufacture lenses. And both doctors and opticians relied on nonmedical staff to operate lensometers.

Furthermore, the court observed that an optician "cannot arbitrarily be divested of a substantial portion of his business *upon the pretext* that such a deprivation is rationally related to the public health." In other words, the Oklahoma law was not a *good faith* effort to promote the public health. Instead, the law was designed to eliminate competition from independent opticians — in this case an out-of-state corporation. The panel found that there was insufficient evidence to prove that the economic regulation actually promoted public health. Therefore, the arbitrary Oklahoma law was unconstitutional.

By 1955, the New Deal was in the rearview mirror. The Supreme Court, now under the leadership of Chief Justice Earl Warren, unanimously reversed the three-judge panel. Justice Douglas's majority opinion made the presumption of constitutionality nearly impossible to rebut. He observed that it was not the role of "the courts to balance the advantages and disadvantages of the" Oklahoma law.

Justice Douglas maintained that it did not matter what the legislature actually intended. It was enough to speculate what the legislature *might* have intended. For example, "the legislature *may* have concluded that eye examinations were so critical, not only for correction of vision but also for detection of latent ailments or diseases, that every change in frames and every duplication of a lens should be accompanied by a prescription from a medical expert."

Of course, the Court acknowledged that "the present law does not require a new examination of the eyes every time the frames are changed or the lenses duplicated." But that reality didn't matter. "The law need not be in every respect logically consistent with its aims to be constitutional," Justice Douglas explained.

Indeed, there is no requirement that the legislature *actually* had a certain intent. Rather, courts are required to uphold laws that are "arbitrary, unreasonable or discriminatory," so long as the government "might" have concluded that the law was reasonable. Justice Douglas offered this simple test: "It is enough that there is an evil at hand for correction, and that it *might* be thought that the particular legislative measure was a rational way to correct it." This form of scrutiny has been dubbed *conceivable basis review*.

In *Carolene Products*, the Court maintained that the due process of law gave a litigant the opportunity to rebut the presumption of constitutionality. She could do so by introducing actual evidence that the law deprived her of life, liberty, or property. But *Lee Optical* held that litigants need not be given an opportunity to rebut the presumption of constitutionality. Justice Douglas made clear that the Court would no longer "strike down state laws, regulatory of business and industrial conditions, because they may be unwise, improvident, or out of harmony with a particular school of thought." He added, "For protection against abuses by legislatures the people must resort to the polls, not to the courts."

STUDY GUIDE

Does the Court only use this sort of deference to review regulations concerning "business and industrial conditions"? Does the Court have the power to set aside "unwise" or "improvident" laws affecting other types of rights?

Let's return to our brief history of the Supreme Court's approach to the Due Process Clause.

- In the first stage, with cases like *Lochner* the Court applied a rebuttable presumption of liberty.
- In the second stage, from *O'Gorman* through *West Coast Hotel*, the Court articulated a rebuttable presumption of constitutionality. This approach resembled Justice Harlan's *Lochner* dissent.
- Third, in Footnote Four of *Carolene Products*, the Court qualified the presumption of constitutionality. Laws that violated express prohibitions in the Constitution — such as those enumerated in the Bill of Rights — would be reviewed with a rebuttable presumption of liberty. However, laws restricting unenumerated rights — especially economic liberties — would still be reviewed with a rebuttable presumption of constitutionality.
- The fourth stage began with *Lee Optical* in 1955. The judiciary would no longer allow challengers to offer evidence to rebut the presumption of constitutionality when laws restricted unenumerated rights. Such laws were now held to be rational, and thus constitutional, if the courts could imagine a conceivable basis for their enactment. The Warren Court's approach to the Due Process Clause now closely resembled Justice Holmes's *Lochner* dissent. In that case, Justice Holmes would have upheld the maximum-hours law because "[a] reasonable man might think it a proper measure on the score of health." Taken literally, such a presumption of constitutionality is nearly impossible to rebut.

PART VIII

EQUAL PROTECTION OF THE LAW: DISCRIMINATION ON THE BASIS OF RACE

The modern story of desegregation begins with *Brown v. Board of Education* and *Bolling v. Sharpe*, both decided in 1954. After these decisions were met with massive resistance, the Supreme Court responded in *Cooper v. Aaron* (1958). Next, in *Loving v. Virginia* (1967), the Supreme Court declared unconstitutional a ban on interracial marriage. The Court then turned to the constitutionality of affirmative action. The Burger and Rehnquist Courts decided three important cases: *Regents of the University of California v. Bakke* (1978), *Grutter v. Bollinger* (2003), and *Gratz v. Bollinger* (2003). More recently, the Roberts Court decided two affirmative action cases: *Fisher v. University of Texas, Austin I* (2013) and *Fisher v. University of Texas, Austin II* (2016).

CHAPTER 36

The School Desegregation Cases

Less than three decades after the ratification of the Fourteenth Amendment, the Supreme Court decided *Plessy v. Ferguson* (1896). This *anti-canonical* case held that the government could segregate public accommodations, such as railroads, so long as the separate facilities were "equal." Over the next five decades, *Plessy* institutionalized racial segregation throughout the country.

That tide, however, would begin to turn in the 1930s. The National Association for the Advancement of Colored People (NAACP) mounted a broad constitutional attack on the "separate but equal" doctrine. Initially, the NAACP asserted that schooling offered to African-American students was not actually equal. The strategy aimed to raise the cost of segregation. The Southern states would have to either spend more money on segregated schools or abolish segregated schools altogether. In a string of victories, the Supreme Court found that the government was not in fact providing "separate but equal" education. Eventually, the NAACP decided the time was right to directly confront *Plessy* itself.

Brown v. Board of Education (1954)

 ConLaw.us/Brown/

In *Brown v. Board of Education* (1954), the NAACP challenged the constitutionality of school segregation laws in Kansas, South Carolina, Virginia, and Delaware. *Brown* was initially argued in December 1952, but the Justices could not reach a decision. The case was then scheduled for reargument the following year.

The decision to have the case reargued likely changed its fate. Chief Justice Fred Vinson died in September 1953. President Eisenhower filled that vacancy with Earl Warren, the Republican governor of California. With his political leadership experience, Warren was able to cajole his colleagues to reach a unanimous, though narrow, decision: school segregation laws violated the Equal Protection Clause of the Fourteenth Amendment. Chief Justice Warren's majority decision had three major parts.

First, the Court found that the case could not be resolved based on the history of the Fourteenth Amendment. The Justices could not determine whether those who wrote or ratified the Fourteenth Amendment expected that it would make segregated schools unconstitutional: "[W]e cannot turn the clock back to 1868 when the Amendment was adopted," Chief Justice Warren explained, "or even to 1896 when *Plessy v. Ferguson* was written." Because history did not provide a clear answer, the Court instead evaluated "public education in the light of its full development and its present place in American life." The Court stressed that education "is the very foundation of good citizenship."

Second, the Justices based their ruling on social science research: "[I]t is doubtful that any child may reasonably be expected to succeed in life if he is denied the opportunity of an education." The Justices concluded that "segregation of children in public schools solely on the basis of race . . . deprive[s] the children of the minority group of equal educational opportunities."

STUDY GUIDE

What role should social science play in the development of constitutional law?

Third, the Court stopped short of overruling *Plessy v. Ferguson*. Rather, the Court found that *Plessy* was inconsistent with the findings of social science. Separate could not be equal because "[s]egregation of white and colored children in public schools has a detrimental effect upon the colored children." In short, when it came to education, "separate" was inherently "unequal." Therefore, the school segregation laws in Kansas, South Carolina, Virginia, and Delaware violated the Equal Protection Clause of the Fourteenth Amendment.

Bolling v. Sharpe (1954)

ConLaw.us/Bolling/

Brown concerned whether *state* school segregation laws violated the Fourteenth Amendment. The Fourteenth Amendment, however, is understood only to restrict the *state's* police powers — not the federal government's powers. The Fifth Amendment's Due Process Clause, however, does limit federal power. It provides that "no person shall be . . . deprived of life, liberty, or property, without due process of law." When *Brown* was decided, federal law segregated public schools in the District of Columbia. In *Bolling v. Sharpe*, decided the same day as *Brown*, the Court found that federal school segregation law violated the Fifth Amendment's Due Process Clause.

Chief Justice Warren also wrote the unanimous opinion in *Bolling*. He admitted that "[t]he Fifth Amendment, which is applicable in the District of Columbia, does not contain an equal protection clause as does the Fourteenth Amendment which applies only to the states." Yet he found "that racial segregation in the public schools of the District of Columbia is a denial of the due process of law guaranteed by the Fifth Amendment to the Constitution." Why? "In view of [our decision in *Brown*] that the Constitution prohibits the states from maintaining racially segregated public schools," he explained, "it would be unthinkable that the same Constitution would impose a lesser duty on the Federal Government."

Because the Equal Protection Clause does not restrict federal power, the Court instead reasoned that racial "discrimination may be so unjustifiable as to be violative of due process." Here, the Court relied on *Buchanan v. Warley* (1917), which we discussed in Chapter 32. This Progressive Era case "held that a statute which limited the right of a property owner to convey his property to a person of another race was, as an unreasonable discrimination, a denial of due process of law."

Segregated schools, the Court held, deprived the children of *liberty*. "Liberty under law extends to the full range of conduct which the individual is free to pursue," the Chief Justice wrote. And that liberty "cannot be restricted except for a proper governmental objective." The Court observed, "Segregation in public education is not reasonably related to any proper governmental objective, and thus it imposes on Negro children of the District of Columbia a burden that constitutes an arbitrary deprivation of their liberty in violation of the Due Process Clause."

STUDY GUIDE

Does the Court's analysis in *Bolling* raise any doubts about its analysis in *Brown*?

The holding in *Brown* was based only on the Equal Protection Clause of the Fourteenth Amendment. Consider a hypothetical scenario in which Section 1 of the Fourteenth Amendment did not include an Equal Protection Clause. In that case, *Brown* should have come out differently. In *Bolling*, however, the Court was willing to reach the same result as it had in *Brown*—segregated schools were unconstitutional—even though there is no Equal Protection Clause that limits the federal government's powers.

This hypothetical scenario raises several questions about the actual reasoning of both cases. First, was *Brown* really based on—much less dictated by—the Equal Protection Clause? After all, the Court did not need that provision in *Bolling* to declare unconstitutional the segregated schools in the District of Columbia. Or was *Bolling* wrongly decided? If the Equal Protection Clause *was* needed in *Brown*, and there is no Equal Protection Clause to constrain federal powers, then Congress should have had the power to segregate schools in the District of Columbia. Can the outcomes of *Brown* and *Bolling* be reconciled with each other and with the scope of the Fifth and Fourteenth Amendments?

In an influential article, Professor Michael McConnell contended that the outcome of *Brown* was consistent with the original meaning of the Fourteenth Amendment.[1] His analysis focused on the debates that led to the Civil Rights Act of 1875. Those debates revealed that most congressional Republicans — and virtually all members who had voted for the Fourteenth Amendment — thought that attendance at public schools was a "privilege" of citizenship. Senator Matthew Carpenter of Wisconsin, for example, stated, "All contribute to the taxes for their support; all are benefited by the education given to the rising generation; and therefore all are entitled to equal *privileges* in the public schools."

If Professor McConnell's historical claim is correct, then *Brown* and *Bolling* can be justified on the *very same grounds*: Neither the federal nor the state government can abridge the privileges of national citizenship.

The Fourteenth Amendment recognized that all persons born in the United States are "citizens of the United States." Professor Akhil Amar explained that the Citizenship Clause "creates rights of equal citizenship that apply against all governments, state and federal."[2] The Fourteenth Amendment also provides that "[n]o State shall make or enforce any law which shall abridge the privileges or immunities of citizens of the United States." This provision gave federal courts the power to review state laws that abridge these rights. (See Chapter 29.) But this provision also affirmed that "citizens of the United States" *have* "privileges or immunities" of citizenship.

If Professor McConnell is correct that attending a public school had become a "privilege . . . of citizens of the United States," then the states could not enact segregation laws that abridged this right. State segregation laws violated the Privileges or Immunities Clause, not the Equal Protection Clause. Specifically, the state segregation laws violated a privilege of *U.S. citizens*. This holding, however, is not limited to state laws. Congress, too, is barred from abridging the privileges of national citizenship. Therefore, federal segregated schools also abridged a privilege of *U.S. citizens* in the District of Columbia.

Instead of relying on the Equal Protection Clause, *Brown* could have held that the state segregation laws violated the Privileges or Immunities Clause of the Fourteenth Amendment. These laws abridged a privilege of U.S. citizens. And, instead of relying on the Due Process Clause of the Fifth Amendment, *Bolling* could have held that the federal segregation law abridged *the very same privilege* of those who the Citizenship Clause of the Fourteenth Amendment declared to be citizens of the United States. If this argument is correct, then the absence of an Equal Protection Clause is no longer problematic for *Bolling*.

---

1. Michael W. McConnell, Originalism and the Desegregation Decision, 81 Va. L. Rev. 947 (1995).

2. Akhil Reed Amar, America's Unwritten Constitution: The Precedents and Principles We Live By 150 (2012).

STUDY GUIDE

After *Brown* and *Bolling*, was segregation unconstitutional in all government institutions nationwide?

In *Brown* and *Bolling*, the Court did not order that all schools nationwide must desegregate immediately. Instead, the Court ordered re-arguments on how to implement the decision. One year later, the Justices decided a case known as *Brown v. Board of Education II* (1955). The Court instructed the lower courts to ensure that public schools would be integrated "with all deliberate speed [as to] the parties to these cases." Alas, that decree would not be heeded. School districts throughout the South, as part of the "Massive Resistance," tenaciously fought against integration. That battle reached the Supreme Court in our next case, *Cooper v. Aaron* (1958).

CHAPTER 37

Cooper v. Aaron (1958)

 ConLaw.us/Cooper/

Brown v. Board of Education was decided in 1954. At the time, nearly two dozen states racially segregated their public schools. *Brown* only considered the constitutionality of the laws in four of those states: Kansas, South Carolina, Virginia, and Delaware. In a unanimous decision, the Warren Court found that segregated public schools violated the Fourteenth Amendment. However, the Court did not order that all schools nationwide must desegregate immediately. Instead, the Court ordered another round of oral argument to decide how *Brown* should be implemented.

One year later, in *Brown v. Board of Education II* (1955) — or simply *Brown II* — the Justices issued an order to the lower courts in Kansas, South Carolina, and Virginia: "enter such orders and decrees consistent with this opinion as are necessary and proper to admit to public schools on a racially nondiscriminatory basis with all deliberate speed the parties to these cases." Officials in these three states were now bound by the Supreme Court's judgment to integrate their schools with "all deliberate speed." (The Delaware courts had already found that the segregated schools were unlawful.) But what about the other states that were not parties in *Brown*? *Cooper v. Aaron* (1958) would resolve this question.

In 1955, the Little Rock, Arkansas, school board approved a plan for gradual integration. However, the so-called "Massive Resistance" spread to Arkansas. Citizens approved an amendment to the state constitution that opposed *Brown* and desegregation. Based on that amendment, a state court judge issued an injunction against members of the Little Rock school board. They were ordered to stop the implementation of the federal court's integration plan at Central High School.

STUDY GUIDE

Brown I only involved cases from Virginia, South Carolina, Kansas, and Delaware. Was the Little Rock school board bound by *Brown I*? By *Brown II*?

In response, a federal district court issued an order to block the state court injunction. The situation escalated quickly. Governor Orval Faubus ordered the Arkansas National Guard to prevent black students from entering Central High School. The National Guard blocked nine African-American students — known as the Little Rock Nine — from entering Central High School. Neither Faubus nor the Guard were bound by the previous court order, which only applied to members of the school board. The situation then escalated further. A federal court enjoined the National Guard from blocking access for the African-American students. In response, the Little Rock Police Department replaced the National Guard. The police had not been included in the prior court order that bound the National Guard.

Two days later, in one of the most dramatic moments of the Civil Rights Movement, President Eisenhower dispatched the 101st Airborne to Arkansas. "Mob rule cannot be allowed to override the decisions of our courts," he said. This storied division of U.S. Army paratroopers had fought their way across Europe in World War II and held their ground at the Battle of the Bulge. Now they were deployed to Little Rock, Arkansas. The troops escorted the Little Rock Nine into Central High School. Throughout the remainder of the year, the students attended class under the supervision of federal paratroopers.

STUDY GUIDE

What would have happened if President Eisenhower chose not to send in federal troops?

Even after the federal intervention, the opposition to the desegregation plan did not subside. As a result, the district court granted the school board a thirty-month extension to integrate Central High School. The judge found that a delay was warranted, because the integration plan had caused "chaos, bedlam, and turmoil" in Little Rock. The Eighth Circuit Court of Appeals reversed the district court's judgment because the school board did not advance a sufficient basis to suspend the integration plan.

Shortly before the start of the semester, the Supreme Court convened for an emergency hearing. The question presented was fairly narrow: Was the thirty-month extension given to the school board consistent with *Brown*'s requirement to integrate with "all deliberate speed"? During oral arguments, the lawyer for the school board told the Court, "It was certainly not anticipated at the time [the] plan was formulated that the Governor of the State of Arkansas would call out troops to keep integration in the schools from taking place." Therefore, he claimed, a delay was warranted. The school board simply needed more time to deal with the unexpected circumstances. The Court was not persuaded by his argument. Chief Justice Earl Warren asked the attorney, "Can we defer a program of this kind merely because there are those elements in the community that will commit violence to prevent it from going into effect?"

Ultimately, the Supreme Court ruled that the delay was not permissible: "The constitutional rights of respondents are not to be sacrificed or yielded to the violence and disorder which have followed upon the actions of the Governor and Legislature." In an unprecedented showing of unanimity, the opinion was signed by each of the nine Justices. However, the Court did not stop there. The Justices then proceeded to "answer the premise of the actions of the Governor and Legislature that they are not bound by our holding in the *Brown* case."

STUDY GUIDE

Article VI provides that the Constitution "shall be the supreme Law of the Land." Does Article VI state that a decision of the Supreme Court is the "supreme Law of the Land"?

The lawyer for the school board suggested that the people of Arkansas believed it did not: "If the Governor of any State says that a United State Supreme Court decision is not the law of the land, the people of that state until it is really resolved have a doubt in their mind and a right to have a doubt." He added, "The School Board, a creature of the State is placed between the millstones and a conflict between the State and federal courts."

Once again, Chief Justice Warren was not persuaded: "I have never heard such an argument made in the Court of Justice before." Thurgood Marshall argued on behalf of the NAACP. He urged the Court to "make it clear even to the politicians in Arkansas, that Article VI of the Constitution means what it says." The Court agreed with Marshall: The "interpretation of the Fourteenth Amendment enunciated by this Court in the *Brown* case is the supreme law of the land." Therefore, *Brown* bound all politicians in Arkansas by virtue of the Supremacy Clause.

STUDY GUIDE

Did *Marbury v. Madison* hold that the decisions of the Supreme Court are the "supreme Law of the Land"?

The immediate aftermath of *Cooper* was bleak. Hours after the case was decided, Governor Faubus leased all of the public schools in Little Rock to a private corporation, which was not bound by the Fourteenth Amendment. After the courts halted this new scheme, the government simply closed public schools for the remainder of the year. Indeed, schools in many states shut down rather than integrate. Having made its decision in *Cooper*, the Court would wait nearly five years before hearing another school desegregation case. Ultimately, schools in Little Rock would not be fully integrated for more than a decade.

CHAPTER 38

Loving v. Virginia (1967)

ConLaw.us/Loving/

In 1924, Virginia enacted the Sterilization Act and the Racial Integrity Act. The former law allowed the government to forcibly sterilize so-called "imbeciles." The latter law prohibited interracial marriage, or "miscegenation." Both Acts were designed to promote scientific eugenics. In *Buck v. Bell* (1927), the Supreme Court upheld the constitutionality of the Sterilization Act. (See Chapter 33.) Four decades later, the Court declared the Racial Integrity Act unconstitutional in *Loving v. Virginia* (1967).

In 1958, Mildred Jeter, a black woman, and Richard Loving, a white man, lived together in Virginia. Under state law, it was illegal for interracial couples to get married or to live together as though they were married. Because of the Racial Integrity Act, the Lovings travelled to the District of Columbia to get married there. Upon their return to Virginia as husband and wife the Lovings were arrested. The police knocked down their door in the dark of night. They were dragged out of bed and jailed. Richard was released on bail, but Mildred was forced to spend the weekend alone in jail. At the time she was pregnant.

Both Richard and Mildred were indicted for violating the Racial Integrity Act. They pleaded guilty to the charges. The Virginia trial judge proudly endorsed the miscegenation ban: "Almighty God created the races white, black, yellow, malay and red, and he placed them on separate continents. And but for the interference with his arrangement there would be no cause for such marriages. The fact that he separated the races shows that he did not intend for the races to mix."

The Lovings were sentenced to one year in prison. However, the trial judge suspended the sentence on the condition that the Lovings leave Virginia and not return for twenty-five years. In 1963, the Lovings filed a motion in state court to set aside their convictions. The couple argued that the state law violated the Fourteenth

Amendment. The state court upheld their convictions. The United States Supreme Court agreed to hear their appeal.

At the time, sixteen states banned interracial marriages through anti-miscegenation laws. Miscegenation is defined as a mixture of races, especially, marriage, cohabitation, or sexual intercourse between a white person and a member of another race.

The Lovings made two primary constitutional arguments. First, they contended that the miscegenation ban violated the Fourteenth Amendment's Equal Protection Clause. That Clause provides that a state cannot "deny to any person within its jurisdiction the equal protection of the laws." Virginia responded that the law did not run afoul of the Equal Protection Clause because it treated the races equally. A white man could not marry a black woman, and a black woman could not marry a white man. In other words, the law "applied" equally to white and black people alike. Moreover, Virginia made a historical argument: Those who framed the Civil Rights Act of 1866 and the Freedmen's Bureau Act did not intend to prevent states from banning interracial marriage.

The Supreme Court agreed with the Lovings' first argument: Virginia's law violated the Fourteenth Amendment's Equal Protection Clause. Chief Justice Warren wrote the majority opinion. He rejected "the notion that the mere 'equal application' of a statute containing racial classifications is enough to remove the classifications from the Fourteenth Amendment's proscription of all invidious racial discriminations." Chief Justice Warren added, "The clear and central purpose of the Fourteenth Amendment was to eliminate all official state sources of invidious racial discrimination in the States."

The Court reviewed the Racial Integrity Act with the "most rigid scrutiny," or what the Court now refers to as "strict scrutiny." Such a racial classification is valid only if it is "shown to be necessary to the accomplishment of some permissible state objective, independent of the racial discrimination which it was the object of the Fourteenth Amendment to eliminate."

Virginia did not dispute that the miscegenation ban was designed to advance racial discrimination. However, Virginia's lawyer offered an alternative justification for the policy: "This statute serves a legitimate, legislative objective of preventing the sociological, psychological evils which attend interracial marriages, and is an expression, a rational expression of a policy which Virginia has a right to adopt." What was that "rational" basis? Virginia's lawyer argued that "interracial marriages are detrimental to the individual, to the family, and to society." These unions, he contended, were especially harmful to the mental health of biracial children. The lawyer stated that "interracial marriages bequeath to the progeny of those marriages, more psychological problems than parents have a right to bequeath to them."

STUDY GUIDE

What police power justification is offered in support of the interracial marriage ban?

During oral arguments, the Justices were skeptical that the Virginia law was in fact a good-faith exercise of the police power to protect the public health. Justice Hugo Black posed the question plainly: "Is there any doubt in your mind that the object of these statutes, the basic premise on which they rest, is that the white people are superior to the colored people and should not be permitted to marry?" Ultimately, the Court concluded that Virginia's law did not pursue any permissible state objective. Rather, the law was "designed to maintain White Supremacy." Therefore, it violated the Equal Protection Clause.

The Lovings' second argument focused on the Fourteenth Amendment's Due Process Clause. It provides, "nor shall any State deprive any person of life, liberty, or property, without due process of law." The Lovings argued that they were being denied "liberty" — in particular, the liberty to marry. In an interview, Mildred Loving stated the issue directly: "I think you can marry who you want to, [this] is a right that no man should have anything to do with. It is a God-given right, I think." "No man" included the men in the Virginia legislature.

The Court held in *Brown v. Board of Education* (1954), and in other cases, that the state did not have a legitimate interest to discriminate. Likewise, the state lacked a legitimate interest to restrict the exercise of the right to marry. Specifically, Virginia's aim of promoting white supremacy was not within the competency of the state legislature.

The Court's Due Process Clause analysis was only two paragraphs long. Let's walk through each step carefully. First, the Court stated that the Virginia law "deprive[s] the Lovings of liberty without due process of law in violation of the Due Process Clause of the Fourteenth Amendment."

Second, Chief Justice Warren explained that "[t]he freedom to marry has long been recognized as one of the vital personal rights essential to the orderly pursuit of happiness by free men." He added, "Marriage is one of the 'basic civil rights of man,' fundamental to our very existence and survival."

STUDY GUIDE

Why is marriage "fundamental to the survival of mankind"?

Marriage was considered a fundamental right because, at the time, it was the only legal means of having children. All other types of sexual activity — especially procreative activity — outside of marriage were barred by laws governing adultery, fornication, sodomy, incest, and bigamy. Indeed, the offspring of unmarried parents were denied certain rights as "illegitimate" children. If the Lovings could not legally marry, they could not legally procreate.

Third, the Court then construed the Due Process Clause in light of "the principle of equality" underlying the Fourteenth Amendment as a whole: "To deny this fundamental freedom on so unsupportable a basis as the racial classifications embodied in these statutes, classifications so directly subversive of the principle of equality at the heart of the Fourteenth Amendment, is surely to deprive all the State's citizens of liberty without due process of law." Based on this reasoning, Chief Justice Warren concluded, "Under our Constitution, the freedom to marry, or not marry, a person of another race resides with the individual and cannot be infringed by the State."

STUDY GUIDE

Is *Loving* consistent with the New Deal Court's "judicial conservatism" and deference to legislative will? The Court relies on Due Process Clause cases from the Progressive Era. Why is this choice significant?

We will return to the state's police power to regulate marriage when we study *Obergefell v. Hodges* (2015). This decision declared unconstitutional state prohibitions on same-sex marriage.

CHAPTER 39

Affirmative Action on the Burger and Rehnquist Courts

Most students are familiar with the concept of "affirmative action" but likely do not know the phrase's origin. In 1961, President John F. Kennedy issued Executive Order No. 10925. It barred government contractors from engaging in racial discrimination. The order, however, did not simply prohibit discrimination. It also required that federal contractors "take *affirmative action* to ensure that applicants are employed, and that employees are treated during employment, without regard to their race, creed, color, or national origin." That is, positive steps must be taken, above and beyond race-neutral hiring practices, to increase employment opportunities for minorities. The concept of affirmative action would soon be extended beyond federal government contracting.

Regents of the University of California v. Bakke (1978)

 ConLaw.us/Bakke/

In *Regents of the University of California v. Bakke* (1978), the Supreme Court considered the constitutionality of affirmative action in higher education. The medical school at the University of California, Davis, denied admission to Allan Bakke, a white man. At the time, there were 100 seats in the entering class. Sixteen seats were set aside for minority applicants. Bakke could not compete for those spots. He argued that the quota system violated the Equal Protection

Clause of the Fourteenth Amendment. Bakke also claimed that the admissions policy violated Title VI of the Civil Rights Act of 1964. That statute prohibited racial discrimination by schools that accept federal funding.

The Supreme Court sharply divided in *Bakke*. The breakdown was somewhat confusing.

- Four Justices found that race-conscious affirmative-action programs did not violate either the Equal Protection Clause of the Fourteenth Amendment or Title VI. Justices Brennan, White, Marshall, and Blackmun would have upheld the admissions policy in its entirety.
- Four other Justices did not reach the constitutional question because they found that Davis's race-conscious policy violated Title VI: Chief Justice Burger and Justices Stewart, Rehnquist, and Stevens.
- Justice Powell was somewhere in the middle. He found that, in theory at least, the College *could* make admissions decisions based on race, if the affirmative-action policy was narrowly tailored — that is, if race was considered as one factor, among other factors — to obtain educational diversity. This conclusion was in accord with that of Justices Brennan, White, Marshall, and Blackmun.
- But Justice Powell found that Davis's race-conscious policy in this case was unconstitutional because it was *not* narrowly tailored. This conclusion was in accord with that of Chief Justice Burger and Justices Stewart, Rehnquist, and Stevens.

Justice Powell approved of affirmative-action admissions policies only when race was used as a factor to achieve educational diversity. This opinion, the most narrow, was considered controlling. He observed that Davis reserved sixteen out of 100 seats exclusively for three categories of racial minorities. Such racial classifications by the state are "inherently *suspect*" and must be subjected to "the most exacting judicial scrutiny." Davis's admissions policy could satisfy strict scrutiny only if it was necessary to "further[] a compelling state interest."

The university argued that it had a compelling interest: to "redress" racial imbalance that was said to result from general societal discrimination against the minority groups selected for preferential treatment. Justice Powell rejected this rationale. There was no evidence that the imbalance was traceable to the university's own discriminatory practices. Discrimination by "society at large" is not sufficient to justify the university's racial classification.

But Justice Powell did identify one compelling interest that could support an affirmative-action policy: "obtaining the educational benefits that flow from an ethnically diverse student body." He grounded this conclusion in the concept of "academic freedom," which "long has been viewed as a special concern of the First Amendment."

Ultimately, then, there was only one interest that was compelling enough to justify a racial classification: the educational benefits that flow from a diverse student body. But Davis's quota system was not narrowly tailored to pursue that interest. The university's quota system totally excluded all applicants who were "not Negro, Asian or Chicano" from sixteen of the 100 seats in the entering class. This policy was not necessary to obtain reasonable educational diversity.

In contrast, Justice Powell praised the Harvard Admissions Program as an example of how race properly could be taken into account. Harvard University did not set a quota. According to Justice Powell, race was merely one factor weighed competitively against a number of other factors deemed relevant. Justice Powell held that "race may be considered as a relevant factor."

In the end, Bakke was admitted and graduated from the medical school. The precise holding of *Bakke*, and status of Justice Powell's solo concurring opinion, would remain unclear for the next twenty-five years.

Gratz v. Bollinger (2003)

 ConLaw.us/Gratz/

In 2003, the Supreme Court decided a pair of affirmative-action cases from the University of Michigan. The first case, *Gratz v. Bollinger*, challenged the university's undergraduate affirmative-action policy. The second case, *Grutter v. Bollinger*, challenged the law school's affirmative-action policy.

The university's undergraduate admissions office employed a selection index. An applicant could score a maximum of 150 points. A score of 100 points guaranteed admission. Each applicant would receive points based on factors such as high school grade point average, standardized test scores, alumni relationship, and personal achievement. The university assigned a numerical value to an applicant's race, which was the single largest factor. The Court observed, "under a 'miscellaneous' category, an applicant was entitled to 20 points based upon his or her membership in an underrepresented racial or ethnic minority group."

The Court found that this policy violated the Equal Protection Clause of the Fourteenth Amendment: "The University's current policy, which distributes 20 points to every underrepresented minority applicant solely because of race, is not narrowly tailored to achieve respondents' asserted interest in diversity." Unlike the Harvard policy, which Justice Powell endorsed, Michigan's "automatic distribution makes race decisive for virtually every minimally qualified underrepresented minority applicant." The vote in *Gratz* was 6-3. Chief Justice Rehnquist wrote the majority opinion, which was joined by Justices O'Connor, Scalia, Kennedy, Thomas, and Breyer. He found that the undergraduate policy was unconstitutional. Justices Stevens, Souter, and Ginsburg dissented.

Grutter v. Bollinger (2003)

 ConLaw.us/Grutter/

The vote in *Grutter v. Bollinger* went 5-4 the other way. Justice O'Connor wrote the majority opinion, which was joined by Justices Stevens, Souter, Ginsburg, and

Breyer. She found that the law school's admissions policy was constitutional. Chief Justice Rehnquist and Justices Scalia, Kennedy, and Thomas dissented.

Why was the University of Michigan's undergraduate policy set aside but the law school policy upheld? The law school did not assign a numerical value to an applicant's race, as did the undergraduate policy. Instead, the law school considered race as a "plus" factor among many other factors. Moreover, the law school gave serious consideration to all the ways besides race that an applicant might contribute to a diverse educational environment. Specifically, the majority found that the law school engaged in a "highly individualized, holistic review of each applicant's file." Furthermore, Justice O'Connor explained that the law school's pursuit of a critical mass of underrepresented minorities did not operate as a quota or a two-track admission system.

STUDY GUIDE

Is there a specific number of minority students that would constitute a "critical mass"? If so, how is that number different from the quota system that was rejected in *Bakke*? If not, how can the university ever know that such a "critical mass" is reached?

The five-member *Grutter* majority adopted Justice Powell's diversity rationale from *Bakke*: It held that the law school's use of race in admissions was "narrowly tailored to further a compelling state interest" in "assembling a diverse student body." Justice O'Connor admitted that "race-conscious admissions policies must be limited in time."

STUDY GUIDE

Are you persuaded that Justice O'Connor was indeed applying strict scrutiny?

Justice Thomas dissented. Racial classifications designed to hurt minorities, he contended, were no different than "benign" racial classifications designed to help minorities. In contrast, progressive Justices have contended that only "invidious," or harmful, uses of race are prohibited. For example, in *Adarand Constructors v. Peña* (1995), Justice Stevens wrote that there was a "difference between a 'No Trespassing' sign and a welcome mat."

Justice Thomas vehemently disagreed with this approach. He quoted Frederick Douglass, the Great Abolitionist: "What I ask for the negro is not benevolence, not pity, not sympathy, but simply justice. The American people have always been anxious to know what they shall do with us. . . . I have had but one answer from the beginning. Do nothing with us." Justice Thomas explained, "Like Douglass,

I believe blacks can achieve in every avenue of American life without the meddling of university administrators." He wrote that "[t]he Constitution abhors classifications based on race" because "every time the government places citizens on racial registers and makes race relevant to the provision of burdens or benefits, it demeans us all."

The Justices on the Burger and Rehnquist Courts remained divided about the proper use of racial classifications in educational admissions programs, as well as in other contexts. In Chapter 40, we will examine how the Justices on the Roberts Court divided over these issues.

Affirmative Action on the Roberts Court

Justice Powell wrote the controlling opinion in *Regents of the University of California v. Bakke* (1978). He found that, under specific circumstances, affirmative action can be a constitutional means to promote educational diversity on campus. Twenty-five years later, the Court decided *Grutter v. Bollinger* (2003). The University of Michigan Law School's "holistic" admissions policy was constitutional because it considered race as a "plus" factor. Justice O'Connor cast the deciding vote in *Grutter*. Chief Justice Rehnquist was in dissent. Two years later, the composition of the Court would change. In 2005, Justice O'Connor announced her retirement. She was replaced by Justice Alito. When Chief Justice Rehnquist passed away in 2005, he was replaced by Chief Justice Roberts. In 2009, Justice Sotomayor replaced Justice Souter. The following year, Justice Kagan replaced Justice Stevens. This newly constituted Roberts Court would revisit the issue of affirmative action in higher education with a pair of cases from the University of Texas at Austin.

Fisher v. University of Texas I (2013)

ConLaw.us/FisherI/

Following *Grutter*, the University of Texas at Austin adopted a race-conscious admissions policy. Race was considered as one of various factors. Abigail Fisher, who is white, sued the university after her application was rejected. She contended that the university's consideration of race in the admissions process violated the Equal Protection Clause of the Fourteenth Amendment.

The lower courts ruled against Fisher. The Fifth Circuit Court of Appeals deferred to the university "both in the definition of the compelling interest in diversity's benefits and in deciding whether its specific plan was narrowly tailored to achieve its stated goal." Therefore, the appeals court upheld the admissions policy.

In 2013, the Supreme Court ruled for Fisher by a 7-1 vote. (Justice Kagan recused.) Because Abigail Fisher would return to the Court in 2016, this decision is called *Fisher I*. Justice Kennedy, who dissented in *Grutter*, wrote the majority opinion. He concluded that the Fifth Circuit's deferential approach was inconsistent with strict scrutiny:

> Once the University has established that *its goal* of diversity is consistent with strict scrutiny, however, there must still be a further judicial determination that the admissions process meets strict scrutiny in *its implementation*. The University must prove that *the means chosen* by the University to attain diversity are *narrowly tailored to that goal*. On this point, the University receives no deference.

The university had the burden to demonstrate that "each applicant is evaluated as an individual and not in a way that makes an applicant's race or ethnicity the defining feature of his or her application." Moreover, the Court observed, "[n]arrow tailoring also requires that the reviewing court verify that it is 'necessary' for a university to use race to achieve the educational benefits of diversity. This [process] involves a careful judicial inquiry into whether a university could achieve sufficient diversity without using racial classifications." But the Court stopped short of declaring the university's policy unconstitutional. Instead, the Court remanded the case so the Fifth Circuit could review the policy with strict scrutiny.

Justice Thomas dissented in *Fisher I*. He urged the Court to overrule *Grutter*, in which he had dissented a decade earlier. In his view, affirmative action did not pursue a "compelling" interest: "There is nothing 'pressing' or 'necessary' about obtaining whatever educational benefits may flow from racial diversity." For Justice Thomas, the University of Texas's "argument that educational benefits justify racial discrimination" was identical to the argument "advanced in support of racial segregation in" *Brown v. Board of Education*.

In June 2013, *Fisher I* was remanded back to the Fifth Circuit Court of Appeals. Notwithstanding Justice Kennedy's admonition that the lower court failed to properly apply strict scrutiny, once again the same three-judge panel upheld the university's affirmative-action policy. And, once again, the Supreme Court granted review.

Fisher v. University of Texas II (2016)

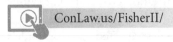 ConLaw.us/FisherII/

Fisher II was argued on December 9, 2015, before eight Justices. (Justice Kagan once again recused.) Justice Scalia seemed like a solid vote to rule against the

University of Texas. Likewise, Chief Justice Roberts, along with Justices Thomas and Alito, have consistently found that affirmative-action programs were unconstitutional. During oral argument, Justices Ginsburg, Breyer, and Sotomayor seemed to support the constitutionality of the university's policy. That breakdown left Justice Kennedy as the deciding vote. But with only eight Justices, at best Justice Kennedy's fourth vote for the liberal wing could yield a tie. A 4-4 vote would simply affirm the lower court ruling, without setting any precedent.

Two months after the case was argued, and after authorship of the majority opinion was assigned, Justice Scalia suddenly passed away. His death almost certainly changed the outcome of *Fisher II*. Instead of a 4-4 tie with no precedential value, the Court upheld the University of Texas's policy by a 4-3 vote. Justice Kennedy wrote the majority opinion, joined by Justices Ginsburg, Breyer, and Sotomayor. He concluded that "[t]he record here reveals that the university articulated concrete and precise goals" with respect to its admissions decisions. These goals, the Court found, were sufficient to satisfy strict scrutiny.

STUDY GUIDE

Did anything in the record change between *Fisher I* and *Fisher II*?

Justice Thomas dissented. He repeated his call from *Fisher I* to overrule *Grutter*. The majority opinion, he wrote, "is irreconcilable with strict scrutiny, rests on pernicious assumptions about race, and departs from many of our precedents."

Justice Alito wrote a separate dissent, joined by Chief Justice Roberts and Justice Thomas. "Something strange has happened since our prior decision in this case," Justice Alito announced from the bench. Following the remand in *Fisher I*, he said, "[t]he University has still not identified with any degree of specificity the interests that its use of race and ethnicity is supposed to serve." Yet the Court in *Fisher II* "effectively defers to the judgment of the University of Texas that its plan is necessary to achieve a vaguely defined objective, the educational benefits of diversity." Justice Alito maintained that "[s]uch deference is inconsistent with *Fisher I* and with the very idea of strict scrutiny." For this reason, he concluded that Justice Kennedy's opinion for four Justices is "simply wrong." Justice Alito also signaled that Justice Scalia's passing may have resulted in the Court's changed direction. He concluded, "I hope this is a one-off attributable to unique circumstances."

STUDY GUIDE

What is the precedential weight of a 4-3 decision by the Supreme Court?

EQUAL PROTECTION OF THE LAW: SEX DISCRIMINATION AND OTHER TYPES

We begin Part IX with a study of two sex discrimination cases decided by the Burger Court: *Frontiero v. Richardson* (1973) and *Craig v. Boren* (1976). Next, we jump to a sex discrimination case decided by the Rehnquist Court: *United States v. Virginia* (1996). We conclude this part with two cases that did not involve race or sex discrimination, yet nevertheless employed "heightened" rational basis scrutiny: *City of Cleburne v. Cleburne Living Center, Inc.* (1985) and *Romer v. Evans* (1996).

CHAPTER 41

Sex Discrimination on the Burger Court

The Fourteenth Amendment provides that a state cannot "deny to any person within its jurisdiction the equal protection of the laws." Generally, popularly elected legislative majorities are trusted to make policy choices without being second-guessed by unelected judges. This approach is known as the *presumption of constitutionality*.

Footnote Four of *United States v. Carolene Products* (1938), however, identified three exceptions to this presumption. (See Chapter 35.) Courts should employ a "more searching judicial inquiry" when they reviews laws that

1. violate an enumerated right, such as those in the Bill of Rights;
2. change the rules by which representatives are elected; and
3. harm "discrete and insular minorities."

The third exception is now reflected in modern Equal Protection Clause doctrine. Courts are very suspicious when the government treats people differently based on their race, nationality, or religion. For example, racial classifications are presumptively unconstitutional. Courts review these *suspect* classifications with *strict scrutiny*.

STUDY GUIDE

The Supreme Court's approach to the Due Process Clause also employs tiers of review and means-ends scrutiny.

When Courts review a law with *strict scrutiny*, they measure the *fit* between the law's purpose, or *ends*, and the *means* it uses to accomplish that goal. Specifically, the government has the burden to show that its law is *narrowly tailored* to achieve a *compelling interest*. This standard is difficult to satisfy.

If the government cannot demonstrate that there is a close fit between the means it has employed and the ends it says it is pursuing, then the court presumes that the government is acting with an improper purpose. In other words, the government did not give the real reason why it enacted the law. Rather, the government's defense was a *pretext* to cover up the real, impermissible justification. This form of means-ends scrutiny is designed to identify, or *smoke out*, an improper legislative objective — for example, laws that are motivated by unconstitutional *animus* towards particular persons or groups.

In Equal Protection Clause cases, courts will only review *suspect classifications* with strict scrutiny. The courts review other *non-suspect* classifications with the more deferential *rational basis scrutiny*. Under rational basis scrutiny, the burden shifts from the government to the challenger. A challenger must demonstrate that the government lacked a *rational basis* to enact the law. The courts will uphold a non-suspect classification if the law is *reasonably related* to accomplish any *legitimate state interest*. This deferential standard of review does not require a close fit between the means and the ends. Indeed, *Williamson v. Lee Optical* (1955) held that the state could deprive a person of a *non-fundamental right* — similar to a *non-suspect classification* — if the government had a "conceivable" basis for acting. (See Chapter 35.) With this form of "conceivable basis review," the challenger always loses.

Is a sex-based classification *suspect*, and thus reviewed with strict scrutiny? Or is it *non-suspect*, and only subject to rational basis review? The Burger Court would resolve this question in two cases: *Frontiero v. Richardson* (1973) and *Craig v. Boren* (1976).

Frontiero v. Richardson (1973)

 ConLaw.us/Frontiero/

Sharron Frontiero was a Lieutenant in the Air Force. She requested certain benefits from the government for her husband, who was a full-time student. The Air Force would have automatically granted those benefits to the wife of a male service member. However, Sharron Frontiero's request was "denied because she failed to demonstrate that her husband was dependent on her for more than one-half of his support." This sex-based classification imposed additional burdens on female service members.

Ruth Bader Ginsburg argued *Frontiero* on behalf of the American Civil Liberties Union. She contended that the law was premised on a stereotype: the government "assumes that all women are preoccupied with home and children." Such stereotypes, she explained, "help keep [a] woman in her place, a place inferior to that occupied by men in our society." Therefore, Ginsburg urged "the Court to declare sex a suspect" classification, which would be reviewed with strict scrutiny.

Frontiero did not have a majority opinion, in which five Justices agreed on a single rationale. Although a majority of the Justices agreed that Frontiero should win, there were only four votes to strictly scrutinize the federal policy. Justice Brennan wrote the plurality opinion, joined by Justices Douglas, White, and Marshall. A plurality opinion is an opinion supported by the greatest number of the Justices who were in the majority: here, four out of nine Justices. A plurality opinion is said to be *controlling*, though it has less precedential value than a majority opinion. Chief Justice Burger filed a concurring opinion, joined by Justices Blackmun and Powell. Justice Stewart wrote his own concurrence.

Justice Brennan observed that "[t]here can be no doubt that our Nation has had a long and unfortunate history of sex discrimination." Over time, he wrote, American statutes "became laden with gross, stereotyped distinctions between the sexes, and, indeed, throughout much of the 19th century, the position of women in our society was, in many respects, comparable to that of blacks under the pre-Civil War slave codes." For example, he cited *Bradwell v. Illinois* (1873), which we discussed in Chapter 28.

Further, Justice Brennan stressed that "sex, like race and national origin, is an immutable characteristic determined solely by the accident of birth." These stereotypes about sex — based on highly visible and unchangeable characteristics — are factually inaccurate. Therefore, the plurality concluded, "classifications based upon sex, like classifications based upon race, alienage, or national origin, are inherently suspect, and must therefore be subjected to strict judicial scrutiny."

STUDY GUIDE

Why would it matter that a characteristic is "immutable"?

Chief Justice Burger, as well as Justices Blackmun and Powell, concurred in the Court's *judgment* — that is, they agreed with the outcome of the case, which held that "the challenged statutes constitute an unconstitutional discrimination against servicewomen." But they did *not* agree with the plurality opinion that sex-based classifications were "inherently suspect," and must therefore be reviewed with strict scrutiny. Three years later, the Court would resolve this disagreement by adopting a middle approach.

Craig v. Boren (1976)

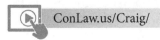 ConLaw.us/Craig/

Craig v. Boren (1976) involved a sex-based classification that treated men worse than it did women. Oklahoma law prohibited the sale of "nonintoxicating" 3.2 percent beer to males under the age of 21. But women could buy the light beer at the age of 18. The state argued that young women were less likely to drive drunk and get into traffic accidents. Therefore, the sex-based classification was related to a legitimate state interest: the improvement of traffic safety on Oklahoma roads.

The Supreme Court rejected this argument. Justice Brennan wrote the majority opinion. He concluded that the means (the sex-based classification) lacked a proper fit with the ends (promoting highway safety). Why? Justice Brennan noted that "Oklahoma's statute prohibits only the selling of 3.2 percent beer to young males and not their drinking the beverage once acquired." In other words, if the state was serious about promoting highway safety, the government would also prohibit young males from drinking beer. The Court found that Oklahoma failed to justify its sex-based classification. This form of "invidious discrimination" violated the Equal Protection Clause.

STUDY GUIDE

Are there relevant differences between the sexes that the government may reasonably take into account?

In *Craig*, a majority of the Justices now agreed that sex-based classifications were subject to a heightened standard of review. But Justice Brennan was still unable to muster a majority of the Court to recognize sex-based classifications as suspect classifications, that are reviewed with strict scrutiny. Instead, the majority adopted a standard that was more rigorous than rational basis scrutiny, though not quite as demanding as strict scrutiny.

Justice Rehnquist dissented. He referred to this new standard as "elevated or 'intermediate' level scrutiny." The latter name stuck. Over time, the Court would clarify that sex-based classifications were "quasi-suspect," and would be reviewed with "intermediate" scrutiny. A quasi-suspect classification will be upheld if the government can show that its law is *substantially related* to an *important interest*.

Under the modern Equal Protection Clause doctrine, there are three tiers of scrutiny:

- **Strict Scrutiny**—A *suspect classification* will be upheld if the government can show that its law is *narrowly tailored* to achieve a *compelling interest.*
- **Intermediate Scrutiny**—A *quasi-suspect classification* will be upheld if the government can show that its law is *substantially related* to an *important interest.*
- **Rational Basis**—A *non-suspect classification* will be upheld unless the challenger can show that a law is not *reasonably related* to accomplish any *legitimate interest.*

First, under strict and intermediate scrutiny, the government has the burden. Generally with rational-basis review, the party challenging the law has the burden.

Second, under strict scrutiny, the government must show that its law achieves a *compelling interest.* That is, a governmental purpose of the highest order, such as national security. For intermediate scrutiny, the government must show that its law is related to an interest that is *important* — not quite compelling, but still weighty. And to survive rational-basis scrutiny, the government's interest must only be *legitimate.*

Third, strict scrutiny requires a very tight fit — that is, *narrow tailoring* — between the suspect classification and the government's compelling interest. Intermediate scrutiny requires a looser fit: The means must be *substantially related* to the government's important interest. Finally, under rational-basis scrutiny, the non-suspect classification needs the loosest of fits — a *reasonable relation* — to survive judicial review. Indeed, according to some cases, there need only be a *conceivable* relation between the means and the ends.

The Court has occasionally departed from these general formulations of the three tiers of scrutiny. At times, the Court uses somewhat different terminology. In *United States v. Carolene Products* (1938), for example, the Court refers to "more exacting scrutiny" rather than "strict scrutiny." In other cases, Justices have questioned whether the Court is actually adhering to the three tiers of scrutiny. In *Fisher v. University of Texas, Austin II* (2016), for example, Justice Thomas's dissent questioned whether the majority faithfully applied the test for strict scrutiny to review a racial classification. (See Chapter 40.) And in *United States v. Virginia* (1996), Justice Scalia's dissent offered a similar criticism: The majority failed to faithfully apply the test for intermediate scrutiny to review a sex-based classification. We will study *Virginia* in Chapter 42.

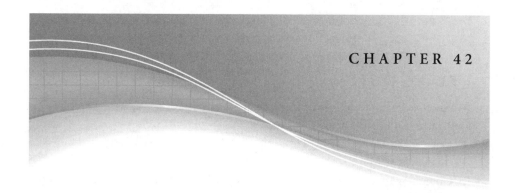

United States v. Virginia (1996)

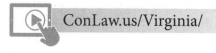

ConLaw.us/Virginia/

The Virginia Military Institute (VMI) is a public college in Virginia. VMI's stated mission was to produce "citizen soldiers." Through the so-called "adversative method," VMI instilled physical and mental discipline in its student body. The students lived in "spartan barracks," wore uniforms, ate together, and had no privacy. Since its founding, VMI had admitted only male students.

The United States filed suit against VMI on behalf of female students who could not apply to the college. The Fourth Circuit Court of Appeals ruled that VMI's admissions policy violated the Fourteenth Amendment. However, the court suggested that the college could cure that constitutional problem by establishing a parallel program for women. As a result, Virginia opened the Women's Institute for Leadership (VWIL) at Mary Baldwin College, a private women's college. That accommodation, however, did not end the litigation. VMI and VWIL offered different programs for men and women.

The United States appealed the case to the Supreme Court. The question presented was whether Virginia "can constitutionally deny to women who have the will and capacity, the training and attendant opportunity VMI uniquely affords" — training and opportunity that the very different VWIL program did not supply. The Court answered no by a 7-1 vote. VMI's admissions policy violated the Equal Protection Clause. Only Justice Scalia dissented. (Justice Thomas recused because his son attended VMI.)

Justice Ginsburg wrote the majority opinion. She acknowledged that there are "'inherent differences' between men and women." However, the Court found, "such classifications may not be used, as they once were, to create or perpetuate the legal, social, and economic inferiority of women." The government may not close entrance gates based on "fixed notions concerning the roles and abilities of males and females."

STUDY GUIDE

Are there ever valid bases for the government to treat men and women differently based on their biological traits?

In Chapter 41, we discussed the standard of review for intermediate scrutiny: A quasi-suspect classification (such as gender) will be upheld if the government can show that its law is *substantially related* to an *important interest*. In *Virginia*, Justice Ginsburg described the test slightly differently. The government must provide an "exceedingly persuasive justification" to impose a sex-based classification. In other words, the government must show that the gender line "serves *important governmental objectives* and that the discriminatory means employed are *substantially* related to the achievement of those objectives." This approach sounds like intermediate scrutiny, but Justice Ginsburg added more: "The justification must be genuine, not hypothesized or invented post hoc in response to litigation. And it must not rely on overbroad generalizations about the different talents, capacities, or preferences of males and females."

STUDY GUIDE

Did *Craig v. Boren* (1976) require the government to identify an "exceedingly persuasive justification" to justify a sex-based classification under intermediate scrutiny? This standard will become significant in future sex-discrimination cases.

Justice Ginsburg found that "Virginia has shown no 'exceedingly persuasive justification' for excluding all women from the citizen-soldier training afforded by VMI." Ultimately, the Court concluded that the Equal Protection Clause "precludes Virginia from reserving exclusively to men the unique educational opportunities VMI affords." And there was only one possible remedy: Women had to be admitted to VMI. Justice Ginsburg observed, "Women seeking and fit for a VMI-quality education cannot be offered anything less, under the Commonwealth's obligation to afford them genuinely equal protection."

Justice Ginsburg's opinion echoed the "separate but equal" principle that was established in *Plessy v. Ferguson* and rejected in *Brown v. Board of Education*. The separate program at VWIL, the majority concluded, was not an equal substitute.

STUDY GUIDE

Can you see how the canonical v. anti-canonical status of cases can work to influence how the Court reasons?

Justice Scalia was the lone dissenter. During oral argument, he contended that VMI excluded women to ensure that men could be trained in the adversative method. The policy, Scalia claimed, had "nothing to do with whether women can take the heat." Rather, he added, forcing VMI to admit women "would interfere with the kind of relationship among the students that produces the adversative method."

Justice Scalia asserted that the majority opinion did not faithfully apply the Court's "intermediate scrutiny" precedents. Instead, he wrote, this new test is "indistinguishable from strict scrutiny." Under conventional intermediate scrutiny, Justice Scalia contended, VMI's policy was obviously valid: "It is beyond question that Virginia has an *important state interest* in providing effective college education for its citizens. That single-sex instruction is an approach *substantially related to that interest* should be evident enough from the long and continuing history in this country of men's and women's colleges."

STUDY GUIDE

After *United States v. Virginia*, is there any difference between how courts review classifications based on sex and classifications based on race? Should sex-based classifications always be treated the same as race-based classifications?

Justices Scalia and Ginsburg often found themselves on the opposite sides of cases; yet, they remained close friends during their entire time together on the Court.

CHAPTER 43

"Heightened" Rational Basis Scrutiny

What is the correct standard of review when the government deprives a person of life, liberty, or property? *United States v. Carolene Products* (1938) held that the person whose rights were violated has the burden. She must show that the law was not reasonably related to a legitimate governmental interest. Critically, the due process of law requires that she be given the opportunity to present evidence to demonstrate that the law was in fact irrational. (See Chapter 35.)

But *Williamson v. Lee Optical* (1955) greatly weakened this standard. (See Chapter 36.) Now, the Court would only review laws with heightened scrutiny if they violated so-called "fundamental" liberties. Laws that violated any other "liberty interest" would be reviewed with a much more deferential standard: Can the court think of a *conceivable* reason why the government might have enacted the law? If so, the law is rational, and therefore is constitutional. Such a presumption of constitutionality is impossible to rebut.

Both *Carolene Products* and *Lee Optical* primarily concerned the Due Process Clause of the Fourteenth Amendment. Soon enough, however, the Court would extend the *conceivable basis* test to Equal Protection Clause cases. Now, courts would afford great deference to classifications that were neither "suspect" nor "quasi-suspect."

Nevertheless, in two Equal Protection Clause cases the Supreme Court took a different approach. In *City of Cleburne v. Cleburne Living Center, Inc.* (1985) and *Romer v. Evans* (1996), the Court applied what is sometimes called heightened rational basis scrutiny, even though the classifications at issue were not suspect or quasi-suspect. In these atypical cases, the Court returned — at least temporarily — to the type of rationality review articulated in *Carolene Products*.

City of Cleburne v. Cleburne Living Center, Inc. (1985)

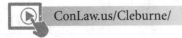 ConLaw.us/Cleburne/

The Cleburne Living Center wanted to operate a group home for thirteen "mentally retarded" people. The city of Cleburne, Texas, told the Center that it needed a special use permit to operate such a facility. Following a public hearing, the City Council voted to deny the permit. The Center filed suit, and argued that the denial violated the Equal Protection Clause. Specifically, the Center contended that if the residents were not mentally retarded, the permit would have been granted.

All nine Justices agreed that the city violated the Constitution. However, they did not agree on a single rationale. Justice White wrote the majority opinion, which was joined by Chief Justice Burger and Justices Powell, Rehnquist, Stevens, and O'Connor. As a threshold matter, the Court found that "mentally retarded" people were not a "quasi-suspect" class. Why not? Justice White found that, collectively, this class was not "politically powerless." Rather, they were adequately represented in the legislative process. Therefore, under the logic of Footnote Four of *Carolene Products*, the "mentally retarded" were not a "discrete and insular minority." As a result, the permit denial for this class—which was neither suspect nor quasi-suspect—would be reviewed with rational basis scrutiny. According to the Court, "[t]o withstand equal protection review, legislation that distinguishes between the mentally retarded and others must be *rationally related* to a *legitimate governmental purpose*."

Rational basis review is extremely deferential. *Williamson v. Lee Optical* (1955), for example, held that rational basis scrutiny was satisfied if there was even a *conceivable* reason why the government *might* have acted as it did. Indeed, the government's actual purpose for treating ophthalmologists differently than opticians was irrelevant.

In *Cleburne*, however, the government's motivation was relevant. The city offered several reasons why it denied the permit. And the Court critically evaluated, and rejected as unreasonable, each of the government's defenses. The rational basis review applied in *Cleburne* was quite different than the approach applied in *Lee Optical*.

Justice White wrote that there was no "rational basis for believing that the [] home would pose any special threat to the city's legitimate interests." For example, the city objected to building a group home for the disabled in a flood plain. Yet, the city permitted other group homes to operate in similar locations. The Court found it "difficult to believe that the groups of mildly or moderately mentally retarded individuals . . . would present any different or special hazard" to the community than other groups of persons.

Ultimately, the Court found that each of the city's justifications was implausible. Therefore, the majority concluded that the permit denial was the result of "an irrational prejudice against the mentally retarded." The Court also found that "[n]egative attitudes, or fear, unsubstantiated by factors which are properly cognizable in a zoning proceeding, are not permissible bases for treating a home for the mentally retarded differently from apartment houses."

STUDY GUIDE

How does the majority's approach to rational basis scrutiny compare with the scrutiny employed in *Williamson v. Lee Optical*?

Justice Marshall, joined by Justices Brennan and Blackmun, concurred in the Court's judgment. Yet, he dissented from Justice White's analysis. He found that the mentally handicapped were a quasi-suspect class. As a result, the city's ordinance should be reviewed with heightened scrutiny. Justice Marshall wrote that "[t]he Court holds the ordinance invalid on rational basis grounds, and disclaims that anything special, in the form of heightened scrutiny, is taking place." Yet, Justice Marshall observed, the city's "ordinance surely would be valid under the traditional rational basis test applicable to economic and commercial regulation."

Justice Marshall contended that the Court was not reviewing the permit denial with rational basis review, as that standard was articulated in *Williamson v. Lee Optical*. Instead, the majority employed what he called "heightened" or "'second order' rational basis review." Justice Marshall also feared that, after *Cleburne*, the Court would carefully scrutinize other economic regulations. *Lee Optical* had foreclosed that approach three decades earlier.

STUDY GUIDE

Why might the majority have been reluctant to find the existence of a suspect class in *Cleburne*?

How exactly does heightened rational basis scrutiny work? No one really knows. The Court has never explained this approach, or even admitted candidly it was a separate form of scrutiny. Justice Marshall's dissent first sounded the alarm that something different was going on. At a minimum, this approach provided an alternative to the three established tiers of scrutiny: some laws motivated by "animus" towards a non-suspect class would be unconstitutional. The Court next employed this form of heightened rational basis scrutiny in *Romer v. Evans* (1996).

Romer v. Evans (1996)

 ConLaw.us/Romer/

In the early 1990s, several cities in Colorado prohibited discrimination on the basis of sexual orientation in housing, employment, and public accommodations. These local ordinances proved to be unpopular statewide. In 1992, the people of Colorado adopted Amendment 2 to the state constitution. This provision repealed the local ordinances, and banned the enactment of new laws that prohibited discrimination on the basis of "homosexual, lesbian, or bisexual orientation, conduct, practices or relationships."

Amendment 2 was challenged in state court. Colorado contended that Amendment 2 was not discriminatory. Rather, the state argued that Amendment 2 put gays and lesbians in the same position as everyone else. That is, the Amendment only denied gays and lesbians "special" rights. The Colorado Supreme Court held that this classification on the basis of sexual orientation triggered strict scrutiny under the Equal Protection Clause.

The Supreme Court affirmed the state court, but on a different rationale. The Justices split 6-3. Justice Kennedy wrote the majority opinion on behalf of Justices Stevens, O'Connor, Souter, Ginsburg, and Breyer. Unlike the Colorado Supreme Court, the majority declined to treat sexual orientation as a suspect class or quasi-suspect class.

STUDY GUIDE

Why do you think the majority in *Romer* refrained from identifying sexual orientation as a suspect or quasi-suspect class?

The Court traditionally employs rational basis review when it reviews a law that burdens a non-suspect class. *Romer* purported to follow this approach. Justice Kennedy stated Amendment 2 was constitutional so long as it "bears a rational relationship to some legitimate end." Yet, he stressed the unprecedented nature of Amendment 2: "[I]t is not within our constitutional tradition to enact laws of this sort." He found that the means adopted, Amendment 2, did not have an adequate fit with this purported end: "A law declaring that in general it shall be more difficult for one group of citizens than for all others to seek aid from the government is itself a denial of equal protection of the laws in the most literal sense."

Justice Kennedy also rejected Colorado's argument that Amendment 2 merely protected the "freedom of association" of "landlords or employers who have personal or religious objections to homosexuality." He added, "The breadth of the Amendment is so far removed from" the justifications Colorado offered "that we find it impossible to credit them. We cannot say that Amendment 2 is directed to any identifiable legitimate purpose or discreet objective." In short, "Amendment 2 classifies homosexuals not to further a *proper* legislative end but to make them unequal to everyone else. This Colorado cannot do. A State cannot so deem a class of persons a stranger to its laws."

Romer, like *Cleburne*, reviewed state action with heightened rational basis scrutiny. Justice Kennedy did not employ the form of rational basis scrutiny described in *Williamson v. Lee Optical*. How do we know? *Romer* rejected Colorado's *conceivable* justifications for Amendment 2. Rather, Justice Kennedy was concerned about whether the classification was *actually* adopted for an improper reason. Like in *Cleburne*, the Court suspected that the law was in fact motivated by animus towards gays and lesbians. For that reason, Amendment 2 was unconstitutional.

Justice Scalia "vigorously" dissented, and read his opinion from the bench. He was joined by Chief Justice Rehnquist and Justice Thomas. Justice Scalia maintained that Amendment 2 would easily satisfy traditional rational basis scrutiny: "The Court gives the back of its hand to the usual test for compliance with the Equal Protection Clause[:] whether the legislation had a rational basis. It is unsurprising that the Court avoids discussion of this question since the answer is so obviously yes."

Moreover, Justice Scalia faulted the majority for its failure to engage with *Bowers v. Hardwick* (1986). That decision upheld the constitutionality of Georgia's criminal prohibition on sodomy. He reasoned:

> Obviously if it is constitutionally permissible for a state to make homosexual conduct criminal, surely it is constitutionally permissible for a State to enact other laws merely disfavoring homosexual conduct, and *a fortiori* it is constitutionally permissible for a State to adopt the provision not even disfavoring homosexual conduct but merely prohibiting all levels of state government from bestowing special protection upon homosexual conduct.

What was the legitimate governmental interest that supported Amendment 2's classification? In *Bowers*, the Court held that "majority sentiments about the morality of homosexuality" provided a rational basis for the criminal prohibition of sodomy. Justice Scalia maintained that "moral disapproval of homosexual conduct" was also a legitimate governmental interest to justify Amendment 2.

In *Cleburne and Romer*—two Equal Protection Clause cases—the Court employed heightened rational basis scrutiny despite the absence of a suspect or quasi-suspect class. The Court would use a similar approach in *Lawrence v. Texas* (2003). This case overruled *Bowers*, and found that Texas's criminal prohibition on sodomy violated the Due Process Clause. Critically, the Court did not find that the sodomy ban violated a "fundamental" right. Yet, the majority still reviewed the Texas law with heightened rational basis scrutiny. We will study *Lawrence* in Chapter 48.

PART X

MODERN SUBSTANTIVE DUE PROCESS

The Court's modern substantive due process case law begins with *Griswold v. Connecticut* (1965), which recognized a right to marital privacy. Next, we turn to three abortion cases: *Roe v. Wade* (1973), *Planned Parenthood v. Casey* (1992), and *Whole Woman's Health v. Hellerstedt* (2016). Finally, we conclude with three cases affecting the liberty of gays and lesbians: *Lawrence v. Texas* (2003), *United States v. Windsor* (2013), and *Obergefell v. Hodges* (2015).

CHAPTER 44

Griswold v. Connecticut (1965)

 ConLaw.us/Griswold/

Following the New Deal, the Supreme Court reviewed most state and federal legislation with a *presumption of constitutionality*. This approach severely restricted how closely courts could scrutinize laws. But in *United States v. Carolene Products* (1938), the Court recognized that the presumption of constitutionality could still be rebutted. How? Litigants could present factual evidence to show that a law was irrational, arbitrary, or discriminatory in a particular circumstance. This form of scrutiny resembles Justice Harlan's *Lochner* dissent. *Carolene Products* described this approach in the body of the opinion.

Williamson v. Lee Optical (1955), however, foreclosed this type of *factual* challenge to a law's rationality. Justice Douglas's majority opinion held that litigants could no longer rebut the presumption of constitutionality with evidence. Now, courts were required to accept any hypothetical or conceivable rationale a legislature might have had for restricting liberty—whether or not that rationale had in fact been considered by the legislature. *Conceivable basis review*, as we call it, is more consonant with Justice Holmes's dissent in *Lochner*.

Yet *Lee Optical* did not disturb Footnote Four of *Carolene Products*. That famous footnote explained that legislation would not be reviewed with the presumption of constitutionality if it:

1. violates a "specific" prohibition of the Constitution, such as those enumerated in the Bill of Rights;
2. restricts those political processes that can ordinarily be expected to bring about repeal of undesirable legislation; or
3. adversely affects discrete and insular minorities who cannot protect themselves in the democratic process.

Through this framework, the New Deal Court shielded most economic regulation from any form of heightened judicial scrutiny. The courts would only employ heightened scrutiny when the government violated a "specific prohibition" on liberty, such as an enumerated right in the Bill of Rights. The liberty of contract, for example, and other economic rights, are not enumerated in the Constitution.

Griswold v. Connecticut (1965) took a momentous step outside this neat framework. In this decision, the Warren Court started to expand the first exception to Footnote Four. The Court would now employ heightened scrutiny, in certain cases where the challenged law did not violate a "specific" prohibition in the Constitution. Specifically, *Griswold* reviewed with heightened scrutiny a law that restricted an *unenumerated* "right to privacy."

Justice Douglas wrote the majority opinion in both *Lee Optical* and in *Griswold*. He no doubt recognized the contradiction between these two decisions. Rather than acknowledging this foundational shift, however, he attempted to disguise it. How? He tried to base the unenumerated "right of privacy" on several enumerated rights in the Bill of Rights. This move, at least superficially, allowed *Griswold* to remain within Footnote Four's framework.

Let's discuss the facts in *Griswold*. Connecticut had an old law that criminalized the use of contraception by married couples. The law also prohibited doctors and others from counseling couples on how to use such products. (There is some debate about how often the law was actually enforced.) In 1961, the Connecticut Birth Control League opened a Planned Parenthood clinic in New Haven. The organization wanted to start a test case as a means to challenge the law's constitutionality. Estelle Griswold was the executive director of the League. Dr. C. Lee Buxton, the chairman of the Yale University Department of Obstetrics and Gynecology, was the medical director of the clinic. Griswold and Buxton counseled married couples on the use of contraception, a clear violation of Connecticut law. They did so deliberately, so they would be arrested. Griswold and Buxton were each fined $100.

On appeal, the Supreme Court reversed their convictions. Seven justices found that Connecticut's contraceptive ban for married couples was unconstitutional: Chief Justice Warren and Justices Douglas, Clark, Harlan, Brennan, White, and Goldberg. Justice Douglas wrote the majority opinion. Justices Black and Stewart dissented.

First, Justice Douglas rejected the argument that *Lochner* was a "guide" to *Griswold*. He wrote, "we decline that invitation, as we did in" *West Coast Hotel* and *Lee Optical*. During oral argument, counsel for Planned Parenthood drew a distinction between laws that regulate personal liberties and laws that violate economic liberties. Before the New Deal, the judiciary closely scrutinized the latter category of laws. Planned Parenthood's theory, the lawyer claimed,

> is not broad due process in the sense in which the issue was raised in the 1930s. In the first place, this is not a regulation that deals with economic or commercial matters. It is a regulation that touches upon individual rights: the right to protect life and health, the right of advancing scientific knowledge, the right to have children voluntarily and therefore, we say we are not asking this Court to revive *Lochner v. New York*, or to overrule *Nebbia* or *West Coast Hotel*.

Justice Douglas followed this lead in his majority opinion. "We do not sit as a super-legislature to determine the wisdom, need, and propriety of laws that touch *economic* problems, business affairs, or social conditions," he wrote. "This law, however, operates directly on an *intimate relation* of husband and wife and their physician's role in one aspect of that relation."

STUDY GUIDE

Does the text of the Constitution draw any distinction between "economic" and "intimate," or personal, liberties?

Before *Griswold* was decided in 1965, *Lochner* remained a rather obscure case. It gained some attention in 1912: Theodore Roosevelt made the decision a campaign issue during his presidential campaign. Yet, five decades later, Justice Black could not quite remember what *Lochner* was about. During oral argument in *Griswold*, he asked if *Lochner* was the case "that held it was unconstitutional . . . for a state to try to regulate the size of loaves of bread." The lawyer replied, "No, no, no." Justice Douglas's opinion in *Griswold* made *Lochner* notorious. After *Griswold*, *Lochner* moved into the *anti-canon*. Cases decided during the Progressive Era became known, generally, as "*Lochner* Era" cases.

Second, Justice Douglas recast *Meyer v. Nebraska* (1923) and *Pierce v. Society of Sisters* (1925) as decisions that involved rights enumerated in the First Amendment. Those cases, however, concerned economic as well as personal liberties protected by the Due Process Clause. And the Court did not rely on the First Amendment in either case. Both decisions relied on the doctrine that came to be known as substantive due process.

Third, Justice Douglas read the Court's precedents to protect a right of "privacy." He wrote, "Specific guarantees in the Bill of Rights have penumbras, formed by emanations from those guarantees that help give them life and substance." An "emanation" refers to a ray of light. During a lunar eclipse, the "umbra" refers to the darkest part of the shadow formed when the Earth passes between the sun and the moon. The "penumbra" refers to the lighter part of the shadow, where some of the "emanations" from the sun are visible.

If you don't understand this analysis, you're not alone. To this day, critics of an unenumerated right to privacy widely deride Justice Douglas's use of "emanations" and "penumbras." Justice Douglas then continued, "Various guarantees" in the Bill of Rights, including the First, Third, Fourth, Fifth, and Ninth Amendments, "create zones of privacy."

Why did Justice Douglas feel compelled to invoke "penumbras" of the Bill of Rights? Perhaps he thought that linking the right of privacy to these express prohibitions of the Bill of Rights would keep his decision within the structure of *Carolene Products*. Footnote Four explained that heightened scrutiny was warranted when a law violates a "specific prohibition" in the Constitution. Here, Douglas invoked the "penumbras" of several express prohibitions in the Bill of Rights.

Fourth, Justice Douglas stated that Connecticut's law "concern[ed] a relationship lying within the zone of privacy created by several fundamental constitutional guarantees." Based on this reasoning, he concluded that the Connecticut law was unconstitutional.

There were three concurring opinions. Justice Goldberg wrote the first concurring opinion. He agreed with Justice Douglas that Connecticut's law was unconstitutional. However, Justice Goldberg provided an alternate analysis. He wrote that the "right of marital privacy" can be "supported" by the "language and history of the Ninth Amendment." The Ninth Amendment provides, "The enumeration in the Constitution, of certain rights, shall not be construed to deny or disparage others retained by the people." Justice Goldberg explained, "the Ninth Amendment shows a belief of the Constitution's authors that fundamental rights exist that are not expressly enumerated in the first eight amendments and an intent that the list of rights included there not be deemed exhaustive."

STUDY GUIDE

Is Justice Goldberg's concurring opinion preferable to Justice Douglas's majority opinion? Does the Ninth Amendment say anything about the scope of state powers?

To be clear, Justice Goldberg does not conclude that the Ninth Amendment directly protects the right to marital privacy in this case. Why not? The Ninth Amendment only places limits on the power of the federal government. Instead, Justice Goldberg cited the Ninth Amendment for a different reason: the text of the Constitution endorses the idea of protecting unenumerated rights.

Justice John Marshall Harlan II wrote the second, and most influential concurring opinion. (He was the grandson of Justice John Marshall Harlan I.) He rejected Justice Douglas's claim that the right of privacy was grounded in the enumerated provisions of the Bill of Rights. Instead, Justice Harlan explained that "the proper constitutional inquiry in this case is whether this Connecticut statute infringes the Due Process Clause of the Fourteenth Amendment because the enactment violates basic values 'implicit in the concept of ordered liberty.'" Justice Harlan's approach here was a distinct break from the logic of Footnote Four. Three decades later in *Washington v. Glucksberg* (1997), several Justices adopted Harlan's framework. They did so to limit judicial scrutiny of laws that violate unenumerated rights.

Justice White wrote the third concurring opinion. He wrote that nothing "justif[ies] the sweeping scope of this statute, with its telling effect on the freedoms of married persons." Like Justice Harlan, Justice White candidly based his reasoning on the Fourteenth Amendment. He concluded that the law "deprives such persons of liberty without due process of law."

There were two dissenting opinions. Justice Black wrote the first dissent. He rejected Justice Douglas's "penumbras" approach, as well as Justices Harlan and

White's Due Process Clause analysis. Rather, Justice Black found that there was no "right of privacy" in the text of the Constitution. "I like my privacy as well as the next one," he wrote, "but I am nevertheless compelled to admit that government has a right to invade it unless prohibited by some *specific constitutional provision.*" Justice Black charged the majority with forgetting *West Coast Hotel*, and returning to the "dangerous" and "discredited" precedent of *Lochner v. New York* — the facts of which he had a hard time remembering during oral argument.

STUDY GUIDE

Can you see how Justice Black's dissent tracks Footnote Four of *Carolene Products*?

Justice Stewart wrote the second dissent. He thought Connecticut's law was "uncommonly silly." However, he could find nothing in the Constitution that rendered the law unconstitutional.

In *Carolene Products*, the New Deal Court established a settlement in which the Court would generally defer to popularly enacted laws. With *Griswold v. Connecticut*, the Warren Court began to crack open that settlement. In the next case, *Roe v. Wade*, the Burger Court would find that the right of privacy limits the state's power to restrict abortions.

CHAPTER 45

Roe v. Wade (1973)

 ConLaw.us/Roe/

Roe v. Wade remains one of the Supreme Court's most controversial opinions. As a general matter, states have the police power to prohibit murder — that is, the taking of a life. Does the police power give states the authority to prohibit abortions? Our analysis starts with the text of the Fourteenth Amendment.

The Due Process Clause provides, "Nor shall any State deprive any person of life, *liberty*, or property, without due process of law." If the choice to terminate a pregnancy constitutes "liberty," then the state cannot deprive a mother of that "liberty" without the due process of law. On this theory, the Fourteenth Amendment would protect the right to an abortion nationwide, unless a state can show that a specific restriction on abortions is justified.

On the other hand, the Fourteenth Amendment may protect more than the mother's rights. The Equal Protection Clause also raises the issue of the legal status of the fetus. It provides: No state shall "deny to *any person* within its jurisdiction the equal protection of the laws." If the fetus is a *person*, does the state have a duty to *equally protect* born and unborn persons alike from murder? If so, on this theory, abortion must be prohibited nationwide. And Congress could then use its powers under Section 5 of the Fourteenth Amendment to enact "appropriate legislation" to prohibit abortion, should a state fail to do so.

The crux of this Equal Protection theory may turn on the point at which a fetus becomes a person, and if abortion is considered to be murder. Even if abortion is not considered murder, however, under one conception of the *police power*, states could still ban the procedure. *If* the police power of states includes the power to prohibit a wide range of conduct that a majority of the public deems immoral, then a majority of their legislative representatives can prohibit this conduct, *regardless* of whether it harms another person. For example, states criminalize animal cruelty, even when no people are harmed, on the sole ground that most people view such cruelty to be immoral.

Furthermore, under this conception of the police power, if a legislature is empowered to speak for the majority to deem some conduct as "immoral," it is not clear how courts are competent to decide otherwise. If this morals-based conception of the police power is correct, then the Fourteenth Amendment does not empower federal courts to review a state legislature's decision to prohibit certain types of immoral conduct. In short, if a statute is a valid exercise of the police power to regulate morality, that law *cannot* violate the due process of law. Accordingly, legislatures in conservative states can ban abortion if they deem it to be immoral, while more liberal states can legalize it.

Whether this *federalism* option is available, therefore, turns on the proper scope of the state's police power. Prior to *Roe v. Wade* (1973), many states banned almost all abortions. Texas, for example, made it a crime to perform an abortion unless the procedure was needed to save the mother's life. Norma McCorvey, who had a healthy pregnancy, could not qualify for that exemption. McCorvey believed that Texas law permitted a woman to get an abortion if she was raped. (It was unclear if the law had such an exemption.) As a result, she told the police she was raped. However, McCorvey later admitted that she had fabricated the allegation. She also attempted to obtain an illegal abortion, but the clinic had already been shut down. Eventually, two attorneys recruited McCorvey to serve as the lead plaintiff to challenge Texas's law. She filed the suit under a pseudonym, Jane Roe.

The case was appealed to the Supreme Court. Roe's attorney argued that Texas's abortion law was unconstitutional under the Fifth, Ninth, and Fourteenth Amendments. The leading precedent was *Griswold v. Connecticut* (1965), which we discussed in Chapter 44. In *Griswold*, Justice William O. Douglas found that "[s]pecific guarantees in the Bill of Rights have penumbras, formed by emanations from those guarantees that help give them life and substance." He added, "Various guarantees" in the Bill of Rights, including the First, Third, Fourth, Fifth, and Ninth Amendments, "create zones of privacy."

Griswold concluded that *married* couples had a right of privacy, which included access to contraception. In *Eisenstadt v. Baird* (1972), however, the Court found that denying this right to *unmarried* couples violated the Equal Protection Clause. The next year, in *Roe v. Wade*, the Court would consider whether this right of privacy also included access to abortions.

The vote in *Roe* was 7-2. Justice Harry Blackmun wrote the majority opinion. He seemed equivocal about the basis of a right to abortion: "This right of privacy, *whether it be founded* in the Fourteenth Amendment's concept of personal liberty and restrictions upon state action, *as we feel* it is, or, as the District Court determined, in the Ninth Amendment's reservation of rights to the people, is broad enough to encompass a woman's decision whether or not to terminate her pregnancy." The Court added, "Only personal rights that can be deemed 'fundamental' or 'implicit in the concept of ordered liberty,' are included in this guarantee of personal privacy."

STUDY GUIDE

Is there a difference between the constitutional basis of the right of privacy in *Griswold* and the right of privacy in *Roe*?

Ultimately, the Court rested its decision on the Due Process Clause of the Fourteenth Amendment, rather than on "penumbras, formed by emanations" from the Bill of Rights. Texas argued that the "State had a compelling interest" to ban abortions as a means to "protect[] . . . fetal life." The Court agreed, in part. The "State retains a definite interest in protecting the woman's own health and safety, when abortion is proposed at a *late stage* of pregnancy." Critically, "at some point in pregnancy," the state's "interests become sufficiently compelling to sustain" prohibitions on abortion to protect fetal life.

The Court found that the scope of abortion rights, as well as the state's interest to regulate abortions, both change throughout the nine months of the pregnancy. In the first trimester, the state can only regulate the qualifications and licensing of doctors and facilities that provide abortions. During this time, the state cannot prohibit, or even restrict, abortions in order to protect fetal life. Prior to the "compelling point" of viability, "the attending physician, in consultation with his patient, is free to determine, without regulation by the State, that, in his medical judgment, the patient's pregnancy should be terminated."

During the second trimester, the state can regulate abortion in ways reasonably related to maternal health. In the third trimester, subsequent to viability, the court can legislate to promote the potentiality of human life. During the final three months of the pregnancy, the state can regulate and even ban abortions, except where the procedure is necessary for preservation of the mother's *life* or *health*. Justice Blackmun explained that his decision "leaves the State free to place increasing restrictions on abortion as the period of pregnancy lengthens, so long as those restrictions are tailored to the recognized state interests."

The Texas law only permitted abortions to save the mother's *life*, and not to protect the mother's *health*. This fact, the Court held, rendered the statute unconstitutional. After *Roe*, courts would find that a mother's health included her mental or emotional well-being. With this broad definition of health, it would become nearly impossible to prohibit all abortions in the third trimester.

There were two dissenting opinions. Justice White wrote the first dissent:

> I find nothing in the language or history of the Constitution to support the Court's judgment. . . . As an exercise of raw judicial power, the Court perhaps has authority to do what it does today; but in my view its judgment is an improvident and extravagant exercise of the power of judicial review that the Constitution extends to this Court.

Chief Justice Rehnquist wrote the second dissent. He contended that the majority opinion was "closely attuned" to *Lochner v. New York*. "As in *Lochner*," he reasoned, "the adoption of the compelling state interest standard will inevitably require this Court to examine the legislative policies and pass on the wisdom of these policies in the very process of deciding whether a particular state interest put forward may or may not be 'compelling.'" In his widely used casebook, Stanford law professor Gerald Gunther paired *Roe* with *Lochner*. He did so to call the legitimacy of *Roe* into question. Justice Rehnquist added, "The decision here to break pregnancy into three distinct terms and to outline the permissible restrictions the State may impose in each one, for example, partakes more of judicial legislation than it does of a determination of the intent of the drafters of the Fourteenth Amendment."

Justice Potter Stewart wrote a concurring opinion. Eight years earlier, he dissented in *Griswold*. Justice Stewart had rejected *substantive due process*. Now, he formally embraced the concept: "As so understood, *Griswold* stands as one in a long line of . . . cases decided under the doctrine of substantive due process, and I now accept it as such."

By the time *Roe v. Wade* was decided in 1973, Norma McCorvey had already carried her pregnancy to term. She gave up the child, her third, for adoption. In the 1980s, she became a pro-choice icon for abortion rights groups. Later in life, however, McCorvey changed her stance on abortion. She became a born-again Christian and served as an advocate for the pro-life movement. She regretted her involvement in *Roe v. Wade*, which she called "the biggest mistake of my life."

In our next case, *Planned Parenthood v. Casey* (1992), the Supreme Court would consider whether *Roe* should be overturned.

CHAPTER 46

Planned Parenthood v. Casey (1992)

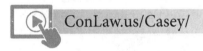

ConLaw.us/Casey/

Roe v. Wade was decided in 1973. At the time, abortion laws were not nearly as politically divisive as they are today. Indeed, when *Roe* was decided, a majority of the Justices on the Supreme Court were appointed by Republican presidents, including four new Nixon appointees. *Roe* attempted to resolve the nationwide debate over abortion. Far from settling the issue, however, *Roe* had the effect of polarizing the nation over this contentious issue.

Many conservatives sought to overturn *Roe* and restore the power of states to prohibit abortions. Short of a constitutional amendment, this goal could only be accomplished if more conservative Justices were nominated to the Supreme Court. Between 1981 and 1991, Presidents Ronald Reagan and George H.W. Bush nominated five new members to the Court: Justices Sandra Day O'Connor, Antonin Scalia, Anthony Kennedy, David Souter, and Clarence Thomas. By 1992, only one member of the Supreme Court, Justice Byron White, had been appointed by a Democratic president. And he had dissented in *Roe*. This gradual change in composition promised a change in the Court's stance on abortion.

In 1989, Pennsylvania enacted five new restrictions on abortion. The most controversial provision required married women to notify their husbands before obtaining an abortion. These laws were challenged in *Planned Parenthood v. Casey*.

During oral arguments, Kenneth W. Starr, the Solicitor General of the United States, contended that the Court should only review abortion laws with rational basis scrutiny: "Under that traditional analysis there must, in fact, be a rational connection with a legitimate State interest, and the State cannot proceed in an arbitrary and capricious fashion." The counsel for Planned Parenthood responded that the government's approach would amount to overruling *Roe*.

Generally, the Justices meet shortly after oral argument at the so-called *conference*, to vote on the case. A vote at conference is not binding, and it can be changed until the final decision is announced to the public. After *Casey* was argued, a five-vote bloc emerged at the conference to overrule *Roe*: Chief Justice Rehnquist and Justices White, Scalia, Kennedy, and Thomas would have upheld all of Pennsylvania's laws. In dissent were Justices Blackmun, Stevens, O'Connor, and Souter. (All four dissenting Justices were appointed by Republican presidents.) But that conference vote would not last. In one of the more famous compromises in Supreme Court history, Justice Kennedy switched sides. Ultimately, he joined with Justices O'Connor and Souter to write the controlling plurality opinion, known as "the joint opinion." Chief Justice Rehnquist, joined by Justices White, Scalia, and Thomas, were now in dissent.

The joint opinion rejected the government's call to overturn *Roe*. Rather, the plurality explained that "the essential holding of *Roe* should be reaffirmed." Yet the plurality departed from *Roe* in four ways. First, the *Casey* plurality abandoned *Roe*'s trimester framework:

> *Roe* established a trimester framework to govern abortion regulations. . . . That trimester framework no doubt was erected to ensure that the woman's right to choose not become so subordinate to the State's interest in promoting fetal life that her choice exists in theory, but not in fact. A framework of this rigidity was unnecessary, and, in its later interpretation, sometimes contradicted the State's permissible exercise of its powers.

Second, the plurality described the right to abortion in a very different fashion than did the *Roe* Court. Instead of focusing on a "fundamental" right of privacy, the joint opinion focused on liberty:

> Our precedents "have respected the private realm of family life which the state cannot enter." These matters, involving the most intimate and personal choices a person may make in a lifetime, choices central to personal dignity and autonomy, are central to the liberty protected by the Fourteenth Amendment. At the heart of liberty is the right to define one's own concept of existence, of meaning, of the universe, and of the mystery of human life. Beliefs about these matters could not define the attributes of personhood were they formed under compulsion of the State. These considerations begin our analysis of the woman's interest in terminating her pregnancy but cannot end it.

Third, the *Casey* plurality found that the State has "legitimate interests" from the outset of pregnancy to protect both the health of the mother *and* the life of the fetus. In contrast, *Roe* held that the state only has an interest to protect fetal life *after* the point of viability — that is, in the third trimester. Now, under the joint opinion's analysis, the state had an interest in protecting fetal life throughout all nine months.

STUDY GUIDE

When is a fetus viable? Will this standard change as neonatal care improves?

Fourth, the *Casey* plurality seemed to abandon *Roe's* application of strict scrutiny to protect the "fundamental" right to abortion. Instead, the joint opinion adopted the "undue burden" framework to protect liberty. The State may enforce restrictions to "persuade the woman to choose childbirth over abortion" throughout all three trimesters, so long as those restrictions do not place a "substantial obstacle" in the path of the woman's choice.

In other words, the state may not place "an undue burden" on the woman's right to choose an abortion. During oral argument, Pennsylvania contended that its law did not violate this test. Justice Scalia mocked the "undue burden" standard. He asked, "How do I go about determining whether it's an undue burden or not? What law books do I look to?"

STUDY GUIDE

Does the adoption of the "undue burden" test make it less likely that the Court would recognize and protect other "fundamental" rights?

With these four changes to *Roe*, the plurality found that four out of the five Pennsylvania laws were constitutional. The joint opinion, however, concluded that the husband notification requirement "unduly burdens" this right and was unconstitutional. Why? "A husband has no enforceable right to require a wife to advise him before she exercises her personal choices." The Court held that the state may not give to a man "the kind of dominion over his wife that parents exercise over their children."

Planned Parenthood v. Casey is a landmark decision concerning abortion rights. But the plurality also provided one of the Court's most important treatments of *stare decisis* — the principle that the Court should stand by its own precedents. The very first sentence of the joint opinion stated, "Liberty finds no refuge in a jurisprudence of doubt."

STUDY GUIDE

What is the relationship between liberty and precedent?

The three members of the plurality admitted that they might not have agreed with *Roe* "as an original matter." But they relied on stare decisis to uphold what they referred to as *Roe*'s "central holding." Yet, other important elements of *Roe*, like the trimester framework, were discarded.

When should the Court overturn a precedent? The plurality identified several "prudential and pragmatic considerations designed to test the consistency of overruling a prior decision with the ideal of the rule of law, and to gauge the respective costs of reaffirming and overruling a prior case":

1. "whether the rule has proven to be intolerable simply in defying *practical workability*";
2. "whether the rule is subject to a kind of *reliance* that would lend a special hardship to the consequences of overruling and add inequity to the cost of repudiation";
3. "whether related *principles of law have so far developed* as to have left the old rule no more than a remnant of abandoned doctrine"; or
4. "whether *facts have so changed*, or come to be seen so differently, as to have robbed the old rule of significant application or justification."

Despite *Roe*'s controversial status, the plurality found that the decision has not proven "unworkable in practice," and has undoubtedly engendered "reliance." The joint opinion observed that many people have "organized intimate relationships" based on *Roe*.

The plurality also contended that the Court would be *weakened* as an institution if *Roe* were now overturned: "[T]o overrule [*Roe*] under fire in the absence of the most compelling reason to reexamine a watershed decision would subvert the Court's *legitimacy* beyond any serious question." For that reason, the plurality found it "imperative to adhere to the essence of *Roe*'s original decision."

Chief Justice Rehnquist wrote the principal dissent, which he delivered from the bench. He chastised the majority for simultaneously abandoning *Roe* yet claiming to reaffirm it under the doctrine of stare decisis:

(1) *Roe* decided that a woman has a fundamental right to an abortion. The joint opinion rejects that view. (2) *Roe* decided that abortion regulations were to be subjected to strict scrutiny and could be justified only in the light of compelling state interests. The joint opinion rejects that view. (3) *Roe* analyzed abortion regulation under a rigid trimester framework, a framework which has guided this Court's decision making for 19 years. The joint opinion rejects that framework and cases following *Roe* are overruled. (4) The analysis in *Roe* is replaced by what is called the 'undue burden test' which does not command the majority of this Court even today. This is surely not stare decisis as we have known it up until now.

Rehnquist also disagreed with the plurality's claim that the Court's "legitimacy" would be undermined if *Roe* was reversed "under fire":

The joint opinion's insistence on preserving the form, if not the substance of the rule, can just as easily be viewed as a surrender to those who have brought political pressure in favor of that decision. Once the Court starts looking to the currents of public opinion regarding a particular judgment, it enters a truly bottomless pit from which there is simply no extracting itself.

Justice Scalia wrote a separate dissent. He offered an even blunter criticism of the joint opinion's approach to stare decisis. The plurality "insists upon the necessity of adhering not to all of *Roe*," he wrote, "but only to what it calls the 'central holding.'" Scalia continued, "It seems to me that stare decisis ought to be applied even to the doctrine of stare decisis, and I confess never to have heard of this new, keep-what-you-want-and-throw-away-the-rest version."

STUDY GUIDE

What value should the Supreme Court give to precedent when it decides a case concerning important constitutional issues?

The right to abortion survived, but *Roe v. Wade* was substantially modified. In *Whole Woman's Health v. Hellerstedt* (2016), a majority of the Court would embrace the *Casey* plurality's "undue burden" approach.

CHAPTER 47

Whole Woman's Health v. Hellerstedt (2016)

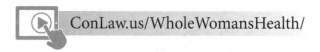

ConLaw.us/WholeWomansHealth/

The Supreme Court's abortion jurisprudence has not followed a straight line. *Roe v. Wade* (1973) held that the right to abortion was fundamental. Accordingly, the Supreme Court reviewed abortion restrictions with strict scrutiny. Under this framework, the state only had a compelling interest to protect fetal life in the third trimester, after the point of viability. Nearly two decades later, *Planned Parenthood v. Casey* (1992) upheld *Roe*'s "central holding" but made several important changes. Critically, the joint opinion adopted the "undue burden" standard. And the plurality found that the state had an interest to protect fetal life throughout all nine months of the pregnancy.

Following *Casey*, the composition of the Court would change. Soon, Justices White and Blackmun retired. They were replaced by Justices Ginsburg and Breyer, in 1993 and 1994, respectively. In 2005, Chief Justice Rehnquist passed away, and was replaced by Chief Justice Roberts. In 2006, Justice O'Connor was replaced by Justice Alito.

In 2007, the new Roberts Court decided its first major abortion case. *Gonzales v. Carhart* upheld the federal ban on partial-birth abortions. The vote was 5-4. Of the three Justices in the *Casey* plurality, only Justice Souter dissented. Justice O'Connor was no longer on the Court. Justice Kennedy wrote the majority opinion. He found that the federal law was consistent with *Casey*:

> We find the Act does not impose an undue burden by reason of its lack of an exception for protecting women's health. . . . The Court has given state and federal legislatures in other cases wide discretion to pass legislation in areas where this medical and scientific uncertainty exists. Physicians are not entitled to ignore regulations that direct them to use reasonable alternative procedures. . . .

After *Carhart* was decided, the composition of the Court would change again. In 2009, Justice Sotomayor replaced Justice Souter. The following year, Justice Kagan replaced Justice Stevens. Soon, the Roberts Court would consider another abortion case.

In 2013, Texas enacted two controversial restrictions on abortion providers. Under the first provision, doctors who performed abortions were required to have admitting privileges at a hospital within thirty miles. As a result, many doctors in rural locations who could not obtain such admitting privileges would have to stop performing abortions. Under the second provision, abortion facilities were required to meet the standards of an *ambulatory surgical center*. Compliance with these standards would be very costly. Further, this requirement was also imposed on clinics that did not perform surgical abortions, but only prescribed abortion-inducing drugs. Taken together, these regulations would shut down most abortion clinics outside of big cities, including Whole Woman's Health.

The District Court declared the law was unconstitutional. It evaluated conflicting evidence about the costs of—and claimed need for—these regulations. The Fifth Circuit Court of Appeals then reversed. The Supreme Court granted certiorari in November 2015. But, in February 2016, Justice Scalia suddenly passed away. The short-handed Court heard oral arguments one month later.

In June 2016, the Court decided *Whole Woman's Health v. Hellerstedt* by a 5-3 vote. The majority declared unconstitutional both provisions of Texas's law because they were inconsistent with *Casey*. Justice Kennedy cast the deciding vote in favor of the challengers. Justice Scalia's vote likely would have made the split 5-4—not enough to change the outcome.

Unlike in *Casey* and *Carhart*, Justice Kennedy would not write the controlling opinion in *Whole Woman's Health*. When the Chief Justice is not in the majority, the most senior Justice in the majority can assign the majority opinion. Here, Justice Kennedy assigned the task to Justice Breyer.

STUDY GUIDE

What level of deference is owed to laws promoting health and safety that regulate abortions?

The majority opinion considered two aspects of the undue burden test with respect to the Texas law: both the claimed health benefits and the burdens imposed on the mother. During oral argument, Justice Breyer posed the question bluntly: "What is the benefit to the woman of a procedure that is going to cure a problem of which there is not one single instance in the nation, though perhaps there is one, but not in Texas?" Scott Keller, the Texas Solicitor General responded that, under *Casey*, the undue burden test solely "examines access to abortion." He conceded that "if a law had no health benefits, presumably, it would be irrational."

However, he countered that consideration of a law's health benefits "has never been the test under *Casey.*"

Justice Breyer disagreed. To determine whether a burden is *undue,* the Court considered "the burden a law imposes on abortion access," as well as "the existence or non-existence of medical benefits." Justice Breyer found that "the admitting privileges requirement brought about no health benefits." Therefore, this requirement "places a burden upon a woman's right which *given the lack of health benefit* is *undue.*"

STUDY GUIDE

Justice Ginsburg wrote a concurring opinion. She suggested that the true motive behind the Texas law was to "strew impediments to abortion." Is there evidence of this improper intent in the record? If not, how are courts to ascertain this intent?

Next, Justice Breyer considered the second provision. He found that mandating abortion facilities to meet the requirements of an ambulatory surgical center would not provide women with "better care" or "more frequent positive outcomes." Yet, enforcement of these requirements would place a "substantial obstacle in the path of a woman seeking an abortion." The majority reasoned that if a law makes obtaining an abortion substantially more difficult, while offering no compensating health benefits, then the law imposes an *undue* burden on the right to an abortion.

STUDY GUIDE

Is the Court's framework in *Whole Woman's Health* the same as that announced in *Planned Parenthood v. Casey*? After *Whole Woman's Health,* is there any meaningful difference between strict scrutiny and the undue burden standard?

Justice Thomas wrote a solo dissent that challenged the modern Court's use of "tiers of scrutiny." First, he charged that the majority applied a level of scrutiny that "bears little resemblance to the undue-burden test" from *Casey.* According to Justice Thomas, *Casey* did not permit the Court to weigh the benefits of the regulations against its costs to determine whether the burden was "undue."

STUDY GUIDE

Is it really possible to determine whether a burden on the exercise of a fundamental right is "undue" without considering the benefits of the regulation, or lack thereof?

Second, Justice Thomas lamented the fact that the Court has a "troubling tendency 'to bend the rules when any effort to limit abortion, or even to speak in opposition to abortion, is at issue.'" Third, he attacked Footnote Four of *Carolene Products*, which "created a new taxonomy of preferred rights." That framework, which was originally designed to protect *enumerated* rights, was later expanded to protect *unenumerated* "putative rights like abortion, which hardly implicate 'discrete and insular minorities.'" He continued, "The Court has simultaneously transformed *judicially created* rights like the right to abortion into preferred constitutional rights, while disfavoring many of the rights actually enumerated in the Constitution." Justice Thomas concluded, "The Court should abandon the pretense that anything other than policy preferences underlies its balancing of constitutional rights and interests in any given case."

CHAPTER 48

Lawrence v. Texas (2003)

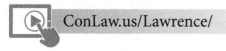

ConLaw.us/Lawrence/

In *Bowers v. Hardwick* (1986), the Supreme Court held that the Fourteenth Amendment did not protect a fundamental right to homosexual sodomy. Therefore, the state could criminalize such acts. However, in *Obergefell v. Hodges* (2015), the Supreme Court held that the Fourteenth Amendment did protect a fundamental right to same-sex marriage. This rapid jurisprudential change was remarkable. How did the Court's precedents transition from *Bowers* to *Obergefell* in just three decades?

During this span, the Supreme Court decided three important Due Process and Equal Protection Clause cases. In Chapter 43, we studied the first case, *Romer v. Evans* (1995). It held that Colorado could not amend its Constitution to deny gays and lesbians certain legal protections. *Romer* did not identify sexual orientation as a "suspect classification." Instead, Justice Kennedy's majority opinion reviewed the state constitutional amendment with heightened rational basis scrutiny under the Equal Protection Clause.

Romer did not, however, overrule *Bowers*. That step was taken in the second case in the trilogy. *Lawrence v. Texas* (2003) held that a criminal prohibition of homosexual sodomy violated the Due Process Clause. The third case, *United States v. Windsor* (2013), declared unconstitutional portions of the federal Defense of Marriage Act (DOMA). We will study *Lawrence* in this chapter. In Chapter 49 we will discuss *Windsor*.

Lawrence began in Houston, Texas. Police officers were dispatched to a private residence in response to a reported weapons disturbance. The officers observed John Lawrence and another man, Tyron Garner, engaging in a sexual act. They arrested the men and charged them with violating Texas's ban on "sodomy," which prohibited sexual acts between members of the same sex. The couple pleaded no contest, and the lower courts upheld their conviction.

On appeal, the Supreme Court held that Lawrence and Garner "were free as adults to engage in the private conduct in the exercise of their liberty under the due process clause of the Fourteenth Amendment." The vote was 6-3. Justice Kennedy wrote the majority opinion. He found "that our laws and traditions in the past half century are of most relevance here. These references show an emerging awareness that liberty gives substantial protection to adult persons in deciding how to conduct their private lives in matters pertaining to sex."

STUDY GUIDE

Do you see any similarity between Justice Kennedy's approach in *Lawrence* and his approach in *Romer*?

Justice Kennedy maintained that the *Bowers* Court had misstated the nature of the right being asserted. The question presented in that case was "whether the federal Constitution confers a fundamental *right upon homosexuals to engage in sodomy.*" Justice Kennedy rejected this characterization of the right:

> To say that the issue in *Bowers* was simply the right to engage in certain sexual conduct demeans the claim the individual put forward, just as it would demean a married couple were it to be said marriage is simply about the right to have sexual intercourse.

To be sure, the laws involved in *Bowers* "purport[ed] to do no more than prohibit a particular sexual act." But this prohibition, Justice Kennedy wrote, touched "upon the most private human conduct, sexual behavior, and in the most private of places, the home." The legislature sought "to control a personal relationship that, whether or not entitled to formal recognition in the law, is within the liberty of persons to choose without being punished as criminals."

Next, Justice Kennedy considered whether the state's police power permitted the government to pursue this purpose. He acknowledged "that the Court in *Bowers* was making the broader point that for centuries there have been powerful voices to condemn homosexual conduct as immoral." This "condemnation has been shaped by religious beliefs, conceptions of right and acceptable behavior, and respect for the traditional family." Yet, Justice Kennedy concluded, the Court had a duty to determine "whether the majority may use the power of the state to enforce these views on the whole society." He then quoted a line from his plurality opinion in *Casey*: "Our obligation is to define the liberty of all, not to mandate our own moral code."

With respect to gays and lesbians, Justice Kennedy continued, the "State cannot demean their existence or control their destiny by making their private sexual conduct a crime. Their right to liberty under the Due Process Clause gives them the full right to engage in their conduct without intervention of the government." Once again, he quoted from his opinion in *Casey*: "It is a promise of the Constitution that there is a realm of personal liberty which the government may not enter." Justice Kennedy concluded that the "statute furthers no legitimate state interest which can justify its intrusion into the personal and private life of the individual."

This approach represented a sharp departure from Justice White's majority opinion in *Bowers*. He found that "heightened judicial protection" was inappropriate when reviewing "rights not readily identifiable in the Constitution's text." *Bowers* identified an important reason to review laws that burden unenumerated rights with rational basis scrutiny: doing so would prevent "the imposition of the Justices' own choice of values on the States and the Federal Government." The *Bowers* test drew upon two prior decisions that characterized "fundamental liberties."

First, *Palko v. Connecticut* (1937) held that heightened judicial scrutiny was appropriate to review restrictions on "those fundamental liberties that are '*implicit in the concept of ordered liberty*,' such that 'neither liberty nor justice would exist if [they] were sacrificed.'" Second, *Moore v. East Cleveland* (1977) explained that heightened judicial scrutiny was appropriate to review restrictions on "those liberties that are '*deeply rooted in this Nation's history and tradition*.'"

Washington v. Glucksberg (1997), decided six years before *Lawrence*, refined this two-fold description of fundamental liberties. *Glucksberg* considered whether the Constitution protected the fundamental right of "a mentally competent, terminally ill adult to commit physician-assisted suicide." The Supreme Court held that the Due Process Clause of the Fourteenth Amendment did not protect this right. Chief Justice Rehnquist wrote the majority opinion. He explained:

> Our established method of substantive due process analysis has two primary features: First, we have regularly observed that the Due Process Clause specially protects those fundamental rights and liberties which are, objectively, "deeply rooted in this Nation's history and tradition," and "implicit in the concept of ordered liberty," such that "neither liberty nor justice would exist if they were sacrificed." Second, we have required in substantive due process cases a "careful description" of the asserted fundamental liberty interest.

In practice, these two "features" are listed in reverse order. First, courts will carefully describe the liberty interest as specifically or concretely as possible. Second, courts will then determine if that narrowly defined liberty interest is "deeply rooted" in this Nation's history and tradition. Generally, when a liberty is defined very narrowly, by definition that right will not be deeply rooted in history and tradition.

Justice Kennedy joined the majority in *Glucksberg*. Yet, in *Lawrence*, Justice Kennedy did not follow *Glucksberg's* reasoning. First, he failed to offer a "careful" or *narrow* description of the right at issue; for example, the right to engage in homosexual sodomy. Rather, he defined the right at issue far more broadly: "When sexuality finds overt expression in intimate conduct with another person, the conduct can be but one element in a personal bond that is more enduring. The liberty protected by the Constitution allows homosexual persons the right to make this choice."

Second, Justice Kennedy did not inquire whether such a right was "deeply rooted" in this Nation's history and tradition. Instead, he recognized "an emerging awareness that liberty gives substantial protection to adult persons in deciding how to conduct their private lives in matters pertaining to sex." History and tradition, he said, "are the starting point but not in all cases the ending point of the substantive due process inquiry."

Bowers v. Hardwick was overruled only seventeen years after it was decided. Justice Kennedy stated, "*Bowers* was not correct when it was decided and it is not correct today. It ought not to remain binding precedent. *Bowers v. Hardwick* should be and now is overruled." Yet the Court did not overrule *Glucksberg*. After *Lawrence* was decided, some of the Justices have continued to follow *Glucksberg*'s "deeply rooted" framework to identify fundamental rights.

For example, in *McDonald v. Chicago* (2010), four Justices found that the right to keep and bear arms was deeply rooted in history and tradition. (See Chapter 61.) Therefore, under the *Glucksberg* approach, the Due Process Clause protected this "fundamental" right. (The *McDonald* plurality did not decide whether the right to bear arms was protected by the Privileges or Immunities Clause.)

Other Justices, however, have declined to apply the *Glucksberg* approach. In *Obergefell v. Hodges* (2015), the majority held that the Due Process Clause of the Fourteenth Amendment protected a right to same-sex marriage. (See Chapter 50.) Here, the majority did not rely on *Glucksberg*'s two-step approach to identify a fundamental right. In contrast, Chief Justice Roberts and Justice Alito — who joined the *McDonald* plurality — dissented. They contended that the right to same-sex marriage was not deeply rooted in history and tradition.

STUDY GUIDE

Does *Lawrence* treat the precedent of *Bowers* the same way *Casey* treated the precedent of *Roe*?

In *Lawrence*, Justice O'Connor concurred in the majority's judgment. But she declined to overrule *Bowers*, which she had joined seventeen years earlier. The Georgia sodomy statute at issue in *Bowers* banned certain sexual acts, regardless of whether the people were of the same or opposite sex. In contrast, the Texas law only criminalized sodomy between people of the *same* sex. Heterosexual sodomy was lawful. This classification, she found, violated the Equal Protection Clause of the Fourteenth Amendment.

Justice O'Connor's analysis relied on *Department of Agriculture v. Moreno* (1973). This case considered whether Congress could prohibit households with "unrelated" family members from receiving food stamps. The stated purpose behind this law was to prevent fraud. But the Court determined that Congress had a different purpose: to block hippies living in communes from receiving food stamps. *Moreno* held that Congress violated the Equal Protection component of the Fifth Amendment's Due Process Clause because its law was motivated by "animus" towards hippies. Justice Brennan's majority opinion established an important test: "For if the constitutional conception of 'equal protection of the laws' means anything, it must, at the very least, mean that a *bare congressional desire to harm* a politically unpopular group cannot constitute a legitimate governmental interest."

In *Lawrence*, Justice O'Connor found that the Texas law was motivated by a *bare desire to harm* gays and lesbians. She contended that "*moral disapproval* [of homosexuality], without any other asserted state interest, is [not] a sufficient rationale under the Equal Protection Clause to justify a law that discriminates among groups of persons." The sodomy statute was unconstitutional, she found, because Texas failed to offer any *other* basis for the law.

Justice Scalia wrote a vigorous dissent. He charged that the Court simply made up a constitutional right: "What Texas has chosen to do is well within the range of traditional democratic action, and its hand should not be stayed through the invention of a brand-new 'constitutional right' by a Court that is impatient of democratic change." He also charged that Justice Kennedy ignored *Washington v. Glucksberg*: "Though there is discussion of 'fundamental proposition[s]' and 'fundamental decisions,' nowhere does the Court's opinion declare that homosexual sodomy is a 'fundamental right' under the Due Process Clause." Because the majority did not make such a finding, he said, the Court should not have subjected "the Texas law to the standard of review that would be appropriate (strict scrutiny) if homosexual sodomy were a 'fundamental right.'"

Generally, in Due Process Clause cases, courts will review laws that violate *fundamental* rights with heightened scrutiny. And in Equal Protection Clause cases, the Court will review laws that use *suspect* or *quasi-suspect* classifications with heightened scrutiny. Yet in *Lawrence*, Justice Kennedy did not identify sexual relations between persons of the same sex to be a fundamental right; nor did he find that gays and lesbians were a suspect or quasi-suspect class. Instead, he seemed to employ the form of *heightened* rational basis scrutiny used in *Cleburne* and *Romer*.

Under rational basis scrutiny, a law that restricts liberty must be reasonably related to a legitimate state interest. Had Texas asserted a legitimate state interest? The Court answered no. Justice Kennedy adopted the reasoning from Justice Stevens's *Bowers* dissent: "[T]he fact that the governing majority of a State has traditionally viewed a particular practice as immoral is not a sufficient reason for upholding a law prohibiting the practice." In short, bare moral disapproval is not a legitimate state interest.

Justice Scalia strongly disagreed with this conclusion. He acknowledged that Texas sought "to further the belief of its citizens that certain forms of sexual behavior are, as the court says, 'immoral and unacceptable.'" But unlike Justices Kennedy and O'Connor, Justice Scalia did not find this purpose problematic. Texas's interest — expressing disapproval of immoral conduct — is "the same interest furthered by criminal laws against fornication, bigamy, adultery, adult incest, bestiality, and obscenity."

In this oft-criticized passage, Justice Scalia was not equating homosexual conduct with incest and bestiality. Instead, he claimed that each of these prohibitions are enforced based solely on moral disapproval of certain types of immoral conduct. These laws are not enforced to prevent conduct that causes demonstrable harm to other people. To this list, he might have added laws against animal cruelty. Justice Scalia found that Texas had a legitimate state interest that justified the enforcement of the sodomy law: preventing sexual behavior that the society believed was "immoral and unacceptable." In other words, bare moral disapproval. Because the Court reached the opposite conclusion, he lamented, *Lawrence* "effectively decree[d] the end of all morals legislation."

Justice Kennedy attempted to limit the scope of his decision. He insisted that *Lawrence* did not present the question "whether the government must *give formal recognition* to any relationship that homosexual persons seek to enter." Justice Scalia was not persuaded. He read his dissent from the bench, and responded:

> Do not believe it. Today's opinion dismantles the structure of constitutional law that has permitted a distinction to be made between heterosexual and homosexual unions. If moral disapprobation of homosexual conduct is as the Court says "no legitimate state interest" . . . [w]hat justification could there possibly be for denying the benefits of marriage to homosexual couples exercising what the Court in today's opinion calls "the liberty protected by the constitution"?

Justice Scalia's prediction would prove to be accurate.

CHAPTER 49

United States v. Windsor (2013)

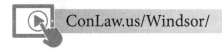

ConLaw.us/Windsor/

In the years following *Lawrence v. Texas* (2003), several states legalized same-sex marriage through judicial decisions, legislation, and popular referendums. During the same time, other states amended their constitutions to prohibit same-sex marriage. This divide created a challenge for the administration of federal law. How should the federal government treat a same-sex couple that was married in one state, but then moves to another state where same-sex marriage was not recognized?

The federal Defense of Marriage Act (DOMA) addressed this problem. Section 3 of the law provided a single federal definition of marriage: one man and one woman. Under DOMA, it did not matter where the couple was married, or where they lived. DOMA was enacted with broad bipartisan support in 1996, four months after *Romer v. Evans* was decided. President Clinton signed DOMA into law shortly before the 1996 presidential election.

In *United States v. Windsor*, the Supreme Court considered the constitutionality of Section 3 of DOMA. The Obama administration concluded that the provision was unconstitutional, and declined to defend it. As a result, the House of Representatives intervened in the litigation to defend DOMA. The House was represented by Paul Clement, the former Solicitor General.

A decade earlier in *Lawrence*, the Court considered whether bare moral disapproval could serve as a rational basis to treat gays and lesbians differently. *Windsor* revisited that debate. During oral argument, Justice Kagan observed that in 1996, the House of Representatives stated that DOMA would "reflect and honor a collective moral judgment" and express "moral disapproval of homosexuality." She asked Paul Clement, "is that what happened in 1996?" Clement replied, "Of course, the House Report says that. And if that's enough to invalidate the statute, then you should invalidate the statute." He then countered that such a test "has never been your approach, especially under rational basis or even rational basis-plus." This colloquy foreshadowed the outcome in *Windsor*.

Solicitor General Donald Verrilli argued on behalf of the Obama administration. He denied that DOMA was "enacted for any purpose of uniformity, administration, caution, pausing, any of that." Instead, he contended Congress had only one purpose: "to exclude same-sex married, lawfully married couples from Federal benefit regimes based on a conclusion that was driven by 'moral disapproval.'" Chief Justice Roberts asked if "that was the view of the 84 Senators who voted in favor of [DOMA] and the President who signed it? They were motivated by animus?"

In a 5-4 decision, the Court found that Congress and President Clinton, in fact, were motivated by animus. Once again, Justice Kennedy wrote the majority opinion in *Windsor*, as he did in *Romer* and *Lawrence*. The Court found that DOMA's purpose was to "impose a disadvantage, a separate status, and so a stigma upon all who enter into same-sex marriages made lawful by the unquestioned authority of the states." As a result, "if any state decides to recognize same-sex marriages, those unions will be treated as second-class marriages for purposes of federal law."

Did it matter that Congress could have also enacted DOMA to resolve difficult choice-of-law questions? Justice Kennedy answered no:

> No legitimate purpose overcomes the purpose and effect to disparage and to injure those whom the state, by its marriage laws, sought to protect in personhood and dignity. By seeking to displace this protection and treating those persons as living in marriage less respected than others, the federal statute is in violation of the Fifth Amendment.

Did DOMA violate the Due Process Clause of the Fifth Amendment? Or did it violate the Equal Protection component of the Fifth Amendment? Justice Kennedy suggested that Section 3 of DOMA violated *both*: The federal law "violates basic Due Process and Equal Protection principles applicable to the Federal Government."

Once again, Justice Scalia wrote a vigorous dissent, which he delivered from the bench. He criticized the majority, which failed to follow the test from *Washington v. Glucksberg* (1997). That case held that for an unenumerated right to be "fundamental," it had to be "deeply rooted in this Nation's history and tradition." And laws that violate fundamental rights would be reviewed with strict scrutiny. However, in Windsor, Justice Kennedy did not determine whether a right to same-sex marriage was "fundamental." Indeed, Justice Scalia observed, "it is difficult to pin down the precise technical legal basis for the majority's conclusion of unconstitutionality." Instead, he continued, "what causes DOMA to be unconstitutional is the fact that it [was] motivated by 'the bare desire to harm' couples in same-sex marriages." Justice Scalia would "require the most extraordinary evidence" before charging that "Congress and the presidency of the United States" were "unhinged members of a wild-eyed lynch mob."

Justice Scalia countered that there was "a perfectly valid justification for the statute." DOMA resolved difficult choice-of-law questions:

> Imagine a pair of women who marry in Albany and then moved to Alabama, which does not recognize as valid any marriage of parties of the same sex. When the couple files their next federal tax return, maybe a joint one, which state's law controls for federal law purposes? The state of celebration (which recognizes the marriage) or their state of domicile (which does not)? . . . DOMA avoided all this uncertainty by specifying which marriages would be recognized for federal purposes.

Justice Alito wrote a separate dissent. He followed the *Glucksberg* approach: "It is beyond dispute that the right to same-sex marriage is not deeply rooted in this Nation's history and tradition." Instead, Windsor and the United States seek "the recognition of a very new right, and they seek this innovation not from a legislative body elected by the people, but from unelected judges."

Justice Kennedy tried to limit his majority opinion. He stressed that *Windsor* was "confined to those lawful marriages." In other words, *Windsor* said nothing about a right to same-sex marriage. Once again, as in *Lawrence*, Justice Scalia did not believe it:

> It takes real cheek for today's majority to assure us, as it is going out the door, that a constitutional requirement to give formal recognition to same-sex marriage is not at issue here — when what has preceded that assurance is a lecture on how superior the majority's moral judgment in favor of same-sex marriage is to the Congress's hateful moral judgment against it. I promise you this: The only thing that will "confine" the Court's holding is its sense of what it can get away with.

He concluded, "The Court has cheated both sides, robbing the winners of an honest victory and the losers of the peace that comes from a fair defeat. We owe both of them better. I dissent."

Shortly after *Windsor* was decided, district court judges across the country did as Justice Scalia predicted. They ruled that prohibitions on same-sex marriage violated the Fourteenth Amendment. In 2015, nearly thirty years after *Bowers v. Hardwick*, the Supreme Court decided *Obergefell v. Hodges*. Now, the Constitution was understood to protect a right to same-sex marriage nationwide. In the three decades from *Bowers* to *Obergefell*, Justice Kennedy wrote each of the major decisions expanding the rights of gays and lesbians.

CHAPTER 50

Obergefell v. Hodges (2015)

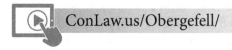

ConLaw.us/Obergefell/

Obergefell v. Hodges (2015) held that the Fourteenth Amendment requires a state to license a marriage between two people of the same sex. The Supreme Court split 5-4. As in *Romer*, *Lawrence*, and *Windsor*, Justice Kennedy wrote the majority opinion.

First, he explained that "[t]he fundamental liberties protected by the Fourteenth Amendment's Due Process Clause extend to certain personal choices central to individual dignity and autonomy, including intimate choices defining personal identity and beliefs."

STUDY GUIDE

What exactly is meant by "dignity"?

This analysis, however, was not limited to deeply rooted rights. "History and tradition" only "guide and discipline the inquiry but do not set its outer boundaries." Rather, "[w]hen new insight reveals discord between the Constitution's central protections and a received legal stricture," he wrote, "a claim to liberty must be addressed." Rather than being a fixed institution, "[t]he history of marriage is one of both continuity and change," especially where "new dimensions of freedom become apparent to new generations." Though the Supreme Court previously addressed marriage as an opposite-sex institution, more recent precedents, such as *Lawrence v. Texas* (2003), "have expressed broader principles."

STUDY GUIDE

Washington v. Glucksberg (1997) held that the Court would only review with strict scrutiny laws that burden those "fundamental" unenumerated rights that are "deeply rooted in this Nation's history and tradition" and are carefully described. Did *Obergefell* overrule *Glucksberg*?

Obergefell did not *expressly* overrule *Glucksberg*. Justice Kennedy wrote, "*Glucksberg* did insist that liberty under the Due Process Clause must be *defined in a most circumscribed manner*, with central reference to specific historical practices." The traditional "right to marry," he insisted, "is *fundamental* as a matter of history and tradition." But he did not, and could not, claim that the more "circumscribed" right of same-sex couples to marry was "deeply rooted in this Nation's history and tradition."

In order to find that the Due Process Clause protected a "fundamental" right to same-sex marriage, Justice Kennedy had to *implicitly* repudiate *Glucksberg*. He wrote that "rights come not from ancient sources alone." Such rights, he explained, rise "from a better informed understanding of how constitutional imperatives define a liberty that remains urgent in our own era." In this case, "same-sex couples seek in marriage the same legal treatment as opposite-sex couples, and it would disparage their choices and diminish their personhood to deny them this right." Thus, the government could not infringe this "fundamental" liberty, protected by the Fourteenth Amendment's Due Process Clause.

Next, the Court concluded that "the right of same-sex couples to marry is also derived from the Fourteenth Amendment's guarantee of equal protection." Yet, Justice Kennedy stopped short of recognizing sexual orientation as a suspect classification. Instead, the Court's analysis intertwined the Equal Protection and Due Process Clauses. "The challenged laws," Justice Kennedy remarked, "burden the *liberty* of same-sex couples, *and* they abridge central precepts of *equality*." The Court dismissed the need to wait for the political process to change the institution because "individuals who are harmed need not await legislative action before asserting a fundamental right."

There were four separate dissenting opinions in *Obergefell*: Chief Justice Roberts, and Justices Scalia, Thomas, and Alito. Chief Justice Roberts rejected the notion that the Court is a "legislature." He explained, "The fundamental right to marry does not include a right to make a State change its definition of marriage." It "can hardly be called irrational," he reasoned, to maintain the traditional definition of marriage that has "persisted in every culture throughout human history."

Chief Justice Roberts repeatedly equated the majority opinion to two anti-canonical cases. First, he wrote, "the majority's approach has no basis in principle or tradition, except for the unprincipled tradition of judicial policymaking that characterized discredited decisions such as *Lochner v. New York* (1905)." He added that in *Lochner* and in similar cases, the Court "invalidated state statutes that presented 'meddlesome interferences with the rights of the individual,' and 'undue interference with liberty of person and freedom of contract.'"

Second, he contended that *Lochner's* "approach to the Due Process Clause" can be traced back to *Dred Scott v. Sandford* (1857). *Dred Scott*, he wrote, was the first time the Court "applied substantive due process to strike down a statute." He continued, "*Dred Scott's* holding was overruled on the battlefields of the Civil War and by constitutional amendment after Appomattox."

STUDY GUIDE

Why would Chief Justice Roberts compare *Obergefell* to *Lochner* and *Dred Scott*?

Chief Justice Roberts then faulted Justice Kennedy for not applying the two-step approach from *Washington v. Glucksberg*. He observed that the Court's "modern substantive due process cases have stressed the need for 'judicial self-restraint'" as a means "[t]o avoid repeating *Lochner's* error of converting personal preferences into constitutional mandates." Specifically, the Court would review with heightened scrutiny only those laws that violate "implied fundamental rights [that are] 'objectively, deeply rooted in this Nation's history and tradition,' and 'implicit in the concept of ordered liberty, such that neither liberty nor justice would exist if they were sacrificed.'" But the majority did not follow these precedents. "It is revealing," Roberts wrote, "that the majority's position requires it to effectively overrule *Glucksberg*, the leading modern case setting the bounds of substantive due process."

Justice Scalia wrote the second dissent. He charged that the majority invented one liberty interest but disregarded another: "the freedom [of the people] to govern themselves." The Court, Justice Scalia wrote, "end[ed] this debate [over same-sex marriage], in an opinion lacking even a thin veneer of law."

STUDY GUIDE

How do you respond to Justice Scalia's concerns about the right of the people to govern themselves?

Justice Thomas wrote the third dissent. He contended that the majority tried to redefine the very notion of liberty: "[L]iberty has been understood as freedom from government action," he wrote, "not entitlement to government benefits." Citing Blackstone and other historical sources, Thomas argued that the phrase "liberty" in the Due Process Clause is limited to "freedom from physical restraint," not an entitlement, such as a marriage license. Because same-sex couples are not physically restrained, Justice Thomas found no constitutional violation. Finally, he concluded, "the Constitution contains no 'dignity' Clause, and even if it did, the government would be incapable of bestowing dignity."

STUDY GUIDE

What are "positive" rights?

Justice Alito wrote the final dissent. He maintained that states possess a sufficient justification to limit marriage to opposite-sex couples: "to encourage potentially procreative conduct to take place within a lasting unit that has long been thought to provide the best atmosphere for raising children." Additionally, Justice Alito warned that this decision may harm religious liberty. "I assume that those who cling to old beliefs will be able to whisper their thoughts in the recesses of their homes," he wrote, "but if they repeat those views in public, they will risk being labeled as bigots and treated as such by governments, employers, and schools."

Obergefell was a landmark decision. But it failed to follow the doctrines the Court had previously used to evaluate Due Process and Equal Protection claims — namely, the identification of a fundamental right or the existence of a suspect class. We must await future decisions to see how the Court resolves this doctrinal tension.

PART XI

FREEDOM OF SPEECH

We begin our study of the First Amendment by analyzing the Sedition Act of 1798. Next, we turn to five foundational free speech cases decided during the early twentieth century: *Schenck v. United States* (1919), *Debs v. United States* (1919), *Abrams v. United States* (1919), *Gitlow v. People of the State of New York* (1925), and *Stromberg v. California* (1931).

With this history in mind, we consider two questions raised by the First Amendment: First, what exactly is *speech*? Three cases consider whether nonverbal conduct is speech: *United States v. O'Brien* (1968), *Texas v. Johnson* (1989), and *R.A.V. v. City of St. Paul* (1992). Three other cases hold that spending money is speech: *Buckley v. Valeo* (1976), *McConnell v. Federal Election Commission* (2003), and *Citizens United v. Federal Election Commission* (2010).

Second, what constitutes *an abridgement* of the freedom of speech? Two cases address whether the First Amendment protects tortious speech: *New York Times Company v. Sullivan* (1964) and *Snyder v. Phelps* (2011). Two other cases consider whether speech that is highly "offensive" is protected: *United States v. Stevens* (2010) and *Brown v. Entertainment Merchants Association* (2011).

CHAPTER 51

Sedition and Prior Restraint

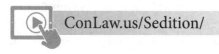

ConLaw.us/Sedition/

The First Amendment was ratified in 1791. It provides, in part, "Congress shall make no law . . . abridging the freedom of speech." This chapter will consider the original meaning of "the freedom of speech."

In 1798, the Federalist party controlled Congress. President John Adams, also a Federalist, favored the enactment of the Sedition Act. This law made it a crime to "write, print, utter or publish . . . any false, scandalous and malicious writing . . . against the government of the United States . . . with intent to defame the said government . . . or to bring [it] . . . into contempt or disrepute . . . or to excite against [it] . . . the hatred of the good people of the United States. . . ." The Adams administration prosecuted its opponents in the Republican party for violating the Sedition Act. At the time, Federalist-appointed judges dominated the federal judiciary and permitted those prosecutions.

The Republican-controlled legislatures in Virginia and Kentucky issued resolutions declaring that the Sedition Act was unconstitutional. James Madison is credited with authoring the Virginia Resolution, and Thomas Jefferson is credited with writing the Kentucky Resolution.

The Virginia Resolution declared that the Sedition Act was "unconstitutional." But it did not claim the power to unilaterally "nullify" the Sedition Act. Instead, the Commonwealth enlisted the opinions of other like-minded states. Virginia also stated that the Commonwealth has "the right, and [is] in duty bound, to *interpose* for arresting the progress of the evil." Through "interposition," the state government intervened to press for the rights of its people against the assertion of power by the federal government. "Interposition" was different from "nullification," though one could favor both interposition and nullification.

The Kentucky Resolution did use the term "nullification." It is not clear, however, that the proponents of the Kentucky Resolution believed that a federal law would become non-operational because one state believed it to be unconstitutional.

Instead, the Resolution authorized a formal protest against the Sedition Act's unconstitutionality. It provided, in part: "That although this commonwealth as a party to the federal compact, will bow to the laws of the Union, yet it does at the same time declare, that it will not now, nor ever hereafter, cease to oppose *in a constitutional manner*, every attempt from what quarter soever offered, to violate that compact."

In early 1800, James Madison — then a Representative from Virginia — published a lengthy report that defended the Virginia Resolution. Madison explained that there is a difference between a state declaring a law unconstitutional and a court declaring a law unconstitutional. "The declarations" by states, he wrote, "are *expressions of opinion*, unaccompanied with any other effect than what they may produce on opinion, by exciting reflection. The expositions of the judiciary, on the other hand, are *carried into immediate effect by force*." The Virginia and Kentucky Resolutions illustrate how the Constitution is interpreted outside of the courts.

Moreover, Madison's report argued that Congress did not have the enumerated powers to enact the Sedition Act. He also argued that the prohibition on sedition violated the First Amendment. This latter discussion illuminates two theories of how the freedom of speech was originally understood.

According to the first theory, the government cannot impose what is called a "prior restraint" on the "freedom of speech." In other words, people cannot be silenced *in advance* of speaking. But on this reading of the "freedom of speech," according to the common law, people can still be punished *after* they speak. In England, the freedom of speech could not be limited through "prior restraints." We call this first theory the British theory of "freedom of speech."

Madison also defended a second theory that is distinctly American. He contended that the British conception of the freedom of speech only prevented prior restraints *by the Crown*. Parliament, however, *could* impose prior restraints, because the British legislature was considered supreme. Madison wrote that the "right of freedom of speech" protected by the First Amendment was much broader. Under the American theory, he argued, it is unconstitutional for the government to constrain the exercise of free expression, both before and after the fact.

The U.S. Constitution rejected *parliamentary supremacy* in favor of *popular sovereignty*. Under the American theory of popular sovereignty, Congress's powers are limited by the Constitution, including the First Amendment. Indeed, the First Amendment begins, "Congress shall make no law . . . ." Therefore, Madison concluded, federal legislation that punishes speech after the fact is *also* unconstitutional.

Later that year, the presidential election of 1800 was held. Thomas Jefferson narrowly defeated John Adams. Jefferson's victory was due, in part, to the controversy surrounding the Sedition Act. This election came to be known as the *Revolution of 1800*. As President, Jefferson pardoned those who had been convicted for violating the Sedition Act.

Although the Supreme Court did not rule on the constitutionality of the Sedition Act, modern courts have accepted Madison's interpretation as the original meaning of "freedom of speech." For example, in *New York Times v. Sullivan* (1964), the Supreme Court favorably cited Madison and Jefferson's criticism of the Sedition Act. Justice Brennan wrote for a unanimous Court: "Although the Sedition Act was never tested in this Court, the attack upon its validity has carried the day in the court of history."

CHAPTER 52

"Clear and Present Danger"

During the eighteenth and nineteenth centuries, the Supreme Court considered very few cases that involved the Free Speech Clause of the First Amendment. The Supreme Court did not begin to develop its modern free-speech doctrine until World War I. During this conflict, Congress enacted the Espionage Act. The Wilson administration tried to silence its critics by prosecuting them under this law.

In 1919, the Supreme Court considered the constitutionality of three convictions for sedition. Justice Holmes wrote the majority opinions in the first two appeals: *Schenck v. United States* and *Debs v. United States*. Both cases, decided in March 1919, upheld the convictions. The third case, *Abrams v. United States*, was decided in November 1919. Justice Holmes dissented. He found that the prosecutions were unconstitutional.

Schenck v. United States (1919)

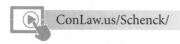 ConLaw.us/Schenck/

During World War I, Charles Schenck circulated literature that urged people to resist the military draft. He wrote that the draft amounted to a form of slavery, in violation of the Thirteenth Amendment. The Wilson Administration charged Schenck under the Espionage Act with "obstruct[ing] the recruitment and enlistment service of the United States, when the United States was at war with the German Empire." Schenck argued that the prosecution violated the Free Speech Clause of the First Amendment.

The Supreme Court upheld the conviction unanimously. Justice Holmes wrote the majority opinion. He explained that during "ordinary times" the defendant would be permitted to oppose the draft. However, "the character of every act depends upon the circumstances in which it is done." Justice Holmes then offered what became a very famous analogy — one that is often misunderstood. He wrote, "The most stringent protection of free speech would not protect a man in falsely shouting fire in a theatre and causing a panic." It is perfectly acceptable to shout fire if there is actually a fire. The government could only prohibit "*falsely* shouting fire in a crowded theater," Holmes found.

Justice Holmes offered another famous test in *Schenck*: "The question in every case is whether the words used are used in such circumstances and are of such a nature as to create *a clear and present danger* that they will bring about the substantive evils that Congress has a right to prevent." During World War I, circumstances were dire. "When a nation is at war many things that might be said in time of peace are such a hindrance to its effort that their utterance will not be endured so long as men fight and that no Court could regard them as protected by any constitutional right." Therefore, Schenck's conviction was constitutional.

To this day, "clear and present danger" is a memorable phrase. But in the 1920s, it was merely a colorful term for what is known as the *bad tendency test*. That test allowed the government to ban speech if "the natural and probable *tendency and effect* of a publication are such as are calculated to produce the result condemned by the statute." Under this relatively deferential test, the defendant's *criminal intent is inferred* from the speech's tendency to lead to violations of the law.

Five decades later, the Supreme Court effectively overturned *Schenck* in *Brandenburg v. Ohio*. This 1969 decision held that the government cannot "forbid or proscribe advocacy of the use of force or of law violation except where such advocacy is directed to inciting or producing *imminent* lawless action and is *likely* to incite or produce such action."

Debs v. United States (1919)

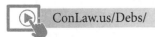 ConLaw.us/Debs/

The second case involved Eugene Debs. He ran for President of the United States five times on the Socialist Party ticket. In 1918, Debs gave a speech to a crowd in Canton, Ohio. He advocated for socialism and argued that the war against Germany was unjustified. The Wilson administration prosecuted Debs for violating the Espionage Act.

Once again, Justice Holmes wrote the majority opinion that upheld the conviction. The Court found that the First Amendment did not protect the obstruction of lawful military recruiting. Holmes concluded that Debs's purpose was to "oppose not only war in general but this war, and that the opposition was so expressed that its *natural and intended effect* would be to obstruct recruiting." Here, Holmes applied the *bad tendency test*. Two years later, in 1921, President Harding commuted Debs's sentence to time served, allowing the Socialist to be released from prison.

Abrams v. United States (1919)

ConLaw.us/Abrams/

In November 1919, eight months after *Schenck* and *Debs* were decided, the Court resolved *Abrams v. United States*. In this case, the defendants distributed leaflets that urged factory workers who made war munitions to go on strike. The federal government prosecuted them for violating the Espionage Act. The Supreme Court upheld their convictions by a 7-2 vote. Justice Clarke wrote the majority opinion. He found that this case was similar to *Schenck* and *Debs*: "The manifest purpose of such publications [the leaflets] was to create an attempt to defeat the war plans of the Government of the United States, by bringing upon the country the paralysis of a general strike, thereby arresting the production of all munitions and other things essential to the conduct of the war."

In *Abrams*, Justices Holmes dissented, along with Justice Brandeis. Justice Holmes did not question his previous majority opinions. Instead, he found that the *Abrams* convictions crossed the line he drew in *Schenck* and *Debs*. Specifically, Justice Holmes concluded that the *Abrams* defendants did not obstruct the lawful military draft: "It is only the present danger of immediate evil or an intent to bring it about that warrants Congress in setting a limit to the expression of opinion where private rights are not concerned." In other words, this case did not present a "clear and present danger."

Justice Holmes also found that the defendants lacked an intent to interfere with the war effort: "It is evident from the beginning to the end that the only object of the [circulated] paper is to help Russia and stop American intervention there against the popular government—not to impede the United States in the war it was carrying on."

Finally, Holmes provided yet another famous principle that animates our modern free speech jurisprudence: "The best test of truth is the power of the thought to get itself accepted in the competition of the market." This test became known as the "marketplace of ideas" theory.

STUDY GUIDE

Justice Holmes adopted the "marketplace of ideas" concept from British philosopher John Stuart Mill. Can this theory be reconciled with Holmes's claim in *Lochner v. New York* that the Fourteenth Amendment "does not adopt Mr. Herbert Spencer's *Social Statics*"?

Gitlow v. People of the State of New York (1925)

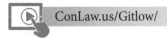

ConLaw.us/Gitlow/

Six years later, the Court decided *Gitlow v. People of the State of New York*. New York convicted Benjamin Gitlow of "criminal anarchy." Like Schenck, Gitlow also distributed Socialist literature.

STUDY GUIDE

The First Amendment provides that "*Congress* shall make no law . . . abridging the freedom of speech." Does this provision also impose limitations on a state's police power? What effect does the Fourteenth Amendment have on this question?

The Supreme Court upheld New York's restriction on speech. *Gitlow*, however, is an important case because it seemed to decide an important constitutional question: the First Amendment limited the state's police power by virtue of the Fourteenth Amendment's Due Process Clause. The Court "*assume[d]* that freedom of speech and of the press—which are protected by the First Amendment from abridgment by Congress—are among the fundamental personal rights and 'liberties' protected by the due process clause of the Fourteenth Amendment from impairment by the States." Ultimately, the Court found that the New York law did not "deprive[] the defendant of his liberty of expression in violation of the due process clause of the Fourteenth Amendment."

Once again, Justice Holmes dissented, joined by Justice Brandeis. He wrote, "there was no present danger of an attempt to overthrow the government by force on the part of the admittedly small minority who shared the defendant's views." For this reason, he believed that the conviction was unconstitutional.

Stromberg v. California (1931)

ConLaw.us/Stromberg/

In *Stromberg v. California* (1931), the defendant raised a red flag, which was a "reproduction of the flag of Soviet Russia." The state convicted him for displaying this anarchist symbol. On appeal, the Supreme Court reversed Stromberg's conviction. For the first time, the Justices found that a state restriction on speech was unconstitutional. Chief Justice Hughes wrote the majority opinion:

> The maintenance of the opportunity for free political discussion to the end that government may be responsive to the will of the people and that changes may be obtained by lawful means, an opportunity essential to the security of the Republic, is a fundamental principle of our constitutional system. A statute which upon its face, and as authoritatively construed, is so vague and indefinite as to permit the punishment of the fair use of this opportunity is repugnant to the guaranty of liberty contained in the Fourteenth Amendment.

The Supreme Court would not find that a federal law violated the Free Speech Clause until 1965.

CHAPTER 53

When Is Conduct Speech?

The three cases in this chapter share one trait: something gets burned. In *United States v. O'Brien* (1968) a draft card is burned. In *Texas v. Johnson* (1989) an American flag is burned. And in *R.A.V. v. St. Paul* (1992) a cross is burned. These cases will answer an important question: When is conduct, such as setting something on fire, considered speech?

United States v. O'Brien (1968)

ConLaw.us/OBrien/

Let's start with *O'Brien*. In the 1960s, all men who registered for the draft received a credit-card size cardboard certificate. The small white "draft card" displayed important information about the registrant, including his name, address, birthday, physical description, draft status, and selective service number. Men were required to carry their draft cards at all times. Before computers were commonly used, these physical records helped the government easily identify people who were eligible for the draft. During wartime, officials could order young men to produce their cards on demand and ensure they were not evading the draft. Congress made it a federal offense to "knowingly destroy, knowingly mutilate, or in any manner change" a draft card. Opponents of the Vietnam War would deliberately violate this law. They publicly burned their draft cards as a symbol of protest.

In March 1966, David Paul O'Brien and three others burned their draft cards on the steps of the South Boston Courthouse in the presence of a sizable crowd. An agent of the Federal Bureau of Investigation asked O'Brien what he had done. He answered that he had burned his draft card, and he knew that this act violated federal law. Yet he did so to persuade others to reevaluate their position about the draft.

O'Brien was charged with destroying his draft card. O'Brien's lawyer argued that burning the draft card was a *symbolic* "expression of dissent." Therefore, this conduct was protected by the First Amendment. Solicitor General Erwin Griswold defended the conviction before the Supreme Court. He conceded that "Congress did not forbid dissent. It could not do that." In this case, however, it did not matter whether or not the conduct was symbolic speech. Why? Because "there was no real impairment of any right to speak." Moreover, Griswold added, "other avenues of communication were always open to the defendant." Congress nevertheless has "the power to do what it regarded as necessary and proper in order to carry out its power granted by the constitution to raise and support armies."

The Court ruled against O'Brien by an 8-1 vote. Chief Justice Warren wrote the majority opinion. Even if O'Brien's conduct was "communicative," the Court held, "it does not necessarily follow that the destruction of a registration certificate is constitutionally protected activity." Why not? Here, Chief Justice Warren announced what came to be known as the four-factor *O'Brien* test. A government regulation "is sufficiently justified

1. if it is within the constitutional power of the Government;
2. if it furthers an important or substantial governmental interest;
3. if the governmental interest is unrelated to the suppression of free expression; and
4. if the incidental restriction on alleged First Amendment freedoms is no greater than is essential to the furtherance of that interest."

As a general matter, if a speech restriction satisfies the four elements of the *O'Brien* test, the law is reviewed with the more-deferential intermediate scrutiny. On the other hand, a speech restriction will be reviewed with strict scrutiny if it does not satisfy the *O'Brien* test — in particular, if the regulation *is* related to "the suppression of free expression."

In *O'Brien*, the first two factors were easily satisfied. Article 1, Section 8, gives Congress the enumerated power "to raise and support Armies." This provision empowers Congress to manage the selective service. The federal law that prohibits the destruction of draft cards, the Court held, improved the operation of the selective service. Second, managing the draft was a very important governmental interest.

With respect to the third element, O'Brien's lawyer argued that the prohibition on burning the draft card *was* related to the suppression of free speech. During oral argument, he contended that "the only congressional purpose here was . . . stamping out dissent." Moreover, he continued, the "congressional action in this case was an act of hysteria rather than act of reflection and there was a desire to do something real fast to punish what they considered to be unpatriotic." The Supreme Court disagreed because the draft card served a practical purpose: It "facilitates communication between registrants and local boards, simplifying the system and benefiting all concerned."

Fourth, the Court found that the restriction on symbolic speech was an "appropriately narrow means of protecting" the government's authority to manage the selective service. Because the four factors were satisfied, the Court reviewed the federal law with a form of intermediate scrutiny. In light of this deferential standard of review, the statute was upheld, and O'Brien's conviction was valid.

The distinction between conduct and speech is not very helpful. After all, speech is a form of conduct. The courts generally use the *O'Brien* test for a different purpose: To decide whether the government is restricting speech based on the content of the message, or if there was a content-neutral reason for restricting the speech.

For example, Congress did not prohibit burning draft cards because that act conveys an anti-war message. Indeed, O'Brien could protest the war by burning every document but his draft card. Rather, Congress prohibited draft card burning to preserve information needed to regulate the armed forces. This restriction satisfied the second and third factors of the *O'Brien* test: The law was (1) aimed at a legitimate government interest, and this interest was (2) "unrelated to the suppression of free expression." As a result, the Court reviewed the law with intermediate rather than strict scrutiny.

Texas v. Johnson (1989)

 ConLaw.us/Johnson/

During the 1984 Republican National Convention in Dallas, Texas, several protesters stole an American flag, which they handed to Gregory Lee Johnson. He marched to City Hall, "doused it with kerosene, and set it on fire." Texas convicted Johnson of burning the American flag.

STUDY GUIDE

What difference, if any, is there between burning a draft card and burning an American flag? Hint: What was the purpose of the two burning bans?

On appeal, the Supreme Court ruled for Johnson by a 5-4 vote. Justice Brennan wrote the majority opinion, and he was joined by Justices Marshall, Blackmun, Scalia, and Kennedy. Chief Justice Rehnquist, and Justices White, Stevens, and O'Connor were in dissent. This case involved expressive conduct, rather than simple speech. As a result, the Court reviewed the Texas law with the four-factor *O'Brien* test. Specifically, the Court had to decide "whether Texas has asserted an interest in support of Johnson's conviction that is unrelated to the suppression of expression." Texas advanced "two compelling state interests. One [was] the preservation of the flag as a symbol of nationhood and national unity. The second [was] the preservation of . . . the peace."

The Court rejected the second interest. Justice Brennan explained that "no disturbance of the peace actually occurred or threatened to occur because of Johnson's burning of the flag." The Court also rejected the first interest: The state's concerns about preserving the flag as a symbol of "national unity" only becomes a problem "when a person's treatment of the flag communicates some message." That is, when someone destroys that flag. In other words, the law was *aimed at* banning the expressive content that is communicated by the conduct of flag burning.

The majority concluded that the third element of the *O'Brien* test was not satisfied: The Texas law was related to the "suppression of free expression." Therefore, the Court would review the law with strict rather than intermediate scrutiny. Did Texas have a compelling interest to preserve the special symbolic character of the flag? No. The law violated the "bedrock principle" that "the government may not prohibit the expression of an idea simply because society finds the idea itself offensive or disagreeable."

The law did more than restrict a message because of its content; the law also discriminated against a particular *viewpoint*. Texas banned flag burning because it viewed the message being conveyed as unpatriotic. During oral argument, Justice Scalia asked, "Will you give me an example where . . . somebody desecrates the flag in order to show that he agrees with the policies of the United States?" He added that a person will never burn a flag "to honor the country. It will always be to criticize the country." A flag-burning ban will censor only one type of speaker: those who are critical of American policies. Viewpoint discrimination is almost *always* unconstitutional.

Justice Scalia would often cite his vote in *Texas v. Johnson* as a case where his constitutional views did not align with his political views. He explained, "If I were king, I wouldn't go about letting people burn the American flag. However, we have a First Amendment which says that the right of free speech shall not be abridged, and it is addressed, in particular to speech critical of the government. I mean, that was the main kind of speech that tyrants would seek to suppress. Burning the flag is a form of expression."

R.A.V. v. City of St. Paul (1992)

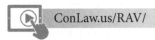 ConLaw.us/RAV/

Our final case, *R.A.V. v. St. Paul*, involves cross burning. In the predawn hours of June 21, 1990, R.A.V., a juvenile, and several other teenagers, allegedly assembled a crudely made cross by taping together broken chair legs. (The defendant was identified by his initials because he was a minor.) They then allegedly burned the cross inside the fenced yard of an African-American family. The City of St. Paul convicted R.A.V. of violating its bias-motivated crime ordinance. This law prohibited the display of a symbol that one knows or has reason to know will "arouse[] anger, alarm, or resentment in others on the basis of race, color, creed, religion, or gender."

During oral argument, St. Paul's lawyer defended the constitutionality of the ordinance: "The First Amendment was never intended to protect an individual who burns a cross in the middle of the night in the fenced yard of an African-American family's home." He added that "the historical context of a burning cross in the middle of the night is a precursor to violence and hatred in this country. . . . Given the historical experience of African-Americans, a burning cross targeted at a black family under the circumstances outlined is an unmistakable threat. Terroristic conduct such as this can find no protection in the Constitution."

STUDY GUIDE

Could the City of St. Paul have prosecuted the defendant for trespassing on private property? Would that prosecution have satisfied the *O'Brien* test? If so, why?

As in *O'Brien* and *Johnson*, the conduct in question here — burning a cross — was an expressive activity. And, as in *Johnson*, the Court found that the restriction was related to the content of the expressive activity. Because of the *O'Brien* test, the St. Paul law would be reviewed with strict scrutiny. The city had to prove that it had a compelling interest to restrict this speech, and that the restriction was narrowly tailored to achieve this interest. All nine Justices agreed that the conviction violated the First Amendment. However, the Court split 5-4 on the rationale.

STUDY GUIDE

What is the difference between *content* and *viewpoint* discrimination?

Justice Scalia wrote the majority opinion. He concluded that the ordinance was "facially unconstitutional." It was a *viewpoint*-based restriction. St. Paul prohibited speech on the "basis of *the subjects* the speech addresses." The law only punished messages that "arouse[d] anger," not messages that aroused happiness. The Court explained that "the First Amendment generally prevents government from proscribing speech or even expressive conduct, *because of disapproval* of the ideas expressed."

Justice Scalia acknowledged that several categories of speech have traditionally been regulated based on their content, such as obscenity, defamation, and fighting words. But these few categories are not "entirely invisible to the Constitution, so that they may be made vehicles for content discrimination unrelated to their distinctively proscribable content." Therefore, he observed, the government may not regulate fighting words "based on hostility — or favoritism — towards the underlying message expressed." In short, the government may suppress these narrowly defined categories of speech based on their *content*. But the state cannot prohibit speech that fits within these categories because of the *viewpoint* being expressed.

The Court concluded that the St. Paul law was facially unconstitutional because it imposed special prohibitions on those speakers who expressed disfavored views about race, color, creed, religion, or gender. The law not only restricted speech based on its content, but it also imposed "actual viewpoint discrimination."

The majority closed on a somber note: "Let there be no mistake about this Court's belief that burning a cross in someone's front yard is reprehensible. But, St. Paul has sufficient means at its disposal to prevent such behavior without adding the First Amendment to the fire." What other means were available? For example, the city could have prosecuted R.A.V. for trespassing on the African-American family's property.

Justice White wrote a concurring opinion, joined by Justices Blackmun, Stevens, and O'Connor. He would have declared the statute unconstitutional on narrower grounds. Specifically, the statute was "overbroad." Justice White wrote that "[a] defendant being prosecuted for speech or expressive conduct may challenge the law on its face if it reaches protected expression, even when that person's activities are not protected by the First Amendment." He maintained that "[a]lthough the ordinance, as construed, reaches categories of speech that are constitutionally unprotected, it also criminalizes a substantial amount of expression that — however repugnant — is shielded by the First Amendment." Therefore, "the ordinance is . . . fatally overbroad and invalid on its face."

STUDY GUIDE

What is *overbreadth*, and why does this doctrine concern the Court?

Generally, when a law violates a person's rights, she has "standing" to challenge that law. However, an overbreadth challenge allows a person to assert that the government has violated the free speech rights of third parties who are not before the court. In other words, the overbreadth doctrine allows someone whose speech *can* be prohibited to assert that a statute is unconstitutional. This approach allows courts to vigorously scrutinize most laws that violate the freedom of speech.

CHAPTER 54

Does Money Equal Speech?

One of First Amendment's core purposes is to protect political speech. This chapter focuses on three cases that concern the regulation of political speech: *Buckley v. Valeo* (1976), *McConnell v. FEC* (2003), and *Citizens United v. FEC* (2010). Alternatively, the laws in these cases could be characterized as imposing restrictions on spending money rather than on speech itself.

Buckley v. Valeo (1976)

 ConLaw.us/Buckley/

Buckley v. Valeo (1976) considered the constitutionality of the Federal Election Campaign Act of 1971. FECA, as it was known, regulated two aspects of campaign finance. First, the law limited *contributions* to a candidate's campaign. Second, the law restricted *expenditures*—that is, money spent by individuals and groups on behalf of a candidate. Shortly after FECA's enactment, the law was challenged by candidates, contributors, political parties, and others. The lead plaintiff was Senator James L. Buckley of New York who had been elected on the Conservative Party ticket. He would later become a judge on the D.C. Circuit Court of Appeals.

The Supreme Court upheld *most* of FECA's restrictions on campaign finance in a long, complicated, and fractured opinion. Chief Justice Burger announced the majority opinion. He found that the *O'Brien* test did not apply to spending money on political campaigns. Chief Justice Burger wrote, "the expenditure of money simply cannot be equated with such conduct as destruction of a draft card." Moreover, the mere fact that speech depends on the expenditure of money does not "reduce the exacting scrutiny required by the First Amendment." As a result, the Court reviewed FECA with strict, rather than intermediate, scrutiny.

First, the Chief Justice determined that FECA's restrictions on contributions were constitutional. The Court observed that candidates will often depend on donors who make large campaign contributions. As a result, such donors may gain an improper influence over the candidate. To avoid even the appearance of such corruption, Congress could restrict the size of contributions. These means were appropriate, the Court found, because contribution limits do not directly restrict the rights of individual citizens and candidates to engage in political debate and discussion.

For example, Citizen A expresses her support for a candidate by contributing $100, and Citizen B expresses his support for the same candidate by contributing $10,000. The latter contribution might reflect the *intensity* of Citizen B's opinion about the candidate, but the amount does not reflect the content of his opinion. Therefore, Congress could restrict *how much* money can be contributed *directly* to a candidate. FECA's restrictions on contributions were narrowly tailored to achieve Congress's compelling interest to prevent corruption or the appearance of corruption.

Second, Chief Justice Burger held that FECA's restrictions on independent expenditures were unconstitutional. These provisions restricted how much money could be spent *independently* of a federal political campaign. The Court also declared unconstitutional FECA's restrictions on how much money could be given to *political parties*. The parties often used expenditures to help in state and federal elections. For example, local get-out-the-vote efforts would assist both state and federal candidates who were on the same ballot.

The Court held that both regulations of expenditures violated the First Amendment. Chief Justice Burger found that these "provisions place substantial and direct restrictions on the ability of candidates, citizens, and associations to engage in political expression" that is protected by the First Amendment. And, because the expenditures were not made directly to the candidate, FECA's restrictions were not narrowly tailored means to prevent corruption or the appearance of corruption.

STUDY GUIDE

Does money equal speech?

Chief Justice Burger explained that "[a] restriction on the amount of money a person or group can spend on political communication during a campaign necessarily reduces the quantity of expression by restricting the number of issues discussed, the depth of their exploration, and the size of the audience reached." He concluded that "the independent expenditure ceiling thus fails to serve any substantial governmental interest in stemming the reality or appearance of corruption in the electoral process." At the same time, that ceiling "heavily burdens core First Amendment expression."

In *Buckley*, the Court did not foreclose the possibility that other interests could support restrictions on campaign finance. But the Court only found one interest that justified restrictions on campaign finance: the prevention of "corruption and the appearance of corruption." In future cases, the limited nature of this interest would prove to be important.

Buckley found that some provisions of FECA were unconstitutional, but the rest of the law was constitutional. This split decision led to several unintended consequences. First, because *Buckley* upheld the limits on contributions, candidates could no longer rely on a small number of high-dollar contributions. As a result, candidates had to spend much more time raising low-dollar contributions from many people. These contributions came to be called *hard money*. Second, the Court declared unconstitutional the limits on independent expenditures for advertising and contributions to political parties for their support of state elections. As a result, high-dollar campaign donors shifted their support to these types of expenditures, which came to be known as *soft money*. Two decades later, this shift gave rise to a political movement to limit soft money in politics.

McConnell v. Federal Election Commission (2003)

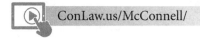
ConLaw.us/McConnell/

In 2002, the efforts to limit soft money culminated in the Bipartisan Campaign Reform Act. BCRA was commonly referred to as "McCain-Feingold" after its sponsors, Republican Senator John McCain of Arizona and Democratic Senator Russ Feingold of Wisconsin. Senator Mitch McConnell of Kentucky, who then served as the Republican Minority Whip, challenged BCRA's constitutionality.

A fractured Court upheld almost all of BCRA. We will focus on the two most significant restrictions that were upheld. First, the Court held that Congress could restrict soft money contributions to political parties through Title I of BCRA. Second, the Court upheld Title II's restrictions on independent expenditures for advertisements.

Justices Stevens and O'Connor jointly wrote the majority opinion. They found that Title I was constitutional because it was "an appropriate response" to two of Congress's legitimate concerns: (1) preventing the *actual and apparent corruption* threatened by large soft money contributions, and (2) preserving the integrity of the federal election process. The majority reasoned that "like the contribution limits . . . upheld in *Buckley*, [Title I's soft money] restrictions have only a marginal impact on the ability of contributors, candidates, officeholders, and parties to engage in effective political speech." The Court observed that the restrictions would primarily "regulate the ability of wealthy individuals, corporations, and unions to contribute large sums of money to influence federal elections."

As in *Buckley*, the Court concluded that Congress could regulate these expenditures to prevent corruption or the appearance of corruption. These interests were deemed compelling: "Both common sense and the ample record in these cases confirm Congress' belief" that "large soft money contributions to national party committees have a corrupting influence or give rise to the appearance of corruption."

Specifically, Justices Stevens and O'Connor explained that candidates who benefited indirectly from expenditures to political parties "would feel grateful for such donations and that donors would seek to exploit that gratitude." In addition, they contended that "corruption" was not limited to "preventing simple cash-for-votes corruption." Congress can also "curb[] 'undue influence on an officeholder's judgment, and the appearance of such influence.'" The leaders of national parties, they said, often "peddl[e] access to federal candidates and officeholders in exchange for large soft-money donations." The majority concluded that "there is substantial evidence to support Congress' determination that large soft-money contributions to national political parties give rise to corruption and the appearance of corruption."

Second, the Court considered the constitutionality of Title II. These provisions restricted independent expenditures made to create "electioneering communications" that referred by name to candidates for office. These issue advertisements included any "broadcast, cable, or satellite communication" that "refers to a clearly identified candidate for Federal office; [and] is made within 60 days before a general, special, or runoff election for the office sought by the candidate; or 30 days before a primary. . . . [and] is targeted to the relevant electorate." BCRA prohibited corporations and labor unions from funding such electioneering communications. The majority held that these restrictions in Title II were a constitutional means to reduce corruption — broadly defined — as well as the appearance of corruption.

This second result in *McConnell* would not stand for long.

Citizens United v. Federal Election Commission (2010)

ConLaw.us/CitizensUnited/

In 2006, Justice O'Connor was replaced by Justice Alito. The Court's changed composition triggered a dramatic reversal: Four years later, in *Citizens United v. FEC* (2010), the Court overruled *McConnell*'s holding about Title II.

Citizens United, a nonprofit corporation, created a film titled *Hillary: The Movie*. The movie provided a critical commentary about then-Senator Hillary Clinton, who was a candidate for president. The company wanted to broadcast the film in 2008 before the election. But doing so would be illegal under BCRA. Why? Section 441b of BCRA prohibited corporations from making certain independent expenditures to support candidates for federal office. Because the movie opposed Clinton's candidacy, and was produced with funds from a corporation, it fell within Title II's definition of an "electioneering communication." Therefore, Citizens United could not broadcast it during an election year. To avoid criminal liability, the corporation asked a federal court to determine whether the First Amendment protected its right to broadcast the film. Citizens United lost in the lower court. The District Court for the District of Columbia concluded that the prohibition on "electioneering communications" was constitutional under *McConnell*. On appeal, the Supreme Court reversed *McConnell* in part. A 5-4 majority held that the ban on electioneering communications was unconstitutional. Justice Kennedy wrote the majority opinion. He was joined by Chief Justice Roberts, and Justices Scalia, Thomas, and Alito.

As a threshold matter, the Court found that Citizens United was protected by the First Amendment, even though it was a corporation. Justice Kennedy observed, "If the First Amendment has any force, it prohibits Congress from fining or jailing citizens, *or associations of citizens*, for simply engaging in political speech." He added, "political speech is 'indispensable to decisionmaking in a democracy, and this is no less true because the speech comes from a corporation rather than an individual.'"

Some of the Justices worried that a precedent upholding a ban on corporate-funded movies could be used to ban corporate-funded books. During oral argument, Justice Alito asked, if the "government's position . . . [would] allow[] the banning of a book if it's published by a corporation?" Malcolm Stewart, the Deputy Solicitor General, candidly replied, "the electioneering communication restrictions . . . could have been applied to additional media as well." Even a book. Justice Alito was taken aback by the answer: "That's pretty incredible. You think that if a book was published, a campaign biography that was the functional equivalent of express advocacy, that could be banned?" The answer was yes.

The government changed its position six months later when the case was re-argued. Justice Ginsburg asked Elena Kagan, the Solicitor General and future-Justice, "if Congress could say 'no TV and radio ads,' could it also say 'no newspaper ads, no campaign biographies'? Last time the answer was, yes, 'Congress could, but it didn't.' Is that still the government's answer?" Kagan answered, "The government's answer has changed." There was audible laughter. She added, "for 60 years a book has never been at issue."

Justice Scalia was not satisfied with that answer. He said, "if you write [BCRA] too broadly, we are not going to pare it back to the point where it's constitutional. If it's overbroad, it's invalid." Chief Justice Roberts added, "we don't put our First Amendment rights in the hands of FEC bureaucrats." Justice Alito was still perplexed by the government's standard: "In light of your retraction, I have no idea where the government would draw the line with respect to the medium that could be prohibited."

In the end, a majority of the Court would not accept the government's assurances. By a 5-4 vote, the Court reversed *McConnell* in part. The majority declared unconstitutional the ban on electioneering communications funded by corporations and unions.

The Court did, however, uphold BCRA's *disclosure* requirements. These provisions, which were previously upheld in *Buckley*, required the disclosure of the identity of those paying for advertisements. Justice Kennedy observed that "disclaimer and disclosure provisions" provide information to the electorate. The "transparency enables the electorate to make informed decisions and give proper weight to different speakers and messages." He added that the disclosure requirements "would be unconstitutional as applied to an organization if there were a reasonable probability that the group's members would face threats, harassment, or reprisals if their names were disclosed." But Citizens United, he said, did not offer any evidence that it faced "harassment and retaliation."

STUDY GUIDE

Can you see how Justice Kennedy's conclusion creates something of a chicken-and-egg problem? A corporation would not be at risk of harassment until its expenditures are disclosed. However, once its expenditures are disclosed, the corporation may already have been harassed. At that point, it would be too late to challenge the constitutionality of the disclosure requirements.

Justices Stevens wrote a dissent. He was joined by Justices Ginsburg, Breyer, and Sotomayor. The dissenters invoked the doctrine of stare decisis. Justice Stevens objected to the reversal of *McConnell* as well as *Austin v. Michigan Chamber of Commerce* (1990). The latter case upheld restrictions on expenditures by corporations and unions. When he read his dissent from the bench, Justice Stevens offered an originalist argument: "At the founding, Americans took it as a given that corporations could be comprehensively regulated in the service of the public welfare." He added that the Founding generation "held a cautious view of corporate power and a narrow view of corporate rights . . . and that they conceptualized speech in individualist terms." He observed that those who "ratified the First Amendment" did not think that "they were laying down a principle that could be used to insulate corporations from even modest restrictions on electioneering expenditures."

Justice Scalia responded to Justice Stevens in a concurring opinion. The dissent's historical discussion, Scalia wrote, was "in splendid isolation from the text of the First Amendment. . . . The Amendment is written in terms of 'speech,' not speakers." Justice Scalia explained that the text of the First Amendment "offers no foothold for excluding any category of speaker, from single individuals to . . . incorporated associations of individuals." He added, "the dissent offers no evidence about the original meaning of the text to support any such exclusion." Justice Scalia concluded, "We are therefore simply left with the question whether the speech at issue in this case is 'speech' covered by the First Amendment. No one says otherwise. A documentary film critical of a potential presidential candidate is core political speech, and its nature as such does not change simply because it was funded by a corporation."

Justice Stevens vehemently disagreed: "Simply put, corporations are not human beings. . . . As the Court has long [recognized,] the distinctive legal attributes of corporations create distinctive threats to the electoral process. The rule announced today that Congress must treat corporate speakers exactly like human beings in the political realm represents a radical strength — a radical change in the law."

Justice Stevens had some difficulty delivering his *Citizens United* dissent from the bench. In an interview, Justice Stevens said "that was the day I decided to resign." Several months later, President Obama nominated Solicitor General Elena Kagan to replace Justice Stevens.

CHAPTER 55

Does the First Amendment Protect Tortious Speech?

All liberty may reasonably be regulated to protect the rights of others. The freedom of speech is no different. For example, no one thinks that the First Amendment protects a right to commit fraud. The two cases in this chapter recognized that the First Amendment limits two types of wrongful acts, or torts, that violate the rights of others. First, *New York Times Company v. Sullivan* (1964) held that the First Amendment restricts the tort of defamation, also known as libel. Second, *Snyder v. Phelps* (2011) held that the First Amendment limits the tort of intentional infliction of emotional distress.

New York Times Company v. Sullivan (1964)

 ConLaw.us/Sullivan/

In March 1960, the Committee to Defend Martin Luther King published a full-page advertisement in the *New York Times*. The advertisement recounted how "thousands of Southern Negro students are engaged in wide-spread non-violent demonstrations . . . [and] they are being met by an unprecedented wave of terror." The lead caption of the advertisement declared "Heed Their Rising Voices," a phrase that was taken from a *Times* editorial. The advertisement was published as a means to obtain financial support. Readers were encouraged to mail a check to the Committee.

The advertisement, however, was factually inaccurate in at least three respects. First, the advertisement stated that African-American students "were expelled from school, and truckloads of police armed with shotguns and tear-gas ringed the Alabama State College Campus." But the police never "ringed" the campus. Second, the advertisement stated that the student "dining hall was padlocked in an attempt to starve them into submission." But the dining hall was never padlocked. Third, the advertisement stated that Martin Luther King, Jr. was arrested "seven times." That assertion was also inaccurate. King was only arrested four times.

L.B. Sullivan sued the *Times* for libel. He was one of the three elected Commissioners in Montgomery, Alabama. Sullivan sought $500,000 in damages. The advertisement did not name Sullivan, but he claimed that the text could "be read as imputing to the police, and hence to him," responsibility for the violent acts against the students. The Alabama Supreme Court applied the conventional standard for the libel tort. It found that the *Times* had published false information, which tended to injure Sullivan's reputation. Therefore, the newspaper was liable for damages. On appeal, the newspaper argued that the First Amendment protected its right to publish the advertisement.

STUDY GUIDE

Should the New York Times Company's advertisement receive heightened protection under the First Amendment? Or should it receive reduced protection as mere "commercial speech"?

Law professor Herbert Wechsler represented the *Times* before the Supreme Court. During oral argument, he contended that a judgment against the newspaper posed "hazards to the freedom of the press of a dimension not confronted since the early days [of] the Republic." He questioned "how far the civil law of libel may be used by state officials to punish the publication of statements critical of their official conduct."

Wechsler drew inspiration from familiar sources. He cited the Virginia and Kentucky Resolutions, authored by James Madison and Thomas Jefferson, respectively. The future Presidents contested the validity of the Sedition Act of 1798. Wechsler explained that "the First Amendment was precisely designed to do away with seditious libel," which he defined as "criticism of the Government and criticism of officials." He claimed that "if James Madison were alive today, so far as anything that I can see . . . in the report on the Virginia resolutions, that the submission that I am making was a submission he would make."

On appeal, the question presented was whether the advertisement "forfeits [First Amendment] protection by the falsity of some of its factual statements and by its alleged defamation of respondent." The Court unanimously ruled in favor of the *Times*. Justice Brennan wrote the majority opinion. He placed limits on libel suits brought by public officials: "The constitutional guarantees require, we think, a federal rule that prohibits a public official from recovering damages for a defamatory falsehood relating to his official conduct unless he proves that the statement was made with 'actual malice'—that is, with knowledge that it was false or with reckless disregard of whether it was false or not." Under traditional tort law, the plaintiff only needs to show that the writer *negligently* made a false statement. This standard is much easier to meet.

Where is the line between a "public" and "private" official? Wechsler admitted the distinction may often be fuzzy. But here there was no doubt that Sullivan was an elected "public official." Did the *Times* act with "actual malice"? No. The newspaper did not publish the false information "with reckless disregard of whether it was false or not." The decision to publish the falsehoods was perhaps *negligent*, but the *Times* did not act with "actual malice." Therefore, Sullivan could not sue the *New York Times* for libel.

Sullivan did not argue that the *Times*, a corporation, lacked First Amendment rights. And the Court did not seem to doubt that the corporation could assert these rights.

STUDY GUIDE

Under the "state action doctrine," constitutional rights are only violated by governmental acts. What was the state action in *New York Times v. Sullivan*?

In the decade after *Sullivan*, the Court held that the "actual malice" standard also limits defamation suits brought by public figures, in addition to suits brought by public officials. The Supreme Court has defined "public figures" as people who do not work for the government but who "are nevertheless intimately involved in the resolution of important public questions or, by reason of their fame, shape events in areas of concern to society at large."

In future cases, the Supreme Court would also extend the *Sullivan* doctrine beyond cases that involve public officials and public figures. The Supreme Court would find that false statements about *matters of public concern* are also entitled to special constitutional protections. In such a defamation lawsuit, a plaintiff still needs to show that the defendant made a false statement about these matters with "actual malice."

The "actual malice" standard, however, does not limit defamation suits brought by private individuals. These plaintiffs can recover if defendants negligently make false statements that damage their reputations.

The next case, *Snyder v. Phelps* (2011) involved the tort of intentional infliction of emotional distress, or IIED. The Court found that the First Amendment limits the IIED tort when the defendant's speech involves matters of public concern.

Snyder v. Phelps (2011)

 ConLaw.us/Snyder/

The facts of *Snyder* are disturbing. The members of the Westboro Baptist Church believe that God hates and punishes the United States for, among other things, its tolerance of homosexuality, particularly in America's military. The group, led by its minister Fred Phelps, protests at military funerals to communicate these views.

Westboro chose to picket the funeral of Marine Lance Corporal Matthew Snyder, who was killed in Iraq in the line of duty. Westboro protested in a public area approximately 1,000 feet from the Catholic church where the funeral was held. The protestors held signs with awful messages: "Thank God for Dead Soldiers," "Fags Doom Nations," "Thank God for 9/11, America is Doomed," "Pope in Hell," and "God Hates You."

Matthew Snyder's father, Albert, did not see the signs during the funeral. He only learned about their presence while watching the evening news. Albert Snyder sued Westboro for the intentional infliction of emotional distress (IIED), a tort defined by state law. After the trial, a jury held Westboro liable for $7 million in compensatory and punitive damages.

On appeal, Westboro argued that the First Amendment fully protected its speech. The Court ruled for Westboro by an 8-1 vote. Chief Justice Roberts wrote the majority opinion. Only Justice Alito dissented.

First, the Court had to decide whether Westboro's speech involved a "public or private concern." Chief Justice Roberts concluded that "[t]he content of Westboro's signs plainly relates to broad issues of interest to society at large." He explained that "the political and moral conduct of the United States and its citizens, the faith of our nation, homosexuality in the military and scandals involving the Catholic clergy are matters of public import."

Justice Alito dissented. He countered that some of the signs were directed at Matthew Snyder. For example, "You're going to Hell" referred to Matthew. In addition to carrying signs at the funeral, Westboro also published a blog post — known as an "epic" — that addressed the Snyder family directly. During oral argument, Justice Alito stated, "The epic specifically referenced Matthew Snyder by name, [and] specifically referenced Matthew's parents by name." He then asked, "Do you think that the epic is relevant as an explanation of some of these arguably ambiguous signs that were displayed at the funeral? For example, 'You are going to hell,' 'God hates you.' Who is 'you'? If you read the epic, perhaps that sheds light on who 'you' is."

The majority declined to consider the relevance of the "epic," because it was "not properly before us." Why? Because "Snyder never mentioned [the epic] in his petition for certiorari." In this way, the majority limited its ruling solely to Westboro's conduct during the funeral. The Court did not resolve whether the sort of message communicated on the Internet by the "epic" could give rise to IIED liability.

Chief Justice Roberts only considered the signs at the demonstration. He observed, "even if a few of the signs — such as 'You're Going to Hell' and 'God Hates You' — were viewed as containing messages related to Matthew Snyder or the Snyders specifically, that would not change the fact that the overall thrust and dominant theme of Westboro's demonstration spoke to broader public issues." By limiting the facts in this way, Chief Justice Roberts made the case easier to decide than perhaps it was.

Second, the majority focused on the fact that Westboro protested "on public land adjacent to public streets." Such spaces have historically occupied a favored position in First Amendment cases. Moreover, "[t]he picketing was conducted under police supervision some 1000 feet from the church out of the sight of those at the church. The protest was not unruly. There was no shouting, profanity, or violence."

Third, the majority observed that "any distress occasioned by Westboro's picketing turned on the content and viewpoint of the message conveyed, rather than any interference with the funeral itself." The Court concluded, "Given that Westboro's speech was at a public place on a matter of public concern, that speech is entitled to 'special protection' under the First Amendment. Such speech cannot be restricted simply because it is upsetting or arouses contempt." Here, Chief Justice Roberts favorably cited *Texas v. Johnson* (1989). That case reversed a conviction for flag burning: "If there is a bedrock principle underlying the First Amendment, it is that the Government may not prohibit the expression of an idea simply because society finds the idea itself offensive or disagreeable."

Justice Alito wrote a solo dissent. He proclaimed, "Our profound national commitment to free and open debate is not a license for the vicious verbal assault that occurred in this case. Petitioner Albert Snyder is not a public figure." According to Justice Alito, Westboro "brutally attacked Matthew Snyder, and this attack, which was almost certain to inflict injury, was central to respondents' well-practiced strategy for attracting public attention."

Justice Alito acknowledged that most of Westboro's speech related to matters of public concern. Had Snyder brought a defamation action, he would have needed to show that Westboro acted with "actual malice." Even though the slain Marine was not a public figure, Westboro's messages were generally related to matters of public concern. But the fact that *some* of Westboro's speech involved matters of public concern, Justice Alito argued, should not decide the case: "I fail to see why actionable speech should be immunized simply because it is interspersed with speech that is protected." He added, "The First Amendment allows recovery for defamatory statements that are *interspersed with* nondefamatory statements on matters of public concern, and there is no good reason why respondents' attack on Matthew Snyder and his family should be treated differently."

The majority, however, disagreed. Chief Justice Roberts explained, "Speech is powerful. It can stir people to action, move them to tears of both joy and sorrow and — as it did here — inflict great pain. On the facts before us, we cannot react to that pain by punishing the speaker. As a nation, we have chosen a different course — to protect even hurtful speech on public issues to ensure that we do not stifle public debate. That choice requires that we shield Westboro from tort liability for its picketing in this case."

CHAPTER 56

Does the First Amendment Protect "Offensive" Speech?

The Supreme Court has held that certain categories of speech are not protected by the First Amendment: for example, speech that incites violence, sexually explicit speech that is "obscene," as well as "fighting words." In two cases, the government asked the Supreme Court to recognize new categories of unprotected speech for extremely graphic or "offensive" depictions of violence: *United States v. Stevens* (2010) and *Brown v. Entertainment Merchants Association* (2011). The Supreme Court disagreed, and found that these categories of speech are protected by the First Amendment.

United States v. Stevens (2010)

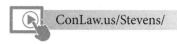

ConLaw.us/Stevens/

Robert Stevens was indicted for selling videos that depicted dog fighting. Federal law made it "a crime to create, sell or possess certain depictions of animal cruelty." This law did not prohibit animal cruelty. Rather, it only prohibited "portrayals of certain acts harmful to animals." Specifically, the statute criminalized any "visual or auditory depiction such as a picture, video, or a sound recording in which a living animal is intentionally maimed, mutilated, tortured, wounded or killed if that conduct is illegal where the creation, sale, or possession takes place." The law exempted depictions of "serious religious, political, scientific, educational, journalistic, historical, or artistic value." Congress enacted this law, primarily, to prohibit so-called *crush videos*. These films depict the torture and killing of helpless animals.

Stevens was convicted and sentenced to more than three years in prison. He argued that his conviction violated the Free Speech Clause of the First Amendment. On appeal, the Court had to decide "whether that prohibition on depictions [of animal cruelty] is consistent with the First Amendment." The vote in *Stevens* was 8-1. Chief Justice Roberts wrote the majority opinion. Justice Alito was the lone dissenter, as in *Snyder v. Phelps* (2011).

First, the government argued that depictions of animal cruelty are categorically unprotected by the First Amendment. The Court had recognized that certain categories of speech receive no protection under the First Amendment, such as "obscenity, defamation, fraud, incitement and speech integral to criminal conduct." Chief Justice Roberts, however, declined to add depictions of animal cruelty to this list. He observed that there was no "similar tradition of excluding depictions of animal cruelty" from the scope of the First Amendment.

Second, the government urged the Court to review the the law with a test that balances "value of the speech against its societal costs." The Court also rejected this deferential form of scrutiny. Chief Justice Roberts explained:

> The First Amendment's guarantee of free speech does not extend only to categories of speech that survive an ad hoc balancing of relative social costs and benefits. The First Amendment itself reflects a judgment by the American people that the benefits of its restrictions on the Government outweigh the costs. Our Constitution forecloses any attempt to revise that judgment simply on the basis that some speech is not worth it. The Constitution is not a document "prescribing limits, and declaring that those limits may be passed at pleasure."

Third, the Court reviewed the statute with the so-called *overbreadth* doctrine. Generally, when a law violates a person's rights, she has "standing" to challenge that law. However, an overbreadth challenge allows a person to assert that the government has violated the free speech rights of third parties who are not before the court. In other words, the overbreadth doctrine allows someone whose speech can be prohibited to assert that a statute is unconstitutional. Chief Justice Roberts explained that a law is overbroad if it can be used to prohibit a substantial number of protected types of expressions.

In *Stevens*, the Court found that the federal statute created a "criminal prohibition of alarming breadth." The statute prohibited depictions of a wide range of conduct, including the treatment of animals that was not even cruel. The government attempted to assure the Court that it would only prosecute "extreme cruelty," but the Court would not "uphold an unconstitutional statute merely because the government promises to use it responsibly." The Court concluded that the federal law was "substantially overbroad and therefore invalid under the First Amendment."

Justice Alito dissented. He would not have declared the entire statute unconstitutional. Rather, he would have determined if the statute was unconstitutional *as applied to* Stevens's dog-fighting videos. The majority declined to "decide whether a statute limited to crush videos or other depictions of extreme animal cruelty would be constitutional."

After *Stevens* was decided, Congress enacted a more narrowly tailored version of the statute. The Animal Crush Video Prohibition Act of 2010, as its name suggests, prohibited the distribution of "crush videos."

Brown v. Entertainment Merchants Association (2011)

 ConLaw.us/EMA/

Today, most video games include ratings, such as "M for Mature." But those ratings, which are issued by the Entertainment Software Rating Board, are not compelled by law. Retailers comply with the voluntary ESRB ratings in much the same way that movie theaters comply with the voluntary movie rating system. The failure to comply with the ratings is not a criminal offense. California sought to change that regime.

In 2005, California enacted Assembly Bill 1179. It prohibited the sale or rental of violent video games to minors. Parents and guardians could still buy the games for their children. The law included a very broad definition of violence. It covered games "[i]n which the range of options available to a player includes killing, maiming, dismembering, or sexually assaulting an image of a human being, if those acts are depicted in a manner that a reasonable person, considering the game as a whole, would find appeals to a deviant or morbid interest of minors, that is patently offensive to prevailing standards in the community as to what is suitable for minors, and that causes the game as a whole to lack serious literary, artistic, political, or scientific value for minors." The violent-video-game law was sponsored by state senator Leland Yee. (Ironically, Yee was later sentenced to five years in prison for "promising votes and guns to an undercover agent who was funneling him contributions.")

The Entertainment Merchants Association (EMA), a trade group for the entertainment industry, challenged the constitutionality of the law. On appeal, the Supreme Court found that the California law was unconstitutional. The vote in *Brown v. EMA* was 7-2. Justice Scalia wrote the majority opinion. Justices Breyer and Thomas wrote separate dissents.

First, the Court held that violent video games are protected by the First Amendment. "The Free Speech Clause exists principally to protect discourse on public matters," Justice Scalia wrote, "but we have long recognized that it is difficult to distinguish politics from entertainment, and dangerous to try." He affirmed that the "government has no power to restrict expression because of its message, its ideas, its subject matter, or its content."

California modeled its law after a New York law that prohibited the sale of "girlie" magazines to minors. In *Ginsberg v. New York* (1968), the Supreme Court held that the state could prohibit retailers from selling such obscene materials to children. In *EMA*, however, Justice Scalia drew an important distinction: "[S]peech about violence is not obscene." It was irrelevant, then, "that California's statute mimic[ked] the New York statute regulating obscenity-for-minors." *Ginsberg*, he explained, "approved a prohibition on the sale to minors of sexual material that would be obscene from the perspective of a child." While "a State possesses legitimate power to protect children from harm," Justice Scalia wrote, this power "does not include a free-floating power to restrict the ideas to which children may be exposed."

Justice Breyer disagreed in his dissent. He queried how the state could prohibit a 13-year-old child from buying a "picture of a naked woman, but the [same] child can go in and buy one of these video games" with similar sexual content. He added, "what's the difference between sex and violence?"

STUDY GUIDE

Should offensive speech involving depictions of violence be treated the same way as offensive speech involving depictions of sex?

The Court, however, declined to "shoehorn speech about violence into" the same category of unprotected "obscenity." Justice Scalia observed that there was no tradition of the state restricting children's access to depictions of violence. He continued, "Certainly the books we give children to read — or read to them when they are younger — contain no shortage of gore." Justice Scalia listed several classic examples, including Grimms' *Fairy Tales*, Homer's *The Odyssey*, and *Lord of the Flies*.

During oral argument, Justice Alito drew a distinction between a violent book and an "interactive" violent video game. He observed that "[w]e have here a new medium that cannot possibly have been envisioned at the time when the First Amendment was ratified." Chief Justice Roberts added, "in these video games the child is not sitting there passively watching something. The child is doing the killing. The child is doing the maiming. And I suppose that might be understood to have a different impact on the child's moral development."

Ultimately, the majority rejected this distinction between "passive" and "interactive" depictions of violence. The Court held that California's content-based restriction did not satisfy the requirements of strict scrutiny. First, the Court found that California had not demonstrated any *direct causal link* between playing violent video games and actual harm to minors. Instead, California could only cite studies that showed "at best some correlation between exposure to violent entertainment and minuscule real-world effects."

Second, the Court determined that the law was *under-inclusive*: "The California Legislature is perfectly willing to leave this dangerous mind-altering material in the hands of children so long as one parent (or even an aunt or an uncle) says it's OK." That sort of inconsistent approach is not how the government would be expected to address a serious social problem.

Third, the Court concluded that the law was *over-inclusive*: "[n]ot all the children who are forbidden to purchase violent video games on their own have parents who care whether they purchase violent video games." Justice Scalia added, "While some of the legislation's effect may indeed be in support of what some parents of the restricted children actually want, its entire effect is only in support of what the State thinks parents ought to want." In the end, the Court concluded that California's approach lacks the "narrow tailoring to 'assisting parents' that restriction of First Amendment rights requires."

Justice Alito, joined by Chief Justice Roberts, concurred in the Court's judgment. They did not decide if the government could ever ban this type of violent content. Rather, they found that the California statute included an unconstitutionally vague definition of "violence." Specifically, the law "fail[ed] to provide . . . clear notice" about what speech is prohibited. The duo wrote that the state could enact a more narrowly tailored statute to protect children from violent video games.

Justice Thomas wrote the first dissent. He found that the "practices and beliefs of the founding generation establish that 'the freedom of speech,' as originally understood, does not include a right *to speak to* minors (or a right of minors to access speech) without going through the minors' parents or guardians."

STUDY GUIDE

Do adults have a constitutional right to speak to other people's children? Does Justice Thomas identify any laws in which the government restricted people from speaking to minors?

Justice Breyer wrote the second dissent. He concluded that the statute survived constitutional scrutiny based on evidence provided by social scientists: "Unlike the majority, I would find sufficient grounds in these studies and expert opinions for this Court to *defer to an elected legislature*'s conclusion that the video games in question are particularly likely to harm children." Justice Breyer would have exercised judicial restraint. He explained, "this Court has always thought it owed an elected legislature *some degree of deference* in respect to legislative facts of this kind, particularly when they involve technical matters that are beyond our competence, and even in First Amendment cases."

Justice Breyer contended that education "is about choices. Sometimes, children need to learn by making choices for themselves. Other times, choices are made for children — by their parents, by their teachers, and by the people acting democratically through their governments." He observed that "the First Amendment does not disable government from helping parents make such a choice here — a choice not to have their children buy extremely violent, interactive video games, which they more than reasonably fear pose only the risk of harm to those children."

Stevens and *Brown* both demonstrate how reluctant the Supreme Court has been to add new categories of unprotected speech.

THE FREE EXERCISE OF RELIGION

The First Amendment provides that "Congress shall make no law . . . prohibiting the free exercise" of religion. Can the government enact laws that substantially burden the free exercise of religion if those laws are generally applicable and do not discriminate among different faiths? At first, in *Sherbert v. Verner* (1963), the Supreme Court answered no. But three decades later, the Court changed course in *Employment Division v. Smith* (1990). What is a neutral law of general applicability? The Court addressed this question in *Church of the Lukumi Babalu Aye v. City of Hialeah* (1993). There, the Court explained that discrimination targeting specific religious practices is still prohibited.

Finally, we consider the Religious Freedom Restoration Act (RFRA). This federal law prevented the federal and state governments from burdening the free exercise of religion. In *City of Boerne v. Flores* (1997), the Supreme Court held that Congress could not use RFRA to limit the state's police power. (See Chapter 20.) Congress, could, however, use RFRA to limit its own power. In *Burwell v. Hobby Lobby Stores* (2014), the Supreme Court held that the Affordable Care Act's so-called "contraceptive mandate" violated RFRA.

CHAPTER 57

Generally Applicable Laws Burdening Free Exercise

The First Amendment begins, "Congress shall make no law respecting an establishment of religion, or prohibiting the free exercise thereof . . . ." The last portion of this provision is known as the Free Exercise Clause. The three cases in this chapter concern two questions. First, can the government substantially burden conduct that is part of a person's religious practice? Second, does the Free Exercise Clause empower the judiciary to create exemptions from such burdensome laws?

Sherbert v. Verner (1963)

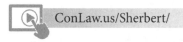 ConLaw.us/Sherbert/

In *Sherbert v. Verner* (1963), the Supreme Court created such an exemption. Adeil Sherbert's employer told her to work on Saturdays. Sherbert, a member of the Seventh-day Adventist Church, declined that assignment because of her religious beliefs. She celebrated the Sabbath on Saturday instead of Sunday. As a result, Sherbert was fired. South Carolina then denied her unemployment benefits because she was unwilling to work on Saturday. Sherbert's attorney explained her position to the Court: "She was willing to work and able to work, in any mill or in any other industry, so long as the job was a decent job, and so long as it did not require her to work on her Sabbath."

The Court ruled for Sherbert by a 7-2 vote. Justice Brennan wrote the majority opinion. First, he found that the state's actions "impose[d] a[] burden on the free exercise of [Sherbert's] religion." The government put "pressure upon her to forego" her religious beliefs, in order to receive unemployment benefits.

Second, the Court determined that South Carolina did not have a "compelling state interest" that "justifie[d] the substantial infringement of [Sherbert's] First Amendment right." The government could not defend its policy by claiming that "unscrupulous claimants feigning religious objections to Saturday work" might file fraudulent claims. Indeed, even if such a problem existed, the state would have "to demonstrate that no alternative forms of regulation would combat such abuses without infringing First Amendment rights."

Finally, in this case, there was no evidence that the state enacted or enforced its law with animus towards Sabbatarians. Rather, the law was generally applicable; it applied equally to people of all faiths. Nonetheless, the Court held that the Free Exercise Clause required South Carolina to exempt Sherbert from the usual requirements of its laws.

This framework came to be known as the *Sherbert* test:

1. If the government imposed a *substantial burden* on the free exercise of religion,
2. the state must demonstrate that its law is the *least restrictive means* to achieve a *compelling state interest*.

If the state interest was not "compelling," or if there was another "less restrictive means" to accomplish that interest, the state cannot enforce its law that imposes a "substantial burden" on the free exercise of religion.

Employment Division v. Smith (1990)

ConLaw.us/Smith/

In our next case, *Employment Division v. Smith* (1990), the Supreme Court would limit, if not effectively overrule, *Sherbert*. Al Smith lost his job as a drug-abuse counselor due to his use of peyote. He ingested the hallucinogenic cactus as part of a ritual in the Native American Church. Oregon denied unemployment benefits to Smith because he was "discharged for work-related 'misconduct'" — that is, using an illegal controlled substance.

The Oregon courts ruled that the Employment Division was required to exempt Smith from its generally applicable law, and grant him unemployment benefits. The state appealed the case to the Supreme Court. The question presented was "whether Oregon's criminal law against the use of certain mind-altering drugs including peyote, can constitutionally be applied to the respondent's sacramental use of peyote in ceremonies of the Native American Church."

The Supreme Court reversed, and ruled against Smith. Justice Scalia wrote the majority opinion. He explained that the Free Exercise Clause prevents the government from penalizing adherence to a religious position or the profession of a religious belief. It also prevents the government from penalizing an action *only because* that action is taken for religious reasons or *only because* of the religious beliefs that action displays. However, the Court found that Smith's ritual did not warrant an exemption:

> Respondents in the present case, however, seek to carry the meaning of "pro-hibiting the free exercise [of religion]" one large step further. They contend that their religious motivation for using peyote places them beyond the reach of a criminal law that is *not specifically directed* at their religious practice, and that is concededly constitutional as applied to those who use the drug for other reasons.

The Court rejected Smith's argument. How did Justice Scalia distinguish *Sherbert*? First, he observed that the Court had "never invalidated any govern-mental action on the basis of the *Sherbert* test except the denial of unemployment compensation." In all other cases, the Court held that the test was satisfied. "The *Sherbert* test," he noted, "was developed in a context that lent itself to individualized governmental assessment of the reasons for the relevant conduct." A "distinctive feature of unemployment compensation programs is that their eligibility criteria invite consideration of the particular circumstances behind an applicant's unem-ployment." Justice Scalia held that "the unemployment cases stand for the proposi-tion that where the State has in place a system of individual exemptions, it may not refuse to extend that system to cases of 'religious hardship' without compelling rea-son." Such decisions, he concluded, "have nothing to do with an across-the-board criminal prohibition on a particular form of conduct."

STUDY GUIDE

Do you find this distinction between *Sherbert* and *Smith* persuasive?

Under the *Sherbert* test, the state must have a "compelling state interest" to justify its imposition of a substantial burden on the free exercise of religion. Justice Scalia rejected Smith's argument that governmental action that burdens religion must be justified by a compelling governmental interest. "The govern-ment's ability to enforce generally applicable prohibitions of socially harmful conduct, like its ability to carry out other aspects of public policy, 'cannot depend on measuring the effects of a governmental action on a religious objector's spiri-tual development.'"

The Court contended that Smith's position "would open the prospect of consti-tutionally required exemptions from civic obligations of every conceivable kind." Justice Scalia admitted that "leaving accommodation to the political process will place at a relative disadvantage those religious practices that are not widely engaged in." In other words, majority faiths would be able to obtain exemptions through the democratic process. Minority faiths, however, would not fare as well. During oral argument, Justice Stevens asked if the state could "outlaw totally the use of alco-hol, including wine, in religious ceremonies." The attorney for Oregon answered, "there might be a religious accommodation argument of an entirely different order than is presented here." Justice Stevens responded, "You mean, just a better-known religion?"

Ultimately, Justice Scalia found this inequity to be an "unavoidable consequence of democratic government [that] must be preferred to a system in which each conscience is a law unto itself or in which judges weigh the social importance of all laws against the centrality of all religious beliefs." The Court refused to create an exemption to a generally applicable law that burdened the free exercise of religion. The government did not need to show that a neutral law was the "least restrictive means" to achieve a "compelling state interest."

Smith proved to be extremely unpopular on all sides of the political spectrum. Three years later, Congress sought to reverse its effect and restore *Sherbert*. In 1993, Congress passed the Religious Freedom Restoration Act (RFRA) by a huge bipartisan majority.

Church of the Lukumi Babalu Aye v. City of Hialeah (1993)

ConLaw.us/Lukumi/

Following *Smith*, courts review neutral, generally applicable laws that burden religion with a deferential form of rational basis scrutiny. The next case examined whether a law was in fact neutral and generally applicable to all people — or whether it targeted a single faith.

Church of the Lukumi Babalu Aye v. Hialeah (1993) involved the Santeria religion. Members of this faith perform animal sacrifices. Professor Douglas Laycock represented the Church before the Supreme Court. He described this ritual: "To believers in Santeria, [animal] sacrifice is directly commanded by the gods in considerable detail on each occasion when it is required."

A new Santeria church was planned in the city of Hialeah, Florida. Members of the community were disturbed by the faith's animal sacrifices. The lawyer for the city explained to the Court, "Animals were being, in effect, tortured in Hialeah and subjected to cruel treatment in the form of possession prior to sacrifice . . . When sacrifices take place . . . as many as 52 animals in a single day are killed, and they are killed in a private residence in many instances, and then they are decapitated, blood is put into pots, the animals are then oftentimes left out in public places."

In response to this practice, the city prohibited sacrificing animals "in a public or private ritual or ceremony not for the primary purpose of food consumption." However, "licensed establishment[s]" could slaughter animals that were "specifically raised for food purposes." The church argued that *Smith's* rational basis review was not appropriate because the law was not neutral and generally applicable. Laycock explained, "This is a case about open discrimination against a minority religion. [The ordinances] were enacted for the express purpose of preventing the central rituals of this faith."

The Court unanimously ruled in favor of the church. Justice Kennedy wrote the majority opinion. The ordinances, he concluded, did not meet *Smith's* dual requirements. "Neutrality and general applicability," he explained, are interrelated. A law lacks neutrality if it targets a specific faith. And a law lacks general applicability if it targets an overly narrow range of conduct.

Justice Kennedy added that the "failure to satisfy one requirement is a likely indication that the other has not been satisfied." Generally, a law that is not neutral is also not generally applicable, and vice versa. The Court found that a law that fails these two "requirements must be justified by a compelling governmental interest and must be narrowly tailored to advance that interest." In other words, if the law was not neutral or not generally applicable, then something like the *Sherbert* test still applied.

First, Justice Kennedy addressed whether the Hialeah ordinances were neutral by focusing on their object or *purpose*. He explained that, "if *the object* of a law is to infringe upon or restrict practices because of their religious motivation, the law is not *neutral*." Justice Kennedy considered how the ordinances were enacted. This record, he found, suggests that the "suppression of the central element of the Santeria worship service *was the object* of the ordinances."

Second, Justice Kennedy considered whether the Hialeah ordinances were laws of general applicability by focusing on their wording. Specifically, he examined whether the law targeted only certain "categories" of activities. A law is not generally applicable if it is enforced in a "selective manner" to prohibit religiously motivated conduct but permits non-religiously motivated conduct.

The government argued that its ordinances were justified as a means to promote public health and prevent animal cruelty. Yet these reasons were seriously *underinclusive* or "selective." For example, the regulations "fail[ed] to prohibit *nonreligious* conduct that endangers these interests in a similar or greater degree than Santeria sacrifice does." Nor did the ordinances prohibit other "types of animal deaths or kills for *nonreligious* reasons." The ordinances allowed hunters to take their kills home, where they can "dispos[e] of animal carcasses in open public places and . . . consum[e] . . . uninspected meat." Although "[i]mproper disposal is a general problem that causes substantial health risks," the ordinances *selectively* address this risk "only when it results from *religious* exercise."

The Court found that the ordinances failed strict scrutiny because the city did not adopt the "least restrictive means" to accomplish its stated goals. Critically, "[t]he legitimate governmental interests in protecting the public health and preventing cruelty to animals could be addressed by restrictions stopping far short of a flat prohibition of all Santeria sacrificial practice." For example, the "city could have imposed a general regulation on the disposal of organic garbage." The Court concluded, "Legislators may not devise mechanisms, overt or disguised, designed to persecute or oppress a religion or its practices. The laws here in question were enacted contrary to these constitutional principles, and they are void."

CHAPTER 58

Burwell v. Hobby Lobby Stores (2014)

ConLaw.us/HobbyLobby/

Employment Division v. Smith (1990), discussed in Chapter 57, proved to be extremely unpopular. In response, Congress enacted the Religious Freedom Restoration Act, or RFRA. Through this 1993 law, Congress sought to use its powers under Section 5 of the Fourteenth Amendment to *restore* the Court's test from *Sherbert v. Verner* (1963).

Under RFRA, the federal and state governments could not impose a "substantial burden" on a "person's exercise of religion even if the burden results from a rule of general applicability," unless the burden "is in furtherance of a compelling governmental interest" and the burden is the "least restrictive means of furthering that compelling governmental interest." Prior to RFRA, courts would review laws of general applicability with rational basis scrutiny. However, RFRA instructed courts to apply a more rigorous test: the state's refusal to make an accommodation for a person's exercise of religion would be reviewed with heightened scrutiny.

In Chapter 20, we studied *City of Boerne v. Flores* (1997). This case held that RFRA was unconstitutional with respect to the states. Congress lacked the power under Section 5 of the Fourteenth Amendment to waive a state's sovereign immunity—that is, to allow the state to be sued in federal court. But Congress had the discretion to limit its *own* power. RFRA continues to impose a statutory — not constitutional — limitation on federal laws that burden religion. As a result, state laws that burden free exercise are reviewed with the deferential *Smith* test, and federal laws that burden free exercise are reviewed with the strict *Sherbert* test.

In *Burwell v. Hobby Lobby Stores* (2014), the Supreme Court considered whether provisions of the Affordable Care Act ran afoul of RFRA. The ACA, or *Obamacare* as it is known, requires that all insurance plans cover "preventive care and screenings" for women, without additional costs. But the federal law did not specify exactly what those services were. To fill this gap, the Obama administration issued a regulation that required insurance plans to cover all FDA-approved forms of contraception. Certain *nonprofit* religious employers were offered accommodations from the mandate. However, *for-profit* employers that did not offer their employees such coverage would be penalized. One of those companies was Hobby Lobby.

Hobby Lobby operated nearly 600 craft stores nationwide. The company was founded by David and Barbara Green. The Green family owned the corporation in a trust. Before the ACA was enacted, Hobby Lobby's insurance policy already covered most forms of birth control. However, board members shared a religious objection to paying for certain other contraceptives, such as Plan B and ella. They considered such products to be "abortifacients," or abortion-inducing drugs. Hobby Lobby and other religious for-profit corporations challenged the so-called "contraceptive mandate" in court. They argued that the regulations imposed a substantial burden on their free exercise of religion, in violation of RFRA.

The Court ruled for Hobby Lobby by a 5-4 vote. Justice Alito wrote the majority opinion, joined by Chief Justice Roberts, and Justices Scalia, Kennedy, and Thomas. He observed that the Greens "believe[d] that they have a religious obligation to run their businesses in accordance with the tenets of their faith." On the basis of that faith, they "object[ed] to offering coverage for four methods of contraception that may operate after conception." The contraceptive mandate "require[d] them to do just that."

First, the Court held "that the language of RFRA makes it clear that" the Court can hear the case of these "closely held for-profit corporations." Justice Alito explained in his oral summary, "The owners of a closely held corporation can exercise religion."

Second, the Court considered whether the contraceptive mandate substantially burdened the free exercise of religion. If the Greens "comply with the HHS Mandate," Justice Alito explained, "they believe they will be facilitating abortions and committing a grave wrong." The Greens were faced with a choice between a $1.3 million daily fine and violating their conscience. "If these consequences do not amount to a substantial burden," Justice Alito asked, "it is hard to see what would."

Third, because there was a substantial burden on free exercise, Justice Alito inquired whether "the Government has a compelling interest in making sure that every woman whose employer is subject to the mandate is able to get every FDA-approved contraceptive without any out of pocket expense." If the interest was not compelling, then the government lacked a sufficient justification to impose a substantial burden on free exercise. The five justices in the majority did not actually decide if the interest was compelling. Rather, they simply assumed "for present purposes that this requirement is satisfied."

The majority could make this assumption because the case would be decided by the fourth issue: whether the mandate was "the least restrictive means" by which the compelling interest could be achieved. The Court found that the government could achieve its interest with a lesser burden on Hobby Lobby's free exercise of religion. "HHS has already devised and implemented a system that seeks to respect the religious liberty of religious non-profit corporations," Justice Alito noted, "while ensuring that the employees of these entities have precisely the same access to all FDA approved contraceptives."

Under the so-called "accommodation," certain religious nonprofits could opt out of having to pay for contraceptive care for their employees. Instead the government, or the insurance company, would pay for the coverage. If the accommodation could work for nonprofit groups like the Little Sisters of the Poor, Justice Alito asked, why could it not "be made available when the owners of for-profit corporations have similar religious objections"?

The Court concluded that "this system constitutes an alternative that achieves all of the Government's aims while providing greater respect for religious liberty." Therefore, the contraceptive mandate could not be enforced against closely held religious corporations, like Hobby Lobby.

Justice Ginsburg wrote the dissent. "In a decision of startling breadth," she began, "the Court holds that commercial enterprises . . . can opt out of any law. . . they judge incompatible with their sincerely held religious beliefs." She was "[p]ersuaded that Congress enacted RFRA to serve a far less radical purpose," and worried about "the havoc the Court's judgment can introduce."

Justice Ginsburg also concluded that RFRA did not protect for-profit corporations; it only protected nonprofits that served a religious community. Only Justice Sotomayor joined this portion of the dissent; Justices Breyer and Kagan did not. All four dissenters, however, agreed that RFRA does not empower the Court to exempt Hobby Lobby from the contraceptive mandate.

Unlike Justice Alito's majority opinion, which focused on how the mandate burdened Hobby Lobby's free exercise, Justice Ginsburg's dissent highlighted the strain a religious accommodation puts on the "employees who do not share their employer's faith." It should make no difference for female employees, she contended, whether they work at Hobby Lobby or the "shop next door."

Justice Ginsburg feared that the majority opinion would lead to a slippery slope. She asked if the government would have to give accommodations to "employers with religiously grounded objections to blood transfusions (Jehovah's Witnesses); antidepressants (Scientologists); medications derived from pigs (certain Muslims, Jews, and Hindus); and vaccinations (Christian Scientists)?"

Justice Alito responded to the slippery-slope objection in his majority opinion. He stressed that there was "no evidence that insurance plans in existence prior to the enactment of ACA excluded coverage for such items." Since the enactment of the ACA, there had been no employers seeking religious exemptions for anything "other than the contraceptive mandate." That it had not happened before, Alito suggested, is a reason not to worry about it happening in the future.

Hobby Lobby was not a constitutional decision based on the Free Exercise Clause of the First Amendment. Rather, the case resolved a statutory dispute based on the Religious Freedom Restoration Act. *Employment Division v. Smith* greatly limited the scope of the *Sherbert* test. Yet, with respect to federal lawmaking, Congress was able to provide greater protections for religious free exercise by limiting its own lawmaking powers.

PART XIII

NO LAW RESPECTING AN ESTABLISHMENT OF RELIGION

Can the government act with a "purpose" to advance religion? Two cases about public displays of the Ten Commandments reached very different results: *McCreary County v. ACLU of Kentucky* (2005) and *Van Orden v. Perry* (2005).

CHAPTER 59

Governmental "Purpose" to Advance Religion

The First Amendment begins, "Congress shall make no law respecting an establishment of religion. . . ." This provision is known as the Establishment Clause. When the First Amendment was ratified in 1791, several states had "established" — that is, official — churches. Some of these states retained their official churches until the mid-nineteenth century.

Law professor Akhil Reed Amar contends that the Establishment Clause performed two functions. First, it prohibited Congress from *establishing* a national church: "Congress shall make no law respecting [a national] establishment of religion." Second, it prevented Congress from *interfering with* established state churches: "Congress shall make no law respecting [a state] establishment of religion." Under Amar's view, the Establishment Clause imposes no limitations on states. Rather, it served as a *structural limit* on federal power. In contrast, the Free Exercise Clause protects *individual* rights.

STUDY GUIDE

If Professor Amar is right, should the Establishment Clause be considered incorporated by the Fourteenth Amendment, or does it resist incorporation like the Tenth Amendment?

The Supreme Court's recent Establishment Clause jurisprudence rejects this Founding-era understanding. Instead, the Court has looked to a much-discussed letter by Thomas Jefferson. In 1802, President Jefferson wrote to the Danbury

Baptist Association in Connecticut. His letter included the now-famous phrase, a "wall of separation between church and state." He wrote:

> Believing with you that religion is a matter which lies solely between man and his God; that he owes account to none other for his faith or his worship; that the legislative powers of the government reach actions only, and not opinions, I contemplate with sovereign reverence that act of the whole American people which declared that their legislature should "make no law respecting an establishment of religion or prohibiting the free exercise thereof," *thus building a wall of separation between church and State.*

To enforce the "separation between church and state," the Supreme Court has identified three kinds of government acts that constitute an "establishment" of religion. First, in *Lemon v. Kurtzman* (1971), the Court prohibited state "entanglement" with religion. Second, in *Marsh v. Chambers* (1983), the Court prohibited state "endorsement" of religion. Third, the Court prohibited a state "purpose" to advance religion.

This chapter will focus on this final test with two related cases: *McCreary County v. ACLU* and *Van Orden v. Perry*. Both cases involved public displays of the Ten Commandments: one in Kentucky and the other in Texas. Both cases were decided on the same day in 2005 by a 5-4 vote. The Kentucky display was declared unconstitutional, while the Texas display was upheld. Justice Breyer joined the majority opinion in *both* cases. How did this split happen? Let's start with the Kentucky case.

McCreary County v. ACLU of Kentucky (2005)

ConLaw.us/McCrearyCounty/

Officials in McCreary County, Kentucky, erected three separate displays of the Ten Commandments in their courthouses. The first display consisted of a large framed copy of the Ten Commandments that was hung in a busy hallway. The American Civil Liberties Union of Kentucky (ACLU) challenged the constitutionality of the first display.

In response, the county erected a second display. It surrounded the framed copy of the Ten Commandments with smaller framed copies of patriotic and legal documents that contained religious references. The district court found that the second display was unconstitutional because it "lacked any secular purpose" and the county's object was instead to advance religion. The phrase *secular*, as opposed to *sectarian*, refers to a non-religious purpose.

After this ruling, the county erected a third display. It included an extended text of the Ten Commandments surrounded by equal-size copies of such documents as the Bill of Rights, a picture of Lady Justice, and the lyrics of The Star-Spangled Banner. The display now included a note explaining that the Ten Commandments influenced the formation of the United States. The lower courts found that the third display was also unconstitutional.

The county appealed that judgment to the Supreme Court. The case presented two questions: (1) to what extent is the government's purpose relevant to evaluate the constitutionality of the current display, and (2) to what extent are the past displays relevant to evaluate the constitutionality of the current display.

The Court ruled for the ACLU by a 5-4 vote. Justice Souter wrote the majority opinion, which was joined by Justices Stevens, O'Connor, Ginsburg, and Breyer. To determine whether the state has violated the Establishment Clause cases, it is "critical" to determine what was the government's *actual* purpose. That motivation, the Court found, directly relates to a central Establishment Clause principle: "neutrality." The majority concluded that McCreary County's displays were predominantly intended to advance religion. This justification was an impermissible purpose under the Court's Establishment Clause doctrine.

Justice Souter's opinion focused on the history of the three displays. The first display consisted of the Ten Commandments in isolation. This display led to the inescapable conclusion that the county intended to convey a religious message. The second display only amplified this religious message, and left no doubt that the county intended to make a religious statement. The third display, which by itself was not problematic, could not be considered in isolation. Rather, the Court had to consider the two displays that immediately preceded it.

Justice Souter concluded that the county had not shown any secular educational purpose to justify the Ten Commandments display. Critically, the Court did not hold that the government would be forever bound, or "tainted," by past purposes.

STUDY GUIDE

Should courts consider political events that come before an official state action? For example, should judges consider statements made on the campaign trail, or a politician's Tweets?

Justice Souter wrote that "although a legislature's stated reasons will generally get deference, the secular purpose required has to be genuine, not a sham, and not merely secondary to a religious objective." McCreary County argued that the display was intended to educate people about the role the Ten Commandments played in developing the rule of law. The majority, however, found this purpose to be "an apparent sham." As a result, the display violated the Establishment Clause. The county's elaborate arrangement of other documents was merely a pretext to promote a specific religious text.

Justice Scalia wrote a dissent that he delivered from the bench. He was joined by Chief Justice Rehnquist and Justice Thomas. Justice Kennedy joined in part. Justice Scalia observed that "[t]oday's opinion ratchets up this Court's hostility to religion." He recounted several instances in which the Founding generation acknowledged the role of religion in society.

First, "George Washington added to the form of presidential oath prescribed by Article II of the Constitution the concluding words 'So help me God.'" Second, "[t]he Supreme Court under John Marshall opened its sessions with the prayer 'God save the United States and this honorable court.'" Third, "[t]he First Congress instituted the practice of beginning its legislative sessions with a prayer." Fourth, "[t]he same week that Congress submitted the Establishment Clause as part of the bill of rights for ratification by the states . . . it enacted legislation providing for paid chaplains in the House and Senate." Fifth, "President Washington authored the first Thanksgiving proclamation . . . on behalf of the American people 'to the service of that great and glorious being who is the Beneficent Author of all the good that is, that was, or that will be.'"

In light of this history, Justice Scalia denied the Court's claim that "'the First Amendment mandates governmental neutrality between . . . religion and non-religion,' and that '[m]anifesting a purpose to favor . . . adherence to religion generally' is unconstitutional." He asked, rhetorically, "Who says so?" That answer, he continued, will surely not be found in "the words of the Constitution," and "surely not [in] the history and traditions that reflect our society's constant understanding of those words." The dissenters would have upheld the constitutionality of the Kentucky display.

Van Orden v. Perry (2005)

 ConLaw.us/VanOrden/

The facts in *Van Orden v. Perry* were different, and so was the vote count. Justice Breyer, who voted *against* the constitutionality of the Ten Commandments display in *McCreary County*, voted *for* the constitutionality of the Ten Commandments display in *Van Orden*. How can we explain the different outcomes? Let's consider the facts.

On the grounds of the Texas State Capitol was a six-foot-high stone monument inscribed with the Ten Commandments and other religious symbols. The Fraternal Order of Eagles donated it to the state in 1961. Greg Abbott, the Attorney General, and future-Governor, defended the monument before the Supreme Court:

> The Texas monument should not be torn down from its historical place for three reasons. First, the Ten Commandments is a historically recognized symbol of law. Second, this monument is one of the smallest of the 17 monuments on the Capitol grounds, and like most of the other monuments, was a gift to the State of Texas and is clearly recognized as such on the monument itself. And third, this monument has stood for more than 40 years without controversy on a national historic landmark.

Law professor Erwin Chemerinsky represented Thomas Van Orden, the challenger. He argued that the monument was unconstitutional:

> When the government puts sacred and solemn texts taken directly from the Bible at the core of its State government, it has to then do something to convey the message that it's not there for religious purposes, that it's there for secular purposes.

By a 5-4 vote, the Court held that the Texas "display of this monument with both the legacy and secular significance does not violate the Establishment Clause." Although Justice Breyer found *Van Orden* to be a "borderline case," he concluded that the Texas display communicates *both* a religious and a secular message, and was therefore constitutional.

STUDY GUIDE

Justice Breyer joined the majority opinion in both *McCreary County* and in *Van Orden*. Can you reconcile his votes?

Justice Breyer's decision seemed to turn on a pragmatic factor: the age of the monument. "This display," he observed, "has stood apparently uncontested for nearly two generations." For this reason, he wrote, keeping "this display is unlikely to prove divisive." Justice Breyer openly feared that a court-ordered removal of this long-standing monument would lead to similar challenges across the nation. Such litigation, he feared, would then generate "the very kind of religiously based divisiveness that the Establishment Clause seeks to avoid."

Justice Souter dissented. He wrote that this "display of an obviously religious text cannot be squared with neutrality." Justice Souter noted that a reasonable observer would "need[] no training in religious doctrine to realize" the religious nature of the display. He acknowledged that there is a relief of Moses and the Ten Commandments in the Supreme Court chamber. However, the Texas display was quite different:

> Moses and the Commandments are displayed in this very Courtroom up on the south and east but Moses stands there in the company of other lawgivers both great and secular demonstrating that the display is about lawgivers, not about religion and was not the product of some religious objective.

When *McCreary County* and *Van Orden* were decided, Justice Rehnquist was quite ill. Cancer would take his life two months later.

PART XIV

THE RIGHT TO KEEP AND BEAR ARMS

The Second Amendment provides, "A well regulated Militia, being necessary to the security of a free State, the right of the people to keep and bear Arms, shall not be infringed." *District of Columbia v. Heller* (2008) held that the Second Amendment protects an individual right to bear arms that was not conditioned on militia service. And *McDonald v. Chicago* (2010) held that state governments are also bound by the Second Amendment.

CHAPTER 60

District of Columbia v. Heller (2008)

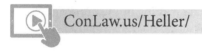

ConLaw.us/Heller/

The District of Columbia criminalized the possession of handguns. Dick Heller, a resident of the District of Columbia, worked as a special policeman. He was required to use a firearm at work to protect federal judges. But the District of Columbia denied his application to register a handgun he wished to keep at home. Heller then challenged the constitutionality of the D.C. handgun ban. He was represented by Alan Gura, a civil rights attorney in Virginia, Robert A. Levy of the libertarian Cato Institute, and Clark M. Neily III of the Institute for Justice.

In 2008, the Supreme Court considered whether D.C.'s handgun ban violated the Second Amendment. It provides, "A well regulated Militia, being necessary to the security of a free State, the right of the people to keep and bear Arms, shall not be infringed." The Court sharply divided, 5-4. Justice Scalia wrote the majority opinion, which was joined by Chief Justice Roberts and Justices Kennedy, Thomas, and Alito. The Court found that the Second Amendment, based on its text and history, guarantees an individual right to possess a gun in the home for self-defense. Justices Stevens, Souter, Ginsburg, and Breyer dissented.

Our analysis starts with the text. The Second Amendment has two portions. The first part is referred to as the *prologue*, the *preamble*, or the *prefatory* clause. It provides, "A well regulated Militia, being necessary to the security of a free State." The second part is known as the *operative* clause. It provides, "the right of the people to keep and bear arms, shall not be infringed."

Justice Scalia concisely summarized his lengthy majority opinion in his oral announcement. He acknowledged that the Second Amendment's prefatory clause creates an "interpretive difficulty." Specifically, "the prologue causes some people to think that [the Second Amendment] confers only a collective, rather than an individual right." Justice Stevens's principal dissent took that position. According to

Justice Stevens, "the preamble clearly contemplates the use of arms in a militia." Yet, Justice Scalia responded, "a prologue cannot limit the scope of the operative text."

Instead, Justice Scalia began his analysis by studying the operative provision:

> We conclude after examining many uses of keep arms and bear arms, contemporaneous with and prior to the adoption of the Second Amendment that it means pretty much what it means today: To *have and carry weapons*. Those old sources refute the notion that bear arms alone or keep and bear arms in combination has an *exclusively* military connotation.

In 1791, he explained, "it was universally understood that the Second Amendment incorporated into the Federal Constitution, a preexisting right of Englishman set forth in the 1689 English Bill of Rights."

With this understanding of the operative clause, the Court returned to the prefatory clause: "The militia consisted of all male citizens capable of military service. That was thought to be a protection against, not only attack from abroad, but tyranny at home. . . . The lesson learned, if the people cannot have arms, there will be no people's militia." The Court found that the original meaning of the prefatory clause was entirely consistent with the original meaning of the operative clause: "The two clauses go together beautifully: Since we need a militia, the right of the people to keep and bear arms shall not be infringed."

In short, the Court held that the Second Amendment protects an individual right that was not conditioned on militia service. Yet, the majority recognized there are certain limits on that right: "Like most rights, the Second Amendment right is not unlimited. It is not a right to keep and carry any weapon whatsoever, in any manner whatsoever, and for whatever purpose."

What types of weapons are protected? Justice Scalia concluded that the operative clause protects weapons that are "'in common use of the time.'" However, he stressed that "dangerous and unusual weapons" are not protected. After *Heller*, lower courts would repeatedly cite this limitation on the types of weapons protected by the Second Amendment.

The Court also gave some examples of other gun regulations that are permissible under the Second Amendment.

> Our opinion should not be taken to cast doubt on longstanding prohibitions on the possession of firearms by felons and the mentally ill, or laws forbidding the carrying of firearms in sensitive places such as schools and government buildings, or laws imposing conditions and qualifications on the commercial sale of arms.

Heller is an otherwise exemplary originalist opinion. But this passage lacked any originalist analysis or support. Why are these regulations, which were not before the Court, consistent with the Second Amendment? Justice Scalia does not say.

STUDY GUIDE

Does Justice Scalia limit the scope of the individual right based on the original public meaning of the Second Amendment? If not, what method does he use?

Next, the Supreme Court had to decide the appropriate level of scrutiny. The Court of Appeals had reviewed the D.C. handgun ban with strict scrutiny. In the Supreme Court, Solicitor General Paul Clement argued the case on behalf of the Bush Administration. He urged the Court *not* to review gun-control laws with strict scrutiny, but to adopt intermediate scrutiny instead. He was concerned that many federal firearms laws, which had long been considered constitutional, would now be in doubt. Clement observed, "if you apply strict scrutiny, I think that the result would be quite different, unfortunately."

Chief Justice Roberts did not think it was necessary to identify the appropriate level of scrutiny: "I don't know why when we are starting afresh, we would try to articulate a whole standard." In contrast, he observed, First Amendment case law "developed over the years."

Ultimately, the Court would follow the Chief Justice's lead. The majority did not adopt strict scrutiny, or intermediate scrutiny for that matter. Rather, the Court found that the District's laws were unconstitutional "under *any* of the standards of scrutiny the Court has applied to enumerated constitutional rights."

But it is important to stress that, by "*any* standard," Justice Scalia meant any standard of *heightened* scrutiny. Justice Scalia did not apply the type of rational basis scrutiny employed in *Williamson v. Lee Optical* (1955). He explained, "the Second Amendment necessarily takes certain policy choices off the table." Justice Scalia added, "This case represents the Court's first in-depth examination of the Second Amendment. One should not expect it to clarify the entire field. There will be time enough to expound upon the historical justifications for these exceptions we have mentioned if and when those exceptions come before us."

Justice Breyer wrote the second dissent. He questioned whether the courts could feasibly review gun control laws with strict scrutiny. Unlike with the freedom of speech, he contended, guns can cause great bodily harm and death. The second part of the strict scrutiny inquiry asks whether the state has a "compelling interest." In light of Justice Breyer's formulation, the state would always have a "compelling interest" to enact gun control laws: to protect people from bodily harm and death. As a result, half of the strict scrutiny analysis would automatically be satisfied. Then, the courts would only have to balance "the interests protected by the Second Amendment on one side and the governmental public-safety concerns on the other."

Justice Breyer would have expressly adopted the sort of "interest-balancing inquiry" that the majority rejected. He wrote that the Court should ask "whether the statute burdens a protected interest in a way or to an extent that is out of proportion to the statute's salutary effects upon other important governmental interests." And such a balancing approach would be quite deferential.

During oral argument, Justice Breyer questioned Alan Gura, Heller's lawyer, about the balance struck by the District of Columbia:

> 80,000 to 100,000 people every year in the United States are either killed or wounded in gun-related homicides or crimes or accidents or suicides. . . . Now, in light of that, why isn't a ban on handguns, while allowing the use of rifles and muskets, a reasonable or a proportionate response on behalf of the District of Columbia? . . . Is it unreasonable for a city with that high crime rate to say no handguns here?

He then asked whether courts should have any role in reviewing gun-control laws: "Do you want thousands of judges all over the United States to be deciding that kind of question rather than the city councils and the legislatures that have decided it in the context of passing laws?"

Gura replied, "When a fundamental right is at stake, there is a role for judicial review, Your Honor." The majority agreed with Gura. Justice Scalia wrote, "We know of no other enumerated constitutional right whose core protection has been subjected to a freestanding 'interest-balancing' approach." Indeed, Justice Breyer's balancing approach does not fit within any of the traditional three tiers of scrutiny: strict, intermediate, or rational basis. "The very enumeration of the right," Justice Scalia concluded, "takes out of the hands of government — even the Third Branch of Government — the power to decide on a case-by-case basis whether the right is really worth insisting upon. A constitutional guarantee subject to future judges' assessments of its usefulness is no constitutional guarantee at all."

Finally, the Court considered the Second Amendment's role in our contemporary society:

> Undoubtedly, some think that the Second Amendment is outmoded in a society where our standing army is the pride of our nation, where well-trained police forces provide personal security, and where gun violence is a serious problem. That is perhaps debatable. But what is not debatable is that it is not the role of this Court to pronounce the Second Amendment extinct.

Justice Stevens wrote the principal dissent. He observed, "the Court is quite wrong today." Throughout the 1980s and 1990s, gun-control advocates had contended that the original meaning of the Second Amendment protected only a *collective* right *of states* to have a militia. By the time *Heller* was argued in 2008, however, these advocates had shifted their position to a new and different theory of original meaning: The Second Amendment only protected an *individual* right to bear arms *in an organized militia*. In his dissent, Justice Stevens defended this new interpretation. He did not contend that the Second Amendment protected a collective right of the states.

STUDY GUIDE

What methods of interpretation are employed in *Heller*?

Both Justices Scalia and Stevens employed originalist arguments, but their methodologies differed. Justice Scalia presented evidence about the original public meaning of the text. He wrote, "In interpreting this text, we are guided by the principle that '[t]he Constitution was written *to be understood by the voters*; its words and phrases were used in their normal and ordinary as distinguished from technical meaning.' Normal meaning may of course include an idiomatic meaning, but it excludes secret or technical meanings that would not have been known *to ordinary citizens* in the founding generation." Most modern-day originalists favor this method, which is called "original public meaning" originalism.

Justice Stevens's approach was more mixed. In contrast with the majority, Justice Stevens concluded that the original public meaning of "bear arms" had an exclusively military connotation. Justice Stevens, who delivered his dissent from the bench, explained that "the most natural reading of the 27-word text" in the Second Amendment "protects the right to keep and bear arms and makes no mention of any non-military use of a firearm. It protects the preexisting right to use guns by members of a militia."

But Justice Stevens also used an alternative method known as "original intent originalism." He contended that "there is no indication that *the Framers* of the Amendment *intended* to enshrine the common-law right of self-defense in the Constitution." Modern-day originalists, as well as non-originalists, have rejected this approach as unworkable. It is simply impossible to identify, and somehow combine, all the differing purposes that were held by different drafters to reach a single "intention of the Framers." In contrast, it is usually possible to identify the single public meaning of the words the framers chose.

Justice Stevens closed the oral summary of his dissent with a plea for judicial restraint: "Regulation of the civilian use of firearms raises complex and critically important questions of public policy that have heretofore been resolved exclusively by the political branches of our Government. This Court should stay out of that political thicket." And he closed his written dissent with a similar plea: "It is . . . clear to me that adherence to a policy of judicial restraint would be far wiser than the bold decision announced today."

In *Heller*, the Court only considered whether the Second Amendment limits the federal government's powers in the District of Columbia. Two years later in *McDonald v. City of Chicago*, the Court would hold that the Second Amendment's "right to keep and bear arms" also limits *state* gun-control laws by virtue of the Fourteenth Amendment.

CHAPTER 61

McDonald v. City of Chicago (2010)

ConLaw.us/McDonald/

In *District of Columbia v. Heller* (2008), the Supreme Court held that the Second Amendment protects an individual right to keep and bear arms in the home for purposes of self-defense. However, *Heller* only considered whether the Second Amendment restricts *federal* gun-control laws. Immediately after *Heller* was decided, Otis McDonald and other Chicago residents challenged ordinances that effectively banned handgun possession in the city. *McDonald v. Chicago* (2010) considered whether the Second Amendment restricts the state's police powers to enact gun-control laws.

The Second Amendment was ratified in 1791. *Barron v. Baltimore* (1833) held that the provisions of what we call "The Bill of Rights," including the Second Amendment, only restricted the federal government's powers. (See Chapter 5.) After the Civil War, however, the ratification of the Thirteenth, Fourteenth, and Fifteenth Amendments changed the relationship between the federal government and the states.

In the late nineteenth and early twentieth centuries, the Court developed the so-called "selective incorporation" doctrine. These cases held that the Due Process Clause of the Fourteenth Amendment *incorporated* some, but not all, of the enumerated rights in the first eight amendments. As a result, states could no longer abridge those rights. For example, *Gitlow v. New York* (1925) affirmed that the Due Process Clause of the Fourteenth Amendment prevented states from violating the freedom of speech protected by the First Amendment. (See Chapter 52.) One by one, or *jot-by-jot*, most of the guarantees in the first eight amendments would be extended to the states in this fashion.

There was, however, another textual basis that prevented state governments from abridging rights in the first eight amendments. The Privileges or Immunities

Clause of the Fourteenth Amendment provides, "No State shall make or enforce any law which shall abridge the privileges or immunities of citizens of the United States." During his hand-down of the opinion, Justice Alito observed, "At the time of the ratification of the Fourteenth Amendment, there were those who thought that the phrase 'Privileges or Immunities of citizens of the United States' protected all of the rights guaranteed by the Bill of Rights." Justice Alito added, "There are prominent scholars today who continue to hold that view." Professors Barnett and Blackman hold that view.

But the Supreme Court rejected that view in two important decisions. First, in the *Slaughter-House Cases* (1873), the Supreme Court interpreted the Privileges or Immunities Clause in a very narrow fashion. Specifically, the majority held that the Clause did not protect an *unenumerated* right to contract. Second, in *United States v. Cruikshank* (1875), the Court held that the Privileges or Immunities Clause did not protect *enumerated* rights, such as those listed in the First and Second Amendments. (We studied both cases in Chapter 28.) To compensate for the all-but-deleted Privileges or Immunities Clause, the Supreme Court would gradually expand the scopes of the Due Process and Equal Protection Clauses beyond their original meaning.

By 2010, the Supreme Court had used the Due Process Clause to incorporate almost all of the rights contained in the first eight amendments. The Second Amendment, however, was one of the few exceptions. *McDonald v. City of Chicago* would change that rule. The vote in this case was complicated. A plurality of four Justices — Chief Justice Roberts and Justices Scalia, Kennedy, and Alito — found that the Second Amendment was a "fundamental right," which should be incorporated through the Due Process Clause. The Chicago handgun ban, like the D.C. handgun ban at issue in *Heller*, was therefore unconstitutional. Justice Alito wrote the plurality opinion. In his oral summary of the case, he explained, "We analyzed the question presented here under the Due Process Clause, that is the practice that the Court has followed now for more than a century and we continue on that path and we hold that the *Heller* right easily meets the standard that the Court has used during the last half century."

Four dissenting Justices — Stevens, Breyer, Ginsburg, and Sotomayor — declined to extend the right to the states. They concluded that the Fourteenth Amendment did not place any limits on the sort of gun-control laws Chicago could enact.

Justice Thomas, standing alone, found that the right to keep and bear arms was a Privilege or Immunity of citizenship. He concurred with the plurality's judgment, but not its reasoning. With this fifth and decisive vote, the Chicago handgun ban was declared unconstitutional.

STUDY GUIDE

How does the Court decide whether the Second Amendment is a "fundamental" right?

Justice Alito used the *Washington v. Glucksberg* (1997) framework to decide that the right to keep and bear arms was "fundamental." (See Chapter 48.) In answering "the question whether the Second Amendment right to keep and bear arms is incorporated in the concept of due process," he wrote, "we must decide whether the right to keep and bear arms is *fundamental* to our scheme of ordered liberty, . . . or . . . whether this right is '*deeply rooted* in this Nation's history and tradition.'"

Justice Alito carefully examined the history of the right to bear arms from the Founding, through Reconstruction, and to the present. Based on this history, the plurality concluded that the Second Amendment satisfied the *Glucksberg* standard. Justice Alito summarized some of this evidence when he announced his opinion:

> Evidence from the Civil War period is particularly instructive. Armed parties often consisting of ex-Confederate soldiers serving in the state militias forcibly took firearms from newly freed slaves and other blacks. The Reconstruction era Congress was alarmed by these practices. Union Army Commanders tried to stop these abuses by issuing orders, securing the right of all people to keep and bear arms, but Congress decided that more was needed. It first turned to ordinary legislation. It enacted the Freedmen's Bureau Act of 1866 which explicitly guaranteed the right of all citizens "to have the full and equal benefit of the constitutional right to bear arms." The Civil Rights Act of 1866 had a similar aim, but Congress feared that these Civil Rights Laws would be held to exceed Congress' power and Congress then proposed the Fourteenth Amendment which was ratified.

Justice Stevens wrote a dissent that no other Justice joined. As in *Heller*, he disputed the plurality's historical account. He also argued that *Lawrence v. Texas* (2003) "plainly renounced" *Washington v. Glucksberg*'s "exclusively historical methodology" to identify fundamental rights. Additionally, Justice Stevens maintained that *Heller* was wrong. He insisted that the Second Amendment, as originally understood, had only a military meaning. Moreover, Justice Stevens contended that "the liberty clause" of the Fourteenth Amendment, as he called it, cuts in both directions. The "liberty" of individuals to own firearms must be weighed against the "liberty" of the people to be safe from gun violence. And the courts should defer to whatever balance of those interests that the states choose.

Justice Breyer wrote the principal dissent, which was joined by Justices Ginsburg, and Sotomayor. In his oral summary of his dissent, Justice Breyer cited five reasons why the right to keep and bear arms was not fundamental:

1. "the framers did not write the Second Amendment in order to protect a private right of armed self-defense;"
2. "there is no consensus if the right is or was fundamental";
3. "no broader constitutional interest or principle supports legal treatment of that right as fundamental";
4. "incorporation is difficult to reconcile with the constitution's allocation of responsibilities between States and the Federal Government, between courts and legislatures"; and

5. "nothing in eighteenth, nineteenth, twentieth or twenty-first century history shows an unambiguous historical consensus that the right is sufficiently fundamental as to warrant incorporation."

He concluded, "*Heller* or no *Heller*, the Fourteenth Amendment does not incorporate a private right of armed self-defense and apply that right against the states."

Neither the conservative plurality, nor the progressive dissenters, was willing to reconsider the *Slaughter-House Cases*. During oral argument, Alan Gura, McDonald's lawyer, contended that the right to keep and bear arms was among the Privileges or Immunities of Citizens of the United States. Chief Justice Roberts retorted, "Of course, [your] argument is contrary to the *Slaughter-House Cases*, which have been the law for 140 years. It might be simpler, but . . . it's a heavy burden for you to carry to suggest that we ought to overrule that decision." Likewise, Justice Scalia—the self-professed originalist—ridiculed Gura's reliance on the original meaning of the Privileges or Immunities Clause:

> Why are you asking us to overrule 150, 140 years of prior law, when you can reach your result under substantive due process. I mean, you know, unless you're bucking for a place on some law school faculty . . . what you argue is the darling of the professoriate, for sure, but it's also contrary to 140 years of our jurisprudence.

Gura replied, "Your Honor, the *Slaughter-House Cases* should not have any stare decisis effect before the Court. The Court has always found that when a case is extremely wrong, when there is a great consensus that it was simply not decided correctly, especially in a constitutional matter, it has less force." Justice Scalia replied, "Why do you want to undertake that burden instead of just arguing substantive due process? Which, as much as I think it's wrong, even I have acquiesced in it."

Only Justice Thomas was willing to reconsider the *Slaughter-House Cases*. He found that the Privileges or Immunities Clause originally "was understood to enforce constitutionally declared rights against the States." What were these rights? The history Justice Alito described points "unambiguously toward the conclusion that the Privileges or Immunities Clause enforces at least those fundamental rights enumerated in the Constitution against the States, including the Second Amendment right to keep and bear arms." Justice Thomas also found that "the ratifying public understood the Privileges or Immunities Clause to protect constitutionally enumerated rights, including the right to keep and bear arms."

As a result, Justice Thomas would have overruled both *Slaughter-House* and *Cruikshank*. The latter precedent, in particular, he wrote, is not "entitled to any respect." Justice Thomas concluded that the Privileges or Immunities Clause prevents the states from abridging the right to keep and bear arms. With this critical fifth vote, a majority of the Court declared Chicago's ordinances unconstitutional.

Why were eight Justices unwilling to overrule *Slaughter-House*? We believe that they were afraid of opening up a Pandora's Box. Both the conservative and progressive justices were uncertain about how to identify unenumerated rights. During oral argument, Justice Kennedy asked, "what are these other unenumerated rights?" Likewise, Justice Ginsburg asked, "what unenumerated rights would we be declaring privileges and immunities under your conception of [the Clause]?"

Attorney Alan Gura answered that "we have wonderful historical guideposts." For example, he looked to "the sort of right[s] that [were] mentioned in the Civil Rights Act of 1866." Gura added, "in 1868, the right to keep and bear arms was understood to be a privilege or immunity of citizenship."

Justice Ginsburg also worried that relying on the original meaning of the Privileges or Immunities Clause could alter the Supreme Court's approach to gender equality. She asked whether "married women at that time across the nation [had] the right to contract, to hold property, to sue and be sued?"

The conservative Justices were also concerned about what other rights might be protected by the original meaning of the Privileges or Immunities Clause. Justice Alito asked a question with a veiled reference to *Lochner v. New York*: "Well, does it include the right to contract?"

Gura replied that the right to contract was an "unenumerated right under the Privileges or Immunities" Clause. He explained that the Civil Rights Act of 1866 expressly protected the rights "[t]o make and enforce contracts; to sue, be parties, and give evidence; to inherit, purchase, lease, sell, hold, and convey real and personal property." Chief Justice Roberts also worried that relying on the Privileges or Immunities Clause would give judges too much discretion to identify unenumerated rights: "Your original approach would give judges a lot more power and flexibility in determining what rights they think are a good idea than they have now with the constraints of the Due Process Clause."

Justice Thomas was not troubled by the fact that the Privileges or Immunities Clause protects unenumerated rights. He wrote in his concurring opinion, "I see no reason to assume that such hazards apply to the Privileges or Immunities Clause. The mere fact that the Clause does not expressly list the rights it protects does not render it incapable of principled judicial application." Why was there no special risk? He answered, "When the inquiry focuses on what the ratifying era understood the Privileges or Immunities Clause to mean, interpreting it should be no more 'hazardous' than interpreting these other constitutional provisions by using the same approach." The Court could determine the original public meaning of the Privileges or Immunities Clause. Doing so, he wrote, is "far more likely to yield discernible answers than the substantive due process questions the Court has for years created on its own, with neither textual nor historical support."

In the end, five Justices found that Chicago's ordinances were unconstitutional because "the right recognized in *Heller* is fully applicable to the states." But the Court did not provide any more guidance on the scope of that right than it had in *Heller*.

PART XV

TAKING PRIVATE PROPERTY FOR PUBLIC USE

The Fifth Amendment prohibits the government from "tak[ing]" "private property" "for public use" without paying "just compensation." This provision implies, conversely, that the government *may* permissibly take private property for public use *with* just compensation. In this part we consider two questions raised by the text of the Fifth Amendment. First, what is a "taking"? *Pennsylvania Coal Company v. Mahon* (1922) and *Penn Central Transportation Company v. New York* (1978) addressed this question. Second, what is a "public use"? *Kelo v. City of New London* (2005) answered this question.

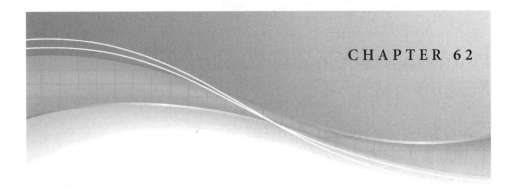

CHAPTER 62

What Is a Taking?

The Fifth Amendment ends with the following clause: "nor shall *private property* be *taken* for *public use*, without *just compensation*." In *Barron v. Baltimore* (1833), the Supreme Court held that the Takings Clause only restricted the federal government's powers. The first eight amendments, now known as the Bill of Rights, did not limit a state's police power. This dynamic would change following the ratification of the Fourteenth Amendment. *Chicago, Burlington & Quincy Railroad Company v. City of Chicago* (1897) held that the state violates the Due Process Clause of the Fourteenth Amendment when it takes property for public use without providing just compensation. That decision did not even cite the Takings Clause of the Fifth Amendment. Yet, under modern doctrine, the Takings Clause of the Fifth Amendment has been deemed *incorporated*. This right, like most of the other rights in the first eight amendments, now limits the states' police powers.

The twelve words of the Takings Clause raise four distinct legal questions. What is the meaning of (1) "property," (2) a "tak[ing]," (3) "public use," and (4) "just compensation"? This chapter will focus on the second question. Chapter 63 will consider the third question.

When the state "take[s]" private property, it must provide "just compensation." When the state uses its police power to regulate property, however, the government does not need to provide "just compensation." How do we distinguish between a taking (which requires just compensation) and an exercise of the police power (which does not)? In some cases, it is fairly obvious when the government takes property. For example, in *Kelo v. City of New London* (2005), the government exercised its power of "eminent domain" to quite literally *take* Susette Kelo's home. In that case, there was unquestionably a *physical* taking for purposes of the Fifth Amendment.

What happens, however, when a regulation merely limits *how* property can be used, and therefore, reduces its value? Does such a reduction, or diminution, in value constitute a *regulatory* taking? Or, is the state merely exercising its police power? The answer is complicated because the Supreme Court has not provided a clear definition of a taking.

Pennsylvania Coal Company v. Mahon (1922)

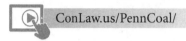

ConLaw.us/PennCoal/

In *Pennsylvania Coal Company v. Mahon* (1922), the Supreme Court attempted to draw the line between a permissible exercise of the police power and an unconstitutional regulatory taking.

Sometimes when coal is mined below the surface, the ground above the surface may collapse. As a result, structures above the surface may sink into the ground. This process is known as "subsidence." In 1921, Pennsylvania enacted the Kohler Act. The law prohibited "the mining of anthracite coal in such way as to cause the *subsidence* of, among other things, any structure used as a human habitation."

Mahon owned the surface rights to a piece of land. Prior to 1921, the Pennsylvania Coal Company had acquired the subsurface right to mine coal below that lot. The Coal Company notified Mahon that it would begin to mine the property. Mahon then sued the company for violating the Kohler Act. The company responded that the Kohler Act took their private property — the subsurface rights — without just compensation. The Supreme Court agreed by an 8-1 vote. Justice Holmes wrote the majority opinion.

STUDY GUIDE

In *Mahon*, Justice Holmes found that the Fourteenth Amendment empowered the courts to carefully scrutinize takings of private property. How does Justice Holmes interpret the Fourteenth Amendment in *Lochner v. New York* (1905)?

Justice Holmes acknowledged that the "Government hardly could go on if, to some extent, values incident to property could not be diminished without paying for every such change in the general law." However, he wrote, the police power is limited. When the "extent of the diminution" in value is too great, there "must be an exercise of eminent domain and compensation to sustain the act." Ultimately, Justice Holmes found that the Kohler Act "is not justified as a protection of personal safety."

Moreover, the "extent of the taking is great." Holmes wrote that the "statute does not disclose a public interest sufficient to warrant so extensive a destruction of the [Coal Company's] constitutionally protected rights." Therefore, "the act cannot be sustained as an exercise of the police power, so far as it affects the mining of coal under streets or cities in places where the right to mine such coal has been reserved."

What is the test? "The general rule, at least, is that, while property may be regulated to a certain extent, if regulation goes *too far*, it will be recognized as a taking." This test is not very helpful.

STUDY GUIDE

Is the regulatory takings doctrine articulated in *Mahon* consistent with the original meaning of the Constitution? Is the government required to provide compensation where an owner keeps his property, albeit with a reduced value?

Justice Brandeis was the lone dissenter in *Mahon*. He wrote that the state has the police "power to prohibit such uses without paying compensation." A "restriction imposed to protect the public health, safety or morals from dangers threatened is not a taking."

Justice Brandeis offered a different test. The Court should not focus on the small parcel of land that the coal company could no longer mine. Instead, the Court should consider the "value of the whole property." Here, the company could *still* mine valuable coal in other areas that would not cause subsidence. This test became known as the "parcel as a whole" test. The Supreme Court would embrace Justice Brandeis's dissent five decades later.

Penn Central Transportation Company v. New York (1978)

ConLaw.us/PennCentral/

The Penn Central Transportation Company wanted to build a tower atop Grand Central Terminal in Manhattan. New York City designated the train station as an historic "landmark" in order to block the redevelopment. Penn Central argued that the landmark designation was an unconstitutional "taking" of its air rights over the terminal. The Supreme Court upheld the designation in *Penn Central Transportation Company v. New York* (1978).

Justice Brennan wrote the majority opinion. Even though New York's law diminished the value of the air rights, Penn Central could still benefit from other portions of Grand Central Terminal. Therefore, there was no taking. In other words, because the Court considered the "parcel as a whole," the diminution in value did not go "too far."

CHAPTER 63

Kelo v. City of New London (2005)

 ConLaw.us/Kelo/

In *Pennsylvania Coal Company v. Mahon* (1922) and *Penn Central Transportation Company v. New York* (1978), the Court divided about when a land-use regulation becomes an unconstitutional *taking*. But no one doubted that both laws pursued a "public use": preventing subsidence and preserving landmarks. In *Kelo v. City of New London* (2005), there was no question that the government wanted to "take[]" a person's home. Yet, the Court sharply divided about whether the property would be taken for a "public use."

The case began in 1990. Connecticut declared that the city of New London was a "distressed municipality." As a means to improve the economy, New London planned to acquire property in the Ft. Trumbull neighborhood and transfer it to Pfizer. The pharmaceutical company pledged to construct a new research facility on this site. The city expected that its plan would create new jobs, increase tax revenues, and improve the area's recreational opportunities.

Initially, New London tried to purchase the homes in Ft. Trumbull, including Susette Kelo's little pink house. However, Kelo and her neighbors—some of whom had lived in their houses for their entire lives—refused to sell. In response, the city commenced condemnation proceedings. New London would use its eminent domain powers to acquire the properties in exchange for "just compensation."

Kelo filed suit in state court to halt the condemnation proceedings. She alleged that the city's taking was not for a "public use." According to the development plan, most of the condemned property would be transferred to private parties.

Justice Scalia aptly summarized Kelo's objection during oral argument:

> What this lady wants is not more money. No amount of money is going to sat-
> isfy her. She is living in this house, you know, her whole life and she does not
> want to move. She said "I'll move if it's being taken for a public use, but by God,
> you're just giving it to some other private individual because that individual is
> going to pay more taxes."

The lower courts ruled against Kelo. On appeal, the question presented was
"whether a city's taking of private property for the purpose of economic development satisfies the public use requirement of the Fifth Amendment." By a vote of
5-4, the Court ruled against Kelo.

The Justices sharply divided on what exactly the Constitution prohibited. The
text of the Fifth Amendment requires that the government have a "public use" to
take "private property." Yet, many Justices equated "public *use*" with "public *purpose*." For example, during oral argument Justice Souter asked, "Why isn't there a
public purpose here?" Justice Scalia interjected, "Does the 'public use' requirement
mean nothing more than that it has a 'public purpose?'"

STUDY GUIDE

What is the difference between taking "private property" for a "public use," and
taking it for a "public purpose"?

New London argued that there was a long line of precedent that equated public
use and public purpose. For example, in *Berman v. Parker* (1954), the government
seized private "distressed" property to promote "community redevelopment" and
the "public welfare." The Supreme Court unanimously found that this taking was
constitutional. Thirty years later, in *Hawaii Housing Authority v. Midkiff* (1984),
the state transferred private property in fee simple from landlords to their tenants.
Justice O'Connor wrote the majority opinion, which upheld the taking. She found
that "the State's purpose of eliminating the 'social and economic evils of a land oli-
gopoly' qualified as a valid public use."

Scott Bullock represented Kelo. He worked for the Institute for Justice, a libertarian
public interest law firm. Bullock did not ask the Court to overrule *Berman* or *Midkiff*.
Instead, at oral argument, he questioned whether a taking to enhance *economic development* was a proper "public purpose." He said:

> Every home, church, or corner store would produce more tax revenue and jobs
> if it were a Costco, a shopping mall, or a private office building. But if that's the
> justification for the use of eminent domain, then any city can take property
> anywhere within its borders for any private use that might make more money
> than what is there now.

Ultimately, the Court found that economic development was a legitimate public
purpose. Justice Stevens wrote the majority opinion, joined by Justices Kennedy,

Souter, Ginsburg, and Breyer. He concluded that "public use" is equivalent to "public purpose." He asked, "Where is the line between 'public' and 'private' property use?" The Court was not prepared to draw this line. Rather, it would "give considerable deference to legislatures' determinations about what governmental activities will advantage the public."

The majority then found that New London's effort to rejuvenate its economy through an "integrated development plan" qualifies as a public purpose. Because New London had such a purpose, the majority reviewed the city's actions with rational basis scrutiny. Ultimately, the Court ruled against Kelo because "the City's proposed condemnations [were] for a 'public use' within the meaning of the Fifth Amendment to the Federal Constitution."

Justice Kennedy wrote a concurring opinion. He found that the Court should review takings with a "deferential standard of review" that echoes "the rational-basis test used to review economic regulation under the Due Process and Equal Protection Clauses." Justice Kennedy favorably cited *Williamson v. Lee Optical* (1955). But he maintained that in some cases, the court could find that the government's stated public use was not the real public use; it was, in fact pretextual. A "court applying rational-basis review under the Public Use Clause should strike down a taking that, by a clear showing, is intended to favor a particular private party, with only incidental or pretextual public benefits, just as a court applying rational-basis review under the Equal Protection Clause must strike down a government classification that is clearly intended to injure a particular class of private parties, with only incidental or pretextual public justifications." Here, Justice Kennedy favorably cited cases that applied *heightened* rational basis scrutiny: *City of Cleburne v. Cleburne Living Center* (1985) and *Department of Agriculture v. Moreno* (1973). (See Chapters 43 and 48.)

Nevertheless, Justice Kennedy contended that "a presumption of invalidity is not warranted . . . simply because the purpose of the taking is economic development." He acknowledged that Pfizer would benefit from New London's "comprehensive" plan. However, Justice Kennedy countered that "benefiting Pfizer was not the primary motivation or effect of this development plan; instead, 'the primary motivation for [the city] was to take advantage of Pfizer's presence'" to enhance the area. Therefore, New London's taking pursued a "public use."

During oral argument, the attorney for New London offered lofty assurances about the forthcoming public benefits: "[T]he expectation is there is going to be a demand for class A office space, which is the best quality office space in this area by 2010. And the expectation is that it will attract the sorts of offices that will feed on Pfizer. They spent $300 million on a site here."

But the *Kelo* majority did not require such rosy predictions about economic development to be accurate or even likely. Justice Stevens wrote, "It is not within our authority as a court to determine the plan's likelihood of success, nor to determine whether New London would have been wiser to pursue economic development in some other way."

Justice O'Connor wrote the first dissent. She was joined by Chief Justice Rehnquist and Justices Scalia and Thomas. Her vote in *Kelo* was a bit of a surprise because she authored the majority opinion in *Midkiff*. Justice O'Connor found that the Court improperly "abandon[ed]" the rule from *Calder v. Bull* (1798). In that case, Justice Samuel Chase explained:

> An act of the Legislature (for I cannot call it a law) contrary to the great first principles of the social compact, cannot be considered a rightful exercise of legislative authority . . . [A] law that takes property from A and gives it to B: It is against all reason and justice, for a people to entrust a Legislature with such powers; and, therefore, it cannot be presumed that they have done it.

During oral argument, Justice O'Connor asked the lawyer for New London if the government could take a "Motel 6" in order to replace it with a "Ritz-Carlton," which would generate "higher taxes. Now, is that okay?" In a gutsy move, the lawyer bit the bullet: "Yes, Your Honor. That would be okay." Justice Kennedy replied, if that were true, then is *Calder* wrong that "you can't take from A to give to B"? Justice Scalia added, "Let me qualify it. You can take from A to give to B if B pays more taxes."

Justice O'Connor explained in her dissent why the majority opinion's rule was so dangerous: "Under the banner of economic development, all private property is now vulnerable to being taken and transferred to another private owner, so long as it might be upgraded — i.e., given to an owner who will use it in a way that the legislature deems more beneficial to the public — in the process." Moreover, she wrote, the Court "wash[ed] out any distinction between private and public use of property — and thereby effectively . . . delete[d] the words 'for public use' from the Takings Clause of the Fifth Amendment."

Justice Thomas wrote the second dissent. He "would revisit [the Court's] Public Use Clause cases and consider returning to the original meaning of the Public Use Clause: that the government may take property only if it actually uses or gives the public a legal right to use the property."

Justice Thomas predicted that "extending the concept of public purpose to encompass any economically beneficial goal guarantees that these losses will fall disproportionally on poor communities. Those communities are not only systematically less likely to put their lands to the highest and best social use, but are also the least politically powerful." Here, Justice Thomas favorably invoked Footnote Four of *United States v. Carolene Products* (1938): "If ever there were justification for intrusive judicial review of constitutional provisions that protect 'discrete and insular minorities,' surely that principle would apply with great force to the powerless groups and individuals the Public Use Clause protects."

After *Kelo* was decided, Pfizer decided not to develop the new research facility in New London after all. Fifteen years later, the former site of Susette Kelo's home remains an empty lot, occupied only by feral cats. Kelo's little pink house was moved, plank by plank, to a new location in New London. It now stands as a monument to eminent domain abuse.

Kelo was a very unpopular decision. More than 40 states enacted some form of eminent domain reform to curb the reach of the Supreme Court's decision. Many of these legislative reforms, however, have proven to be largely ineffective.

APPENDIX A
Annotated Constitution of the United States

Preamble

We the People of the United States, in Order to form a more perfect Union, establish Justice, insure domestic Tranquility, provide for the common defence, promote the general Welfare, and secure the Blessings of Liberty to ourselves and our Posterity, do ordain and establish this Constitution for the United States of America.

Article I

Section 1. All legislative Powers herein granted shall be vested in a Congress of the United States, which shall consist of a Senate and House of Representatives.

> *McCulloch v. Maryland* (1819)
> *Hepburn v. Griswold* (1870)
> *Schechter Poultry Corp. v. United States* (1935)
> *NLRB v. Jones & Laughlin Steel Corp.* (1937)

Section 2. The House of Representatives shall be composed of Members chosen every second Year by the People of the several States, and the Electors in each State shall have the Qualifications requisite for Electors of the most numerous Branch of the State Legislature.

No Person shall be a Representative who shall not have attained to the Age of twenty five Years, and been seven Years a Citizen of the United States, and who shall not, when elected, be an Inhabitant of that State in which he shall be chosen.

[Representatives and direct Taxes shall be apportioned among the several States which may be included within this Union, according to their respective Numbers, which shall be determined by adding to the whole Number of free Persons, including those bound to Service for a Term of Years, and excluding Indians not taxed, three fifths of all other Persons.]* The actual Enumeration shall be made within three Years after the first Meeting of the Congress of the United States, and within every subsequent Term of ten Years, in such Manner as they shall by Law direct. The number of Representatives shall not exceed one for every thirty Thousand, but each State shall have at Least one Representative; and until such enumeration shall be made, the State of New Hampshire shall be entitled to chuse three, Massachusetts eight, Rhode-Island and Providence Plantations one, Connecticut five, New-York six, New Jersey four, Pennsylvania eight, Delaware one, Maryland six, Virginia ten, North Carolina five, South Carolina five, and Georgia three.

When vacancies happen in the Representation from any State, the Executive Authority thereof shall issue Writs of Election to fill such Vacancies.

The House of Representatives shall chuse their Speaker and other Officers; and shall have the sole Power of Impeachment.

Section 3. The Senate of the United States shall be composed of two Senators from each State, [chosen by the Legislature thereof,]** for six Years; and each Senator shall have one Vote.

Immediately after they shall be assembled in Consequence of the first Election, they shall be divided as equally as may be into three Classes. The Seats of the Senators of the first Class shall be vacated at the Expiration of the second Year, of the second Class at the Expiration of the fourth Year, and of the third Class at the Expiration of the sixth Year, so that one third may be chosen every second Year; [and if Vacancies

---

* Changed by Section 2 of the Fourteenth Amendment.
** Changed by the Seventeenth Amendment.

happen by Resignation, or otherwise, during the Recess of the Legislature of any State, the Executive thereof may make temporary Appointments until the next Meeting of the Legislature, which shall then fill such Vacancies.]*

No Person shall be a Senator who shall not have attained to the Age of thirty Years, and been nine Years a Citizen of the United States, and who shall not, when elected, be an Inhabitant of that State for which he shall be chosen.

The Vice President of the United States shall be President of the Senate, but shall have no Vote, unless they be equally divided.

The Senate shall chuse their other Officers, and also a President pro tempore, in the Absence of the Vice President, or when he shall exercise the Office of President of the United States.

The Senate shall have the sole Power to try all Impeachments. When sitting for that Purpose, they shall be on Oath or Affirmation. When the President of the United States is tried, the Chief Justice shall preside: And no Person shall be convicted without the Concurrence of two thirds of the Members present.

Judgment in Cases of Impeachment shall not extend further than to removal from Office, and disqualification to hold and enjoy any Office of honor, Trust or Profit under the United States: but the Party convicted shall nevertheless be liable and subject to Indictment, Trial, Judgment and Punishment, according to Law.

Section 4. The Times, Places and Manner of holding Elections for Senators and Representatives, shall be prescribed in each State by the Legislature thereof; but the Congress may at any time by Law make or alter such Regulations, except as to the Places of chusing Senators.

The Congress shall assemble at least once in every Year, and such Meeting shall be [on the first Monday in December,]** unless they shall by Law appoint a different Day.

NLRB v. Noel Canning (2014) ——— **Section 5.** Each House shall be the Judge of the Elections, Returns and Qualifications of its own Members, and a Majority of each shall constitute a Quorum to do Business; but a smaller Number may adjourn from day to day, and may be authorized to compel the Attendance of absent Members, in such Manner, and under such Penalties as each House may provide.

Each House may determine the Rules of its Proceedings, punish its Members for disorderly Behaviour, and, with the Concurrence of two thirds, expel a Member.

Each House shall keep a Journal of its Proceedings, and from time to time publish the same, excepting such Parts as may in their Judgment require Secrecy; and the Yeas and Nays of the Members of either House on any question shall, at the Desire of one fifth of those Present, be entered on the Journal.

Neither House, during the Session of Congress, shall, without the Consent of the other, adjourn for more than three days, nor to any other Place than that in which the two Houses shall be sitting.

Section 6. The Senators and Representatives shall receive a Compensation for their Services, to be ascertained by Law, and paid out of the Treasury of the United States. They shall in all Cases, except Treason, Felony and Breach of the Peace, be privileged from Arrest during their Attendance at the Session of their respective Houses, and in going to and returning from the same; and for any Speech or Debate in either House, they shall not be questioned in any other Place.

No Senator or Representative shall, during the Time for which he was elected, be appointed to any civil Office under the Authority of the United States, which shall have been created, or the Emoluments whereof shall have been increased during such time; and no Person holding any Office under the United States, shall be a Member of either House during his Continuance in Office.

Section 7. All Bills for raising Revenue shall originate in the House of Representatives; but the Senate may propose or concur with Amendments as on other Bills.

---

* Changed by the Seventeenth Amendment.

** Changed by Section 2 of the Twentieth Amendment.

Every Bill which shall have passed the House of Representatives and the Senate, shall, before it become a Law, be presented to the President of the United States; If he approve he shall sign it, but if not he shall return it, with his Objections to that House in which it shall have originated, who shall enter the Objections at large on their Journal, and proceed to reconsider it. If after such Reconsideration two thirds of that House shall agree to pass the Bill, it shall be sent, together with the Objections, to the other House, by which it shall likewise be reconsidered, and if approved by two thirds of that House, it shall become a Law. But in all such Cases the Votes of both Houses shall be determined by Yeas and Nays, and the Names of the Persons voting for and against the Bill shall be entered on the Journal of each House respectively. If any Bill shall not be returned by the President within ten Days (Sundays excepted) after it shall have been presented to him, the Same shall be a Law, in like Manner as if he had signed it, unless the Congress by their Adjournment prevent its Return, in which Case it shall not be a Law.

Every Order, Resolution, or Vote to which the Concurrence of the Senate and House of Representatives may be necessary (except on a question of Adjournment) shall be presented to the President of the United States; and before the Same shall take Effect, shall be approved by him, or being disapproved by him, shall be repassed by two thirds of the Senate and House of Representatives, according to the Rules and Limitations prescribed in the Case of a Bill.

Section 8. The Congress shall have Power To lay and collect Taxes, Duties, Imposts and Excises, to pay the Debts and provide for the common Defence and general Welfare of the United States; but all Duties, Imposts and Excises shall be uniform throughout the United States; — *McCulloch v. Maryland* (1819)

— *McCulloch v. Maryland* (1819)

To borrow Money on the credit of the United States;

To regulate Commerce with foreign Nations, and among the several States, and with the Indian Tribes;

Gibbons v. Ogden (1824)
United States v. Dewitt (1869)
Hepburn v. Griswold (1870)
United States v. E.C. Knight (1895)
Champion v. Ames (1903)
Hammer v. Dagenhart (1918)

To establish an uniform Rule of Naturalization, and uniform Laws on the subject of Bankruptcies throughout the United States;

To coin Money, regulate the Value thereof, and of foreign Coin, and fix the Standard of Weights and Measures; — *Hepburn v. Griswold* (1870)

To provide for the Punishment of counterfeiting the Securities and current Coin of the United States;

To establish Post Offices and post Roads;

To promote the Progress of Science and useful Arts, by securing for limited Times to Authors and Inventors the exclusive Right to their respective Writings and Discoveries;

To constitute Tribunals inferior to the supreme Court;

To define and punish Piracies and Felonies committed on the high Seas, and Offenses against the Law of Nations;

To declare War, grant Letters of Marque and Reprisal, and make Rules concerning Captures on Land and Water;

To raise and support Armies, but no Appropriation of Money to that Use shall be for a longer Term than two Years;

To provide and maintain a Navy;

To make Rules for the Government and Regulation of the land and naval Forces;

To provide for calling forth the Militia to execute the Laws of the Union, suppress Insurrections and repel Invasions;

To provide for organizing, arming, and disciplining, the Militia, and for governing such Part of them as may be employed in the Service of the United States, reserving to the States respectively, the Appointment of the Officers, and the Authority of training the Militia according to the discipline prescribed by Congress; — *District of Columbia v. Heller* (2008)

To exercise exclusive Legislation in all Cases whatsoever, over such District (not exceeding ten Miles square) as may, by Cession of particular States, and the Acceptance of Congress, become the Seat of the Government of the United States, and to exercise like Authority over all Places purchased by the Consent of the Legislature of the State in which the Same shall be, for the Erection of Forts, Magazines, Arsenals, dock-Yards and other needful Buildings; — And

McCulloch v. Maryland (1819)
Prigg v. Pennsylvania (1842)
United States v. Dewitt (1869)
Hepburn v. Griswold (1870)
United States v. E.C. Knight (1895)
Champion v. Ames (1903)
Hammer v. Dagenhart (1918)

To make all Laws which shall be necessary and proper for carrying into Execution the foregoing Powers, and all other Powers vested by this Constitution in the Government of the United States, or in any Department or Officer thereof.

Section 9. The Migration or Importation of such Persons as any of the States now existing shall think proper to admit, shall not be prohibited by the Congress prior to the Year one thousand eight hundred and eight, but a Tax or duty may be imposed on such Importation, not exceeding ten dollars for each Person.

Marbury v. Madison (1803)
Barron v. City of Baltimore (1833)
Ex Parte Merryman (1861)

The Privilege of the Writ of Habeas Corpus shall not be suspended, unless when in Cases of Rebellion or Invasion the public Safety may require it.

No Bill of Attainder or ex post facto Law shall be passed.

[No Capitation, or other direct, Tax shall be laid, unless in Proportion to the Census or Enumeration herein before directed to be taken.]*

No Tax or Duty shall be laid on Articles exported from any State.

No Preference shall be given by any Regulation of Commerce or Revenue to the Ports of one State over those of another: nor shall Vessels bound to, or from, one State, be obliged to enter, clear, or pay Duties in another.

No Money shall be drawn from the Treasury, but in Consequence of Appropriations made by Law; and a regular Statement and Account of the Receipts and Expenditures of all public Money shall be published from time to time.

No Title of Nobility shall be granted by the United States: And no Person holding any Office of Profit or Trust under them, shall, without the Consent of the Congress, accept of any present, Emolument, Office, or Title, of any kind whatever, from any King, Prince, or foreign State.

Barron v. City of Baltimore (1833)
Hepburn v. Griswold (1870)

Section 10. No State shall enter into any Treaty, Alliance, or Confederation; grant Letters of Marque and Reprisal; coin Money; emit Bills of Credit; make any Thing but gold and silver Coin a Tender in Payment of Debts; pass any Bill of Attainder, ex post facto Law, or Law impairing the Obligation of Contracts, or grant any Title of Nobility.

No State shall, without the Consent of the Congress, lay any Imposts or Duties on Imports or Exports, except what may be absolutely necessary for executing its inspection Laws: and the net Produce of all Duties and Imposts, laid by any State on Imports or Exports, shall be for the Use of the Treasury of the United States; and all such Laws shall be subject to the Revision and Controul of the Congress.

No State shall, without the Consent of Congress, lay any Duty of Tonnage, keep Troops, or Ships of War in time of Peace, enter into any Agreement or Compact with another State, or with a foreign Power, or engage in War, unless actually invaded, or in such imminent Danger as will not admit of delay.

Article II

Youngstown Sheet & Tube Co. v. Sawyer (1952)
Morrison v. Olson (1988)

Section 1. The executive Power shall be vested in a President of the United States of America. He shall hold his Office during the Term of four Years, and, together with the Vice President, chosen for the same Term, be elected, as follows:

Each State shall appoint, in such Manner as the Legislature thereof may direct, a Number of Electors, equal to the whole Number of Senators and Representatives to which the State may be entitled in the Congress: but no Senator or Representative, or Person holding an Office of Trust or Profit under the United States, shall be appointed an Elector.

[The Electors shall meet in their respective States, and vote by Ballot for two Persons, of whom one at least shall not be an Inhabitant of the same State with themselves. And they shall make a List of all the Persons voted for, and of the Number of Votes for each; which List they shall sign and certify, and transmit sealed to the Seat of the

---

* See the Sixteenth Amendment.

Government of the United States, directed to the President of the Senate. The President of the Senate shall, in the Presence of the Senate and House of Representatives, open all the Certificates, and the Votes shall then be counted. The Person having the greatest Number of Votes shall be the President, if such Number be a Majority of the whole Number of Electors appointed; and if there be more than one who have such Majority, and have an equal Number of Votes, then the House of Representatives shall immediately chuse by Ballot one of them for President; and if no Person have a Majority, then from the five highest on the List the said House shall in like Manner chuse the President. But in chusing the President, the Votes shall be taken by States, the Representation from each State having one Vote; A quorum for this Purpose shall consist of a Member or Members from two thirds of the States, and a Majority of all the States shall be necessary to a Choice. In every Case, after the Choice of the President, the Person having the greatest Number of Votes of the Electors shall be the Vice President. But if there should remain two or more who have equal Votes, the Senate shall chuse from them by Ballot the Vice President.]*

The Congress may determine the Time of chusing the Electors, and the Day on which they shall give their Votes; which Day shall be the same throughout the United States.

No Person except a natural born Citizen, or a Citizen of the United States, at the time of the Adoption of this Constitution, shall be eligible to the Office of President; neither shall any person be eligible to that Office who shall not have attained to the Age of thirty five Years, and been fourteen Years a Resident within the United States.

[In Case of the Removal of the President from Office, or of his Death, Resignation, or Inability to discharge the Powers and Duties of the said Office, the Same shall devolve on the Vice President, and the Congress may by Law provide for the Case of Removal, Death, Resignation or Inability, both of the President and Vice President, declaring what Officer shall then act as President, and such Officer shall act accordingly, until the Disability be removed, or a President shall be elected.]**

The President shall, at stated Times, receive for his Services, a Compensation, which shall neither be increased nor diminished during the Period for which he shall have been elected, and he shall not receive within that Period any other Emolument from the United States, or any of them.

Before he enter on the Execution of his Office, he shall take the following Oath or Affirmation: "I do solemnly swear (or affirm) that I will faithfully execute the Office of President of the United States, and will to the best of my Ability, preserve, protect and defend the Constitution of the United States."

Section 2. The President shall be Commander in Chief of the Army and Navy of the United States, and of the Militia of the several States, when called into the actual Service of the United States; he may require the Opinion, in writing, of the principal Officer in each of the executive Departments, upon any Subject relating to the Duties of their respective Offices, and he shall have Power to grant Reprieves and Pardons for Offenses against the United States, except in Cases of Impeachment.

Ex Parte Merryman (1861)
Youngstown Sheet & Tube Co. v. Sawyer (1952)
Morrison v. Olson (1988)
NLRB v. Noel Canning (2014)

He shall have Power, by and with the Advice and Consent of the Senate, to make Treaties, provided two thirds of the Senators present concur; and he shall nominate, and by and with the Advice and Consent of the Senate, shall appoint Ambassadors, other public Ministers and Consuls, Judges of the supreme Court, and all other Officers of the United States, whose Appointments are not herein otherwise provided for, and which shall be established by Law: but the Congress may by Law vest the Appointment of such inferior Officers, as they think proper, in the President alone, in the Courts of Law, or in the Heads of Departments.

---

* Changed by the Twelfth Amendment.
** Changed by the Twenty-Fifth Amendment.

The President shall have Power to fill up all Vacancies that may happen during the Recess of the Senate, by granting Commissions which shall expire at the End of their next Session.

Section 3. He shall from time to time give to the Congress Information of the State of the Union, and recommend to their Consideration such Measures as he shall judge necessary and expedient; he may, on extraordinary Occasions, convene both Houses, or either of them, and in Case of Disagreement between them, with Respect to the Time of Adjournment, he may adjourn them to such Time as he shall think proper; he shall receive Ambassadors and other public Ministers; he shall take Care that the Laws be faithfully executed, and shall Commission all the Officers of the United States.

Section 4. The President, Vice President and all civil Officers of the United States, shall be removed from Office on Impeachment for, and Conviction of, Treason, Bribery, or other high Crimes and Misdemeanors.

Article III

Marbury v. Madison (1803)

Section 1. The judicial Power of the United States, shall be vested in one supreme Court, and in such inferior Courts as the Congress may from time to time ordain and establish. The Judges, both of the supreme and inferior Courts, shall hold their Offices during good Behaviour, and shall, at stated Times, receive for their Services, a Compensation, which shall not be diminished during their Continuance in Office.

Chisholm v. Georgia (1793)
Marbury v. Madison (1803)
Hans v. State of Louisiana (1890)
*Seminole Tribe of Florida
    v. Florida* (1996)

Section 2. The judicial Power shall extend to all Cases, in Law and Equity, arising under this Constitution, the Laws of the United States, and Treaties made, or which shall be made, under their Authority; — to all Cases affecting Ambassadors, other public Ministers and Consuls; — to all Cases of admiralty and maritime Jurisdiction; — to Controversies to which the United States shall be a Party; — to Controversies between two or more States; — [between a State and Citizens of another State; —]* between Citizens of different States; — between Citizens of the same State claiming Lands under Grants of different States [and between a State, or the Citizens thereof; — and foreign States, Citizens or Subjects.]**

In all Cases affecting Ambassadors, other public Ministers and Consuls, and those in which a State shall be Party, the supreme Court shall have original Jurisdiction. In all the other Cases before mentioned, the supreme Court shall have appellate Jurisdiction, both as to Law and Fact, with such Exceptions, and under such Regulations as the Congress shall make.

The Trial of all Crimes, except in Cases of Impeachment; shall be by Jury; and such Trial shall be held in the State where the said Crimes shall have been committed; but when not committed within any State, the Trial shall be at such Place or Places as the Congress may by Law have directed.

Section 3. Treason against the United States, shall consist only in levying War against them, or in adhering to their Enemies, giving them Aid and Comfort. No Person shall be convicted of Treason unless on the Testimony of two Witnesses to the same overt Act, or on Confession in open Court.

The Congress shall have Power to declare the Punishment of Treason, but no Attainder of Treason shall work Corruption of Blood, or Forfeiture except during the Life of the Person attainted.

Article IV

Section 1. Full Faith and Credit shall be given in each State to the public Acts, Records, and judicial Proceedings of every other State. And the Congress may by

---

* Changed by the Eleventh Amendment.
** Changed by the Eleventh Amendment.

general Laws prescribe the Manner in which such Acts, Records and Proceedings shall be proved, and the Effect thereof.

Section 2. The Citizens of each State shall be entitled to all Privileges and Immunities of Citizens in the several States.

Prigg v. Pennsylvania (1842)

A Person charged in any State with Treason, Felony, or other Crime, who shall flee from Justice, and be found in another State, shall on Demand of the executive Authority of the State from which he fled, be delivered up, to be removed to the State having Jurisdiction of the Crime.

[No Person held to Service or Labour in one State, under the Laws thereof, escaping into another, shall, in Consequence of any Law or Regulation therein, be discharged from such Service or Labour, but shall be delivered up on Claim of the Party to whom such Service or Labour may be due.]*

Section 3. New States may be admitted by the Congress into this Union; but no new State shall be formed or erected within the Jurisdiction of any other State; nor any State be formed by the Junction of two or more States, or Parts of States, without the Consent of the Legislatures of the States concerned as well as of the Congress.

The Congress shall have Power to dispose of and make all needful Rules and Regulations respecting the Territory or other Property belonging to the United States; and nothing in this Constitution shall be so construed as to Prejudice any Claims of the United States, or of any particular State.

Section 4. The United States shall guarantee to every State in this Union a Republican Form of Government, and shall protect each of them against Invasion; and on Application of the Legislature, or of the Executive (when the Legislature cannot be convened) against domestic Violence.

Article V

The Congress, whenever two thirds of both Houses shall deem it necessary, shall propose Amendments to this Constitution, or, on the Application of the Legislatures of two thirds of the several States, shall call a Convention for proposing Amendments, which, in either Case, shall be valid to all Intents and Purposes, as Part of this Constitution, when ratified by the Legislatures of three fourths of the several States, or by Conventions in three fourths thereof, as the one or the other Mode of Ratification may be proposed by the Congress; Provided that no Amendment which may be made prior to the Year One thousand eight hundred and eight shall in any Manner affect the first and fourth Clauses in the Ninth Section of the first Article; and that no State, without its Consent, shall be deprived of its equal Suffrage in the Senate.

Article VI

All Debts contracted and Engagements entered into, before the Adoption of this Constitution, shall be as valid against the United States under this Constitution, as under the Confederation.

This Constitution, and the Laws of the United States which shall be made in Pursuance thereof; and all Treaties made, or which shall be made, under the Authority of the United States, shall be the supreme Law of the Land; and the Judges in every State shall be bound thereby, any Thing in the Constitution or Laws of any State to the Contrary notwithstanding.

Cooper v. Aaron (1958)
Printz v. United States (1997)

The Senators and Representatives before mentioned, and the Members of the several State Legislatures, and all executive and judicial Officers, both of the United States and of

---

* Changed by the Thirteenth Amendment.

the several States, shall be bound by Oath or Affirmation, to support this Constitution; but no religious Test shall ever be required as a Qualification to any Office or public Trust under the United States.

Article VII

The Ratification of the Conventions of nine States, shall be sufficient for the Establishment of this Constitution between the States so ratifying the Same.

Done in Convention by the Unanimous Consent of the States present the Seventeenth Day of September in the Year of our Lord one thousand seven hundred and Eighty seven and of the Independence of the United States of America the Twelfth.

In Witness whereof We have hereunto subscribed our Names,

Go. Washington — Presidt. and deputy from Virginia
New Hampshire: John Langdon, Nicholas Gilman
Massachusetts: Nathaniel Gorham, Rufus King
Connecticut: Wm. Saml. Johnson, Roger Sherman
New York: Alexander Hamilton
New Jersey: Wil. Livingston, David Brearley, Wm. Paterson, Jona: Dayton
Pennsylvania: B Franklin, Thomas Mifflin, Robt Morris, Geo. Clymer, Thos. FitzSimons, Jared Ingersoll, James Wilson, Gouv Morris
Delaware: Geo. Read, Gunning Bedford jun, John Dickinson, Richard Bassett, Jaco. Broom
Maryland: James McHenry, Dan of St. Thos. Jenifer, Danl. Carroll
Virginia: John Blair, James Madison Jr.
North Carolina: Wm. Blount, Richd. Dobbs Spaight, Hu Williamson
South Carolina: J. Rutledge, Charles Cotesworth Pinckney, Charles Pinckney, Pierce Butler
Georgia: William Few, Abr Baldwin
Attest William Jackson Secretary

In Convention Monday September 17th, 1787. Present The States of New Hampshire, Massachusetts, Connecticut, Mr. Hamilton from New York, New Jersey, Pennsylvania, Delaware, Maryland, Virginia, North Carolina, South Carolina and Georgia.

Resolved,

That the preceeding Constitution be laid before the United States in Congress assembled, and that it is the Opinion of this Convention, that it should afterwards be submitted to a Convention of Delegates, chosen in each State by the People thereof, under the Recommendation of its Legislature, for their Assent and Ratification; and that each Convention assenting to, and ratifying the Same, should give Notice thereof to the United States in Congress assembled. Resolved, That it is the Opinion of this Convention, that as soon as the Conventions of nine States shall have ratified this Constitution, the United States in Congress assembled should fix a Day on which Electors should be appointed by the States which shall have ratified the same, and a Day on which the Electors should assemble to vote for the President, and the Time and Place for commencing Proceedings under this Constitution.

That after such Publication the Electors should be appointed, and the Senators and Representatives elected: That the Electors should meet on the Day fixed for the Election of the President, and should transmit their Votes certified, signed, sealed and directed, as the Constitution requires, to the Secretary of the United States in Congress assembled, that the Senators and Representatives should convene at the Time and Place assigned; that the Senators should appoint a President of the Senate, for the sole Purpose of receiving, opening and counting the Votes for President; and, that after he shall be chosen, the Congress, together with the President, should, without Delay, proceed to execute this Constitution.

By the unanimous Order of the Convention
Go. Washington — Presidt.

W. JACKSON Secretary.

AMENDMENTS TO THE CONSTITUTION OF THE UNITED STATES

The Preamble to The Bill of Rights

Congress of the United States begun and held at the City of New-York, on Wednesday the fourth of March, one thousand seven hundred and eighty nine.

THE Conventions of a number of the States, having at the time of their adopting the Constitution, expressed a desire, in order to prevent misconstruction or abuse of its powers, that further declaratory and restrictive clauses should be added: And as extending the ground of public confidence in the Government, will best ensure the beneficent ends of its institution.

RESOLVED by the Senate and House of Representatives of the United States of America, in Congress assembled, two thirds of both Houses concurring, that the following Articles be proposed to the Legislatures of the several States, as amendments to the Constitution of the United States, all, or any of which Articles, when ratified by three fourths of the said Legislatures, to be valid to all intents and purposes, as part of the said Constitution; viz.

ARTICLES in addition to, and Amendment of the Constitution of the United States of America, proposed by Congress, and ratified by the Legislatures of the several States, pursuant to the fifth Article of the original Constitution*

McCreary County, Kentucky v. ACLU of Kentucky (2005)
Van Orden v. Perry (2005)

Sherbert v. Verner (1962)
Employment Division v. Smith (1990)
Church of the Lukumi Babalu Aye v. City of Hialeah (1993)

Amendment I

Congress shall make no law respecting an establishment of religion, or prohibiting the free exercise thereof; or abridging the freedom of speech, or of the press; or the right of the people peaceably to assemble, and to petition the Government for a redress of grievances.

Schenck v. United States (1919)
Debs v. United States (1919)
Abrams v. United States (1919)
Gitlow v. People of the State of New York (1925)
Stromberg v. California (1931)
New York Times Co. v. Sullivan (1964)
United States v. O'Brien (1968)
Buckley v. Valeo (1976)
Texas v. Johnson (1989)
R.A.V. v. City of St. Paul (1992)
McConnell v. Federal Election Commission (2003)
Citizens United v. Federal Election Commission (2010)
United States v. Stevens (2010)
Snyder v. Phelps (2011)
Brown v. Entertainment Merchants Association (2011)

Amendment II

A well regulated Militia, being necessary to the security of a free State, the right of the people to keep and bear Arms, shall not be infringed.

Amendment III

No Soldier shall, in time of peace be quartered in any house, without the consent of the Owner, nor in time of war, but in a manner to be prescribed by law.

Amendment IV

The right of the people to be secure in their persons, houses, papers, and effects, against unreasonable searches and seizures, shall not be violated, and no Warrants shall issue, but upon probable cause, supported by Oath or affirmation, and particularly describing the place to be searched, and the persons or things to be seized.

District of Columbia v. Heller (2008)
McDonald v. City of Chicago (2010)

---

* The first ten amendments were ratified December 15, 1791, and form what is known as the "Bill of Rights."

Amendment V

No person shall be held to answer for a capital, or otherwise infamous crime, unless on a presentment or indictment of a Grand Jury, except in cases arising in the land or naval forces, or in the Militia, when in actual service in time of War or public danger; nor shall any person be subject for the same offence to be twice put in jeopardy of life or limb; nor shall be compelled in any criminal case to be a witness against himself, nor be deprived of life, liberty, or property, without due process of law; nor shall private property be taken for public use, without just compensation.

Amendment VI

In all criminal prosecutions, the accused shall enjoy the right to a speedy and public trial, by an impartial jury of the State and district wherein the crime shall have been committed, which district shall have been previously ascertained by law, and to be informed of the nature and cause of the accusation; to be confronted with the witnesses against him; to have compulsory process for obtaining witnesses in his favor, and to have the Assistance of Counsel for his defence.

Amendment VII

In suits at common law, where the value in controversy shall exceed twenty dollars, the right of trial by jury shall be preserved, and no fact tried by a jury, shall be otherwise reexamined in any Court of the United States, than according to the rules of the common law.

Amendment VIII

Excessive bail shall not be required, nor excessive fines imposed, nor cruel and unusual punishments inflicted.

Amendment IX

The enumeration in the Constitution, of certain rights, shall not be construed to deny or disparage others retained by the people.

Amendment X

The powers not delegated to the United States by the Constitution, nor prohibited by it to the States, are reserved to the States respectively, or to the people.

Amendment XI*

The Judicial power of the United States shall not be construed to extend to any suit in law or equity, commenced or prosecuted against one of the United States by Citizens of another State, or by Citizens or Subjects of any Foreign State.

Amendment XII**

The Electors shall meet in their respective states and vote by ballot for President and Vice-President, one of whom, at least, shall not be an inhabitant of the same state with themselves; they shall name in their ballots the person voted for as President, and in distinct ballots the person voted for as Vice-President, and they shall make distinct lists of all persons voted for as President, and of all persons voted for as Vice-President, and of the number of votes for each, which lists they shall sign and certify, and transmit sealed to the seat of the government of the United States, directed to the President of

---

* Passed by Congress March 4, 1794. Ratified February 7, 1795. Article III, section 2, of the Constitution was modified by the Eleventh Amendment.

** Passed by Congress December 9, 1803. Ratified June 15, 1804. A portion of Article II, section 1 of the Constitution was superseded by the Twelfth Amendment.

the Senate; — the President of the Senate shall, in the presence of the Senate and House of Representatives, open all the certificates and the votes shall then be counted; — The person having the greatest number of votes for President, shall be the President, if such number be a majority of the whole number of Electors appointed; and if no person have such majority, then from the persons having the highest numbers not exceeding three on the list of those voted for as President, the House of Representatives shall choose immediately, by ballot, the President. But in choosing the President, the votes shall be taken by states, the representation from each state having one vote; a quorum for this purpose shall consist of a member or members from two-thirds of the states, and a majority of all the states shall be necessary to a choice. [And if the House of Representatives shall not choose a President whenever the right of choice shall devolve upon them, before the fourth day of March next following, then the Vice-President shall act as President, as in case of the death or other constitutional disability of the President. —]* The person having the greatest number of votes as Vice-President, shall be the Vice-President, if such number be a majority of the whole number of Electors appointed, and if no person have a majority, then from the two highest numbers on the list, the Senate shall choose the Vice-President; a quorum for the purpose shall consist of two-thirds of the whole number of Senators, and a majority of the whole number shall be necessary to a choice. But no person constitutionally ineligible to the office of President shall be eligible to that of Vice-President of the United States.

The Slaughter-House Cases (1873)
The Civil Rights Cases (1883)
Plessy v. Ferguson (1896)

The Slaughter-House Cases (1873)
Bradwell v. Illinois (1873)
McDonald v. City of Chicago (2010)

United States v. Cruikshank (1875)
Yick Wo v. Hopkins (1886)
Lochner v. New York (1905)
Muller v. Oregon (1908)
Buchanan v. Warley (1917)
Meyer v. Nebraska (1923)
Pierce v. Society of Sisters (1925)
Gitlow v. People of the State of New York (1925)
Buck v. Bell (1927)
O'Gorman & Young, Inc. v. Hartford Fire Insurance Co. (1931)
Stromberg v. California (1931)
Nebbia v. New York (1934)
West Coast Hotel v. Parrish (1937)
Williamson v. Lee Optical (1955)
Griswold v. Connecticut (1965)
Roe v. Wade (1973)
Planned Parenthood v. Casey (1992)
Lawrence v. Texas (2003)
McDonald v. City of Chicago (2010)
Obergefell v. Hodges (2015)
Whole Woman's Health v. Hellerstedt (2016)

Amendment XIII**

Section 1. Neither slavery nor involuntary servitude, except as a punishment for crime whereof the party shall have been duly convicted, shall exist within the United States, or any place subject to their jurisdiction.

Section 2. Congress shall have power to enforce this article by appropriate legislation.

Amendment XIV***

Section 1. All persons born or naturalized in the United States, and subject to the jurisdiction thereof, are citizens of the United States and of the State wherein they reside. No State shall make or enforce any law which shall abridge the privileges or immunities of citizens of the United States; nor shall any State deprive any person of life, liberty, or property, without due process of law; nor deny to any person within its jurisdiction the equal protection of the laws.

Section 2. Representatives shall be apportioned among the several States according to their respective numbers, counting the whole number of persons in each State, excluding Indians not taxed. But when the right to vote at any election for the choice of electors for President and Vice-President of the United States, Representatives in Congress, the Executive and Judicial officers of a State, or the members of the Legislature thereof, is denied to any of the male inhabitants of such State, being twenty-one years of age,**** and citizens of the United States, or in any way abridged, except for participation in rebellion, or other crime, the basis of representation therein shall be reduced in the proportion which the number of such male citizens shall bear to the whole number of male citizens twenty-one years of age in such State.

Section 3. No person shall be a Senator or Representative in Congress, or elector of President and Vice-President, or hold any office, civil or military, under the United

United States v. Cruikshank (1875)
Yick Wo v. Hopkins (1886)
Brown v. Board of Education (1954)
Loving v. Virginia (1967)
Frontiero v. Richardson (1973)
Craig v. Boren (1976)
Regents of the University of California v. Bakke (1978)
City of Cleburne v. Cleburne Living Center, Inc. (1985)
United States v. Virginia (1996)
Romer v. Evans (1996)
Grutter v. Bollinger (2003)
Gratz v. Bollinger (2003)
Fisher v. University of Texas at Austin I (2013)
Fisher v. University of Texas at Austin II (2016)

---

*   Superseded by section 3 of the Twentieth Amendment.

**   Passed by Congress January 31, 1865. Ratified December 6, 1865. A portion of Article IV, section 2, of the Constitution was superseded by the Thirteenth Amendment.

***   Passed by Congress June 13, 1866. Ratified July 9, 1868. Article I, section 2, of the Constitution was modified by section 2 of the Fourteenth Amendment.

****   Changed by section 1 of the Twenty-Sixth Amendment.

States, or under any State, who, having previously taken an oath, as a member of Congress, or as an officer of the United States, or as a member of any State legislature, or as an executive or judicial officer of any State, to support the Constitution of the United States, shall have engaged in insurrection or rebellion against the same, or given aid or comfort to the enemies thereof. But Congress may by a vote of two-thirds of each House, remove such disability.

Section 4. The validity of the public debt of the United States, authorized by law, including debts incurred for payment of pensions and bounties for services in suppressing insurrection or rebellion, shall not be questioned. But neither the United States nor any State shall assume or pay any debt or obligation incurred in aid of insurrection or rebellion against the United States, or any claim for the loss or emancipation of any slave; but all such debts, obligations and claims shall be held illegal and void.

The Civil Rights Case (1883)
Plessy v. Ferguson (1896)
Heart of Atlanta Motel v. United States (1964)
City of Boerne v. Flores (1997)
United States v. Morrison (2000)
Board of Trustees of University of Alabama v. Garrett (2001)
Nevada Department of Human Resources v. Hibbs (2003)

Section 5. The Congress shall have the power to enforce, by appropriate legislation, the provisions of this article.

Amendment XV*

Section 1. The right of citizens of the United States to vote shall not be denied or abridged by the United States or by any State on account of race, color, or previous condition of servitude.

Section 2. The Congress shall have the power to enforce this article by appropriate legislation.

Amendment XVI**

The Congress shall have power to lay and collect taxes on incomes, from whatever source derived, without apportionment among the several States, and without regard to any census or enumeration.

Amendment XVII***

The Senate of the United States shall be composed of two Senators from each State, elected by the people thereof, for six years; and each Senator shall have one vote. The electors in each State shall have the qualifications requisite for electors of the most numerous branch of the State legislatures.

When vacancies happen in the representation of any State in the Senate, the executive authority of such State shall issue writs of election to fill such vacancies: Provided, That the legislature of any State may empower the executive thereof to make temporary appointments until the people fill the vacancies by election as the legislature may direct.

This amendment shall not be so construed as to affect the election or term of any Senator chosen before it becomes valid as part of the Constitution.

Amendment XVIII****

Section 1. After one year from the ratification of this article the manufacture, sale, or transportation of intoxicating liquors within, the importation thereof into, or the exportation thereof from the United States and all territory subject to the jurisdiction thereof for beverage purposes is hereby prohibited.

Section 2. The Congress and the several States shall have concurrent power to enforce this article by appropriate legislation.

---

* Passed by Congress February 26, 1869. Ratified February 3, 1870.

** Passed by Congress July 2, 1909. Ratified February 3, 1913. Article I, section 9, of the Constitution was modified by the Sixteenth Amendment.

*** Passed by Congress May 13, 1912. Ratified April 8, 1913. Article I, section 3, of the Constitution was modified by the Seventeenth Amendment.

**** Passed by Congress December 18, 1917. Ratified January 16, 1919. Repealed by the Twenty-First Amendment, December 5, 1933.

Section 3. This article shall be inoperative unless it shall have been ratified as an amendment to the Constitution by the legislatures of the several States, as provided in the Constitution, within seven years from the date of the submission hereof to the States by the Congress.

Amendment XIX*

The right of citizens of the United States to vote shall not be denied or abridged by the United States or by any State on account of sex.

Congress shall have power to enforce this article by appropriate legislation.

Amendment XX**

Section 1. The terms of the President and the Vice President shall end at noon on the 20th day of January, and the terms of Senators and Representatives at noon on the 3d day of January, of the years in which such terms would have ended if this article had not been ratified; and the terms of their successors shall then begin.

Section 2. The Congress shall assemble at least once in every year, and such meeting shall begin at noon on the 3d day of January, unless they shall by law appoint a different day.

Section 3. If, at the time fixed for the beginning of the term of the President, the President elect shall have died, the Vice President elect shall become President. If a President shall not have been chosen before the time fixed for the beginning of his term, or if the President elect shall have failed to qualify, then the Vice President elect shall act as President until a President shall have qualified; and the Congress may by law provide for the case wherein neither a President elect nor a Vice President shall have qualified, declaring who shall then act as President, or the manner in which one who is to act shall be selected, and such person shall act accordingly until a President or Vice President shall have qualified.

Section 4. The Congress may by law provide for the case of the death of any of the persons from whom the House of Representatives may choose a President whenever the right of choice shall have devolved upon them, and for the case of the death of any of the persons from whom the Senate may choose a Vice President whenever the right of choice shall have devolved upon them.

Section 5. Sections 1 and 2 shall take effect on the 15th day of October following the ratification of this article.

Section 6. This article shall be inoperative unless it shall have been ratified as an amendment to the Constitution by the legislatures of three-fourths of the several States within seven years from the date of its submission.

Amendment XXI***

Section 1. The eighteenth article of amendment to the Constitution of the United States is hereby repealed.

Section 2. The transportation or importation into any State, Territory, or Possession of the United States for delivery or use therein of intoxicating liquors, in violation of the laws thereof, is hereby prohibited.

Section 3. This article shall be inoperative unless it shall have been ratified as an amendment to the Constitution by conventions in the several States, as provided in the

---

* Passed by Congress June 4, 1919. Ratified August 18, 1920.

** Passed by Congress March 2, 1932. Ratified January 23, 1933. Article I, section 4, of the Constitution was modified by section 2 of this amendment. In addition, a portion of the Twelfth Amendment was superseded by section 3.

*** Passed by Congress February 20, 1933. Ratified December 5, 1933.

Constitution, within seven years from the date of the submission hereof to the States by the Congress.

Amendment XXII*

Section 1. No person shall be elected to the office of the President more than twice, and no person who has held the office of President, or acted as President, for more than two years of a term to which some other person was elected President shall be elected to the office of President more than once. But this Article shall not apply to any person holding the office of President when this Article was proposed by Congress, and shall not prevent any person who may be holding the office of President, or acting as President, during the term within which this Article becomes operative from holding the office of President or acting as President during the remainder of such term.

Section 2. This article shall be inoperative unless it shall have been ratified as an amendment to the Constitution by the legislatures of three-fourths of the several States within seven years from the date of its submission to the States by the Congress.

Amendment XXIII**

Section 1. The District constituting the seat of Government of the United States shall appoint in such manner as Congress may direct:

A number of electors of President and Vice President equal to the whole number of Senators and Representatives in Congress to which the District would be entitled if it were a State, but in no event more than the least populous State; they shall be in addition to those appointed by the States, but they shall be considered, for the purposes of the election of President and Vice President, to be electors appointed by a State; and they shall meet in the District and perform such duties as provided by the twelfth article of amendment.

Section 2. The Congress shall have power to enforce this article by appropriate legislation.

Amendment XXIV***

Section 1. The right of citizens of the United States to vote in any primary or other election for President or Vice President, for electors for President or Vice President, or for Senator or Representative in Congress, shall not be denied or abridged by the United States or any State by reason of failure to pay poll tax or other tax.

Section 2. The Congress shall have power to enforce this article by appropriate legislation.

Amendment XXV****

Section 1. In case of the removal of the President from office or of his death or resignation, the Vice President shall become President.

Section 2. Whenever there is a vacancy in the office of the Vice President, the President shall nominate a Vice President who shall take office upon confirmation by a majority vote of both Houses of Congress.

Section 3. Whenever the President transmits to the President pro tempore of the Senate and the Speaker of the House of Representatives his written declaration that he is unable to discharge the powers and duties of his office, and until he transmits to them

---

* Passed by Congress March 21, 1947. Ratified February 27, 1951.

** Passed by Congress June 16, 1960. Ratified March 29, 1961.

*** Passed by Congress August 27, 1962. Ratified January 23, 1964.

**** Passed by Congress July 6, 1965. Ratified February 10, 1967. Article II, section 1, of the Constitution was affected by the Twenty-Fifth Amendment.

a written declaration to the contrary, such powers and duties shall be discharged by the Vice President as Acting President.

Section 4. Whenever the Vice President and a majority of either the principal officers of the executive departments or of such other body as Congress may by law provide, transmit to the President pro tempore of the Senate and the Speaker of the House of Representatives their written declaration that the President is unable to discharge the powers and duties of his office, the Vice President shall immediately assume the powers and duties of the office as Acting President.

Thereafter, when the President transmits to the President pro tempore of the Senate and the Speaker of the House of Representatives his written declaration that no inability exists, he shall resume the powers and duties of his office unless the Vice President and a majority of either the principal officers of the executive department or of such other body as Congress may by law provide, transmit within four days to the President pro tempore of the Senate and the Speaker of the House of Representatives their written declaration that the President is unable to discharge the powers and duties of his office. Thereupon Congress shall decide the issue, assembling within forty-eight hours for that purpose if not in session. If the Congress, within twenty-one days after receipt of the latter written declaration, or, if Congress is not in session, within twenty-one days after Congress is required to assemble, determines by two-thirds vote of both Houses that the President is unable to discharge the powers and duties of his office, the Vice President shall continue to discharge the same as Acting President; otherwise, the President shall resume the powers and duties of his office.

Amendment XXVI*

Section 1. The right of citizens of the United States, who are eighteen years of age or older, to vote shall not be denied or abridged by the United States or by any State on account of age.

Section 2. The Congress shall have power to enforce this article by appropriate legislation.

Amendment XXVII**

No law, varying the compensation for the services of the Senators and Representatives, shall take effect, until an election of representatives shall have intervened.

---

* Passed by Congress March 23, 1971. Ratified July 1, 1971. The Fourteenth Amendment, section 2, of the Constitution was modified by section 1 of the Twenty-Sixth Amendment.

** Originally proposed Sept. 25, 1789. Ratified May 7, 1992.

Members of the Supreme Court of the United States

Name	State Appointed From	Appointed by President	Date Judicial Oath Taken	Date Service Terminated
CHIEF JUSTICES				
Jay, John	New York	Washington	(a) October 19, 1789	June 29, 1795
Rutledge, John	South Carolina	Washington	August 12, 1795	December 15, 1795
Ellsworth, Oliver	Connecticut	Washington	March 8, 1796	December 15, 1800
Marshall, John	Virginia	Adams, John	February 4, 1801	July 6, 1835
Taney, Roger Brooke	Maryland	Jackson	March 28, 1836	October 12, 1864
Chase, Salmon Portland	Ohio	Lincoln	December 15, 1864	May 7, 1873
Waite, Morrison Remick	Ohio	Grant	March 4, 1874	March 23, 1888
Fuller, Melville Weston	Illinois	Cleveland	October 8, 1888	July 4, 1910
White, Edward Douglass	Louisiana	Taft	December 19, 1910	May 19, 1921
Taft, William Howard	Connecticut	Harding	July 11, 1921	February 3, 1930
Hughes, Charles Evans	New York	Hoover	February 24, 1930	June 30, 1941
Stone, Harlan Fiske	New York	Roosevelt, F.	July 3, 1941	April 22, 1946
Vinson, Fred Moore	Kentucky	Truman	June 24, 1946	September 8, 1953
Warren, Earl	California	Eisenhower	October 5, 1953	June 23, 1969
Burger, Warren Earl	Virginia	Nixon	June 23, 1969	September 26, 1986
Rehnquist, William H.	Virginia	Reagan	September 26, 1986	September 3, 2005
Roberts, John G., Jr.	Maryland	Bush, G. W.	September 29, 2005	
ASSOCIATE JUSTICES				
Rutledge, John	South Carolina	Washington	(a) February 15, 1790	March 5, 1791
Cushing, William	Massachusetts	Washington	(c) February 2, 1790	September 13, 1810
Wilson, James	Pennsylvania	Washington	(b) October 5, 1789	August 21, 1798
Blair, John	Virginia	Washington	(c) February 2, 1790	October 25, 1795
Iredell, James	North Carolina	Washington	(b) May 12, 1790	October 20, 1799
Johnson, Thomas	Maryland	Washington	(a) August 6, 1792	January 16, 1793
Paterson, William	New Jersey	Washington	(a) March 11, 1793	September 9, 1806
Chase, Samuel	Maryland	Washington	February 4, 1796	June 19, 1811
Washington, Bushrod	Virginia	Adams, John	(c) February 4, 1799	November 26, 1829
Moore, Alfred	North Carolina	Adams, John	(a) April 21, 1800	January 26, 1804
Johnson, William	South Carolina	Jefferson	May 7, 1804	August 4, 1834
Livingston, Henry Brockholst	New York	Jefferson	January 20, 1807	March 18, 1823
Todd, Thomas	Kentucky	Jefferson	(a) May 4, 1807	February 7, 1826
Duvall, Gabriel	Maryland	Madison	(a) November 23, 1811	January 14, 1835
Story, Joseph	Massachusetts	Madison	(c) February 3, 1812	September 10, 1845
Thompson, Smith	New York	Monroe	(b) September 1, 1823	December 18, 1843
Trimble, Robert	Kentucky	Adams, J. Q.	(a) June 16, 1826	August 25, 1828
McLean, John	Ohio	Jackson	(c) January 11, 1830	April 4, 1861
Baldwin, Henry	Pennsylvania	Jackson	January 18, 1830	April 21, 1844
Wayne, James Moore	Georgia	Jackson	January 14, 1835	July 5, 1867
Barbour, Philip Pendleton	Virginia	Jackson	May 12, 1836	February 25, 1841
Catron, John	Tennessee	Jackson	May 1, 1837	May 30, 1865

Name	State Appointed From	Appointed by President	Date Judicial Oath Taken	Date Service Terminated
McKinley, John	Alabama	Van Buren	(c) January 9, 1838	July 19, 1852
Daniel, Peter Vivian	Virginia	Van Buren	(c) January 10, 1842	May 31, 1860
Nelson, Samuel	New York	Tyler	February 27, 1845	November 28, 1872
Woodbury, Levi	New Hampshire	Polk	(b) September 23, 1845	September 4, 1851
Grier, Robert Cooper	Pennsylvania	Polk	August 10, 1846	January 31, 1870
Curtis, Benjamin Robbins	Massachusetts	Fillmore	(b) October 10, 1851	September 30, 1857
Campbell, John Archibald	Alabama	Pierce	(c) April 11, 1853	April 30, 1861
Clifford, Nathan	Maine	Buchanan	January 21, 1858	July 25, 1881
Swayne, Noah Haynes	Ohio	Lincoln	January 27, 1862	January 24, 1881
Miller, Samuel Freeman	Iowa	Lincoln	July 21, 1862	October 13, 1890
Davis, David	Illinois	Lincoln	December 10, 1862	March 4, 1877
Field, Stephen Johnson	California	Lincoln	May 20, 1863	December 1, 1897
Strong, William	Pennsylvania	Grant	March 14, 1870	December 14, 1880
Bradley, Joseph P.	New Jersey	Grant	March 23, 1870	January 22, 1892
Hunt, Ward	New York	Grant	January 9, 1873	January 27, 1882
Harlan, John Marshall	Kentucky	Hayes	December 10, 1877	October 14, 1911
Woods, William Burnham	Georgia	Hayes	January 5, 1881	May 14, 1887
Matthews, Stanley	Ohio	Garfield	May 17, 1881	March 22, 1889
Gray, Horace	Massachusetts	Arthur	January 9, 1882	September 15, 1902
Blatchford, Samuel	New York	Arthur	April 3, 1882	July 7, 1893
Lamar, Lucius Quintus C.	Mississippi	Cleveland	January 18, 1888	January 23, 1893
Brewer, David Josiah	Kansas	Harrison	January 6, 1890	March 28, 1910
Brown, Henry Billings	Michigan	Harrison	January 5, 1891	May 28, 1906
Shiras, George, Jr.	Pennsylvania	Harrison	October 10, 1892	February 23, 1903
Jackson, Howell Edmunds	Tennessee	Harrison	March 4, 1893	August 8, 1895
White, Edward Douglass	Louisiana	Cleveland	March 12, 1894	December 18, 1910*
Peckham, Rufus Wheeler	New York	Cleveland	January 6, 1896	October 24, 1909
McKenna, Joseph	California	McKinley	January 26, 1898	January 5, 1925
Holmes, Oliver Wendell	Massachusetts	Roosevelt, T.	December 8, 1902	January 12, 1932
Day, William Rufus	Ohio	Roosevelt, T.	March 2, 1903	November 13, 1922
Moody, William Henry	Massachusetts	Roosevelt, T.	December 17, 1906	November 20, 1910
Lurton, Horace Harmon	Tennessee	Taft	January 3, 1910	July 12, 1914
Hughes, Charles Evans	New York	Taft	October 10, 1910	June 10, 1916
Van Devanter, Willis	Wyoming	Taft	January 3, 1911	June 2, 1937
Lamar, Joseph Rucker	Georgia	Taft	January 3, 1911	January 2, 1916
Pitney, Mahlon	New Jersey	Taft	March 18, 1912	December 31, 1922
McReynolds, James Clark	Tennessee	Wilson	October 12, 1914	January 31, 1941
Brandeis, Louis Dembitz	Massachusetts	Wilson	June 5, 1916	February 13, 1939
Clarke, John Hessin	Ohio	Wilson	October 9, 1916	September 18, 1922
Sutherland, George	Utah	Harding	October 2, 1922	January 17, 1938
Butler, Pierce	Minnesota	Harding	January 2, 1923	November 16, 1939
Sanford, Edward Terry	Tennessee	Harding	February 19, 1923	March 8, 1930
Stone, Harlan Fiske	New York	Coolidge	March 2, 1925	July 2, 1941*
Roberts, Owen Josephus	Pennsylvania	Hoover	June 2, 1930	July 31, 1945
Cardozo, Benjamin Nathan	New York	Hoover	March 14, 1932	July 9, 1938
Black, Hugo Lafayette	Alabama	Roosevelt, F.	August 19, 1937	September 17, 1971
Reed, Stanley Forman	Kentucky	Roosevelt, F.	January 31, 1938	February 25, 1957
Frankfurter, Felix	Massachusetts	Roosevelt, F.	January 30, 1939	August 28, 1962
Douglas, William Orville	Connecticut	Roosevelt, F.	April 17, 1939	November 12, 1975
Murphy, Frank	Michigan	Roosevelt, F.	February 5, 1940	July 19, 1949
Byrnes, James Francis	South Carolina	Roosevelt, F.	July 8, 1941	October 3, 1942

Name	State Appointed From	Appointed by President	Date Judicial Oath Taken	Date Service Terminated
Jackson, Robert Houghwout	New York	Roosevelt, F.	July 11, 1941	October 9, 1954
Rutledge, Wiley Blount	Iowa	Roosevelt, F.	February 15, 1943	September 10, 1949
Burton, Harold Hitz	Ohio	Truman	October 1, 1945	October 13, 1958
Clark, Tom Campbell	Texas	Truman	August 24, 1949	June 12, 1967
Minton, Sherman	Indiana	Truman	October 12, 1949	October 15, 1956
Harlan, John Marshall	New York	Eisenhower	March 28, 1955	September 23, 1971
Brennan, William J., Jr.	New Jersey	Eisenhower	October 16, 1956	July 20, 1990
Whittaker, Charles Evans	Missouri	Eisenhower	March 25, 1957	March 31, 1962
Stewart, Potter	Ohio	Eisenhower	October 14, 1958	July 3, 1981
White, Byron Raymond	Colorado	Kennedy	April 16, 1962	June 28, 1993
Goldberg, Arthur Joseph	Illinois	Kennedy	October 1, 1962	July 25, 1965
Fortas, Abe	Tennessee	Johnson, L.	October 4, 1965	May 14, 1969
Marshall, Thurgood	New York	Johnson, L.	October 2, 1967	October 1, 1991
Blackmun, Harry A.	Minnesota	Nixon	June 9, 1970	August 3, 1994
Powell, Lewis F., Jr.	Virginia	Nixon	January 7, 1972	June 26, 1987
Rehnquist, William H.	Arizona	Nixon	January 7, 1972	September 26, 1986*
Stevens, John Paul	Illinois	Ford	December 19, 1975	June 29, 2010
O'Connor, Sandra Day	Arizona	Reagan	September 25, 1981	January 31, 2006
Scalia, Antonin	Virginia	Reagan	September 26, 1986	February 13, 2016
Kennedy, Anthony M.	California	Reagan	February 18, 1988	July 31, 2018
Souter, David H.	New Hampshire	Bush, G. H. W.	October 9, 1990	June 29, 2009
Thomas, Clarence	Georgia	Bush, G. H. W.	October 23, 1991	
Ginsburg, Ruth Bader	New York	Clinton	August 10, 1993	
Breyer, Stephen G.	Massachusetts	Clinton	August 3, 1994	
Alito, Samuel A., Jr.	New Jersey	Bush, G. W.	January 31, 2006	
Sotomayor, Sonia	New York	Obama	August 8, 2009	
Kagan, Elena	Massachusetts	Obama	August 7, 2010	
Gorsuch, Neil M.	Colorado	Trump	April 9, 2017	
Kavanaugh, Brett M.	Maryland	Trump	October 6, 2018	

Notes: The acceptance of the appointment and commission by the appointee, as evidenced by the taking of the prescribed oaths, is here implied; otherwise the individual is not carried on this list of the Members of the Court. Examples: Robert Hanson Harrison is not carried, as a letter from President Washington of February 9, 1790 states Harrison declined to serve. Neither is Edwin M. Stanton who died before he could take the necessary steps toward becoming a Member of the Court. Chief Justice Rutledge is included because he took his oaths, presided over the August Term of 1795, and his name appears on two opinions of the Court for that Term.

The date a Member of the Court took his/her Judicial oath (the Judiciary Act provided "That the Justices of the Supreme Court, and the district judges, before they proceed to execute the duties of their respective offices, shall take the following oath . . .") is here used as the date of the beginning of his/her service, for until that oath is taken he/she is not vested with the prerogatives of the office. The dates given in this column are for the oaths taken following the receipt of the commissions. Dates without small-letter references are taken from the Minutes of the Court or from the original oath which are in the Curator's collection. The small letter (a) denotes the date is from the Minutes of some other court; (b) from some other unquestionable authority; (c) from authority that is questionable, and better authority would be appreciated.

[The foregoing was taken from a booklet prepared by the Supreme Court of the United States, and published with funding from the Supreme Court Historical Society.]

———————

* Elevated.

Index

Acknowledgments

Customarily, the lead author's acknowledgment goes first. But here, I'll take the lead. Randy will finish.

This project began a decade ago. In 2009, I began to blog photographs of the people and places behind famous Supreme Court cases. Soon enough, other SCOTUS wonks sent me pictures from their own collections. And then the idea hit: publish a coffee table book! *Constitutional Places, Constitutional Faces* would be filled with rich photographs and compelling narratives about the Supreme Court's most important cases.[1] And, each book would come with a password: Readers could access a special website with photographs, videos, and other multimedia features.[2] My good friend Yaakov Roth and I developed the concept, retained a literary agent, and shopped a proposal.[3] Yaakov, who recently finished a clerkship with Justice Scalia, even secured an endorsement from the Boss.[4] "If the public good is of any concern to your publisher," he wrote, "it is surely true that such a book can bring the Court and the Constitution to life."

Alas, the bottom line trumped the public good. We got bupkis. A coffee table book for attorneys—even in 2010—was not a profitable endeavor. Securing permissions for the photographs, as well printing the glossy photographs, would have been far too costly. Plus, we were young lawyers without a following. Yaakov and I abandoned the coffee table book.

Yet, over the ensuing years, I continued to develop this project in three ways. First, I routinely blogged and tweeted about #ConstitutionalPlaces. My collection grew. Second, I highlighted these photographs in class.[5] (Many law professors, with and without credit, tapped my library.) And third, I developed podcasts (JoshCasts) and videos (JoshVlogs) about these landmark cases—I incorporated audio from oral arguments and conducted interviews with famous litigants. At some point, I hoped to unify this pedagogy into a single multimedia platform. But I couldn't quite figure out how and when.

Fast-forward to 2016. Randy Barnett invited me to be a co-author on his constitutional law casebook. I accepted this opportunity of a lifetime, and—as I am wont to do—quickly proposed another project. No, not a coffee table book. Rather, I pitched Randy on my long-dormant project: develop a series of videos to teach students about the most important cases in the constitutional canon. These films would incorporate photographs of the parties, as well as audio from oral arguments and opinion hand-downs. Students would even be able to *binge watch* a semester of constitutional law in a single sitting. Randy enthusiastically backed the project.

---

1. http://bit.ly/2Ir5zFJ
2. http://bit.ly/2UrIwBL
3. http://bit.ly/2UHvZti
4. http://bit.ly/2UcWZg5
5. In 2011, I discussed the 300 most important Supreme Court cases in a single lecture: https://youtu.be/W3Aq-D--u7Q.

365

In April 2017, we pitched Wolters Kluwer, our publisher. As originally conceived, students who purchased our casebook would be able to stream these videos online. We are grateful to Vikram Savkar, Joe Terry, and Maureen Kenealy at WK who saw the potential in the idea, and green-lit a pilot program. Over the summer, Randy and I developed the concept and wrote the scripts.

Soon, production day came. In September 2017, Randy and I spent eight hours at Trivision Studios in Chantilly, Virginia. After sitting through hair and makeup—thank you Dyneisha Felder—we took our position under the bright lights and in front of the green screen. The Trivision team skillfully manned the cameras, adjusted the lighting, positioned the microphone, and rolled the teleprompter. After we wrapped, Trivision produced eight beautiful pilot videos that showcased the great potential of the project. Wolters Kluwer was convinced, and green-lit a full catalogue of sixty videos. Over the next year, Randy and I would spend over sixty hours at Trivision, shooting and reshooting all of the segments. We are indebted to Sean, Joey, Wahid, and Mustafa for their professionalism, talent, and patience.

As we were filming, this time Randy had an epiphany. No, not a coffee table book, but close. We would expand the scripts into chapters of a book. Again, Wolters Kluwer was sold. *An Introduction to Constitutional Law* was born. And, as with my initial proposal a decade ago, each book would come with a password to access the online video library. #ConstitutionalPlaces finally came full circle. And the public good, as Justice Scalia hoped, prevailed.

I am forever grateful to Randy for being a champion for my vision. Randy is *always* willing to listen to new ideas, and, when he is persuaded, change course. The same can't be said for most people in his position. Also, I am thankful to Randy for his patience. Summarizing a complicated case in a few pages is no easy task. We spent countless hours debating about what should be included, and excluded. And we didn't always see eye-to-eye on prose. Randy likes longer sentences. I don't mind starting sentences with "however." But, in the end, we knew that any content that satisfied both of our meticulous standards was ready for primetime. We hope this book, and the videos, will be used for generations to come.

I am also in debt to my colleagues on the South Texas College of Law Houston faculty. You have guided me throughout my career to become the best professor I can be; I promise, I am still not quite there yet. And to my students. Every semester, I tell my classes that I learn more from them than they learn from me. Though they never believe me, my contributions to this book are proof. Thank you all for teaching me so much about teaching. Whatever insights I bring to this endeavor, I owe to my students.

Finally, and most importantly, I owe a debt to my amazing family. To Militza, thank you for believing in me, and supporting my never-ending quest to share my knowledge with the world. I love you. To Mom, Dad, and Alix, I am who I am because of what you have done for me. And to Miriam, you bring me so much joy every day. I can't wait until you are old enough to read this book, and share my love of the Constitution.

J.B.

When relating the journey we have been on these past two years to bring this project to fruition, Josh speaks for me. I should add that he has been a fire hose of ideas for the videos and the resulting book. And it fell to him to handle all the logistics of negotiating and scheduling their production. Were it not for his initiative and creativity, this intellectual product would simply not exist. This project vindicates my decision to bring him on board my constitutional law casebook.

At Wolters Kluwer, we are grateful to John Devins, Maureen Kenealy, and everyone else at Wolters Kluwer. We are particularly grateful to Joe Terry for embracing and advocating the concepts of the videos and the book that grew out of them. At The Froebe Group, we are indebted to Darren Kelly, who allowed us to turn this edition out in less than six months, from start to finish.

I thank my dean, William Treanor, for providing the research support that made writing this book possible. Josh and I also thank Betsy Kuhn at Georgetown, for her superlative proofreading talents. And we are indebted to research assistance from Katherine "Casey" Norman and Miranda Granchi. As always, I am grateful to my students in my Con Law I and II courses at the Georgetown University Law Center for their willingness, not only to be pushed by me, but to push back. They make teaching a worthwhile and enjoyable endeavor. This book should really be dedicated to them.

Finally, I thank my wife, Beth, for putting up with yet another writing project.

R.B.

About the Authors

Randy E. Barnett is the Carmack Waterhouse Professor of Legal Theory at the Georgetown University Law Center, where he teaches constitutional law and contracts, and is Director of the Georgetown Center for the Constitution. Professor Barnett's publications include twelve books, more than one hundred articles and reviews, as well as numerous op-eds.

Josh Blackman is an Associate Professor of Law at the South Texas College of Law Houston. Josh is the author of two books, one casebook, four dozen law review articles, and his commentary has appeared in national publications. Josh is the President of the Harlan Institute and founder of FantasySCOTUS.